MYTH AND POETICS

A series edited by
GREGORY NAGY

Poetry and Prophecy: The Beginnings of a Literary Tradition
edited by James L. Kugel

Also in the series

The Language of Heroes: Speech and Performance in the Iliad
by Richard P. Martin

Greek Mythology and Poetics
by Gregory Nagy

Homer and the Sacred City
by Stephen Scully

POETRY AND PROPHECY

The Beginnings of a Literary Tradition

EDITED BY

JAMES L. KUGEL

CORNELL UNIVERSITY PRESS

ITHACA AND LONDON

First published 1990 by Cornell University Press.

International Standard Book Number 0-8014-2310-4 (cloth)
International Standard Book Number 0-8014-9568-7 (paper)
Library of Congress Catalog Card Number 90-2154
Printed in the United States of America
Librarians: Library of Congress cataloging information appears on the last page of the book.

♾ The paper in this book meets the minimum requirements of the American National Standard for Information Sciences—Permanence of Paper for Printed Library Materials, ANSI Z39.48-1984.

Dedicated to the memory of
two great scholars,
Morton Bloomfield and Dan Pagis

Contents

Foreword

Poetry and Prophecy, edited by James Kugel, is the fourth book in the Myth and Poetics series. My goal, as series editor, is to encourage work that will help integrate literary criticism with the approaches of anthropology and that will pay special attention to problems concerning the nexus of ritual and myth. In the case of poetry and prophecy, the very pairing of these terms raises questions that can be answered only through an integration of approaches. Kugel's collection, interdisciplinary in the best sense of the word, addresses some of these questions and offers challenging answers.

GREGORY NAGY

POETRY AND PROPHECY

CHAPTER I

Poets and Prophets: An Overview

James L. Kugel

That poets and prophets have something in common with each other is an idea with a long history. Certainly anyone acquainted with the Western literary tradition knows that some of its greatest poets—Dante, Milton, Blake (to name only three of the most celebrated examples)—have in one way or another viewed themselves, and presented themselves to the world, as endowed with prophetic gifts or divinely inspired speech. What is perhaps less well known is that such figures were themselves the inheritors of an earlier tradition associating poetry and prophecy, one that winds back through the Middle Ages in Christian Europe and Muslim Spain and the East, and back still further to ancient Greece and biblical Israel. This tradition hardly speaks with one voice. At times, it seems, there have been those who would utterly separate the offices of poet and prophet, sometimes seeking quite consciously to exalt the latter through specific contrast with the former. At other times, quite the opposite operation has been performed, and the prophetlike nature of the poet—indeed, the identity of poet and prophet—has just as willfully been asserted. In either case, the position of poetry vis-à-vis prophecy has not infrequently been the subject of debate or polemic: the makers of poetry have more than once been attacked as usurpers or falsifiers of the Divine Word, and defended as following nothing less than Scripture's own dictates and models of prescribed behavior—perhaps most explicitly in the Renaissance, when the "defense of poetry" by Petrarch, Sidney, and others was conducted along just such lines.

The more recent high points of this tradition are, as noted, generally well known; but what of its earlier stages? Were poetry and prophecy seen as cognate concerns in the biblical world or in classical Greece and Rome—and in what ways? And when Judaism and Hellenism met, in the centuries following Alexander's conquest of the ancient Near East in 332 B.C.E., did not poet and prophet thereafter stand in a somewhat altered relationship? To what extent was this tradition passed on to emergent Christianity, with its own ongoing synthesis of the classical and biblical heritage; and did the rise of Islamic civilization, with *its* particular Near Eastern and classical heritage, give currency to a somewhat different set of views (views subsequently passed on to medieval Europe)? Meanwhile, what of the legacy of old European traditions of seers and wizards, visions and dreams—did not these also have a role in shaping the encounter between poetry and prophecy, poetic and divine inspiration, in the Middle Ages and beyond? Exploring these questions, an important undertaking in its own right, should seem all the more so in that it must ultimately touch upon the poet's whole stance—the poet's "mythology," one might say—as it developed in the formative period of the Western literary tradition.

To approach an answer to these questions and, perhaps still more basically, to perform a preliminary "naming of parts" (through which at least some of the main points of reference might be identified), a conference entitled "Poetry and Prophecy" was convened at Harvard University in the spring of 1986, and the essays in the present volume are in large measure the product of that undertaking. Conference participants were asked to focus on individual works or questions within their own fields, but in so doing to seek to address as well a series of larger questions common to all: To what extent were poetry and prophecy felt to be fundamentally similar activities, perhaps even identified with each other? What sorts of similarities were conceived to exist between the two, and how were these explained? How was poetic inspiration viewed in the light of prophecy, and what effect did the existence of prophecy have on the poet's self-presentation? The answers might obviously vary in accordance with the literature and period under consideration; indeed, one purpose of the conference was to assemble specific answers from a variety of contexts in order both to understand better how poetry itself was conceived of in antiquity and the Middle Ages and to identify the sources of a theme that has continued to be central to the European literary tradition from the Renaissance through the Romantic movement, and even to the present day. What emerged was that the twin halves of our theme—the prophet-as-poet and the poet-as-prophet—have indeed been the subject of an uninterrupted inquiry that stretches from biblical times to our own.

The essays that follow certainly speak for themselves: as noted, their purpose is to examine particular foci of our topic and, in so doing, to illuminate the development and background from which the later, better-known poet-prophets of Western literature emerged. Rather than seek to summarize the individual contributions in this volume or to articulate the transition from one to the next, it seems to me most appropriate in an introduction such as this to present, however roughly and inadequately, something of an overview of the topic considered as a whole and, via a näive introductory question or two, to try to set the stage for the essays that follow.

The first question that might be posed is a formal one, or at least might best be approached through the issue of form: Are biblical prophecies written in verse—that is, is there something in the form itself of the prophetic corpus in Hebrew which might encourage the identification of poetry and prophecy? This may seem a rather simple-minded approach to our topic, but this formal question has many far-reaching consequences and connections, and it is one that has occupied the attention of a number of recent studies.[1] To begin with, the notion "in verse" requires clarification. There is no prosodic structure in biblical poetry which quite corresponds to those well-known structural elements of our own poetry, meter and rhyme. What does characterize most songs, proverbs, sayings, and the like in the Bible is the repeated use of a generally binary sentence

______________________ | ______________________ ||
(*A*) (*B*)

in which part *A* is separated from part *B* by a slight (and usually syntactic) pause, and part *B* is separated from the next line by a fuller stop (the two pauses thus often corresponding to a comma and period in an English sentence). This alternating series of partial and full stops is usually apparent even in translation:

> Happy the man who fears the Lord | who greatly delights in His commandments || (Ps. 112:1)

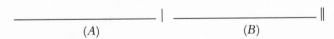

This pattern of stops is responsible for much of the feeling of regularity found in biblical poetry.

The task of the biblical poet thus consisted of creating a series of such two-part sentences, in which *B* is both clearly separable from *A* (hence the "slight pause"), yet just as clearly *A*'s continuation or partner. The feeling of connection between the two parts is often achieved (as in the preceding example) by having *B* parallel *A* in some fashion, through similar syntax, repetition or restatement, and the like or by ellipsis of some element found in *A* and implied in *B*; this *binding* feature of the binary style has caused it to be called, somewhat misleadingly, "parallelism." Although scholars for centuries have tried to discover a metrical scheme underlying such sentences, none has been found to exist, at least none susceptible to precise formulation. The most one can say is that parts *A* and *B* often consist of three or four words each—a mark of the terseness that, in other ways as well, is characteristic of poetic speech in Hebrew—although clauses of as few as two words or as many as five are not rare.

Given this somewhat loose structure, it should not be surprising that the dividing line between what we call biblical "poetry" and biblical "prose" is far from clear.[2] Indeed, the same sort of terse, binary sentence is to be found here and there in the midst of biblical "prose"—in narrative (especially in dialogue or when introducing or epitomizing incidents), in speeches of all kinds, in laws, blessings, curses, and so forth. What is more, whereas the consistent use of these terse, binary sentences is easily recognizable in such biblical books as Psalms or Proverbs or Jeremiah—and easily distinguished from the narrative style of Kings or the exhortations of Deuteronomy—there is not infrequently a kind of stylistic "middle ground" in which terse, binary sentences of the type seen above blend in with longer, less easily characterized sentences. Such "middle ground" passages are to be found in many of these same books—Psalms or Kings or Deuteronomy—but are particularly characteristic of long sections of the prophetic utterances of the books of Jeremiah, Ezekiel, and many of the twelve minor prophets. Such passages make particularly difficult the work of modern editors and translators of the Bible, who often seek to distinguish typographically between biblical poetry and biblical prose (such a distinction, incidentally, was never made consistently for the whole Bible by earlier typographers or scribes): their efforts tend to run aground, particularly in the prophetic books, where "prosaic" and "poetic" styles sometimes overlap to produce a frustrating indeterminacy, and the many variations between one editor's decisions and another's testify to the subjectivity that must govern them.

To return, then, to our question: Are biblical prophecies written in verse? Well, if we are willing to identify this loose, binary sentence structure as that which constitutes "verse" in the Bible, then the answer must be yes and no. Yes, most of the book of Isaiah and plenty of Jeremiah and Ezekiel and smaller prophetic collections are written in this biblical "high style." But at the same time, no: whole sections of Jeremiah and Ezekiel and Hosea and Joel and Amos and so forth are not. These sections are either simply (but is it ever simple?) "prose" or else composed of the sort of "middle ground" utterances described above.

Nor of course ought the question "Were the prophets poets?" be left to such purely formal criteria. Certainly there is much outside the realm of prosody proper that suggests a certain kinship between prophets and poets in biblical Israel. A passing reference in 1 Samuel 10.5 mentions a "band of prophets coming down from the high place with harp, tambourine, flute and lyre, prophesying." Similarly, the prophet Elisha is presented in 2 Kings 3:14–16 in these terms:

> And Elisha said, "As the Lord of hosts lives, whom I serve, were it not that I have regard for Jehoshaphat the king of Judah, I would neither look at you, nor see you. But now, bring me a musician." And when the musician played, the power of the Lord came upon him, and he said, "Thus says the Lord."

The pictures of prophecy found within the Bible are scarcely harmonious: prophecy in the north was different from prophecy in the south, and prophecy in its incipient stages was apparently quite different from what it became in the eighth and seventh and sixth centuries (and that, in turn, rather different from prophecy after the return from the Babylonian exile at the end of the sixth century). Nevertheless, it is noteworthy that these two passages, at least, presume some connection between the act of prophesying and the accouterments of music making (which is to say, the accouterments of poetry). Equally interesting is the presence within the Psalter of a number of psalms that seem to contain prophetic oracles, that is, psalms in which God is presented as speaking in the first person and addressing himself to

Israel or other nations or deities (see, for example, Ps. 81:6–16; 82:2–7). The existence of such psalms likewise argues a connection that must have existed at one time between cultic psalmody and prophecy.[3]

The tale of the Eastern soothsayer Balaam presents a detailed picture of the divinely inspired speaker at work: though Balaam has been engaged for the purpose of cursing Israel, he warns his employers in advance, "The word that God puts in my mouth, that must I speak" (Num. 22:38), and indeed, instead of cursing, he ends up blessing. It is therefore all the more interesting that the text repeatedly refers to Balaam's utterances by the word *māšāl,* "proverb," a term elsewhere generally reserved for the pithy, binary sentences of wisdom literature—that is, the carefully crafted utterances of the sage and the psalmist, those two Israelites who most closely approximate the person of the poet in other societies.[4] It is also interesting to note that, while Balaam is, like other prophets, presented primarily as a divine spokesman or messenger, the mere bearer of a word from on high (and so, for example, "the Lord put a word in Balaam's mouth" [Num. 23:5]; later he is asked, "What has the Lord spoken?" [Num. 23:17]), he nonetheless seems to have some role in shaping those divine words. After receiving God's message, he travels some distance back to his hosts, and there "takes up his parable"; does this formulation and accompanying scenario indicate that it is Balaam who turns a basic message he has received from God into the cadenced, balanced utterances that he then proclaims? If so, then he seems to be something more than a mere messenger, something of a "maker" himself.

If the famous comparison of Amos—"When a lion roars, who is not fearful? When God speaks, who does not prophesy?" (Amos 3:8)—suggests that there is something automatic, even mechanical, about being a prophet, we must balance this picture against others, such as that of Isaiah 50:4, where "the Lord has given me the tongue of those who are taught [better, "the language of learning"], that I may know how to sustain with a word him that is weary." Indeed, even the figure of Amos presents arguments for either side: although such verses as that just cited, along with the prophet's "rustic" origins, led Augustine to exalt him as a model of "untutored eloquence" (*De doctrina christiana* 4.8), the very type of the prophet *malgré lui,* modern scholars have noted strong resemblances between Amos's speech and the scholarly wisdom sayings found in the book of Proverbs—in particular his repeated use of the "graded numerical saying" (Amos 1:3, 6, 9, 11, 13;

2:1, 4, 6), a device otherwise characteristic of proverbs (Prov. 30:15, 18, 21, 24, 29) and songs (Song of Songs 6:8).

Within the biblical orbit, figurative language, bold imagery, and the like were conceived to belong specifically to the world of "song" (*šîr*) or "proverb" (*māšāl* or *ḥîdāh*), and it is certainly of significance that prophets sometimes invoked these genres in introducing their oracles. "Let me sing for my beloved a love song concerning his vineyard," Isaiah says in introducing a famous parable concerning the fate of his people (Isa. 5); later on in the same book, the prophet's words of consolation take up a well-worn introductory trope known to us from the Psalter, "Sing to the Lord a new song, his praise from the end of the earth!" (Isa. 42:10). "Son of man," God orders his prophet Ezekiel, "speak a proverb and say a riddle," and Ezekiel complies with the allegory of the eagles (Ezek. 17:1–10). It is hard to know just what to make of such evidence. Does the presence of these prominently identified songs and parables within the corpus of prophetic oracles argue a fundamental kinship between the ways of prophets and those of songsters and proverbists? Or does the very fact that these passages *are* so clearly identified as belonging to other genres imply on the contrary that they are somehow foreign to the normal stuff of prophecy, so that the prophet, in calling them by their name, seeks to prepare his listeners for what might otherwise shock or confuse them? In any case, perhaps one of the most interesting passages for our subject comes in the book of Ezekiel, when the prophet's place among his countrymen receives this sharp characterization:

> As for you, son of man, your people who talk together about you by the walls and at the doors of the houses say to one another, each to his brother, "Come and hear what the word is that comes forth from the Lord." And they come to you as people come, and they sit before you as my people, and they hear what you say but they will not do it; for with their lips they show much love, but their heart is set on their gain. And lo, you are to them like one who sings love songs with a beautiful voice and plays well on an instrument, for they hear what you will say, but they will not do it. But when this comes—and come it will—then they will know that a prophet has been among them. (Ezek. 33:30–33)

In this passage lie the seeds of one-half of the argument pursued in the rest of this volume—the suggestion that, at least in the perception of many, a prophet may be mistaken for a mere poet, "one who sings love songs with a beautiful voice," but, along with it, the fervent assertion that there is all the difference in the world between prophet and poet, a difference soon to be brought home by public events.

·

An issue as important as the foregoing evidence itself is how that evidence was construed by the Bible's early interpreters in the centuries before and just after the start of the common era, since these interpreters were in no small measure responsible for the reputation that prophecy enjoyed vis-à-vis poetry for the next millennium and more. Here too, there is something of a mixed picture, but the bulk of material ought to lead one to conclude that, on balance, there was something of a bias in this early period against associating poetry with prophecy, merely human artifice with divine oracles.

One might begin with the mute testimony of our oldest biblical manuscripts, the so-called Dead Sea Scrolls from Qumran and elsewhere, which date from the last pre-Christian centuries. It was the practice of medieval scribes sometimes to set off the Psalms and a few other parts of the Bible in various forms of graphic arrangement (generally called stichometry or stichography),[5] and this is the case as well with some of the biblical manuscripts at Qumran. To my knowledge, however, none of the manuscripts from there or indeed from the entire corpus of Jewish biblical manuscripts and books extending from the early Middle Ages almost to the present day adopts this "poetic" writing system for the oracles of Isaiah or Jeremiah or the other prophets. Apparently (although the significance of such stichographic arrangements is hardly beyond dispute) such prophetic books belonged to a class apart.[6]

Another sort of testimony is found in the very order of books that make up the biblical canon. In fact there is not one order but several. It is noteworthy that in the order ultimately adopted by rabbinic Judaism the canon is divided into three parts, *Tôrāh* (that is, the Pentateuch), *Nĕbîʾîm* (Prophets, itself subdivided into "former prophets" comprising the historical books from Joshua to Kings, and "latter prophets," comprising the prophetic corpora of Isaiah, Jeremiah, Ezekiel, and the twelve minor prophets), and *Kĕtûbîm* ("[other] writings"), including the Psalms and other traditionally "poetic" books. Perhaps one ought not to make too much of the significance of this separation, which may have more to do with the manner and order in which elements of the future biblical canon were brought together than with judgments about genre, but prophecy again seems to be treated here as a thing apart.[7] In the other widely diffused system of canonical arrangement, a section of "historical books," Pentateuch through Esther, is followed by a purely "poetic" section consisting of Job, Psalms, Proverbs, Ecclesiastes, and the Song of Songs, which in turn is followed by the "prophetic" section—here, too, clearly distinguished as something separate.

The system of punctuation marks used in the Hebrew text (known in Hebrew as *tĕʿāmîm*) sets off three books—Psalms, Proverbs, and Job—with a special system of notation. The reason for the use of this special system (present not only in the later, Tiberian system but in its predecessors as well) is hardly clear: perhaps it had something to do with the manner in which these books were recited. Nor, it should be noted, did these three constitute the only biblical books to which the label "poetry" came to be accorded: certainly the Song of Songs, for example, or Lamentations might as justly bear that title. But this particular feature of the Hebrew textual tradition must in some measure have solidified the separation between prophecy and poetry, putting these prominently poetic compositions in a box of their own. Later on, during the Renaissance, when Christian Europe began to read Hebrew and study Scripture in the original, these three books, because of their special *tĕʿāmîm,* were not infrequently referred to as the *Libri metrici.*

There were, of course, forces pulling in the other direction. The very idea of a biblical canon, that is, a corpus of sacred writings, implied to early Jewish readers a certain homogeneity of content: all the books included in the Bible were not only in harmonious accord with one another but were all "given from one Shepherd" (Eccles. 12:11), dictated or inspired by the same God. In that case, distinctions between biblical prophecy and biblical psalmody were bound to be superficial. Strictly speaking, a prophet may be defined simply as the bearer of a message from God. If so, then the Bible as a whole became, via the doctrine of divine inspiration, one long prophetic corpus, including, of course, the biblical poetry of the Psalter. This view is already clearly espoused in the interpretive literature of Qumran, where psalms as well as songs such as the "Song of the Well" (Num. 21:17–18) are interpreted as prophecies. The promotion of David from psalmist to prophet (on which see my essay herein) similarly aided the blurring of the distinction between mere poetry and prophecy. But no doubt the matter was far from clear, and the idea of a canon of uniformly divine provenance raised great interpretive problems as well. Centuries later, the medieval scholar Seʿadya Ga'on was to ask how words addressed *to* God (he meant specifically the supplications and praises contained in the book of Psalms) could at the same time be held to have come *from* God; and the answer that he proposed—that pleas for divine mercy and the like in the Psalms were really intended to inform the reader about the nature of God, that He is indeed merciful etc.—was only one of various contemporaneous attempts to grapple with this issue.[8]

Were the prophets poets in the eyes of early Judaism? If one considers the corpus of classical rabbinic writings about the Bible, stretching from the second century C.E. on to the sixth and beyond, one might well conclude that although the Rabbis held what might be called the *phenomenon* of song and singing in high esteem,[9] any association of the Divine Word (all of it being, in the sense seen above, prophecy) with mere song was generally offensive to them. As a consequence, connecting the words revealed to prophets with those created by mere poets was bound to encounter rabbinic disapproval. Consider, for example, the rabbinic handling of Ps. 119:54, "Your statutes have been as songs to me within my dwelling-place." At face value, this verse (like all of Psalm 119) is a pious assertion of the psalmist's total devotion to divine law; here he relates that his zeal is such that he recites, even sings, the sacred statutes within his own house, just as others might sing some popular song. But in the Talmud, this verse is treated, quite to the contrary, as a presumptuous statement for which David (the presumed author of this psalm) received divine punishment.

> Why was David punished? Because he called Scripture "songs," as it is written, "Your statutes have been as songs to me . . ." God said to David: Scripture, about which it is said "If your eyes light upon it, it will disappear" [Prov. 23:5, i.e., it must be treated with utmost sanctity], you refer to as "songs"! Here I will cause you to trip up on something even little schoolchildren know about, [for they learn the verse] "But to the sons of Korah he gave no [wagons], because they were charged with the care of holy things, which had to be carried on the shoulder" [again, an expression of the sanctity with which "holy things" (including Scripture) are to be treated]. (*Soṭa,* 35a)

In the same vein: The prophetess Deborah utters a militant hymn in Judges 5, the so-called Song of Deborah. In the course of describing the terrible conditions under which the people had theretofore lived, she adds, "until I, Deborah, arose, until I arose, a mother in Israel" (Jud. 5:7).[10] This apparent lack of modesty was unbecoming one to whom the gift of prophecy had been granted, and rabbinic exegetes saw in a later verse in the same song a hint that Deborah was consequently "demoted":

> R. Judah said that Rav had said: Anyone who acts arrogantly, if he is a scholar his wisdom departs from him, and if a prophet, his prophecy departs from him. . . . [The latter is learned] from the case of Deborah, as it is written, "The peasantry ceased in Israel, they ceased, until I, Deborah, arose, until I arose, a mother in Israel," [after which] it is written, 'Awake, awake, oh Deborah, awake, awake, sing a song!' [Jud. 5:12] (Babylonian Talmud, *Pesaḥim* 66b).

Rav's interpretation of the latter verse is as an announcement of punishment: because of her arrigance, Deborah is now enjoined only to "sing a song," prophecy being henceforth denied to her.

The well-known injunction of Rabbi Akiba with regard to the Song of Songs perhaps also illustrates something of the same mentality. The *Ṭosefta* (*Sanhedrin* 12:10) cites this second century C.E. teacher as holding that "anyone who sings the Song of Songs in melodic fashion at a banquet and treats it as an ordinary song [*kĕmîn zemer*] forfeits his portion in the world to come." In its rabbinic interpretation, of course, the Song of Songs was a divinely given allegory concerning relations between God and Israel, and treating it like an "ordinary song" might seem, as it were, to deny that interpretation and was thus tantamount to equating sacred Scripture with secular compositions.

It has been noted that although rabbinic exegesis pursued the expounding of Scripture to its minutest details and textual scholarship per se of the Hebrew Bible early on reached a level of exactitude quite unsurpassed in the transmission and study of other contemporary texts, the Rabbis themselves showed remarkably little interest in the poetic structure or rhetoric of Scripture *as such*. While their Hellenistic contemporaries explored in detail the prosodic and rhetorical features of *their* texts and while, soon enough, Greek- and Latin-speaking Christians were to import these same concerns and methods to their study of the Bible,[11] rabbinic exegesis remained largely oblivious to this "human" side of biblical expression. There is no rabbinic treatise on the binary, "seconding" style of biblical song described above, nor is there any catalogue of tropes and figures used in the Sacred Writ (such as was, in fact, compiled by Cassiodorus [ca. 487–580] for the Psalter, and by various later writers for the Bible as a whole). It certainly would not have been impossible for Jewish homilists in the early centuries to compare Moses—who is frequently likened in rabbinic homilies to a teacher or private tutor, military figure, householder, and the like—to a poet or maker of songs, if only in discussing the two biblical songs associated with him (Exod. 15 and Deut. 32), or to compare the activities of Isaiah or Jeremiah or other prophets to the occupation of poet; yet this is nowhere done. Indeed, as I have suggested, biblical "poetry" is not a category of rabbinic exegesis, nor am I aware of any hint within the rabbinic corpus that human artifice is responsible for even one word of Scripture. So: were the prophets "poets"? Heaven forfend!

•

But there certainly were other Jews in late antiquity and opinions other than those preserved in rabbinic texts. Philo of Alexandria (ca. 20 B.C.E. to ca. 50 C.E.), the great expositor of Hebrew Scripture to the Greek-speaking Jewish community of Egypt, asserts that the prophet Moses had learned the "study of rhythm, harmony, and meters" from the Egyptians, and goes on to report on the singing of (biblical?) "hymns and psalms to God composed of many meters and melodies."[12] The mention of metrical study in connection with Moses served principally to show that he had received a proper education,[13] and to a Greek-speaking audience, the idea that biblical hymns and psalms had been composed in meter was only to be expected; nevertheless, remarks such as these certainly suggest that in Philo's eyes, at least, the offices of poet and prophet were not utterly foreign to each other. A little less than a century later, the Jewish historian Josephus did not hesitate to compare Moses or David to Greek-style poets, even specifying the meters (hexameter, trimeter, pentameter) in which their songs were written.[14] These ideas in turn were passed on to the early Church and came to exercise great influence on various Christian writers of late antiquity, notably Jerome and Augustine, and through them on the entire structure of Western Christianity throughout the

Middle Ages. Here Scripture, albeit divinely revealed, was frequently compared to secular literature (if only to be exalted over it), and one third-century tract, the *Didascalia apostolorum,* even addressed readers potentially tempted by pagan literature: "If you wish to read histories, take those of the Book of Kings; if you want poetry and wisdom, take the Prophets . . . if you desire songs, you have the Psalter."[15] In the world of Western Christianity, Scripture in effect became a "surrogate literature," for a time rivaling classical texts in the curriculum; although the classics managed, more or less, to stay on in their educational role, learned churchmen from Jerome to the Renaissance did not tire of exalting the literary values of Scripture over classical (pagan) models. In all this, the "poetic" side of prophecy did, at times, gain wide attention.

•

And were not poets sometimes prophets? Here, on the other side of our medallion, certainly the whole Greek tradition of the divinely inspired poet-prophet (admirably exposed herein in an essay by Gregory Nagy) came into play, for those of Greek speech and education could scarcely doubt that the two were related. Were not the inspiring messages of the Muse what stood behind Greek verse, just as the prophetic oracles of Delphi had found expression in dactylic hexameter? True enough, with the rise of Christianity, much that smacked of pagan religion and matters of similarly un-Christian orientation were roundly condemned, but (just as frequently, it seems) such things were adroitly Christianized (most prominently in Eusebius's *Preparatio evangelica*) or apologized for, so that in the end not only did prophets appear somewhat poetlike, but poets—at least some of them—were held to have enjoyed powers bordering on the prophetic. Early Christian apologists frequently cited Homer, Hesiod, Euripides, and others as having "spokenly darkly of God," "sung of the true sacred word," and so forth.[16] In one instance, treated in detail in Wendell Clausen's delightful essay herein, a "prophecy" of Virgil's vouchsafed his place among the prophetic poets for centuries to come.

In approaching the phenomenon of the poet-prophet during this early period, one must mention a change in the scope of divinely inspired texts, a change perhaps not unrelated to the influx of Greek ideas into the Semitic world at the time of Alexander's conquest—ideas that were later integrated with Jewish views via Christianity and then spread to points far and wide. In preexilic Israel, the prophet was a man with a message straight from God. Indeed, as some of the sources reviewed in Alan Cooper's essay suggest, the prophet's *messenger* status has come to be understood by scholars in the most literal terms: they have drawn convincing parallels between the functions of prophets and those of ordinary messengers commissioned by kings or other officials in the Hebrew Bible—right down to the "messenger formula" that initiated the speech of both prophets and ordinary emissaries. Whatever actual scenario lay behind the ancient Israelite conception of prophecy (and this is part of what Cooper's essay sets out to describe, in the light not only of modern scholarship but of some answers given by medieval Jewish commentators), it seems, at least much of the time, worlds away from our notion of "inspiration": for again and again biblical texts inform us that the prophet has been physically transported on high, to the Divine Council or to some other site where the substance of the divine decree was delivered to him, or has been quite simply addressed by God in words sounding, as in the case of Samuel, so much like an external, ordinary human voice as to be mistaken for one—not once but three times (1 Sam. 3). Elsewhere, the divine voice did not speak so much as thundered—so that the myriad Israelites gathered at the foot of Mount Sinai trembled at its sound and pleaded with Moses to converse with God on their behalf, lest the experience of hearing Him result in their death (Exod. 20:18–20; cf. Deut. 18:15–17); again, this conception seems somewhat removed from what is suggested to most people by the phrase "divine inspiration."[17] (Indeed, the use of that phrase by Christian theologians apparently owes its origin to the New Testament, 2 Timothy 3:16, and belongs precisely to the period of expansion and change that I am discussing.)[18] And certainly all this is at some remove from the "divine inspiration" that might cause a Greek bard to recount the exploits of ancient heroes or push a lyric poet to song. Moreover, if one considers the biblical texts themselves, there is nothing in, for example, the great histories of Judges or Samuel or Kings even to indicate that the teller of the tale regards himself as in any way an *inspired* teller: he is simply going about the business of recording facts.

Given this orientation, it seems that a prophet like Isaiah or even Jeremiah might not only have had some difficulty in grasping the notion of divine inspiration which came to underlie many of the Jewish compositions written several hundred years after the Babylonian exile (that is, in the centuries just before and after the turn of the common era) but might have been particularly perplexed at the very idea of the Hebrew Bible—specifically, the notion that a group of the most diverse sort of texts, legends, histories, prayers, prophecies, songs, and proverbs might all, somehow, be held to be of divine provenance or sanction. For by the end of the biblical period, not only had there sprung up a whole new class of apocalyptic visions rather different from classical prophecies, but all manner of ancient compositions, works that had gradually become part of Israel's sacred library, were now being accorded, however obliquely, something akin to prophetic status. In the latter case, at least, the unquestioned antiquity of many of the texts involved, their long tradition of preservation and revered status, indeed, their unrivaled standing as the record of earliest times, certainly must have favored the conferral upon them of a divine character as if by fiat. Radiating outward from the Pentateuchal nucleus and the specifically God-spoken and God-prompted oracles of the prophets, divine inspiration (and with it, the connection of the names of distingushed, often divinely chosen human authors—David, Solomon, the prophets—to anonymous old works) came to adhere to a highly diverse literary miscellany. And along with these, wholly new works, attributed to ancient worthies (whether in a sincere attempt to defraud or as a pro forma gesture is a good question, and the answer no doubt varies from work to work), so began to proliferate that it became necessary finally to draw the borders of Israel's officially sanctioned sacred library—this was the "canonization" proper.[19]

What brought about this great expansion of divinely inspired writing? The answer is a complex one, connected to the political and theological aspirations of the Jewish people throughout that period, but no doubt the influence of Greek ideas about inspiration was likewise of some importance, not only in regard to inspired poetry, as we have seen briefly, but (as came to be alleged) in the supernatural boost that might underlie such diverse activities as philosophy and mathematics. Nor was inspiration here necessarily of the rather muted and dim character that might seem plausible to modern sensibilities. On the contrary, the inspired speaker or singer was as if wholly possessed: inspiration came easily and was total. Such a picture emerges, for example, in Plato's *Ion,* a brief dialogue in which poetic inspiration is compared to the force of a great magnetic stone, which can then be transferred from the stone itself (that is, the inspiring deity) to a series of magnetized rings: the poet, the reciter of his poems, and the audience all receive and emit the inspiring power. Later Socrates observes:

> All good poets, epic as well as lyric, compose their beautiful poems not by art, but because they are inspired and possessed. . . . For the poet is a light and winged and holy thing, and there is no invention in him until he has been inspired and is out of his senses, and the mind is no more in him. When he has not attained to this state he is powerless and unable to utter his oracles. . . . And therefore God takes away the minds of the poets, and uses them as his ministers, as he also uses diviners and holy prophets, in order that we who hear them may know them to be speaking not of themselves who utter these priceless words in a state of unconsciousness, but that God himself is the speaker, and that through them he is conversing with us. Tynnichus the Chalcidian affords a striking instance of what I am saying: he wrote nothing that anyone would care to remember but the famous paean that is in everyone's mouth, one of the finest poems ever written, simply an invention of the Muses, as he himself says. For in this way the God would seem to indicate to us and not allow us to doubt that these beautiful poems are not human or the work of man, but divine and the work of God; and that the poets are only the intermediaries of the gods by whom they were severally possessed.[20]

Similar views soon came to be expressed by Jews with regard to their own prophets. Here is Philo on Deut. 18:18: "A prophet possessed by God will suddenly appear and give prophetic oracles. Nothing of what he says will be his own, for he that is truly under the control of divine inspiration has no power of apprehension when he speaks, but serves as the channel of the insistent words of Another's promptings. For prophets are interpreters of God, Who makes full use of the organs of their speech to set forth what He wills."[21] And on the mention of the sun's setting when Abraham is visited by God in Gen. 15:12, Philo writes: "When the light of God shines, the human light sets; when the divine light sets, the human dawns and rises. This is what regularly befalls the fellowship of prophets. The mind is evicted at the arrival of the divine Spirit, but when that departs the mind returns to its tenancy. Mortal and immortal may not share the same home."[22]

How much ordinary Jews subscribed to such a view of divine inspiration or even the extent to which the role of ready inspiration in postexilic Jewish writings is the result of conscious reflection on the part of their authors is difficult to assess. But it is noteworthy in any case that among many of these authors, the gift of inspiration was held to be neither middling nor all that rare. Thus, for example, the story of the miraculous simultaneous divine inspiration of the Septuagint translators—all of whom, working independently and cut off from all communication, produced absolutely identical translations of the Bible—was clearly not an embarrassment to a writer like Philo.[23] Indeed, he does not mince words: "They became as it were possessed, and, under inspiration, wrote not each individual scribe something different, but the same word for word, as though dictated to each by an invisible prompter."[24]

A crucial figure here was that of the Sibyl, whose oracular writings mark the exact point of confluence of the two traditions, I have been examining, Greek and Jewish.[25] In general, sibylline oracles are writings of a prophetic character composed in Greek hexameters and held to be the work of various old women (of Greek or "Asiatic" origin) endowed with the gift of predicting future events. Earliest uses of the name Sibyl (in the fifth and fourth centuries B.C.E.) seem to refer to a single individual: perhaps the word's origin is to be connected with the actual name of a particular prophetess. There were collections of various sibylline oracles made in antiquity, including an official one at Rome, which was entrusted to special guards and which could be consulted only by decree of the Roman senate—a mark of the prestige these writings enjoyed. This collection, however, has not survived: the sibylline oracles that we actually possess (save for some brief fragments) are all essentially Jewish or Christian works (though attributed to the pagan Sibyl) and constitute a lengthy body of material, divided into twelve books and apparently composed over a span of more than seven centuries.

Their significance to our topic, of course, is that they constituted a body of prophet-like utterances (clearly modeled, in some cases, on biblical prophecy and Jewish apocalyptic writings) but spoken in verse by an ecstatic pagan poet, one nonetheless inspired by the true God. She was a prophetess in the style suggested by the Greek views of inspiration: "I will speak the following with my whole person in ecstasy/For I do not know what I say, but God bids me utter each thing" (2.4–5). Her mellifluous exhortations, delivered from a mouth both "honey-voiced" and "holy" (4.3, 23), told of the history of the world (including events and information recounted in the Hebrew

Bible) and of the future of peoples and their leaders, prophecies of doom or salvation. That such oracles existed was of great importance to early Christian writers, who cite sibylline verses both in order to drive a particular point home in Greek hexameters and, still more important, to show that the One God's message had also been delivered outside of biblical Israel, indeed, in a form readily accessible to a Greek-speaking audience. "Just as God wished to save the Jews by giving them prophets," wrote Clement of Alexandria (ca. 150–ca. 215) "so too, by raising up prophets out of their own [Greek] tongue, as they were able to receive God's bounty, He distinguished the most excellent of the Greeks from the common herd."[26]

But beyond this message was another, concerning poetry and prophecy: for did not the "truth" of the Sibyl's vaticinations—asserted hundreds of times to nascent Christianity—solidify once and for all the identification of poet and prophet, hexameter and revelation, and bind tightly together two offices that under different circumstances might have gone on to pursue quite separate and distinct careers? If the Sibyl's verses had brought true teachings from God into the Greek language, could not the same be maintained of other apparently "pagan" poets? Certainly it was the Sibyl's example that opened the way to the Christian reading of verses from Homer, Hesiod, and the other Greek poets, which in turn proved to be an important element in the presentation of Christianity in the West. The Latin writer Lactantius (ca. 240–ca. 320), a Christian apologist who pursued this approach at some length, seems to have connected the very calling of poet with the ability (or occasion) to grasp Christian truth, as it were, *avant la lettre:*

> Poets, therefore, however much they may have celebrated the gods with their songs or magnified their deeds with greatest praise, nevertheless admit rather often that all things are contained and ruled by a single Spirit or Mind. Orpheus, who is the very oldest of the poets and peer of the gods themselves . . . called the true and great God *Protogonos* [firstborn], because nothing was born before Him, but all things are engendered out of Him. . . . Thus, with the help of nature and reason, he was able to grasp the existence of a preeminent power, the Founder of Heaven and Earth.[27]

The promotion of Virgil in particular to "Christian prophet"[28] and the whole later course of commingling classical and biblical voices in Western thought owes not a little to this most significant poet-prophet of late antiquity.

The case of Virgil is striking for (among other things) what it shows about later Christian attitudes. Virgil was, of course, a classic before Christianity took hold in Rome, and it was not long (as Clausen's essay relates) before Christians, at least some Christians, turned his writings to pious purpose. The *idea* of a divinely guided Virgil may not always have been necessary for this conversion; after all, his words were simply around, in everyone's mouth. But it was not long before they turned up (slightly altered) in Prudentius's Christian epic *Psychomachia* and similar poetic undertakings. Striking indeed is the Christian cento of Virgil composed by Faltonia Proba in the middle of the fourth century. A cento, as is well known, is a patchwork poem made up of individual lines or fragments taken from another poet (in this case, Virgil). The result is a kind of putting-words-into-Virgil's-mouth, for by cleverly assembling pieces from here and there, the author is able to create an entirely new work out of scraps, a literary mosaic. Invoking divine aid to "unlock the inner chambers of my soul so that I, Proba, *as a prophetess* may return whole mysteries," the author reassembled Virgilian fragments into a narration of Old Testament tales up to the Flood, then turned to New Testament themes. If the achievement itself is impressive, more so is the undertaking, at least for what it says about our theme. Indeed, while some people (as Clausen notes) were skeptical about the notion of a pagan prophet of Christ, Augustine at one point even finds scriptural warrant for the idea. Citing an apparent pleonasm in Romans 1:2 ("which He promised beforehand through His prophets in the holy Scriptures"), Augustine asserts that "there were prophets that were not His," and that these too had sung of the coming of Christ:

> Which I should not easily believe, were it not that the noblest of poets in the Roman language long ago spoke these things concerning the coming of a new age, which may be seen to fit and accord rather well with the kingdom of our Lord Jesus Christ, as in the verse (Eclogue 4:4) "Now comes the last age of the Cumaean song." No one can doubt that Cumaean song to be that of the Sibyl.[29]

Such endorsement notwithstanding, knowledge of Virgil's writings was apparently a slightly racy commodity for ecclesiastical writers in later centuries. Jerome's famous dream (recounted in his *Letters* 22), in which he renounces his "Ciceronian" standing and his collection of Latin classics, became a model for later generations, and it is not uncommon to find medieval churchmen who simultaneously let on that they know the *Aeneid* well (perhaps from a misspent youth) and yet, like Jerome, have renounced it in order to devote themselves wholly to Scripture, the lives of the saints, and equally suitable reading.[30]

•

Poet and prophet continued their uneasy relationship in other contexts, most notably within Islam, whose Scripture had been communicated through one most anxious to distinguish himself from mere poets but in a language and within a cultural tradition already rich in poetry, which held the poet's calling to be akin to that of visionaries and the divinely possessed. The Islamic heritage came to affect—profoundly—Judaism and Christianity in these matters, and the synthesis of all these (and other) sources of influence can be seen in the works of medieval and Renaissance creativity in Western Europe which are the subject of the essays in the latter part of this volume. There is not much that I might add to what has already been said on these themes—and surely not to the contributions that follow, the masterful treatments of poet and prophet in the Islamic orbit by Michael Zwettler and Wolfhart Heinrichs, Dan Pagis's colorful survey of the poet-prophet in medieval Hebrew, and the essays by Jan Ziolkowski and Lawrence Rhu which return our focus to European letters in the Middle Ages and beyond.

This is certainly not to say that there is nothing more that could be written about our subject even within the overall time frame covered by these essays, for there are works of undeniable significance to our theme which, however, for want of space or because of the overall aim of this book, have not been treated as fully as they might otherwise have deserved. (In one instance, the omission of significant material was hardly voluntary: Morton Bloomfield's death deprived us of an essay that not only would have shed new light on the theme of poetry and prophecy within *Piers Plowman* but would likewise have illuminated the whole tradition of medieval prophetic visions, whether dream visions like that of the anonymous *Pearl*-poet or, for that matter, the waking revelation of Dante's *Divine Comedy*.) And of course beyond the period covered by these essays lies that of the great fulfillment of the poetry-prophecy theme in European letters from the Renaissance to the present day. But having invoked all that which, alas, could not be said in the present collection, I might do best now to conclude these introductory thoughts by returning to the question with which we began—"Did the prophets write in verse?"—and in so doing to invoke the name of one last figure whose influence in this matter is still felt nowdays, that of the great eighteenth-century scholar Robert Lowth.

Lowth was a scholar of broad learning and great intelligence, and it was he, perhaps more than any other modern, who solidified the connection between poetry and prophecy which became so important two or three generations later in the whole enterprise of Romantic poetry in England and on the Continent—not, of course, that the connection per se was a late innovation. As we have seen briefly, medieval piety (not unlike that of an earlier age) was of two minds with regard to both parts of our theme, the prophet-as-poet and the poet-as-prophet, and some of this ambivalence was to become the capital of those in the Renaissance who sought to defend poetry against its pious detractors. "David was a poet" is a refrain that resounds in the Renaissance, starting as early as Boccaccio and Petrarch in Italy and on to poetry's later defenders in France, England, and elsewhere; the versified psalms translations (as well as verse translations of other biblical books) undertaken by poets great and small bear witness to the hold this identification had on the imagination in this period. "And may I not presume a little further to show the reasonableness of this word *vates,* and say that the holy David's Psalms are a divine poem? If I do, I shall not do it without the testimony of great learned men, both ancient and modern. But even the name Psalms will speak for me, which, being interpreted, is nothing but 'Songs'; then, that it is fully written in metre, as all learned Hebricians agree, although the rules be not yet fully found out. Lastly and principally, his handling his prophecy, which is merely poetical."[31]

As these words of Sir Philip Sidney's defense attest, David was equally poet and prophet, a *vates,* as he says (and so he had been since late antiquity). If so, then Isaiah, Jeremiah, et al. could fall in step quite naturally behind him. George Puttenham (1532–1590) felt it clear that "King David also and Solomon his sonne and *many other of the holy Prophets* wrate in meeters, and used to sing them to the harpe, although to many of us, ignorant of the Hebrue language and phrase, and not observing [that is, scanning] it, the same seeme but a prose."[32] Similarly, Thomas Lodge in his defense of poetry commanded his readers: "Ask Josephus, and he will tell you that Esay [Isaiah], Job and Salomon voutsafed poetical practices, for (if Origen and he fault not) theyre verse was Hexameter, and Pentameter."[33] Not too long after, John Donne wrote these words:

> Thy Eagle-sighted Prophets too,
> Which were thy churches Organs, and did sound
> That harmony, which made of two
> One law, and did unite, but not confound;
> Those heavenly Poëts which did see
> Thy will, and it expresse
> In rythmique feet, in common pray for mee,
> That I by them excuse not my excesse
> In seeking secrets, or Poëtiquenesse.
>
> ("The Litanie")

But the metrical question, alluded to by all these men, continued to perplex scholars, as poetry and some consistent meter seemed to them inextricably allied. What was that metrical system which certainly existed, "as all learned Hebricians agree, although the rules be not yet fully found out," the one that might save the prophets' utterances from seeming "but a prose"?

Many answers were put forward: from Greek-style quantitative meters whose endlessly complex rules of substitution only proved, at least to some, the superiority of the ancient Hebrews to other peoples, to isosyllabic metrical systems that mirrored what was then being done in vernacular European verse, to "pure stress" meters on the Germanic model, to a free-verse system tied together by a system of rhyme (something in the manner of Ogden Nash). Into this array of conflicting claims came Robert Lowth, and his solution, put forward in a series of lectures at Oxford and later published under the title *De sacra poesi hebraeorum praelectiones* (1753), conquered the imagination of many contemporary and subsequent biblical scholars.

Lowth's was a wide-ranging work of scholarship that treated a number of issues then currently in debate among biblicists and, as well, brought to the Bible some of the sensibilities and concerns of eighteenth-century literary criticism. But from this array of seemingly separate subjects and pursuits emerged a single, overriding theme to the book, an idea that, Lowth thought, was of immense importance and on which the success or failure of his whole enterprise depended: It was that biblical prophecy was itself a form of poetry, indeed, that poetry and prophecy had "one common name, one common origin, one common author, the Holy Spirit." If so, then not only was one free to inquire into the poetics of Isaiah, Jeremiah, and Ezekiel—the first "at once elegant and sublime, forceful and ornamented," indeed, "the most perfect model" of a poetic prophet; and the three together "as far as relates to style, may be said to hold the same rank among the Hebrews as Homer, Simonides and Aeschylus among the Greeks"—but indeed the very essence of prophesying was thereby asserted to belong to the same order of being as the business of making poems.[34]

However: did the prophets actually write in *verse?* This old question still required an affirmative answer in order for Lowth's argument to be accepted, and it was here that Lowth's concept of *parallelismus membrorum,* "the parallelism of the clauses," came into play. (Lowth, incidentally, is still often credited with the "discovery of biblical parallelism"; however, as I have suggested above, "parallelism" is actually something of a misnomer and his misled scholars in their attempts to understand the dynamics of the binary, "seconding" style of biblical poetry—and in any case, Lowth was hardly the first to remark on this paralleling feature. Lowth's answer to the old question of meter was indeed yes: the prophets, just like other biblical (and nonbiblical) poets, composed their poetry in some sort of meter. That meter, however, was unrecoverable. The reason why previous scholars had not been able to reduce biblical poetry to a fixed system was that the Hebrew texts themselves were most likely in many respects defective as a result of having been transmitted from generation to generation by Jews no longer aware of the original prosodic structure. In any case, since the original texts had been written without vowels (the "vowel-points" that now accompany it being, again, an innovation of Jews living far after the biblical period), the precise quantities of individual syllables, or even the precise number of syllables in any given line, was, Lowth believed, forever lost. Little wonder that scholars had been unable to make the Psalms and other biblical songs scan! The very texts on which they tried out their systems were fundamentally flawed.

This argument was not entirely new with Lowth, but what followed was: How then, Lowth asked, can one know for sure that biblical poetry was written in verse if the metrical system is unknown and unrecoverable? The structure of biblical poetry is indicated by another feature, he argued, whereby one clause is connected to the next (that is, *A* to *B* in our terminology), so that "like answers to like" through a series of semantic correspondences. Lowth claimed that this "parallelism of the clauses" is a regular feature of Hebrew poetry, and he went on to catalogue the three different types of it in the Hebrew Bible, "synonymous," "antithetical," and "synthetic" parallelism.[35] Now the brief clauses as marked off by the parallelism will, Lowth said, appear on examination to be of roughly equal length even in the present (debased) form of the texts, whether one count the number of words or accents or whatever. This rough equality could hardly be the work of chance, he argued, and indeed, if the texts were only in their pristine state and the vowel quantities correctly understood, then a still sharper form of correspondence might be easily demonstrated to all.

> But of this particular [Hebrew meter] we have at present so little information, that it is utterly impossible to determine whether it were modulated by the ear alone, or according to any settled or definite rules of prosody. Since, however, this [parallelism] and other marks or vestiges, as it were, of the metrical art are alike extant in the writings of the prophets and in the books which are commonly allowed to be poetical, I think there is sufficient reason to rank them in the same class.

In short, Isaiah and the Psalms obey the same prosodic rules, for both are poetry; and no less than Job, Proverbs, or other specimens of the poet's art in the Bible, "the predictions of the prophets are metrical."[36]

Lowth's solution, as I have implied, was composed of equal parts insight and legerdemain, but no matter: it conquered the world. Indeed, soon enough parallelism alone was being advanced as the "meter" of biblical verse. His views on biblical poetics continue to influence biblical scholars to this day, and in broader ways too—especially in his valuation of the Bible's poetry in its various species over mere prose—he has had great impact on the course of later biblical scholarship. And of course Lowth's legacy to poetry itself, to Romanticism, was manifold: certainly one of his book's most important "children" was a volume written quite consciously in answer to it and which was to have a direct impact on Goethe and Romanticism in Germany—I mean J. G. von Herder's *Spirit of Hebrew Poetry,* which exalted biblical verse's "childlike" and primitive appeal to the emotions (only appropriate for a poetry written, by Herder's reckoning, in the childhood of humanity, when passions were all). But of all the matters taken up in Lowth's book and developed by later writers, it is certainly the equation of prophet and poet that had the most immediate and widespread effect. Although his arguments may have been restricted to a relatively small circle of scholars, the conclusions to which they led certainly received widespread attention, and it is not much of an exaggeration to say that the great poet-prophets of Romanticism, as well as Romantic views of inspiration (and the descendants of these views, down to surrealism and perhaps beyond), were all beneficiaries of Lowth's equation of poet and prophet. So it is perhaps fitting to end this survey of some high points of our theme with him, and with a broad gesture to the two and a quarter centuries that have followed publication of his *De sacra poesi hebraeorum*.

•

There only remains for me to perform a last, sad duty in introducing this volume, and that is to mention the names of two participants in our conference who did not live to see its publication. Dan Pagis was a major figure in Hebrew letters in the twentieth century, the author of several outstanding volumes of verse, as well as a pioneering critic who expounded the poetics of secular Hebrew verse in medieval Spain and Renaissance Italy at the Hebrew University in Jerusalem. His essay herein is his last published work of scholarship; he died only a few short weeks after returning to Israel from our conference. Morton Bloomfield of Harvard was an equally outstanding scholar, a student of early English literature whose accomplishments and reputation are well known throughout the world. The essay he contributed to our conference, "Poetry in Prophecy and Apocalypse," brought together insights about his beloved *Piers Plowman* with broader reflections on Messianism and the "apocalyptic temper" and their role in literature of different periods. The essay as he read it to us at the conference was complete and full of wisdom, but Morton was dissatisfied with it and, he said, wished to add substantially to it before allowing it to be published. Unfortunately, his death prevented him from making the desired changes, and so his contribution is not represented in the present volume.

Bloomfield and Pagis, so different in their training and fields of interest, nevertheless shared a common fascination with the intersection of poetry and prophecy, an interest manifest in their major works of scholarship. It is fitting, then, and an honor to all the scholars represented herein to be able to dedicate this volume to the memory of these two men.

CHAPTER 2

Imagining Prophecy

Alan Cooper

In a supposedly disenchanted world, it is, perhaps, surprising how the idiom of prophecy flourishes—and not merely in its banal association with prognostication. A music critic fancifully ascribes a pianist's remarkable performance to "some disembodied controlling spirit" that "seems to hover over the keyboard."[1] A modern poet writes that his poems are produced when he is "jolted out of [his] habitual state of mind" into a "poetic" state by "no apparent cause."[2] Another says that the "first emergence" of a poem "involves the divining, oracular, vatic function" and that the role of technique is merely to ensure "that the first gleam attains its proper effulgence."[3] And a third yearns for "some backtalk from the mute sky," so that she might "patch together a content of sorts."[4]

This idiom, with its intimations of revelation, inspiration, and possession, seems peculiarly applicable to people with extraordinary gifts. Indeed, the encounter with creative genius is no less mystifying today than it must have been twenty-seven hundred years ago, when the prophet Amos—the first whose oracles were preserved in a prophetic book—addressed the Israelites at Bethel. "The Lord roars from Zion," he proclaimed to an audience that heard not a sound (1:2). When he ingenuously asked, "Can misfortune come to a town if the Lord has not caused it?" (3:6), the reply ("No") was self-evident to him and, apparently, to him alone. Amos himself was answerable only to the authority of his vision, which he claimed to be divine: "My Lord God has spoken, who can but prophesy?" (3:8; cf. 7:15).

The prophets, with their magnificent oracles and strange performances, must have been, as Abraham Heschel remarks, "some of the most disturbing people who have ever lived."[5] They "arose," Northrop Frye observes, "out of a . . . reverence for people with ecstatic powers." Reverence, to be sure, but also fear and wariness; like all geniuses, such people "represent an authority . . . that most societies find the greatest difficulty in absorbing." It is the authority of those who perceive more than their fellows and who perceive things differently. They have what Frye calls "a comprehensive view of the human situation, . . . a view which marks the extent of what in other contexts we could call the creative imagination."[6]

Without gainsaying Amos's self-assurance, how might his present-day readers (not to mention his ancient auditors), without the remotest empathy, understand his claim of divine inspiration? Is it literally true, and if so, exactly what does it mean? Or is it a metaphor for some other kind of experience or perhaps a delusion or simply a lie?

If the analogy of the prophetic gift with poetic or musical genius has any validity (as it did for Robert Lowth, for example), then we must assume that the prophetic "art" is some peculiar combination of "inspiration" and "technique."[7] That assumption, of course, scarcely enables us to understand genius, or to become artists (or prophets) ourselves, but it does preclude simplistic explanations. We can say neither that Amos was an unselfconscious medium for transmitting divine messages nor, on the contrary, that he was a clever and well-schooled poseur.[8] Give up those handy explanations, and the mystery of prophetic consciousness comes to the fore. It may well be, as Herder long ago asserted, that it is futile "to aim at penetrating and working ourselves into the subjective condition of the Prophets."[9] That sentiment is echoed by one of the great modern students of prophecy, Johannes Lindblom: "The supernatural mystery of the religious experiences of the prophets is concealed from us and inaccessible to scientific inquiry."[10] Yet inquiry into those experiences—albeit *un*scientific—is, in my view, the heart of the matter, even if critical biblical scholarship has neglected it for good reason.[11]

·

For ancient Jewish and Christian commentators, it was essential to comprehend the nature of inspiration; the truth of their faith depended on the veracity of the revelations to Moses and the prophets. From the very beginning, as Harry Wolfson has shown, those commentators mustered four types of arguments to prove that the laws of the Torah and the teachings of the prophets were of divine origin: "(1) the miracles performed by the prophets; (2) the prophetic power to predict future events; (3) the revelation on Mount Sinai; (4) the intrinsic excellency of the laws and teachings of the prophets."[12] Three of the four proofs, it will be noted, depend on the character of the prophets and their writings. And these three turn up repeatedly in Hellenistic and medieval defenses of Scripture.

The sundering of modern critical scholarship from traditional interpretation began with Spinoza's repudiation of those ancient proofs.[13] Biblical miracles, he argued, are proof of nothing except human credulity, and no more excellence inheres in the Bible than in any book that inculcates virtue. The biblical accounts of history, filled as they are with implausibility and contradiction, are unreliable except in broad outline. As Morton Smith wryly remarks, in the wake of the "great change in our notion of the way the world works . . . O[ld] T[estament] scholars committed to Judaism or Christianity have now some difficulty in explaining how it happens that this revelation of divine truth is mostly incredible."[14]

Whereas traditional study of prophecy concentrated on the nature of divine revelation and human receptivity to it, modern scholarship has moved in two directions: literary history and phenomenology.[15] The first is the attempt to recover the authentic prophetic sayings embedded in the extensively edited prophetic books, to locate those sayings in their original historical and social settings, and to account for their transmission and preservation. The goal of this act of recovery is historical reconstruction—either the correlation of the prophetic writings with the history of Israel or the composition of a history of Israelite religious ideas.[16]

The literary-historical approach posits five stages in the development of the prophetic books: (1) the original prophetic speeches, delivered orally; (2) the transmission of those speeches, either orally or in writing; (3) the composition of the speeches, together with supplementary material (biographical, for example) into books; (4) the compilation of those books into the canonical collection known simply as "Prophets" (Hebrew *nĕbîʾîm,* the plural of *nābîʾ,* "prophet"); (5) the fixing of the text of the collected books.

The earliest speeches, recorded in the books of Amos, Hosea, Micah, and Isaiah, date from the middle to late eighth century B.C.E., and the first edition of Prophets was probably "published" by Nehemiah about three centuries later.[17] That publication asserted the sanctity and authority of a specific collection of books, but the individual books were still subject to editing and circulated in divergent editions.[18] The process of standardizing the text extended from the end of the last century B.C.E. until early in the third century C.E.[19]

In order to understand the prophetic books in their historical development, scholars rely on three methods: *form criticism* for recovering the original speeches; *tradition history* for explaining the processes of transmission and composition; and *text criticism* for establishing the best text of the finished product.

Form critics assume that the original prophetic speeches were brief oracles that were delivered orally. When the oracles are similar in content (for example, threats of judgment or promises of salvation), they also exhibit formal similarities. It is thus possible to isolate the "basic forms of prophetic speech" and to demarcate the conventional elements in prophetic utterances. Each of the idealized forms can then be located in a specific sociohistorical setting (the so-called *Sitz im Leben*), usually cultic or juridical. It is this last element of form criticism that finds it at its weakest and most speculative.[20]

The task of the tradition historian is to account for the transition from discrete oracular utterances to integrated prophetic books.[21] In the case of Isaiah, for example, the scholarly consensus is that it took about half a millennium of oral transmission and literary activity for the book to assume its present shape. As Joseph Blenkinsopp writes, "While the nucleus of this collection goes back, directly or indirectly, to Isaiah ben-Amoz, to whom the entire book is attributed (1:1), at least two thirds of the text derives from anonymous disciples, seers, scholiasts, and interpreters of either the First or the Second Temple period."[22]

The "domain assumptions" of the tradition-historical approach are well summarized in the recent commentary on Isaiah by John Hayes and Stuart Irvine, with special reference to chapters 1–39 (so-called First Isaiah):

> (1) These chapters are the product of a process of exegetical supplementation, editorial redaction, expansive interpolation, and creative reinterpretation that extended over centuries. . . . (2) This material is reflective of the religious and theological developments of the Judean people

> throughout the period in which the work was being produced and thus is a theological anthology of the monarchical period, late first temple times, the exile, and the second temple era. (3) As the material was in transmission and [in] the process of formation, it was added to and edited to reflect practically every significant event in Judean history. (4) The successive phases through which the material has passed can, in general, be isolated, and the literary elements from the various phases can be related to particular historical and sociological contexts. Thus it is possible to outline the general process by which Isaiah 1–39 came into being and thereby to decompose the collection. (5) The process of decomposing the material leaves a deposit of isolated units and fragments that may be considered the original preaching of the eighth-century prophet and reflective of his views and thought.[23]

The first three assumptions pertain to the nature of the biblical material itself, and they are all debatable. (Indeed, one of the main purposes of Hayes and Irvine is to challenge them.) The fourth and fifth assumptions do little more than presume the claims of tradition history and form criticism. They have engendered a bewildering array of literary-historical reconstructions of Isaiah 1–39.[24] Bringing chapters 40–66 into the discussion complicates matters even further. It is generally recognized that they are not the work of the eighth-century prophet.[25] But that observation only begs the tradition-historical question: why were the anonymous sayings of the so-called Deutero-Isaiah (chapters 40–55) and Trito-Isaiah (56–66) attributed to Isaiah of Jerusalem and appended to "his" book? One widespread solution, that the original oracles were preserved, reinterpreted, and augmented by communities of prophetic disciples, has foundered for lack of evidence, and scholarly consensus is now lacking.[26] All that is certain is that the book of Isaiah was in more or less its present form by the second century B.C.E. That is the probable date of the great Isaiah Scroll (1QIsa^{a}) discovered at Qumran and also of the Greek translation of Isaiah.

The evaluation of such ancient evidence for the biblical book is part of the third and last phase of literary-historical scholarship—text criticism. The text critic tries to establish the best text of the *book* of Isaiah. This task is obviously far removed from the search for the *ipsissima verba* of the eighth-century prophet. As the text critic Emanuel Tov remarks, in general "textual criticism deals with the transmission of the finished works."[27] That is because it is based, for the most part, on ancient witnesses to the text of the book which reflect only the latest stages of composition.[28] These witnesses include Hebrew manuscript evidence from the Hellenistic and medieval periods, as well as ancient translations from the Hebrew into various languages (especially Greek, Latin, and Aramaic). When none of the extant evidence appears to offer a satisfactory text, scholars often resort to conjectural emendation.[29] In principle, there is no denying the desirability of working from the best possible biblical text, but as Moshe Greenberg comments, "our present state of knowledge and art in these [text-critical] tasks is very imperfect, with opinion and whim dominating decisions in the absence of a body of systematically developed knowledge."[30]

A complement or, for some, an alternative to literary-historical study is what I have called the phenomenological approach—that is, the examination of prophecy in relation to comparable ancient and modern religious manifestations from the Near East and elsewhere. Robert R. Wilson, a staunch advocate of this approach, defends it this way:

> To be sure, there is a sense in which every society's religion is unique, for it is shaped by a distinctive history and a particular set of cultural forces. However, once this uniqueness has been recognized, the fact remains that the same general religious phenomena appear in a number of different societies. Even more important, these phenomena tend to play similar roles in their respective cultures. For this reason comparative anthropological studies can help us to understand more clearly the interaction between religion and society in a particular culture, such as ancient Israel, without requiring that we ignore the religion's distinctive features.[31]

The essence of the phenomenological study of prophecy is the recognition that the Israelite prophet is but one specimen of a well-attested religious "type." In Lindblom's words, "The prophets belong unmistakably to the 'visionary type' of *homines religiosi,* of which we have countless examples in many different countries and periods."[32] He compares medieval Christian visionaries. Wilson cites a broad range of prophetic types from modern societies, together with every sort of divine intermediary that can be found in the ancient Near East.[33] Following Wilson, Thomas W. Overholt has prepared an extensive reader to introduce students to prophecy as a cross-cultural phenomenon. Overholt expresses the hope that his anthology will inspire readers "to pursue the rewards of reading the Bible and anthropological materials in a way that stimulates dialogue between them. Such study may lead to a better understanding of the Bible, and perhaps also of our human situation."[34]

Once the prophetic type is identified in many cultural contexts, it is possible to specify the social role of the prophet. The fundamental assumption is that similar religious phenomena will function similarly in their respective societies. Wilson identifies some prophets as mainstream figures whose oracles tend to bolster the status quo and others as peripheral gadflies who would foment social change.[35] At this level of generalization, I find the social-scientific study of prophecy to be instructive and illuminating.

Problems with the approach emerge when its advocates attempt more detailed analysis. Wilson's sociohistorical survey of Israelite prophecy is, in my view, far less persuasive than the theoretical generalizations on which it is based.[36] As one of his critics has asserted, "even a brief review of Wilson's study reveals the unmistakable impact that relativism and determinism have had upon his view of prophetic religion, and that positivism and reductionism have had upon his cross-disciplinary method."[37] Wilson's work is, nevertheless, superior to the regrettably mechanical application of social-scientific theory which turns up in much recent scholarship.[38]

A forceful argument against the phenomenological approach can be found in the writings of Abraham Joshua Heschel, particularly *The Prophets*. For him, any "understanding" that is derived from it tends to be demystifying and reductionistic: "In the profound embarrassment caused by the prophets' claim to have received the word of God, persistent efforts have been made to interpret that claim in a way which would take from it all element of mystery" (2.190). Heschel himself is prepared to reject one of the axioms of modern scholarship, namely, "the certainty that there is no supernatural element in the prophets" (2.192).

Heschel's aim is to formulate a nonreductionistic theory of prophecy.[39] In doing so, he inevitably (and, in my view, profitably) reverts to the typical concerns of traditional theories: the nature of revelation and the character of human receptivity to it. "A person's perception," he writes, "depends upon his experience, upon his assumptions, categories of thinking, degree of sensitivity, environment, and cultural atmosphere. A person will notice what he is conditioned to see. The prophet's perception was conditioned by his experience of inspiration" (2.2).

What the prophet perceives, according to Heschel, is the divine pathos, which is the expression of God's concern for the world. Heschel calls this pathos the "fundamental feature of divine reality, present in the prophets' consciousness" (2.87). It evokes the prophet's sympathy, which is an intense emotional identification with the divine Other: "The pathos of God is upon him. It moves him. It breaks out in him like a storm in the soul, overwhelming his inner life. . . . It takes possession of his heart and mind, giving him courage to act against the world" (2.88). Imbued with a constant attitude of sympathy, the prophet is "attuned to God" (2.91).

Armed with his understanding of the prophetic experience, Heschel challenges alternative explanations. He rejects comparison of the biblical prophets with religious figures from other times and places, arguing that "the comparative method . . . must be supplemented by an *immanent method,* by the attempt to go beyond the general features of incidental externals to the unique aspects of religious phenomena" (2.229). He also attacks the various efforts to characterize the prophets as ecstatics, inspired poets, psychotics, and political agitators (2.104–46, 147–69, 170–89, 201–4). And he positively disdains the idea that the prophets' claim to divine inspiration might be mere literary artifice (2.194–97).

For the most part I agree with Heschel's rejection of the phenomenological approach to biblical prophecy. I also find myself utterly out of sympathy with the literary-historical approach (text criticism excepted). As I have written elsewhere, "I do not deny the validity of historical-critical claims. . . . But I am troubled by virtually all the historical-critical presuppositions about what the Bible is and about how and why it ought to be read." I have argued that "we do not understand a text by placing it in *its* 'historical context,' but in *ours,*" and that we do so by assessing our own understanding of the text in the light of the history of interpretation.[40] In making that claim, I have associated myself with those biblical scholars who eschew historical reconstruction in favor of synchronic analysis of the received text.[41] Where I depart from most current "literary study of the Bible," however, is in my constant recourse to traditional biblical commentary for its insights. My goal is a form of biblical scholarship which is connected with the *entire* history of the discipline (not just the critical scholarship of the past two centuries) and, at the same time, in touch with the broader world of humanistic discourse.

•

In order to illustrate my approach, I would like to consider the problem of true and false prophecy in the light of some medieval exegetical and philosophical treatments of the problem. The issue has, to be sure, been discussed at length by modern scholars. Robert R. Wilson has enumerated no fewer than seven approaches to the problem, and Wilson himself takes a new anthropological tack.[42] No critical biblical scholar, to my knowledge, has seriously examined "precritical" accounts of false prophecy. Yet such an examination can, in my view, significantly contribute to a modern biblicist's understanding of the prophetic experience.[43]

Two fascinating passages in prophetic literature which raise the issue of false prophecy are the polemics against prophecy in Jeremiah 23 and Ezekiel 13. Jeremiah attacks those prophets who are "deluding" Israel, because "the prophecies they speak are from their own minds [*ḥăzôn libbām yĕdabbērû*], and not from the mouth of the Lord" (23:16); Ezekiel condemns those who "prophesy out of their own minds [*nĕbîʾê millibbām*]" as "degenerates . . . who follow their own fancy [*rûḥām*] without having had a vision" (13:1–2).[44]

Most traditional and modern commentators on these texts have taken them more or less at face value. The twelfth-century exegete Eliezer de Beaugency, for example, glosses Ezekiel's *millibbām* with *wĕlōʾ mimmennî,* "and not from me [that is, God]." He takes *rûḥām* to mean *bĕdîyat daʿatām,* "the invention of their own minds."[45] In other words, the purported "prophets" are frauds. As a modern scholar puts it, "Their visions are conjured up out of their own minds rather than constructed from Yahweh's words."[46] Once that interpretation is accepted, discussion can turn to the ways in which pseudoprophecy and its practitioners can be distinguished from their genuine counterparts.[47]

The usual tests for true prophecy emphasize two factors: the prophet's miraculous gifts and the excellence of his or her character and teachings. These tests are based on the biblical teachings in Deuteronomy 13:2–6 and 18:15–22. In the latter text, where prophecy is contrasted with divination, the test of the true prophet is that his or her "word" must come to pass. Deuteronomy 13 adds a qualification, namely that the prophet must not promote "other gods." Although such prophets may produce a "sign or wonder," they are not to be followed, for God is "testing" Israel to assess its "love" for Him.

Later commentators explain the prophetic gift in various ways. Some appeal to the miraculous sign as proof of prophecy.[48] God gives the prophet the power either to subdue or to transform elements of nature. The Karaite sage Yaqub al-Qirqisani also invokes a Muslim proof (rarely used by Jewish authorities) to defend the notorious false Messiah Abu-Isa al-Isfahani: Abu-Isa was author of many books although he was unlettered.[49] Such phenomena as automatic writing and books dictated by angels were common enough in the Middle Ages, but their value as proof of prophetic inspiration is eloquently dismissed in a famous responsum by Shelomo ben Adret (Rashba).[50]

The typical Jewish view, inherited from the rabbis, is that prophets were supposed to be "wise, strong, and wealthy."[51] As Rashba comments, "Prophecy and the Holy Spirit inspire only an upright, pious man of the highest moral and intellectual attainment." Maimonides bluntly asserts that fools and ignorant people are unfit to prophesy: "It is as impossible for any one of these to prophesy as it is for an ass or a frog."[52] As for the case of Jeremiah, supposedly called by God while still in his mother's womb (Jer. 1:5), Maimonides argues that "this is the case with all prophets; there must be a physical preparation from the beginning of their existence."[53]

Most commentators note the prophet's talent for prognostication. But although that is the Bible's principal test of true prophecy, the medieval authorities tend to downplay it. Joseph Albo, for example, asserts that God inspired the prophets so that those who would heed them "might attain human perfection by doing God's will, not merely to provide knowledge of the future, as is the case with diviners."[54] Still, true prophets, according to Maimonides, "tell things which men could not tell by reason and ordinary imagination alone," including future events.[55] Ramban (Naḥmanides), in his commentary on Deuteronomy 18:22, takes it for granted that "we expect any prophet to foretell the future." As the young philosopher in Isaac Polgar's *Ezer ha-Dat* explains, a sagacious person may correctly reason out the future, but the prophet "apprehends the matter without knowing how or why it was revealed to him. And if someone were to ask him about it, he could not answer him." Polgar later claims that the prophet's grasp of the matter is, nevertheless, more complete than the sage's.[56] And, for

Shimon ben Ṣemaḥ Duran, the ability to foretell the future does indeed distinguish the prophet from the sage.[57]

The emphasis on the prophet's moral character emerges naturally from the strictures in Deuteronomy 13 and even more clearly from Jeremiah 23. John Skinner's classic study of Jeremiah, for example, emphasizes this point.[58] Among the medievals, Maimonides is notable for his insistence on moral perfection as preparation for prophecy.[59] Other commentators argue that the "perfect righteousness" of the prophet even excuses violating the law "out of momentary necessity." Thus Elijah was justified in offering a sacrifice at the forbidden high place on Mount Carmel.[60] Still, to return to Maimonides, only "some ignorant people" think that God inspires anyone He pleases with the spirit of prophecy as long as that person is morally good.[61] The same ignorant people declare it impossible that God would so inspire a wicked person.

Ḥasdai Crescas raises the problem of the wicked Balaam in view of the strange rabbinic statement that places Balaam on a par with Moses.[62] Crescas interprets that statement to mean that Balaam and Moses have one extraordinary thing in common: their prophetic gifts transcend natural explanation. Only a miracle can account for Moses, and only a miracle can account for prophecy by an evil man lacking all "preparation and perfection."[63]

Examples could, of course, be multiplied, but they would all lead to the same conclusion, namely, that any "objective" test for true prophecy can be challenged if not falsified.[64] Polgar, for instance, recognizes that astrologers often accurately predict the future, while some true prophecies, such as Jonah's, never come to pass.[65] Magicians may at least give the appearance of contravening nature.[66] Insistence on the prophet's moral character seems presumptuous on the part of the commentator and fails to account for revelations to such individuals as Balaam's ass.

Finally, the most fundamental criterion, which contrasts the external stimulus of true prophecy with the internal fabrication of the false variety, runs afoul on both ancient and modern psychology. In the Maimonidean scheme, all visions except those of Moses are imagined.[67] As the anonymous author of the popular *Ruaḥ Ḥen* avers, "These things are not real, and it is well known that they have neither form nor structure." Still, the author continues, "they appear to [the prophet] as if they had come to him from external stimuli."[68] Maimonides himself ascribes this confusion to the "efficiency" of the imaginative faculty.[69]

Modern psychological experiments have shown that mental imagery and actual perception can hardly be distinguished at all.[70] People can be made to mistake real stimuli for images, and anyone who has dreamed will have mistaken illusion for reality. But the physiological processes of perception are about the same in both cases.[71] The subjective means by which most people are able to discriminate between reality and illusion is a mystery.[72] It cannot, therefore, be invoked to distinguish Jeremiah from the "prophets." Jeremiah might well have thought otherwise, but how could he *know*? More to the point, how can *we*?

•

On the face of it, it seems strange for Jeremiah and Ezekiel to apply the title "prophets" to mere charlatans. A. G. Auld has recently advanced the suggestion that Jeremiah, at least, did not think of himself as a prophet.[73] References in the book of Jeremiah to "Jeremiah the prophet," then, are secondary, and pertain to the book's canonical setting rather than to Jeremiah's self-understanding.[74] In this light, pejorative references to "prophets" need not lead to a test of one prophet's claims against another's (unlike the situation in 1 Kings 22), because Jeremiah is condemning the whole institution of prophecy from without. In a response to Auld, Robert P. Carroll argues that "the individuals traditionally known as prophets should not be regarded as prophets . . . but require a different description. They were certainly poets, probably intellectuals, and possibly ideologues."[75]

While I am sympathetic to that rejection of the standard view, I find the proposed alternative uncomfortably facile. My own approach to the problem of those "prophets" is closer to that of some of the aforementioned medieval Jewish authorities. Certainly no one has taken the prophetic experience more seriously than they, since, as Seymour Feldman comments, "prophecy was the very foundation of the belief system of the medieval thinker."[76]

My starting point is Isaac Abravanel's commentary on Ezekiel 13.[77] Abravanel argues that the term *nebîʾîm,* "prophets," is actually a homonym with two contrasting meanings. True prophets "bring forth [*mĕbîʾîm*—the putative etymology of *nĕbîʾîm*] and draw out the revelation of the Most High"; others merely "speak to people." In the latter case the word *nĕbîʾîm* is related to the idiom *nîb śĕpātāyim* (Isaiah 57:19), which is understood to mean "speech."[78] Ezekiel's "prophets" obviously belong to this second category: they "prophesy" (*mĕnabbĕʾîm*) in the sense that they "speak" (*mĕdabbĕrîm*), but Abravanel declares that "the only inspiration they have is what they invent with their own minds [*bôdîm millibbām*]." It is tempting to see in this second type of prophecy Abravanel's response to the outbreak of prophecy during his own lifetime: it was just talk.[79]

While Abravanel offers a fascinating answer to the question "When is a prophet not a prophet?" he still falls back on that unsatisfying interpretation of false prophecy as delusion or fraud. It remained for Meir Arama, a generation after Abravanel (and no friend of the older scholar), to appreciate the potential of Abravanel's distinction. The following commentary on Jeremiah 23:16 is from Arama's *Sefer Urim ve-Tummim*:

> After [Jeremiah] calls them "prophets" he says that they obtain the opposite of knowledge; therefore he continues by saying "the prophecies they speak are from their own minds." When he calls them "prophets" he means that they bring forth [*môṣîʾîm ûmĕbîʾîm*] on their tongues what is in their minds. The tongue is the mind's emissary and agent of expression—in effect the "prophet" of one's own mind [*kĕnābîʾ libbô*; cf. Ps. 90:12], in the sense of *nîb śĕpātāyim* [that is, ordinary speech]. This is how [Jeremiah] can call a wicked and delusive person a "prophet": while true prophets perfect and actualize their reason, these others corrupt it, making nothing out of something.[80]

Simply put, Arama effects a brilliant accommodation of Abravanel's interpretation to the Maimonidean theory of prophecy. For Arama, the truth of prophecy seems to depend not on the presence or absence of inspiration but on the creativity of the prophet's mind. Especially piquant is Arama's way of styling false prophecy, "making nothing out of something," which inverts the standard formula for creation *ex nihilo*. The prophet who self-consciously "creates" actually destroys the revealed word.

The crux of the matter is clearly that basis of all the neo-Aristotelian theories of prophecy, the imagination (*dimyôn*) or imaginative faculty (*kôaḥ hammĕdammeh*). Maimonides defines prophecy as "the most perfect development of the imaginative faculty," and it is the "greatest perfection man can attain." Without the "highest natural excellence of the imaginative faculty," no amount of intellectual and moral attainment will enable a person to prophesy.[81]

Maimonides' clearest definition of imagination is in the first chapter of his *Shemonah Peraqim*. It is, he says, "the power that preserves the impressions of sensibly perceived objects after they vanish from the immediacy of the senses that perceived them. Some impressions are combined with others, and some are separated from others. Therefore, from things it has perceived, this power puts together things it has not perceived at all and which are not possible for it to perceive. . . . [It] puts together many . . . impossible things and makes them exist in the imagination." Maimonides concludes by attacking those philosophers who hold "that everything that can be imagined is possible."[82]

There are two kinds of imagination combined into Maimonides' definition; Harry Wolfson dubbed them the "retentive imagination" and the "compositive imagination."[83] The former is, as Wolfson notes, barely distinguishable from memory. Abraham Ibn Daud, in his *Sefer ha-Emunah ha-Ramah,* calls it *mĕṣayyēr,* "formative": "through which we can recall the form of someone who is hidden from our eyes."[84] Animals have this faculty, which explains how a bird can return to its nest.

The other kind of imagination Ibn Daud calls *mĕdammeh ûmĕḥaššēb,* "imaginative and inventive"; it is "a loving gift of God." Animals do not have it: "Only man can bring forth in his mind many inventions of all kinds, to the point that he has the capacity to create [*librô*', an allusion to what God does in Genesis 1] what has never been created before." Similarly, the author of the *Ruaḥ Ḥen* stresses the unique power of this creative imagination: "From the human imagination come forth many crafty plans for the attainment of something desired; this is beyond the capacity of the animals."[85]

The danger of imagination, as Ibn Daud puts it, is that "sometimes it creates a false form. . . , and sometimes it brings forth a true form." It is active primarily during sleep, combining and separating the images retained in the memory.[86] The newly created forms impress themselves on the senses as if they were actually perceived. This kind of perception is the cause of "lying visions or dreams." Since it is not the task of the imagination to preserve the truth, some things that are imagined will be true and others false.

A "lying dream" is the opposite of a "true dream," which, according to Ibn Daud, is one of the three kinds of prophetic vision.[87] But how can one distinguish a lying dream from a true dream? Obviously, says the *Ruaḥ Ḥen,* by that prerequisite for prophecy, the "perfection of the imaginative faculty" (*šĕlēmût kôaḥ hammĕdammeh*], which means, in Levi ben Gershom's words, that "the imagination of the recipient is perfectly prepared to represent what has been transmitted of the cognition to the material intellect."[88] But how does one test for a perfected imagination?

Ḥasdai Crescas insists that a prophet *can* identify a dream of divine origin by the "force of its impression on his imagination." Non-prophetic dreams leave little impression once the dreamer has awakened; prophetic dreams are "close to real sense impressions," and the prophet can therefore rely on them.[89] Crecas amplifies his point with a poignant and instructive account of Hananiah ben Azzur, the "false prophet" in Jeremiah 28: "I think that Hananiah ben Azzur, who was taken to be a prophet as Scripture plainly teaches, erred in the measure of the force of his imagination; he imagined that his dream about the king of Assyria [*sic*] was a prophetic dream. For an ordinary person does not lie when he can easily be found out, and neither does a prophet. Indeed, Scripture terms [Hananiah] a 'prophet' plain and simple. But there is no doubt that his error in measuring the force of his imagination brought him to this."[90] Hananiah, who incurs the punishment of death for his false prophecy, emerges in Crescas's version of the story as a tragic, or at least pathetic, figure.

There is a continuum of prophetic experiences, along which those experiences and, therefore, the prophets themselves can be placed. At one end stands Moses, whose prophecy was unique because it was unmediated by imagination. Ḥoṭer ben Shelomo describes this prophetic ideal in one of his questions, which is an inquiry into the meaning of a difficult passage in Genesis *Rabba*. The text in question begins: "Great is the power [*kôḥān*] of the prophets, for they liken the form to its Creator [*haṣṣûrâ lĕyôṣĕrô*]." In context the saying probably refers to the ability of the prophets to describe God anthropomorphically. But Ḥoṭer turns it into a philosophical allegory. The "form" is the human intellect, and the "Creator" is the Active Intellect. The "perfection" of the prophets is their "faculty" (that is, the *kôaḥ* of the Midrash), which "likens" the one to the other, thus "attaining the conjunction of the human intellect with the Active Intellect."[91] This ideal, which sounds rather like a mystical experience, corresponds to Maimonides' description of Moses, who "did not receive prophetic inspiration through the medium of the imaginative faculty, but directly through the intellect."[92] The absence of imagination from Mosaic prophecy, of course, guarantees the truth of the Torah.[93]

Next along the continuum come the remainder of the prophets, whose prophecy is, in the words of Shimon ben Ṣemaḥ Duran, "through the medium of the imaginative faculty."[94] The clarity or obscurity of their messages, according to Levi ben Gershom, depends on the relative "perfection or imperfection" of their imaginations.[95] Maimonides describes the variability of their prophetic experiences. They do not prophesy continuously, or always with the same degree of inspiration. "It may happen that the highest degree is reached by a prophet only once in his lifetime, and afterwards remains inaccessible to him, or that a prophet remains below the highest degree until he entirely loses the faculty." To retain the faculty, the prophet must maintain a high level of intellectual and moral perfection, which will in turn sustain the imagination with which he or she is naturally endowed.[96]

The role of imagination in this sort of prophecy is beautifully captured by Nissim ben Moses in his *Sefer ha-Nissim*: "The habits and manner of being of the prophet are present in his imaginative faculty and color the prophetic vision. The prophet who has devoted himself to the intelligibles [that is, a philosopher] will thus have imaginative perceptions that are colored by his intellectual preoccupations."[97] In the light of Maimonides and Nissim, then, non-Mosaic prophecy is an unstable mixture of inspiration, imagination, and experience.

It is now clear that false prophecy is a *kind* of prophecy, not a phenomenon distinguishable from prophecy. One might say that it stands at the opposite end of the continuum from Moses, but it is not possible to place a mark somewhere along the continuum and declare all prophecy on one side to be true and all on the other side false. All non-Mosaic prophecy is imagined. True prophecy arises from an imagination closely attuned to the Divine Will, as in Heschel's prophetic "sympathy" (2.87–103) or the medieval "conjunction with the Active Intellect." False prophecy is the product of the creative imagination. False prophets might imagine that they are inspired, as in Crescas's account of Hananiah ben Azzur. But what is the difference between "real" inspiration and imagined inspiration if all prophecy is imagined? Or conversely, the false prophet's imagination might falsify a true inspiration, as in Meir Arama's "making nothing out of something." Either way, the false prophets are real prophets and no frauds. That is why Jeremiah and Ezekiel call them "prophets," and it is also why those prophets are so dangerous.

•

The false prophet properly belongs with that other class of individuals whose creative imaginations produce lies, namely, the poets. In fact, to return full circle to Abravanel, there is another answer to the question "When is a prophet not a prophet?"—when he is a poet. The Midrash on Psalm 90 anticipates this kind of answer, noting the placement of that "Prayer of Moses" in the book of Psalms rather than in the Torah.[98] In his well-known discussion of prophecy and poetry, Abravanel declares: "Be aware that every 'poem' [*šîrâ*] that you find among the words of the prophets is something that they were inspired to compose autonomously. They did not see it in prophecy like the rest of their visions. . . . It is not the work of God but solely the work of the prophet who composed it."[99] Abravanel's prophet-poet, of course, is no liar, but any distinction between prophecy and poetry inevitably begs the question of the relationship between poetry and truth. After all, as the aphorism has it, *mêṭab haššîr kĕzābô,* "The best part of the poem is what is false in it."

The more basic question is, once again, whether the imagination can be a source of truth. The pendulum has swung back and forth on that question throughout the history of philosophy and poetics.[100] In poetics the imagination (*fantasia*) gets short shrift as long as the Aristotelian ideal of imitation (*mimēsis*) holds sway. Contrast, for example, Horace, who "would not allow either imagination or emotion to pass from under the sway of Reason," with Proclus, who ranked the imaginative faculty higher than reason.[101] That medieval aphorism about the "best part of the poem" can, of course, be understood in two contradictory ways: either it disparages the poet for playing fast and loose with the "facts" (the mimetic view) or it extols the poet's ability to transcend the facts, as it were, in order to achieve a nobler purpose (the imaginative view).[102]

Even critics who recognize that imagination is the soul of poetry are often, like Plato, unwilling to acknowledge its truth.[103] Poetry and prophecy, then, raise essentially the same question concerning the relationship between imagination and truth: Is the imagination the source of truth or its corrupter? For the sake of religious truth, one would expect accounts like Abravanel's, which place prophecy and poetry at opposite poles. For the same reason, Muslims insist that there is no poetry in the Qur'ān.[104] But since the Renaissance, as James Kugel has shown, there has been a persistent tendency to equate the two, to shrink the gulf between the Bible and human works.[105]

This equation has moved from both ends toward the middle. On the one hand, biblical scholars argue for the formal and theoretical identification of prophetic literature as poetry. This is the signal achievement of Robert Lowth (*not* the classification of poetic parallelism for which he is best remembered), who was influenced by the "orientalism" that so captivated eighteenth-century poetry and criticism.[106] After asserting that poetry "is found to pervade the predictions of the prophets," Lowth explicitly attacks Abravanel and Jerome for denying the poetical character of prophetic writing: "A thinking person . . . will not be misled by such authorities as these, before he examines whether they are to be accounted competent judges in this case, and what weight and credit is due to their testimony."[107]

Lowth's equation of prophecy with poetry, with all its profound problems, is no mere intellectual relic; biblical scholars are still worrying over the matter. Heschel, for example, calls the attempt to substitute aesthetics for theology "an evasion of a challenge" (2.157).[108] David Noel Freedman rightly argues that the question is important because of "the larger underlying problem of inspiration, which in turn is related to questions of authority and canonicity."[109] Stephen Geller claims that the Bible's poetic/aesthetic aspect continues to be "morally repugnant" to the pious.[110] Anyone who would identify prophecy with poetry, therefore, must tread warily. Robert Alter begins his discussion of prophecy and poetry with a well-worn question: "Why did the Hebrew prophets cast their urgent messages in verse?" His answer, in my view, hardly advances beyond Lowth's.[111]

On the other hand, poets explicitly and implicitly identify themselves with prophets. This side of the equation will not be elaborated here, beyond the mere mention of such familiar examples as William Wordsworth's comparison of the Bible with Milton and Gerard Manley Hopkins's famous description of poetic inspiration.[112]

·

Even in these disenchanted times, all but devoid of both prophecy and poetry, there are signs of yearning for the prophetic experience: the creative imagination longing to hear and speak for "God" with existential certainty and a confident sense of mission. This yearning stems, I think, from a belated recognition of the real power of enchantment. As Howard Nemerov writes, "Supernatural entities may be easily enough derided and mocked into nonexistence by the skeptical under their traditional names, such as Jehovah, Lucifer, Michael, Ahriman, and so on; but at some peril to all of us, for if those names are fictitious names, and they are, they nevertheless name perfectly real forces able to produce perfectly real and spectacular results in what we call the real world." Poetry, Nemerov continues, "was once the place where these entities did their proper work, where the exact degree of their fictitiousness could be measured against the exact degree of their quite real powers, and both could be experienced ideally, not fatally in the world of action." Nemerov extols the poet as a mythmaker, in contrast to those philosophers, historians, and scientists who cannot grasp "the whole of things rather than their division into categories."[113]

What Nemerov calls the "proper work" of enchantment strikes me as an epigrammatic definition of the Bible's place in the modern world. If I may be permitted to quote myself, "Engagement with the opaque (even esoteric) biblical text enables the willing reader to participate in the creation of a remarkable world of imagination."[114] And the encounter with that world, in my view, often has more to teach us than does immersion in grim reality.

At one point, Heschel remarks that "the certainty of being inspired by God . . . is the basic and central fact of the prophet's consciousness" (2.206). The longing for that kind of certainty, even if only imagined, is surely manifest in the spiritual struggle of the prophets and in the attempts of the medievals to comprehend the prophetic experience as well. It can even be found in the writings of those few modern scholars who, like Heschel, are willing to confront that experience head on. Of course, as T. R. Hobbs comments, Heschel's metaphor is "inadequate" and "unexplained," and it "bears the burden of too many unexamined presuppositions."[115] One could say the same of the medievals, or of all those prophet-poets, past and present, striving for illumination. Their inability to explain strikes me as proper deference to the topic. My inclination is to suspend explanation and to discard facile distinctions—between true and false prophets, between prophecy and poetry, between imagination and reality—rather than to seek labels that foster an illusion of understanding. One can, I think, do no better than to try to imagine prophecy—at least until the world to come, when, as the Midrash says, "every person will be a prophet."[116]

CHAPTER 3

David the Prophet

James L. Kugel

Viewed from the standpoint of our present understanding of the phenomenon of prophecy in ancient Israel, David is a most unlikely candidate for the title of prophet. He is, after all, a king, indeed, the founder of the great and enduring Davidic dynasty; and kings are in some sense the prophets' opposite number. Prophets, that is, messengers sent by the God of Israel with some divine commission, are dispatched *to* kings with words of divine reproach, encouragement, or advice; sometimes they are the out-and-out enemies of the king, as Elijah is to Ahab and Jezebel. When relations between king and prophet are better, the prophet is often a fixture in the royal court, functioning not only as a mediator of the divine word, but as court adviser and counselor. It is in precisely such a role that we see the prophet Nathan in the court of David. So Nathan is *David's prophet;* the division of roles, and of powers, could not be clearer in the narratives of Samuel and Kings. And it goes without saying, David himself is never specifically referred to in these narratives as a prophet, or soothsayer. Given these facts, to set out on the theme of "David the prophet" might seem a most unpromising undertaking.

Yet the fact is that this theme—in fact, almost this very phrase—does emerge, certainly by the end of the first century of the common era. The New Testament and other early Christian writings contain multiple references to David as a prophetic figure. "David . . . being therefore a prophet [προφήτης οὖν ὑπάρχων]" it says clearly in Acts 2:29–30, and the same book amply attests the conviction that the Holy Spirit "spoke beforehand by the mouth of David" (1:16) and that God spoke "by the mouth of our father David his servant" (4:25), just as in Mark 12:36–37 and parallels David speaks "in the Holy Spirit"; similarly, the epistle of Barnabas 12:10 holds that "David himself prophesies."[1]

One might seek to explain these references as Christian *Tendenz*. After all, passages of the Psalms (traditionally attributed to David) are cited in the same accounts as foretelling one or another aspect of the message of Christianity; this being the case, it follows that David must have foreseen the future and/or given voice to a divinely sent message in his Psalms, both aspects of the prophetic task as it was then understood. In other words, for Christians to assert that this or that Davidic psalm was to be interpreted in terms of the Gospels was *ipso facto* a claim that David spoke through some form of prophecy, and to assert that he was a prophet was to put him on a par with Isaiah, Jeremiah, Daniel (incidentally, another case of promotion to prophet) and others who had foretold the coming of a Messiah.

"David the prophet" is not merely an ad hoc Christian invention, however. It is widely attested in rabbinic writings and in several earlier texts, perhaps most directly in a Psalms scroll found among the Dead Sea Scrolls in Cave 11 at Qumran (that is, 11 Q Ps.[a]). This scroll, in addition to containing about a third of the psalms known to us from the biblical Psalter, as well as a few apocryphal compositions, also contains a brief note inventorying the literary oeuvre of King David, whom it describes as "wise, and a light like the light of the sun, and a sage [*sôpēr*] and discerning and perfect in all his ways before God and men." Among his literary works are some 4,050 liturgical compositions (apparently written for the Jerusalem Temple), falling into various categories listed by the scroll. It concludes: "All these he spoke through prophecy given to him by the most High God [*kōl'ēlleh dibbēr binbû'āh 'ašer nātan lô millipnê hā'elyôn*]." Here, we might note, there is no question that certain psalms foretell later events and thereby belong to the general sphere of prophecy (as in the aforementioned Christian texts).[2] Rather, it is asserted as a blanket statement that all of David's listed compositions were written with divine aid, *binbû'ah,* "in prophecy."

Of a similarly prophetic character is the David presented in an allied text, the "Songs of David," preserved in a medieval manuscript from the Cairo Geniza which was discussed in a recent article by David Flusser and Shemuel Safrai.[3] They date the original of these pseudo-Davidic psalms to the first century C.E. or earlier and compare them to our Qumran fragment, suggesting that the original from which the medieval copy emanated came from the Qumran sect. At the end of the first century of the common era, Josephus clearly considered David a prophet (*Jewish Antiquities* 8.109–10). Of course David the prophet went on to flourish in later times under Christian auspices, but as noted, the theme is found in rabbinic writings as well, and one recent study has highlighted the fact that, while David's standing in medieval Judaism was not beyond dispute, certainly one view held him to be a prophet no less than Moses, and his five-part Psalter therefore comparable to the Pentateuch of Moses.[4] It should not therefore be surprising (but somehow it nonetheless is) to find Naḥmanides in the introduction to his commentary on the Pentateuch referring to David as "the illustrious prophet in kingly garb and crown." This side of David the prophet in medieval Judaism might elsewhere be explored in greater detail, but my purpose here is to focus on the very beginning of this tradition and to ask, more precisely, what factors gave rise to this twofold (Jewish and Christian) elaboration of David's prophetic gifts and whether we can isolate specific elements or stages in the development of this tradition.

One thing is clear and has already been pointed out by previous scholars: although the biblical accounts do not specifically designate David as a prophet, a number of late biblical texts open the door, as it were, to this interpretation. Perhaps most insistent of all is the book of Chronicles, with its repeated identification of David as the Temple impresario, the one who ordered the appointment of Levites "as singers who should play loudly on musical instruments, on harps and lyres and cymbals, to raise sounds of joy" (1 Chron. 15:16) and "as ministers before the ark of the Lord, to invoke, to offer thanks, to praise the Lord the God of Israel" (1 Chron. 16:4). David it was who made musical instruments used for divine praise (1 Chron. 23:6; 2 Chron. 7:6; cf. Amos 6:5), and he who established the orders to duty. Moreover, in this function he is described as, if not quite a *nābîʾ* (the word for prophet used elsewhere in Chronicles), then at least, *ʾîš hāʾelohîm,* literally "man of God" (for example, in 2 Chron. 8:14; as in Neh. 12:24, 36), a term used as a prophetic title elsewhere in biblical narrative. So here we have David at least exalted and halfway to prophecy. His other title, "the anointed of the Lord," might well have pulled in the same direction, since its specifically royal connections (kings were the "anointed ones" par excellence) began to be blurred in the late biblical period, and the term was used in connection with anointed priests and (as J. A. Fitzmyer has aptly pointed out), in two Qumran texts specifically for prophetlike figures.[5] One recalls, in this connection, the verse of Psalms 105:15 (cf. 1 Chron. 16:22), "Do not touch my anointed ones, nor harm my prophets." So David, long known as God's "anointed one," might have acquired a quasi-prophetic coloring as the lexical range of this term broadened.

Added to these relatively local bits of terminology is the figure of David himself as presented on the lively canvas of 1 and 2 Samuel. In one version of David's rise, he is summoned to the court of King Saul as a musician, for the Spirit of the Lord had departed from Saul and a divinely sent evil spirit now tormented the king. Now, David's lyre playing here could not but summon the image of prophets who elsewhere are said to take up the lyre to bring on their visions (for example, 1 Sam. 10:5; 2 Kings 3:14–16). What is more, in the case of David's playing the text observes, "And whenever the evil spirit from God was upon Saul, David took the lyre and played it with his hand, so Saul was refreshed, and was well, and the evil spirit departed from him" (1 Sam. 16:23). If so, and in view of the assertion that the evil spirit was itself sent from God, David's playing could hardly have seemed less than divine if it was capable of driving that spirit away. Given the lyre's prophetic associations, David the divine musician could also urge in the direction of David the prophet.

Perhaps most important of all is the matter of 2 Samuel 23: 1–7, the "last words of David." This is certainly a curious composition, and scholars are divided as to its provenance, some arguing that it is an extremely ancient piece of Hebrew writing, others that it is a relatively modern pastiche of archaisms stuck into the mouth of David by a later narrator or editor. Whatever the case, David is certainly presented in prophetic language: he begins his last words with a rare formula—(*nĕʾum* X-son-of-Y, *nĕʾum haggeber*)—used, however, in the case of the soothsayer Balaam (Num. 24:3, 15). He is further described as the "anointed of the God of Israel" (on which see above) and *nĕʿîm zĕmirôt yisrāʾēl*. The latter phrase, sometimes still translated "sweet singer of Israel," almost certainly does not mean that; it may mean "the hero of the songs of Israel," though one recent study proposes "the one granted an affirmative omen by the Mighty One of Israel."[6] The passage then continues: "The Spirit of the Lord speaks through me, his word is upon my tongue; the God of Israel utters, to me speaks the Rock of Israel." Again, although the date of this passage (or its insertion here) is in dispute, there can be no doubt that to readers and listeners living at the end of the biblical period, the combination of assertions and epithets, together with David the divine harpist and the double-entendres "David the anointed" and "David the man of God" seen elsewhere in the Bible, must have encouraged, if not led straight to, "David the prophet," even if this particular phrase is not found in the Hebrew Bible.

There remains, finally, the tradition of David's authorship of some, and later all, of the psalms in the biblical Psalter. This tradition is obviously connected with the many psalm headings or superscriptions that specifically mention David (it seems clear, incidentally, that such headings were by and large added on at some time after the original composition of the psalms themselves). In the traditional Hebrew text, just less than half of the one hundred and fifty psalms of the Psalter bear some form of the superscription *lĕdāwid,* "to [or "of" or "for"] David." The precise significance of this phrase has been debated since antiquity: it may indicate that the psalm in question belonged to a smaller collection of psalms somehow associated with David, that is, "of the Davidic collection"; it may indicate that the psalm or collection of psalms was intended "for David" or for the Davidic king, perhaps for public recitation by him; it may even be that the *subject* in some cases was the Davidic king, that is, "of David." In fact, it seems certain that this phrase had no static existence but, having been used for one purpose early on, was reused and added on to other compositions later, perhaps with a new understanding of its meaning. (It is noteworthy that the Old Greek translation of the Psalter has more Davidic attributions than the traditional Hebrew text, and this apparently bespeaks a later development, as does the great expansion of titles in the Syriac apocryphal psalms and in Aramaic Bible translations.) Perhaps the least likely hypothesis about this mysterious phrase is that it was originally an attribution of authorship, but that is precisely the sense in which it came to be taken. It may be that the editorial note at Psalm 72:20, "The prayers of David son of Jesse are concluded," is evidence of such an interpretation (which evidence certainly predates the final editing of the Psalter, since there are psalms that occur after this note which are nonetheless attributed "to David"). Other, more expansive psalm headings such as those of Psalm 18 or 34 or 51, which mention the supposed circumstances in David's life history which occasioned the psalm's composition, likewise strongly imply a claim of Davidic authorship. The occasional secondary change in the Greek translation of the Bible from "to David" (dative) to "of David" (gene-tive) also appears to be an attempt to make a less ambiguous statement of authorship.[7] In any case, the notion that David wrote many of the psalms—not only attested by the psalm headings and by the insertion of a victory psalm into the narrative of David's life (2 Sam. 22=Ps. 18) but supported by such apparently corroborative incidents as David's composing a lament over Saul and Jonathan, David's dancing before the ark, and so forth—seems to be rooted at least fairly early in Second Temple times, and it was an idea that (as our Qumran psalms scroll, with its mention of 4,050 Davidic compositions, attests) kept expanding. But here David the poet almost inevitably becomes David the prophet, for how else was one to interpret the tradition of the Davidic authorship of psalms (for example, Ps. 137) that seem to be set in a period far more recent than David's—how else but that their author, David, a true prophet of God, was able to foresee conditions centuries, nay ages, after his own time? The Christian evocation of David the prophet seen above was only an expansion of an interpretive tack that was certainly much older.

•

All these certainly constitute the grounds for David's promotion to prophet, but I daresay merely listing them falls short of the task I have assigned myself. For what is necessary is to understand them, and to understand specifically their relationship to one another. To put it differently, David's rise to prophet is not simply the result of all the factors mentioned having accumulated until they attained sufficient critical mass to persuade the Bible's earliest readers that David was in fact that which the text somehow neglects to call him, a prophet. Instead of such a gradual slide, it seems more proper to view the data assembled in terms of three distinct phases or movements in David's reputation, each phase motivated by rather distinct concerns.

I have alluded to the somewhat tendentious picture of David presented in Chronicles, in which his life is simultaneously air-brushed of embarrassing detail (his sin with Bathsheba, Absalom's rebellion, etc.) and, more relevant to our subject, his depiction as the designer of the music and song used in the Jerusalem Temple. Surely the latter element derives from the Chronicler's desire to give music and song in the Temple a distinguished founder. Now it is curious that although the Pentateuch goes into painstaking detail about how different classes of sacrifices are to be offered, the festive calendar, laws of purification, and so forth, it makes no mention of music or songs in its prescriptions of Temple ritual. Whether this omission indeed means, as some have argued, that psalmody was a relative newcomer to that ritual or, as I believe, that it had a somewhat different status from the rest of what went on, especially in priestly eyes, the fact that music and song are not mentioned may have helped to determine the Chronicler's choice for founder of the Temple music and singers.[8] It is David, the ideal king, who establishes these rituals, a David who, as the chosen ruler of God, the "anointed of the Lord," can confer on music making almost the same glory and honor, indeed, the same divine commission as Moses might have.[9] For this is what is on the Chronicler's mind—he is anxious to show that these musical elements of the Temple service, perhaps looked down upon or less respected in other quarters, in truth go back not only to the very one first inspired to build a temple in Jerusalem but to a man who was nothing less than God's chosen servant or, in the Chronicler's telling phrase, a "man of God." This first "promotion" for David does not aim at prophecy or even authorship: it is not a divine message that David brings but a divine plan of how things are to be in the completed Temple. Thus it is to be noted that there is no reference to David as the composer of the words to be spoken or sung in the Temple; he is presented just as I have described him, as the Temple impresario. I would say that all this makes great sense in the context of Israel's worship in postexilic times: the Temple in Jerusalem is the focus of Jewish piety, the meeting place of human and divine. It is important to assert that what goes on in the Temple is utterly in keeping with God's will, even if it had not been spelled out in the great corpus of priestly law—hence the insistence on David's ideal qualities, his status as divinely chosen man, and his role in establishing the Temple music. At the same time, since the actual words spoken or sung in the Temple were not supposed to be utterly standardized but (this was apparently the operating fiction)[10] tailor-made for a variety of speakers and circumstances, there was no stress on David's authorship of the words spoken or sung there.

That concern—the Davidic authorship of the Psalms—bespeaks a somewhat later period, when Israel's ancient texts began to be promoted to something higher, to Scripture. This is a crucial moment for such texts, and it arrives historically at different periods, depending on the text. But in general we can say that at a certain point it was no longer considered sufficient that a particular text had been used or written down in earlier ages and lovingly preserved; now what was demanded was the certain knowledge that the words had indeed been uttered by one of God's chosen servants and not merely some anonymous historian or scribe. The question of authorship was certainly first raised about the Pentateuch, but soon all other sacred texts also required an established, chosen author. (The case made for such authorship need not have been airtight—the "Solomonic" authorship of Proverbs or especially Ecclesiastes was not without problems—but it had at least to be possible; the beloved book of Ben Sira was excluded from the rabbinic canon precisely because its true authorship was too well known.)[11] A famous passage in the writings of Josephus, the first-century Jewish historian, connects the reliability of Israel's historical sources with their exclusive authorship by prophets: "It therefore naturally, or rather necessarily, follows, seeing that with us it is not open to everyone to write the records, that there is no discrepancy in what is written; seeing that, on the contrary, the prophets alone had this privilege, obtaining their knowledge of the most remote and ancient history through inspiration which they owed to God" (*Against Apion* 1.7.37).

Divine inspiration may have vouchsafed the authority of, for example, Moses' account of the Creation and other early events; but it is just as important that the compilers of Israel's later history were prophets, hence reliable recorders.[12] So, similarly, the more the Psalms were looked to as Scripture and not (or not merely) cultic pieces, the more important it was to know who their author was, indeed, to know that their author had been a fit bearer of sacred speech. Anonymity in the case of the Psalms was most troubling, and certainly the psalm headings, whatever their original purpose, were taken as reassuring assertions of authorship in the closing centuries before the common era. There is a reflection of the problems raised by anonymous psalms even later on, in a passage (dated to the first century C.E.) of the apocryphal *Martyrdom of Isaiah* (4:22): "And all these things, behold they are written in the Psalms, in the parables of David the son of Jesse and in the Proverbs of Solomon his son, and in the words of Korah and Ethan the Israelite, and in the words of Asaph, and in the rest of the Psalms which the angel of the spirit has inspired, namely, in those which have no name written." All the names listed in this sentence (David, Solomon, Korah, etc.) appear in the psalm headings, and it is apparently for that reason that they are mentioned here: the text invokes these "authors" and their authority to bolster its own. But what of those psalms that have no name attached to them? It was apparently necessary for the writer of this text to insist that they too enjoyed the same status as the others, that the omission of a name does not mean that they were written by just some uninspired anybody. Unable, however, to connect them with David or any other known individual (to connect them exactly as the authors of our pseudepigrapha had connected their visions and treatises with the names of ancient worthies), the writer is forced to the somewhat awkward assertion that these anonymous psalms originate from the "angel of the spirit."

When exactly did this second stage, the shift to David the divinely chosen one as a fit author for the "scripturescent" Psalms, begin? The date is bound to be inexact, both because "Judaism" hardly spoke with one voice on this issue (different Jewish sects and communities felt different demands) and because what we are dealing with in any case is not an event but a trend, a trend whose history is further complicated by the existence of such psalm headings as *lĕdāwid* which must have seemed to answer the question of authorship even before it became a crucial issue. But certainly the fact that we see scant evidence of David the psalmist in Chronicles is significant. It is interesting as well that the book of Ben Sira (Ecclesiasticus), which we can date with some precision to the beginning of the second century B.C.E., has in its paean of praise to David relatively little to say about him as the author of the Psalms: "In all that he did he gave thanks to the Holy One, Most High, with ascriptions of glory; he sang praise with all his heart, and he loved Maker." Though this does seem to be an allusion to the Davidic authorship of some psalms, it is still far from an assertion that he wrote all of them, or even many; nor yet is there evidence of the association of psalm writing with prophecy or divine inspiration. Indeed, the whole section on David in Ben Sira begins, "And after him [that is, Samuel], Nathan rose up to prophesy in the days of David." That is the last that is said of Nathan, but presumably he is there for the sake of stressing the succession of prophets, *for which purpose, it must still have seemed obvious to Ben Sira, David himself could not serve.*

On the positive side, we do have the evidence of the expanded "biographical" psalm headings (such as the aforementioned ones in Psalms 18, 34, 51) and evidence in the Old Greek Psalter and other ancient version of the increase in Davidic attributions and the "of David" which, as we have seen, seems to aim more specifically at the attribution of authorship. It is noteworthy that so many of these later attributions center on David: for David is now God's chosen one and the quasi-prophetic "man of God." The text of 11 Q Ps.[a] is also interesting in this connection: it does not quite say that David wrote all the Psalms but apparently seeks to overwhelm us with numbers (4,050!). Most interesting is the fact mentioned above that the songs and praises in question in this Qumran text all seem to be associated with the cult. Might not this be seen as an attempt to connect (perhaps "harmonize" would be too strong a word) the growing tradition of the Davidic authorship of many or all the Psalms with the already well-established picture of David the Temple impresario presented in Chronicles?

There is another ancient text relevant to my inquiry, one I have never seen cited in this connection. It is a passing reference in the writings of Philo of Alexandria to the author of Psalm 84—presumably David—as τις προφητικὸς ἀνὴρ, "a certain prophetic man."[13] Whether Philo is thinking specifically of David or simple (as we say) "the Psalmist," his choice of words is a wonderful bit of testimony: it indicates both a desire to connect the author of the psalm with prophecy and yet a reluctance to go all out and say "prophet." Is it not the perfect Greek equivalent of the Qumran Cave 11 Psalter's somewhat hedged description, cited earlier, which, having qualified David as "wise" and "luminous"—in other words, a sage but not a prophet (*nābî'*)—goes on to attribute to him authorship of liturgical pieces composed, it asserts, "in prophecy" (*binbû'āh*). Such indeed is τις προφητικὸς ἀνὴρ.

What conclusions can be drawn from all of this? It seems reasonable to say that there was pressure, but not enormous pressure (witness Ben Sira), in the second century B.C.E. to attribute more and more psalms to David's authorship, and this in consequence of a general abhorrence of anonymous authorship in texts held to be sacred, for sacred here meant not only sanctified by use but also of sacred provenance, transmitted by a specially selected servant of God. This pressure ultimately led to David the prophet in unvarnished form (the third phase I alluded to earlier), and one can identify its inauguration with the fence-sitting of both Alexandrian Philo and the Palestinian author of the note inserted in 11 Q Ps.[a]. This scroll is usually dated to the middle of the first century C.E., the Philo passage slightly earlier. But Philo the exegete, sitting in Alexandria, is probably neither the source of this tradition nor even at the crest of its breaking wave. Therefore it would not seem unreasonable to conclude that David the prophet, that is, the prophetic author of the Psalms, was a notion already in the air at the turn of the era, if not earlier.[14] On the other hand, the utter absence of "David the prophet" not only in the fiercely pro-Davidic book of Chronicles but (far more relevant for purposes of dating) in the second-century B.C.E. book of Ben Sira, which adheres to the clear distinction between king and prophet precisely in regard to David and Nathan, suggests that the theme of "David the prophet" had at least not *imposed itself* until after Ben Sira's time. All this might suggest a period of roughly one hundred and fifty years, the century and a half that preceded the start of the common era, as the time during which the widespread attribution of most, if not all, of the psalms to David's authorship—combined with the desirability of having a "prophetic," divinely commissioned author for the Psalms, as well as the prima facie prophetic nature of psalms "of David" that allude to or best suit events that took place long after his death—all made "David the prophet" seem not only palatable but necessary, indeed, inevitable.

If I have correctly reconstructed the sequence of events that led up to "David the prophet," then it will be seen to have been the product of a rather long chain of events and shifts in sensibilities, a construct whose origins lie in the pro-Davidic sympathies of certain early postexilic writers and editors (the Chronicler, the authors of various psalm headings) moved by rather political or exegetical necessities. Their promotion of David was later elaborated by Jews grappling with the issue of the authorship of sacred texts as part of the canonization process and further refined by those for whom the Psalms were now sacred Scripture, divine revelation. But if this chain of events seems to have been rather fortuitous and quite unpredictable at its outset, its ultimate effect ought not to be understated for all that. "David the prophet" had an afterlife. It concretized the connection of poetry and prophecy for later ages as no other biblical figure or theme did. Thenceforth, a poet, at least a divinely inspired one, might *eo ipso* also be a prophet, and poetry itself (soon: "verse") was thus at least one of the forms that prophecy might take.[15] Corroborated, as it were, by the classical heritage of Greece and Rome, which was so influential (even when being resisted) in the development of Western Christianity, this association of poetry and prophecy went on to play a major role in the intellectual and, particularly, literary life of Europe for two millennia.

CHAPTER 4

Ancient Greek Poetry, Prophecy, and Concepts of Theory

Gregory Nagy

Even in the earliest literary evidence about Greek society, it is clear that a distinction was regularly being made between poetry and prophecy, as reflected by the word *aoidos,* "singer," on one side, and by the words *mantis,* "seer," and *kērux,* "herald," on the other.[1] The notion of *aoidos* corresponds to our notion of poet, while the notions of *mantis* and *kērux,* taken together, correspond roughly to our notion of prophet. Such a pattern of distinction, however, was preceded by an earlier stage in which poet and prophet were as yet undifferentiated. This stage is evident in the self-references of Hesiod's *Theogony,* where the Muses of Mount Helicon are represented as endowing Hesiod with a sacral voice that enables him not only to sing a theogony (*Theogony* 33–34) but also to tell the future and present as well as the past (32); in addition, the Muses give Hesiod a *skēptron,* "staff, scepter," as a symbol of his sacral authority to proclaim the absolute truth (30, in the context of 26–29). In effect, then, the figure of Hesiod presents himself as *mantis,* "seer," and *kērux,* "herald," as well as *aoidos,* "singer," whereas a figure such as Homer is strictly an *aoidos,* a poet.[2]

The words *mantis* and *kērux,* as I shall argue presently, had once been appropriate designations for an undifferentiated poet-prophet; after

Shorter and longer versions, with different frameworks of argumentation and presentation, have appeared respectively in the following two larger works written by the same author: "Early Greek Views of Poets and Poetry," *Cambridge History of Literary Criticism,* vol. 1, ed. G. Kennedy (Cambridge: Cambridge University Press, 1989), pp. 1–77; and *Pindar's Homer: The Lyric Possession of an Epic Past* (Baltimore: Johns Hopkins University Press, 1990), esp. chap. 6.

differentiation set in, the word *aoidos* filled the need for designating a general category, as distinct from *mantis* and *kērux,* which became specialized subcategories. I should add that, by the time of the classical period, another round of differentiation had led to a new general category, *poiētēs,* the ancestor of our word *poet.* Unlike *mantis* and *kērux,* however, which had become specialized subcategories of *aoidos, aoidos* in its own turn did not become a specialized subcategory of the word that replaced it as a general category, *poiētēs.* Whereas the *aoidos* had remained in the sacral realm of prophecy, as evidenced by the institutional dependence of the *aoidos* on the divine inspiration of the Muse, the *poiētēs* entered the secular realm of poetry as we are used to it, where the notion of inspiration is but a literary convention.[3] In the sacral realm of prophecy, however, there survived such specialized subcategories as the designations *prophētēs* and *theōros,* which are the ancestors but not equivalents of our own words *prophet* and *theory.* These designations, as we shall see, maintained the inherited sacral links between poetry and prophecy.

Before turning to the words *prophētēs* and *theōros* and what they meant, I must proceed with my argument concerning the parting of ways between *mantis* and *kērux* on one hand and *aoidos* on the other. To repeat, my claim is that *mantis* and *kērux* had once been appropriate designations for an undifferentiated poet-prophet; after differentiation set in, the word *aoidos* became a general category, while *mantis* and *kērux* became specialized subcategories. Such a pattern of semantic evolution corresponds to what is known in linguistic theory as Kuryłowicz's Fourth Law of Analogy: when two forms come into competition for one function, the newer form may take over that function while the older form may become relegated to a subcategory of its earlier function.[4] In the case of *mantis, kērux,* and *aoidos,* we find the clearest illustration in the realm of myth, where the patterns of differentiation between poet and prophet are reenacted in the patterns of differentiation between various gods who preside over various activities. I cite in particular the division of functions as dramatized in the *Homeric Hymn to Hermes:* in the sphere of prophecy, the older god, Hermes, becomes the specialist, and the newer god who displaces him, Apollo, becomes the generalist. To put it in terms of Prague School linguistics: there is an opposition between the functions of Hermes and Apollo in which Hermes is the marked member of the opposition, and Apollo is the unmarked.[5]

In the *Hymn to Hermes,* the god Hermes is represented as singing the first theogony ever, thereby *krainōn,* "authorizing," the gods, that is, confirming their authority (*HH* 427).[6] In this respect, Hermes is analogous to Hesiod as an undifferentiated poet-prophet. Later, Hermes enters into an agreement with Apollo, in which he cedes to that god the lyre with which he had sung the theogony, along with all the powers that go with it (*HH* 434–512); in return, Apollo gives Hermes a *rhabdos,* "staff," described as *epikrainousa,* "authorizing," the ordinances that Apollo had learned from Zeus (531–32). Again we see an analogy with Hesiod, who received the *skēptron,* "scepter, staff," of authority to proclaim the *Theogony.* But we must note carefully that while Hermes is allowed this much authorization, he is explicitly excluded from the sphere of prophecy that is associated with the Oracle of Apollo at Delphi (*HH* 533–49), being restricted to the sphere of prophecy associated with the Bee Maidens of Mount Parnassus (*HH* 550–66). These Bee Maidens also *krainousin,* that is, "authorize" (*HH* 559), but only if they are fed fermented honey: then they are in ecstasy and tell *alētheiē,* "truth" (560–61), though they *pseudontai,* "lie," when deprived of this stimulant (562–63).[7]

In this "exchange" between Hermes and Apollo, myth formalizes the specialization of Hermes and the generalization of Apollo. The division of attributes between them reenacts the evolutionary separation of functions that are pictured as still integral at the time when Hermes sang the theogony. But then Hermes cedes the lyre to Apollo and confines himself to the primitive shepherd's pipe (*HH* 511–12). In this way, Apollo can take over the sphere of the poet. Apollo also takes over the sphere of the prophet on a highly evolved Panhellenic level (his oracle at Delphi), leaving Hermes the more primitive sphere of the prophet as a local exponent of the sort of "truth" that is induced by fermented honey. The affinity of Hermes with an undifferentiated stage of poetry-prophecy and his actual inauguration of Apollo's poetic art by way of singing a theogony suggest that Hermes is an older god than Apollo and that his "authorizing" staff and his "authorizing" Bee Maidens are vestiges of an older and broader poetic realm. From a historical point of view, Apollo and his Olympian Muses are the newer gods: they represent a streamlining of this older realm into the newer and narrower one of Panhellenic poetry.[8]

It bears stressing that I am applying the words *old* and *new* from a diachronic standpoint: it is a matter of *Religionsgeschichte* that Hermes presides over older institutions and Apollo over the newer ones.[9] From the synchronic point of view of the myth itself, however,

Hermes *seems* to be the younger god and Apollo, the older: in the narrative, after all, Hermes is a newborn infant when he discovers the tortoise, constructs the first lyre out of its shell, and sings the first theogony. To this extent, the sequence of myth reverses the sequence of *Religionsgeschichte:* the older figure is represented as junior and the younger as senior.[10] And yet, even in terms of the myth, Hermes is latently older than Apollo, though he is overtly younger.[11]

Just as Hermes is a specialist by comparison to Apollo, Apollo in turn is a specialist by comparison to the Muses. He is their *khorēgos,* their leader in the choral context of singing, dancing, and instrumental accompaniment (for example, in *Homeric Hymn to Apollo* 189–203).[12] But *he* is the one who primarily dances and plays the instrument, while the Muses' function is more generally that of singing or reciting (as in *Hymn to Apollo* 189–90). It is a Muse, not Apollo, who inspires the *Iliad* (1.1) and the *Odyssey* (1.1). In the realm of prophecy, as in the realm of poetry, it is Apollo, not the Muses, who is a specialist. Whereas the Muses can be described in general as guarantors of prophetic powers to tell the future (again, Hesiod, *Theogony* 32), it is Apollo in particular who presides over prophecy, within such overarching frameworks as the Oracle at Delphi.

The affinities of Apollo with prophecy are reflected even in the etymology of his name, which is *Apollōn* in Ionic, *Apellōn* in Doric, and *Apeilōn* in Cypriote: these forms are apparently related to the Homeric verb *apeileō,* "hold out, authoritatively, in the way of either promise or threat."[13] As for the affinities of Apollo with poetry, they are indirectly reflected in another connection of the name, this time with the noun *apellā,* a Doric term referring to the institution of the coming together of Dorian phratries.[14] The relationship of Apollo with the institution of the *apellā* corresponds to the function of the Muses in their conventional role as integrators of society (Theognis 15–18).[15]

The differentiation between Apollo as a specialist in prophecy and the Muses as generalists in poetry is reflected in Plato's treatment of the distinction between *mantis,* "seer," and *prophētēs,* a word that can best be described in the passage that follows as "declarer":

> For the authors of our being, remembering the command of their father when he bade them create the human race as good as they could, that they might correct our inferior parts and make them attain a measure of *truth* [*alētheia*], placed in the liver the *seat of mantic power* [*manteion*]. And

herein is a proof that the god has given *mantic skill* [*mantikē*] not to the wisdom, but to the foolishness of man. No man, when in his wits, attains *mantic skill* [*mantikē*] that is *inspired* [*entheos*] and *true* [*alēthēs*], but when he receives the [mantic skill], either his intelligence is enthralled in sleep or he is demented by some distemper or *possession* [*enthousiasmos*]. And he who would understand what he remembers to have been said, whether in a dream or when he was awake, through a *mantic* [*mantikē*] and *inspired* [*enthousiastikē*] nature, or would determine by reason the meaning of the apparitions which he has seen, and what *indications* [=verb *sēmainō*] they afford to this man or that, of past, present, or future good and evil, must first recover his wits. But, while he continues *demented* [*maneis*], he cannot *discriminate* [*krīnō*] the visions which he sees or the words which he utters; the ancient saying is very true—that "only a man who has his wits can act or judge about himself and his own affairs." And for this reason it is customary to appoint the lineage of *declarers* [*prophētēs* pl.] to be *judges* [*kritēs* pl.] over the *inspired* [*entheos* pl.] *mantic utterances* [*manteia* pl.]. Some persons call them *seers* [*mantis* pl.], being blind to the fact that they [=the *prophētēs* pl.] are only the expositors of *riddles* [*ainigmos* pl.] and visions, and are not to be called *seers* [*mantis* pl.] at all, but only *declarers* [*prophētēs* pl.] of *what the seers say* [*manteuomena*]. (Plato, *Timaeus* 71e–72b [after B. Jowett's trans.])

In this passage, we must distinguish between the complex philosophical points being made and the relatively simple institutional reality upon which they are predicated: it is clear that the *mantis,* "seer," is being recognized as one who speaks from an altered mental state, let us call it *inspiration,* while the *prophētēs* does not. The philosophical connection being made in this passage between *mantis,* "seer," and *maniā,* "madness, dementia," is in fact etymologically correct: the etymology of *mantis* is "one who is in a special [that is, marked or differentiated] mental state" (from the root **men-,* as in Latin *mens, mentis*), while that of *maniā* is "a special [that is, marked, differentiated] mental state" (again, from root **men-*).[16] The word *mantis* has been semantically specialized in conveying the altered mental state of a seer or prophet, within the framework of Greek religious institutions, while the word *maniā* retains the general notion of being "out of one's mind," being in a state of mind other than the everyday one. From the standpoint of the Platonic passage at hand, the inspiration of the *mantis* is a given, a matter of Greek religious institutions. The noninspiration of the *prophētēs* is also a given, again a matter of Greek religious institutions, as we have seen in the explicit wording of Plato: "and for this reason it is customary to appoint the lineage of *declarers* [*prophētēs* pl.] to be *judges* [*kritēs* pl.] over the *inspired* [*entheos* pl.] *mantic utterances* [*manteia* pl.]."[17]

The prime example is the *prophētēs* of the Oracle of Apollo at Delphi (cf. Herodotus 8.36, 37).[18] The *prophētēs* declares, formalizes as a speech-act, the words of the inspired *mantis*.[19] In the case of the Oracle at Delphi, the office of the inspired *mantis* was traditionally held by a priestess, known as the *Puthiā*, "Pythia."[20] From stories about famous attempts to bribe the Pythia (for example, Herodotus 6.66.3, 6.75.3), we know that it was the Pythia, not the *prophētēs*, who controlled the *content* of the mantic utterance.[21] I infer that the *prophētēs* controlled the *form*. The standard transmission of this form, as we see most clearly in the many quotations of the Delphic Oracle in Herodotus, was the *poetic* form of dactylic hexameter. I see no reason to doubt, therefore, that the *prophētēs* was involved in the poetic formalization of prophecy.[22]

The *mantis*, then, is the intermediary between the source of inspiration and the *prophētēs*, the recomposer of the inspired message in poetic form. Alternatively, in the realm of myth, there are situations where we see no intermediary. Thus the seer par excellence, Teiresias, who declares the will of Zeus, is the "*prophētēs* of Zeus" (Pindar, *Nemean* 1.60). Here we are witnessing a relic of an earlier and undifferentiated stage, in that Teiresias is generally known as a *mantis* (for example, *Odyssey* 11.99). In other words, the figure of Teiresias represents a stage in which the *prophētēs is* the *mantis*. The diction of poetry preserves further relics of such an undifferentiated stage, in which the prophecy of the *mantis* and the poetry formulated by the *prophētēs* are as yet one: in some instances the word *prophētēs* designates the poet as the one who declares the voice of the *Mousa*, "Muse" (Pindar, *Paean* 6.6; Bacchylides, *Epinician* 8.3). A particularly striking example is Pindar fr. 150: "Be a *mantis*, Muse, and I shall be the *prophētēs*." The very form *Mousa* (⟨**mont-ia*; possibly **month-i̯a*) may well be derived from the same root **men-* as in *maniā*.[23] If this etymology is correct, then the very word for Muse reflects an earlier stage when not only the one who is inspired and the one who speaks the words of inspiration are the same, but even the type of mental state marked by *maniā* is not yet differentiated from the type of mental state marked by formations with **men-t-* and **men-*h_2*-*, "remember," "have the mind connected with."

There is yet another pertinent use of *prophētēs*: this word also designates the herald who declares the winner at athletic games (for example, in Bacchylides, *Epinician* 9.28, where the reference is to the Isthmian Games). This usage is crucial for our understanding of another word, *theōros,* "one who observes the vision [*theā*]" in the specific sense of *theōros* as designating the official delegate of a given *polis,* "city-state," who is sent out to observe the athletic games and to bring back the news of victory (Herodotus 1.59.1, 8.26, which refers to the Olympic Games). Thus the *prophētēs* is the one who declares the message of victory at the games, and the *theōros* is the one who witnesses the message and takes it back to the polis to declare it.

Similarly, the *theōros* is the official delegate of a given polis who is to bring back the message of the oracle: there are many examples, the most famous of which is Kreon in Sophocles' *Oedipus Tyrannus* 114. Thus the *prophētēs* is the one who declares the message in the Oracle at Delphi, and the *theōros* is the one who witnesses the message, takes it back to the polis and declares it.

The word *theōros,* to repeat, designated a person who was specifically assigned by the community, the polis, to go to Delphi in order to consult the oracle about a given matter that concerned the community. After the consultation, the *theōros* was to return to the community to impart the communication of the oracle. There were severe sanctions against any *theōros* who would divulge the message of the oracle to outsiders before returning home (*Suda* s.v. τὰ τρία). This message, moreover, was a privileged kind of communication. As Heraclitus declares (22 F 93DK), the god at Delphi neither *legei,* "speaks," nor *kruptei,* "conceals,": rather, he *sēmainei,* "indicates." The verb *sēmainō,* "indicate," is derived from the noun *sēma,* which means "sign" or "signal" and derives from a concept of inner vision (as attested in the Sanskrit cognate *dhyāma,* derived from the verb *dhyā-*).[24] Correspondingly, as we have seen, the word *theōros* means literally "he who sees [root *hor-*] a vision [*theā*]." Thus the god Apollo of the Oracle at Delphi, when he *sēmainei,* "indicates," is conferring an inner vision upon the *theōros,* the one who consults him. Both the encoder and the decoder are supposedly operating on the basis of an inner vision. Greek usage makes it clear that the *prophētēs,* who communicates the words of Apollo to those who consult the god, likewise *sēmainei,* "indicates" (cf. Herodotus 8.37.2).

The Greek word *sēmainō,* "indicate, make a sign [*sēma*]," has been appropriated in such modern lexical creations as *semantics* and *semiotics.* As for *theōriā,* which designates the activity of being a *theōros,* we find it resurrected in another word borrowed from the Greek, that is, *theory*.

In Greek usage, someone *sēmainei*, "indicates," that is, "makes a *sēma*," when he or she speaks from a superior vantage point, as when a scout goes to the top of a hill and then comes back down to indicate what he or she saw (Herodotus 7.192.1, 7.219.1).[25] By extension, someone *sēmainei*, "makes a *sēma*," when he or she speaks from a metaphorically superior vantage point, as when an authoritative person makes a pronouncement that arbitrates between contending points of view (Herodotus 1.5.3). But the ultimate voice of authority belongs to the god of the Oracle at Delphi, whose supreme vantage point confers upon him the knowledge of all things, even the precise number of all grains of sand in the universe (cf. Herodotus 1.47.3).

Thus it is most appropriate for poets, when they speak with the voice of authority, to compare themselves to a *theōros*, one who consults the oracle and to whom the oracle *sēmainei*, "makes a *sēma*," through the intermediacy of the priestess of Apollo, the Pythia. Here is an explicit example from the poetry of Theognis of Megara:

> A man who is *theōros*
> must be more straight, Kyrnos, being on his guard,
> than a carpenter's pin and rule and square
> —a man to whom the priestess [the Pythia] of the god at Delphi
> makes a response, as she *sēmainei* [indicates] the *omphē*[26] [voice = sacred
> utterance] from the opulent shrine.
> You will not find any remedy if you add anything,
> nor will you escape from veering, in the eyes of the gods, if you take
> anything away.
>
> (Theognis 805–10)

Just as the priestess, through her intermediacy, *sēmainei*, "indicates," the message of the god, so also the poet speaks authoritatively, as if he were a lawgiver. Again I quote from Theognis:

> I must render this judgment, Kyrnos, along [the straight line of] a
> carpenter's rule and square,
> and I must give to both sides their equitable share,
> with the help of seers, portents, and burning sacrifice,
> so that I may not incur shameful reproach for veering.
>
> (Theognis 543–46)

By implication, the poet is a *theōros* who *sēmainei,* "indicates," to the community what the god indicates to him or her. To be a *theōros,* as Theognis declares, you may not change for your audience one iota of what the god had imparted to you, just as whoever consults the oracle must report to the community exactly what the priestess had said. In these examples from Theognis, there is no intermediary, no *prophētēs,* between the Pythia and the *theōros,* because the *theōros is* the *prophētēs* as well. The poetry here collapses the attested differentiation between the one who formulates the inspired word as poetry and the one who takes it back to the community.

That the poet is truly speaking here in the mode of a lawgiver is clear from the traditions reported by Herodotus 1.65.4 about Lycurgus, the lawgiver of Sparta: it is the Pythia of the Oracle of Apollo at Delphi who indicates (φράσαι) to Lycurgus the law code of Sparta (*kosmos*).[27]

So we have seen the following differentiations: (1) *mantis:* "one who is in a special mental state, one who is inspired [*entheos*=having the god within], one who communicates in a sacred medium"; (2) *prophētēs:* either number 1 (for example, Teiresias) or, more specifically, "one who communicates the message of the *mantis* in a poetic medium" (for example, the official who turns the inspired message of the Pythia into dactylic hexameters or the poet who turns the inspiring message of the Muse into a variety of meters); (3) *theōros:* either number 2 (for example, Lycurgus or Theognis in the stance of a lawgiver) or, more specifically, "one who is officially delegated by the polis to communicate the message of the *mantis*/*prophētēs* to the polis."[28]

From the sacral standpoint of its archaic Greek etymological legacy, theory must take the place of the long-lost poet who speaks as an author, that is, with the authority of the *theōros.* Theory, then, must recapture exactly what was intended by the poetry. To put it another way, theory must recapture the very essence of the communication between the poet and the poet's community, as proclaimed by the *prophētēs.*

CHAPTER 5

Virgil's Messianic Eclogue

Wendell Clausen

> Vltima Cumaei uenit iam carminis aetas;
> magnus ab integro saeclorum nascitur ordo.
>
> (Virgil, *Eclogues* 4.4–5)

The last age of the Cumaean prophecy has now come and with it a great new temporal order. The year is 40 B.C. Why Virgil took notice of this portentous annunciation, which otherwise would be unknown to us, and made it the occasion of a poem, we can only guess. At any rate, he unhesitatingly defines the last age (whatever the Sibyl had meant[1]) with reference to Hesiod and Aratus as the mythical golden age:[2]

> iam redit et Virgo, redeunt Saturnia regna.
>
> (6)
>
> Now too the Virgin returns, the reign of Saturn returns.

In the *Works and Days* (106–73) Hesiod introduces, after the story of Prometheus and Pandora, another story that men tell (he says) to account for the human condition. It is a story of progressive degeneration from a golden race of men who lived like gods in the reign of Cronus, through the intermediate races of silver and bronze to the iron race, the present debased and corrupt race of which Hesiod despairs. To this symbolic, traditional scheme Hesiod adds, between the bronze and iron races, the race of heroes; theirs being, he notes, the generation before ours. Although necessary, as Hesiod must have felt, to a more comprehensive view of the Greek past, his interpolation evidently disrupts an original pattern, for the heroes are associated with no metal and are out of place besides in this descending scale of value. They were the great warriors, demigods, who fought and died at Thebes and Troy, passing thereafter to the Isles of the Blest, where they enjoy Nature's spontaneous and unfailing bounty forever—a condition indistinguishable, save for its duration, from that of the golden race.[3]

iam redit et Virgo, redeunt Saturnia regna.

Virgil assumes a knowledge of the story that Aratus tells in describing the constellation of the Virgin (Παρθένος, Virgo).[4] She once lived on earth and mingled freely with the men of the golden race, who called her Justice (Δίκη),[5] for she would gather the elders of the people together in the marketplace or in the streets and exhort them to be more just. There was no strife then, no hatred, no tumult of battle, only an innocent and easy existence. With the silver race she mingled less freely, longing as she did for the men of old. She would come alone, in the late afternoon, from the echoing hills to rebuke them for their wickedness, then withdraw again to the hills as they gazed after her. They too died and were succeeded by the bronze race. Loathing them—the first men to forge the highwayman's dagger, to eat the flesh of the ploughing ox—she fled to heaven; yet still in the night she appears to men, to remind them of their ancient sin, near the far-seen constellation of Boötes.

The Virgin is synonymous with the golden race, and by implication therefore—an implication Virgil exploits—with the reign of Cronus. Hence "Saturnia regna," for the Latins had long since identified Cronus with Saturn,[6] who reigned in that golden springtime (as Virgil imagines it)[7] of primitive Latium.

Two surprising innovations are involved in Virgil's vision of the golden age: the golden age is about to be—indeed is now being[8]—restored to mankind; and the restoration coincides with the birth of a child. Ever so slightly Virgil labors the coincidence: with the birth of the child (8 "nascenti") is born (5 "nascitur") a new order of time. The ancients imagined no such prodigious birth or rebirth; for them the golden age was a vague paradise lost in the mythical past and never to be regained.

tu modo nascenti puero, quo ferrea primum
desinet ac toto surget gens aurea mundo,
casta faue Lucina: tuus iam regnat Apollo.

(8–10)

Lucina, chaste goddess, bless the boy, at whose birth the iron age at last will cease and a golden rise up throughout the world: now your Apollo reigns.

The tender, almost homely appeal to Lucina, the old Roman goddess of childbirth,[9] is immediately qualified with the statement that her brother is now gloriously reigning—"tuus iam regnat Apollo"—which reestablishes the elevation of the opening line.[10]

This blessed event will take place—we now approach contemporary reality—when Pollio is consul; that is, in the year 40 B.C. Virgil is alluding to the pact of Brundisium, a political settlement between Antony and Octavian, which was soon disregarded or violated but which, for the moment, offered hope of lasting peace, or at least freedom from lasting fear (14 "perpetua . . . formidine"), to a world burdened with guilt and despair. The pact was negotiated in September, with Asinius Pollio acting as Antony's lieutenant.[11]

The pact of Brundisium was solemnized, in the high Roman fashion, with a dynastic wedding: Antony took to wife Octavian's sister, the chaste Octavia. To contemporary readers the vexed question "Who is the boy?" would not have occurred. They knew well enough who was meant: the expected son of Antony and Octavia, the heir to Antony's greatness—the son that never was; a daughter was born instead. Antony claimed descent from Hercules as proudly as Julius Caesar (and Octavian) claimed descent from Venus;[12] thus the boy would have been descended on his father's side from Hercules, on his mother's from Venus: a symbol incarnate of unity and peace. Like the deified Hercules (Virgil implies) he will be exalted to heaven and there see gods mingling with heroes:

ille deum uitam accipiet diuisque uidebit
permixtos heroas et ipse uidebitur illis,
pacatumque reget patriis uirtutibus orbem.

(15–17)

Scholars have failed to recognize that the allusion to Hercules in lines 15–16 is continued in line 17: "pacatumque reget patriis uirtutibus orbem [and he will rule a world pacified by his father's valor]." The verb *pacare* is ordinarily used of military conquest, as it is by Caesar, "omni pacata Gallia" (*Bellum Gallicum* 1.6.2); but it has also a peculiar sense or reference: to Hercules and the labors by which he pacified the world.[13] Virgil was to use this verb only once again, years later, in a similar, if far more elaborate, context, the encomium of Augustus in book 6 of the *Aeneid;* Augustus is extolled for the magnitude of his achievements and compared favorably with Hercules and Dionysus.[14]

> nec uero Alcides tantum telluris obiuit,
> fixerit aeripedem ceruam licet, aut Erymanthi
> pacarit nemora et Lernam tremefecerit arcu.
>
> (801–3)

> Not even Hercules traversed so much of earth, though he shot the brazen-footed deer, though he pacified the grove of Erymanthus and made Lerna tremble at his bow.

The larger reference in line 17 and at the end of the eclogue, where again there is an allusion to Hercules, is to Hellenistic ruler-worship. For a hundred and fifty years Roman proconsuls in the East had been paid divine honors; a subservient people merely transferred the language and gestures of such worship from Greek potentates—Alexander's successors and their successors—to Roman magistrates, men like Pompey, Julius Caesar, Antony. But in the West, in Rome, there was no such tradition or, as yet, practice—hence the conciseness and indirection of Virgil's references.

The eclogue closes on a note of tenderness and intimacy as the poet addresses the newborn child, urging him to smile at his mother:

> Incipe, parue puer, risu cognoscere matrem
> (matri longa decem tulerunt fastidia menses)
> incipe, parue puer.
>
> (60–62)

> Begin, little boy, to recognize your mother with a smile (ten long months have wearied your mother); begin, little boy.

Much in the tone and manner of these lines is Hellenistic—is owing, that is to say, to Hellenistic poetry, and especially to two poets Virgil had much in mind at the time, Callimachus and Theocritus. In Callimachus's *Hymn to Delos* a travel-weary and impatient Leto speaks to her unborn child, the god Apollo:

> *τί μητέρα, κοῦρε, βαρύνεις; . . .*
> *γείνεο, γείνεο, κοῦρε, καὶ ἤπιος ἔξιθι κόλπου*
>
> (212, 213)

Why, child, do you burden your mother? . . . Be born, be born, child, and come gentle from the womb.

Closer in tone, certainly, is Theocritus 24, *The Infant Heracles;* after bathing and nursing Heracles and his little brother Iphicles, Alcmena puts them to bed in a great bronze shield; then speaks as she strokes their heads:

εὕδετ', ἐμὰ βρέφεα, γλυκερὸν καὶ ἐγέρσιμον ὕπνον·
εὕδετ', ἐμὰ ψυχά.

(7–8)

Sleep, my babes, a light and delicious sleep. Sleep, soul of my soul.[15]

The tenderness of the scene at the end of the eclogue is qualified to a degree by the last line, with its grander reference:

nec deus hunc mensa, dea nec dignata cubili est.

No god invites him to table nor goddess to bed—the sort of child, that is, who refuses his poor mother a smile. It was the deified Hercules who enjoyed these transcendent privileges, and Virgil seems to be thinking of Theocritus 17, which begins with an encomium of Ptolemy:

Ἐκ πατέρων οἷος μὲν ἔην τελέσαι μέγα ἔργον
Λαγείδας Πτολεμαῖος. . . .
τῆνον καὶ μακάρεσσι πατὴρ ὁμότιμον ἔθηκεν
ἀθανάτοις, καί οἱ χρύσεος θρόνος ἐν Διὸς οἴκῳ
δέδμηται· παρὰ δ' αὐτὸν Ἀλέξανδρος φίλα εἰδώς
ἑδριάει, Πέρσαισι βαρὺς θεὸς αἰολομίτρας.
ἀντία δ' Ἡρακλῆος ἕδρα κενταυροφόνοιο
ἵδρυται στερεοῖο τετυγμένα ἐξ ἀδάμαντος·
ἔνθα σὺν ἄλλοισιν θαλίας ἔχει Οὐρανίδῃσι,
χαίρων υἱωνῶν περιώσιον υἱωνοῖσιν. . . .
τῷ καὶ ἐπεὶ δαίτηθεν ἴοι κεκορημένος ἤδη
νέκταρος εὐόδμοιο φίλας ἐς δῶμ' ἀλόχοιο,
τῷ μὲν τόξον ἔδωκεν ὑπωλένιόν τε φαρέτραν,
τῷ δὲ σιδάρειον σκύταλον κεχαραγμένον ὄζοις·
οἱ δ' εἰς ἀμβρόσιον θάλαμον λευκοσφύρου Ἥβας
ὅπλα καὶ αὐτὸν ἄγουσι γενειήταν Διὸς υἱόν.

(17.13–14, 16–23, 28–33)

> What a man was Ptolemy the high-born son of Lagus to accomplish some great deed. . . . Him Zeus made equal to the blessed immortals, for him a golden throne is erected in Zeus's halls, and beside him in friendship sits Alexander, god of the bright-colored turban, the Persians' bane. Opposite them, and wrought of solid adamant, is placed the chair of Heracles, slayer of the Centaurs, and there with the other celestials he keeps revel, rejoicing exceedingly in the sons of his sons. . . . And when he has drunk his fill of fragrant nectar and leaves the feast for his dear wife's house, he hands his bow and quiver to one, and to the other his knotted club of iron, and to the chamber of white-ankled Hebe they escort, with his weapons, Zeus's bearded son.[16]

In the year 40 B.C.—on earth—Antony, not Octavian, was "the greatest prince o' the world," and of this their contemporaries, spectators of the mighty drama, could be in no doubt. In the year 40 B.C., Octavian was a sickly, if determined and ruthless young man, the future Augustus unimaginable. Failure of historical perspective vitiates much that has been written about the fourth eclogue.[17]

The golden age coincides, as already remarked, with the birth of the child. While he is still in his cradle—his miraculously flowering cradle—Earth will pour forth her gifts of plants and flowers; she-goats will return home of their own volition with udders full; and the snake will perish and the treacherous poison herb. But the golden age is not yet completely realized: it will be perfected as the child develops. (The perfectibility of the golden age is another of Virgil's innovations.) When the boy becomes old enough to read of the glories of heroes and of his father's deeds, and to understand what true manhood (*uirtus*) is, the fields will gradually turn golden with grain, the reddening grape hang on the wild briar, and stubborn oaks exude dewdrops of honey. Yet some few traces of ancient wrong will remain. Men will sail the sea, build walled cities, and inflict deep furrows on the Earth. There will be a second *Argo* to transport chosen heroes; new wars, and again mighty Achilles will be sent to Troy. During this period of military expansion in the eastern Mediterranean and beyond, the golden age will insensibly be merged, as the boy grows to manhood, with the age of heroes; like the golden, in Hesiod, an age of preternatural felicity but, unlike the golden, immune to change and deterioration. Now the merchantman will quit the sea, because Earth will produce everything everywhere in abundance. Agricultural labor too will cease; there will be no dyeing of wool—symbolic of decadence—for the ram in the meadow will change the color of his own fleece, sometimes to glowing sea-purple, sometimes to saffron yellow:

ipse sed in pratis aries iam suaue rubenti
murice, iam croceo mutabit uellera luto.

(43–44)

(The portentous Sibylline tone seems very faint and faraway as we contemplate Virgil's polychromatic ram.)

Since the fourth eclogue was not originally conceived as an eclogue, it has, or rather had, no distinctively pastoral features, not even—a significant technical detail noticed by Walter Savage Landor—the bucolic diaeresis.[18] When Virgil published it, some five years later, in his *Book of Eclogues,*[19] he prefixed a brief pastoral apologia:[20]

Sicelides Musae, paulo maiora canamus!
non omnis arbusta iuuant humilesque myricae;
si canimus siluas, siluae sint consule dignae.

(1–3)

Sicilian Muses, let us sing a somewhat grander song. Not all delight in trees and lowly tamarisks; if we sing of the woods, let the woods be worthy of a consul.

—and added, I suspect, the emphatic—the rather too emphatic—reference to Pan and Arcadia near the end:

Pan etiam, Arcadia mecum si iudice certet,
Pan etiam Arcadia dicat se iudice uictum.

(58–59)

Even Pan, if with Arcadia as judge he should challenge me,
Even Pan, with Arcadia as judge, would own himself vanquished.

In the absence of these lines a slight emphasis falls on "Apollo" at the end of line 57, "Lino formosus Apollo," which recalls the earlier mention of Apollo with Lucina—"tu modo nascenti puero . . . casta faue Lucina: tuus iam regnat Apollo" (8, 10)—and thus prepares for the intimacy of the closing scene: "Incipe, parue puer."

Much had happened in the years after the pact of Brundisium while Virgil was writing and rewriting his eclogues and meditating his book. After his consulship, Pollio departed to govern Macedonia for Antony; Virgil was drawn into the circle of Maecenas and became acquainted with Octavian. And so, when Virgil decided to represent his epithalamium (so to call it) as an eclogue and publish it, some five years later, as the fourth in his book, it is likely that he made certain changes[21]—not merely the changes already noticed, but certain subtle changes. Hence, it may be, something of the mystery, or mystification perhaps, of the fourth eclogue. Time obliterates; the expectations of the year 40 B.C. were forgotten, and in the next generation Pollio's son, the rash and ambitious Asinius Gallus, could assert that he was the marvelous child.[22]

·

The fourth eclogue was accessible and attractive to Christian apologists for several reasons: it was beautifully, conveniently mysterious, for they, like their pagan contemporaries, were unable to appreciate its poetic or political context;[23] it referred to the Sibyl, whose prophecies, in large part Jewish and Christian forgeries, the Christians so triumphantly adduced;[24] and, above all, it proposed to imagination a new birth of time with a child, a virgin, and a perfected Edenic world.

Here are a few examples of Christian exegesis from the fourth and fifth centuries:

6:"iam redit et uirgo": the Virgin Mary, who returns after Eve.

7:"noua progenies": baptized Christians, as distinct from Jews; or Christ; more precisely, for Prudentius, the new Adam.

22:"nec magnos metuent armenta leones": Christian congregations will no longer fear persecution from pagan emperors, the great lions.

24:"occidet et serpens": the Old Serpent, the Devil.

25:"Assyrium uulgo nascetur amomum": this prized exotic, which will spring up everywhere, prefigured for the Emperor Constantine—if he did indeed expound the fourth eclogue to the Assembly of Saints on Good Friday A.D. 313–the propagation of the Christian faith.[25]

Jerome and Augustine of course knew better. Jerome characterizes the Christian interpretation of "iam redit et uirgo" as puerile; Augustine identifies the fourth eclogue as an adulatory poem to a Roman noble but supposes that the Sibyl may have divined the advent of Christ.

The Christian, or Messianic, interpretation prevailed unchallenged for centuries, supported by, and supporting, Virgil's reputation as a seer, a Christian before Christ. Virgil's first great modern commentator, the Spanish Jesuit Juan Luis de la Cerda (1617), accepted it in principle but did not allow it to influence his own interpretation in any important way. Virgil's second great modern commentator, the German Protestant Christian Gottlob Heyne (1776) rejected the Christian interpretation in a characteristically vigorous, plain statement, noting, however, that most learned men still accepted it. It would be difficult, if not impossible, to determine exactly when the Christian interpretation was given up. Samuel Johnson, Heyne's contemporary, firmly believed it, but in 1858, in the preface to his commentary on the fourth eclogue, John Conington dismissed it with a brief reference: "The coincidence between Virgil's language and that of the Old Testament prophets is sufficiently striking: but it may be doubted whether Virgil uses any image to which a classical parallel cannot be found."[26] In England, however, a sense of the fourth eclogue as inspired utterance seems to have persisted through most of the nineteenth century, perhaps even longer.

In 1907 a small book was published at London with the title *Virgil's Messianic Eclogue;* it contained three essays by three well-known English classicists. The author of the first essay, R. S. Conway, begins by expressing regret at "the complete decay of the reverence with which Virgil's Fourth Eclogue was once regarded." Conway knows that as a scholar he cannot accept the Christian interpretation, and yet he can hardly bring himself to reject it. The occasional involution of his prose suggests, it seems to me, some distress of spirit: "Understood in the only way possible to the early centuries, that Eclogue made him a direct prophet, and therefore an interpreter of Christ; and it is not the deepest students of Virgil who have thought him unworthy of that divine ministry."[27]

Seventeen years later, however, in 1924, a book was published at Leipzig that made something like the discredited Christian interpretation acceptable: Eduard Norden's *Die Geburt des Kindes.* Norden attempted to explain the fourth eclogue in terms of Eastern theology and ritual, in particular by connecting it with two religious festivals celebrated annually in Alexandria, that of Helios on December 24–25 (Christmas Eve) and that of Aion on January 6 (Epiphany).[28] *Die Geburt des Kindes,* though not a large book, is impressive—profoundly learned, occasionally enlightening, the consistent aberration of a great scholar. It is not necessary to reconstruct Norden's elaborate argument, since it was never, I suppose, accepted in detail, certainly not by very many;[29] and in any case was largely demolished by Guenther Jachmann in 1952.[30] But the general effect of *Die Geburt des Kindes* is still powerfully felt; and to this extent Norden was successful. He succeeded, that is, in the view of many, in making a religious or mystical interpretation of the fourth eclogue intellectually respectable. In my view, however, Norden reintroduced the Babylonian darkness into the interpretation of this brilliant little poem: brilliant and playful, with overtones of grandeur, delicate, intentionally vague perhaps—at once insistent and elusive.

CHAPTER 6

A Mantic Manifesto: The Sūra of "The Poets" and the Qur'ānic Foundations of Prophetic Authority

Michael Zwettler

The traditional view that has determined most Muslim and non-Muslim scholarship on the Qur'ān holds that the text as it has come down to us consists essentially of utterances conceived as discontinuous revelations of varying length received from God by the Prophet Muḥammad and proclaimed by him seriatim over a period of roughly twenty to twenty-five years until his death in A.D. 632. In this essay I subscribe, by and large, to that view.[1] I would hold also that an understanding of the internal dynamics of qur'ānic discourse might best be based, whenever possible and feasible, upon analytic study of whole sūras,[2] with some concern for their approximate place in the historical scheme of unfolding revelation and in the discernible evolution and crystallization of qur'ānic patterns of thought, perception, and expression over the course of the Prophet's career.[3]

With these considerations in mind, I wish to give some attention,

I dedicate this essay to Professor M. J. Kister, with affection, admiration, and deep appreciation: "Wa in kunta ʿan-hā dhā ghinan fa -ghna wa -zdadī."

I thank the Harvard University Center for Jewish Studies and the Yale University Whitney Humanities Center for their generous sponsorship of the conference "On Poetry and Prophecy" (20–21 April 1986), at which an earlier version of this essay was read, and Professor James Kugel, in particular, for his cordial hospitality, efficient organization, and understanding patience. The essay has benefited greatly from the comments and suggestions of the other participants and from general discussions with them. Above all I must thank the many students in my classes over the years whose intelligent questions, observations, and objections have sharpened my own understanding and prompted me to venture on this endeavor.

first, to the phenomenon of mantic inspiration as it seems to have been known to Muḥammad's hearers in early seventh-century Mecca; second, to the biblical (and nonbiblical) prophet or messenger in the Qur'ān as an alternative—and superior—type of mantic; and third, to "The Poets" (sūra 26) as the ideological foundation and locutionary paradigm for the principle of prophetic rule through revealed law—a principle vital to the constitution of the community of believers at Medina, the *umma*.[4]

•

As in many other traditions, those pre-Islamic Arabs whose circumstances and attitudes are reflected in the Qur'ān, classical Arabic poetry, and early narrative reports were aware of a class of individuals who would at times be subject to the influence of some supernatural or paranormal entity. Such individuals would receive through the agency of that entity communications and perceptions inaccessible to ordinary folk and would relay these communications and perceptions to others in a verbal form that differed markedly from conventional everyday speech.[5] The most prominent representatives of the class susceptible to these mantic influences were the shamanistic soothsayers or seers, known as *kuhhān* (sing. *kāhin*), and the poets, whose very name in Arabic—*shuʿarāʾ* (sing. *shāʿir*)—seems to have signified those adept at a special mode of *knowing*, endowed with a special kind of *knowledge*.[6]

The entity, the mantic force that influenced a *kāhin* or a *shāʿir*, was personified as a rational, subtle-bodied being, often permanently associating with (though not necessarily always in fact "possessing") its subject and sometimes of the opposite sex. Such beings were called collectively *jinn* or *jinna* or, rarely, *jānn*, words often infelicitously translated "demons" (whereas "daemons" seems quaintly more acceptable and will sometimes be used here, especially to render the term *shayāṭīn*, to be taken up in a moment.)[7] One of them was called a *jinnī* (fem. *jinnīya*). The jinn were also regularly (and etymologically)[8] linked with insanity: one afflicted with madness was called *majnūn* ("beset, possessed by jinn"). But a *majnūn* could also be one only temporarily under the influence of a jinni or one merely to be dismissed, colloquially and derisively, as no more than "crazy." During the Jāhilīya, or pre-Islamic period, too, the term *shayāṭīn* (sing. *shayṭān*) was used almost synonymously with jinni, apparently with special reference to poetic inspiration. Qur'ānic usage, however, while by no means unambiguous, progressively lent to the term *shayāṭīn* the connotation of jinn of an evil, irreligious, or unbelieving nature, adding to it the older monotheistic senses of "devils" or "demons" par excellence and (in its defined singular form *ash-shayṭān*) "THE Devil" or "Satan." According to both Nöldeke's and Blachère's chronological arrangements, for instance, by the end of the Meccan period (that is, shortly before the Hijra in 622), we find the qur'ānic statement that there are *shayāṭīn,* "daemons," of both humankind and jinn appointed by God as enemies to prophets, "one inspiring the other with embellished discourse to deceive" (6:112).[9]

Paul Eichler has shown that to denote more strictly a person subject to inspiration by jinn the Qur'ān employs the phrase *bi-hi jinna* or, negatively, *mā bi-hi min jinna* (literally, "jinn are with, by, or in him" or "no jinn are . . .") and that these must be distinguished from expressions such as *majnūn,* signifying possession or madness.[10] And Toshihiko Izutsu has analyzed the distinctly unilateral, generally verbal, and always private or secret character of communication through mantic inspiration—whether by daemons (jinn or *shayāṭīn*), angels, or God—as its semantic structure emerges from early Arabic sources, especially poetry and the Qur'ān itself.[11]

When performing as such, then, each of the two best-known mantic figures, the *kāhin* and the poet (*shāʿir*), was presumed to be operating under the control of an invisible being that communicated directly and privately to him words that he then repeated verbatim not as his own but as those of his controlling agent, words that he could not have been expected to have produced of his own volition. These words, as discourse, bore witness to their unnatural or paranormal origin not only by their extraordinary content and often difficult style but above all by their very linguistic medium: rhymed and cadenced periods (*sajʿ*) for the *kāhin,* rigorously rhymed and isometric verse (*shiʿr*) for the poet, and—if my hypothesis is correct regarding the oral-poetical foundations of the classical Arabic language[12]—a special nonvernacular, intertribal, case- and mood-inflective speech-form for both. Yet, at the time of Muḥammad certainly and probably for some time before that, the *kāhin* and the poet were pretty clearly differentiated from each other, both in the nature of their activities and their verbal products and in the minds of their audiences.

In simplest terms, the *kāhin* was a consultant on the occult, a soothsayer or oracle whose short, cryptic, rhymed, jinn-inspired pronouncements on such matters as lost camels, launching of raids, determination of paternity, and especially dream interpretation and other kinds of auguries were seldom volunteered but were besought and usually compensated.[13] Judging from many of the early Arabic narrative sources, it seems that the pre-Islamic *kuhhān,* with few exceptions, were frequently depicted as something of social misfits, sometimes deformed or defective in body, dwelling outside the pale of normal urban and nomadic communities. One might think, Jean Lecerf suggests, "that there existed in the popular imagination a connection between physical infirmities or disabilities of whatever kind and the possession of superior powers to establish contact with demons, the souls of the ancestors, or hidden realities."[14] While the oracular incantations of the *kuhhān* of the Jāhilīya may have been valued for whatever advice, information, or prognostication they might enigmatically have conveyed, in few, if any, instances that we know of did they urge—much less command—a course of action or a moral stance. It may be true that some tribal leaders, or sayyids, could have been touched with some of the *kāhin*'s mantic or shamanistic endowments (though that such a state of affairs was common during the sixth and early seventh centuries is by no means so evident as Henri Lammens and others have alleged).[15] But I am aware of no record from the last century or so before Islam of an individual's being elevated to a position of leadership *by virtue of* such abilities or the inspired communications resulting from them.

Contrasted with the rhymed and cadenced *saj*ʿ of the *kuhhān,* the utterances of the poets were far more regular and patterned in their formal structure, having both a considerably more complex and demanding system of rhyme and a rigorously isometric prosody. And their verse productions tended to be far more substantial, extensive, coherent, thematically and generically diversified, and aesthetically satisfying than the vaticinations of the *kuhhān*. Poets themselves seem to have participated to a much greater extent in the social life of the Jāhilīya, serving sometimes as respected spokesmen for their own tribes, feared hurlers of invective verse at enemies, welcome panegyrists before kings and chieftains, and admired masters of verbal art in any assembly. Theirs, too, was a discourse believed to be inspired and conditioned by jinn or *shayāṭīn;* and the exceptional verbal and linguistic virtuosity and creative variety that even a middling poet could command so far exceeded the capacities of the average speaker of Arabic that it would have been but a short step to attribute such qualities to some external, superhuman source.[16] It may well be, as

Eichler and Izutsu have speculated, that by the end of the sixth century the relatively primitive shamanistic idea of involuntary, daemon-inspired, daemon-directed speech as applied to the newer breed of professional poets no longer retained quite the cogency that it may once have held when applied to the earlier tribal poets and still held as applied to the *kuhhān*.[17] Nevertheless, the idea unquestionably did retain tremendous power and popularity as an etiological myth accounting for the singularity and wonder of poetic creativity—a myth that has been embraced, recounted, and embellished by many later Arab and Muslim writers with tongue only half in cheek.[18] And yet, again, as with the kuhhān, the poems of the pre-Islamic shuʿarāʾ which communicated their special, privileged jinn- or *shayāṭīn*-inspired knowledge bore no moral imperative. Edify, exhort, advise, deplore, condemn, embarrass, scorn, extoll, lament—all of these and more the poets' words might do! But as discourse their words neither commanded what was good and reputable nor forbade what was evil and reprehensible: poems were not framed nor poets fit to be obeyed. Accordingly, although some famous sayyids of the late Jāhilīya, such as Labīd and Durayd b. aṣ-Ṣimma, may also have been celebrated poets, it was never *because* they were poets that they became sayyids. It was more likely *despite* or *regardless of* their being poets.

Izutsu writes that "in the latter Jahili period just preceding the rise of Islam, the social position of the poet was no longer so high" as it may have been "in the most ancient days of Arab heathenism,"[19] when the poet's magical jinn-impelled words were launched against the enemy like poisoned arrows.[20] One might question whether the social position of poets had ever actually been as high as Izutsu supposes, however much honored, admired, and valued they might have been. Or perhaps the increasing professionalism of many of the poets, together with their perennial journeys from one court or camp to another, trading their talents and their praises for patronage and recognition, severely reduced, within their own communities, whatever leadership potential they might once have had. Or it may be that, as Lecerf ventures with reference to both kinds of mantic practitioners, poet and *kāhin*, "perhaps a bond did exist, or at least was presumed to exist, between an inability to fulfill a normal function in society and an aptitude for supranormal functions."[21]

What is clear is that whatever special knowledge the jinn or *shayāṭīn* might have communicated to poets and *kuhhān* and however useful, pertinent, accurate, and wondrous it might on occasion have seemed, it was essentially a situation-specific, morally neutral kind of knowledge of relatively little practical value in ordering the behavior, affairs, lives, and communities of human beings over the long term. At their most prescriptive and normative, these mantic communications might take the form of cryptic advisories or warnings, aphoristic exhortations, bitter condemnations, affective appeals, satirical tirades, or idealized portrayals of exemplary conduct or character that could be adduced on an ad hoc basis to confirm or discredit something in terms of its conformity to established convention, received opinion, and shared experience. The discourse of *kuhhān* and especially poets might have incorporated much that was true and valuable, and leaders—tribal chieftains and even kings—may have found it expedient to consult and patronize them; but certainly no one who operated under the control of such capricious, unreliable, antisocial, and often downright misanthropic powers as jinn and *shayāṭīn* could be expected to act dependably and consistently for the welfare of those who would follow his lead.[22] Early Arabic tradition certainly gives us enough instances of nonconformity, impetuosity, recklessness, irresponsibility, alienation, and lawlessness on the part of pre-Islamic and even early Islamic poets—such as Imra'alqays, Ṭarafa, ʿAmr ibn Kulthūm, Shanfara, Kaʿb ibn Zuhair, and the Prophet's own poet Ḥassān ibn Thābit—to support the view that poets *as poets* were not commonly considered fit leadership material by their contemporaries.[23]

•

To proceed from these considerations to the question of the Prophet Muḥammad, the sūra of "The Poets," and the foundations of prophetic authority, I will first refer briefly to what I have said elsewhere in a not entirely dissimilar context: "The Qur'ān, as is well known, most insistently denies that Muḥammad was either a poet or a *kāhin*."[24] In Mecca it quite soon became imperative that the qur'ānic revelations be absolutely dissociated from the verses of the former and the vatic incantations of the latter. "One is made aware that comparisons—invidious or otherwise—had been drawn by Muḥammad's Meccan detractors between his revelations, admittedly inspired by a supranormal agent, and the familiar mantic utterances of poets and soothsayers; and one generally and, I believe, correctly assumes that such comparisons had their basis in some sort of perceived similarities of form and style and, to unsympathetic observers, source of inspiration as well."[25]

That these comparisons would have been prompted by a fairly natural response on the part of Muḥammad's fellow Meccan tribesmen to his self-evidently mantic experiences and pronouncements is attested in one of the earliest preserved reports of his call as Messenger and his first revelation. Transmitted by Muḥammad ibn Isḥāq (d. 150/767), the report depicts Muḥammad himself as appalled at the prospect that he had been afflicted by daemonic possession and that he might have been being coerced into the role of poet or *kāhin*. In words assigned directly to him, we are told of his initial reaction to his encounter with the divine messenger (traditionally identified as the angel Gabriel): "Of all God's creatures there was none more odious to me than a poet or one possessed! I couldn't bear to look at them. . . . I said, 'Oh, wretched me! A poet or a man possessed? Never shall Quraysh say that about me! Let me climb to the mountain's bare peak, hurl myself off, and kill myself! Then shall I surely have rest!' So I went forth with that intention."[26] But Gabriel prevents this rash act, and through the compassionate trust of his wife and the wise counsel of her Christian (or monotheist) kinsman, Muḥammad comes to recognize and accept the divine rather than daemonic source of that which had been communicated to him.

Such a distinction, however, between divine revelation and inspiration by jinn or *shayāṭīn* seems to have been totally beyond the grasp of most of Muḥammad's Meccan compatriots. For them the facts—namely, that his recited discourse indisputably originated as mantic communication, that it shared the formal features of the rhymed prose (*saj*ʿ) heard in the vaticinations of the jinn-directed *kuhhān,* and that it was couched in a linguistic medium, the inflective ʿarabīya, which was inseparable in their minds from the discourse of the *kuhhān* and, above all, the poets—were sufficient to implicate him conclusively as one of their ilk or at least to lend such accusations credibility.

Among revelations explicitly addressed to these accusations one of those dated earliest occurs in sūra 52, "The Mount" (B22/N40):

> Therefore remind! by thy Lord's
>   bounty thou [Muḥammad] art
>   not a *kāhin* nor possessed [*majnūn*].
> Or do they say, "He is a poet for
>   whom we expect the vagaries of the
>   'fates.' "

Say: "Expect! I shall be with you
among the expectant."

(29–31)[27]

At about the same time (according to Blachère's chronology: B24/N38), an even more emphatic denial was issued in sūra 69, "The Inevitable":

No! I swear by what you see
and by what you do not see:
It is indeed the discourse [*qawl*] of
a noble Messenger—
it is not a poet's discourse (little
do you believe!)
nor a *kāhin*'s discourse (little do
you recall!)—
a sending-down from the Lord of the
Worlds.

(38–43; cf. 26:192)

But perhaps even earlier than either of these passages, a powerful and passionate assertion of the reality and truth of Muḥammad's visions was revealed in sūra 81, "The Envelopment" (B18/N27), sharply differentiating between the source of his prophetic communications and that of the mantic communications familiar to contemporaries:

It is indeed the discourse of a
noble Messenger,
one having power and with the Lord
of the Throne firmly placed,
one to be obeyed there and
trustworthy [*muṭāʿin thamma amīn*].
Your comrade [Muḥammad] is not
possessed [*majnūn*]:
He did see him on the clear horizon.
Nor with the Mystery [*al-ghayb*] is
he stingy [*ḍanīn*].
It is not the discourse of an
accursed demon [*shayṭān rajīm*].

(19–25)[28]

Although these three important passages certainly merit serious attention and explication, at this time only a very few salient points will be considered. In the second and third passages, particularly, we find introduced the figure of "a noble Messenger" (*rasūl karīm*)—not, here, Muḥammad but his inspiring agent, who subsequently becomes identified with "the Spirit" of revelation—"the Holy Spirit" (*rūḥ al-qudus*) or "the trustworthy Spirit" (*ar-rūḥ al-amīn*)—and, in Islamic tradition, with Gabriel.[29] From the outset the predication of this figure would immediately have given to the mantic event of qur'ānic revelation a structure radically different from that of poetic or divinatory inspiration. For to adapt Izutsu's point of view, whereas the familiar unilateral, unidirectional act of communication by jinni or *shayṭān* through poet or *kāhin* to audience could be characterized as a three-person relationship (A→B→C), the communication predicated in these and similar qur'ānic verses—namely, the "Lord of the Worlds" to a "noble Messenger" to Muḥammad to his audience—would represent a four-person relationship (G→A→B→C).[30]

A communicational relationship such as this lay altogether beyond the standard conception of mantic experience. Setting God prior to jinn or *shayāṭīn* as the party initiating the communicative act completely changed its character and quality, since among the Arab populations of central and northern Arabia at the time, God—*Allāh,* "THE God"— was generally acknowledged as creator, sky dweller, supreme god, and patron of Mecca's sanctuary, albeit for most of the nonmonotheists He had become a *deus otiosus* to be venerated and called upon only in moments of dire need.[31] In addition, setting an angelic "noble Messenger" in place of jinn or *shayāṭīn* as the intermediary agent communicating from God to Muḥammad further defamiliarized the qur'ānic event. While little in the structure of this unique mantic relationship or in the content of early Meccan revelations could be said to presuppose an *essential* difference between the Prophet's inspiring "noble Messenger" and the jinn or *shayāṭīn,* nevertheless, the very terms with which the divine agent is described—"noble [*karīm*]. . . , having power [*dhū qūwa*] and . . . firmly placed [*makīn*], . . . to be obeyed [*muṭāʿ*], . . . trustworthy [*amīn*]"—could never in any normal circumstances have been applied to jinn, much less to *shayāṭīn*.[32] These terms are charged with social and political significance. They are evocative of a degree of respectability, prestige, reliability, and authority not ordinarily associated with the mantic experience and the mantic practitioner in sixth- and early seventh-century Arabia.

But these early revelations, directly confronting and refuting accusations that Muḥammad was a poet or a *kāhin* (or just plain crazy), seem not to have had the intended effect upon most of their hearers, for revelations dated later continued to be addressed to such accusations with just as much urgency. Furthermore, those revelations also introduced a new and vitally important theme: namely, that preceding messengers and prophets—Noah, Moses, and others—had met with comparable accusations leveled against them by the peoples to whom they had been sent and that their precurrent similar experiences could be understood to have adumbrated and validated Muḥammad's present situation and could be adduced to corroborate the authenticity of his mission and the truth of his message (for example, 21:3–5; 36:35–36; 51:52; etc). Nowhere in the Qur'ān are the two disparate agents of mantic activity—seventh-century Arabian *kuhhān* and poets, on the one hand, and ancient Near Eastern prophets and messengers, on the other—more directly and effectively brought together, counterposed, and distinguished from one another than in sūra 26, "The Poets."

•

According to scholarly consensus, it is during what is called the "middle Meccan period" of qur'ānic revelation (roughly perhaps around 617 or so) that the sūra of "The Poets" (*sūrat ash-shuʿarā'*) can be dated.[33] Like many other sūras dated to this period, it takes the form of a three-part homiletically structured elocution or homilylike "recitation-text," consisting of 227 verses (*āyāt;* sing. *āya*) of varying length.[34]

The first of the three major sections is a proem of seven āyas, consoling the Prophet Muḥammad for the unbelief of most of his compatriots and their rejection of the evidential "sign" of God's production:

Ṭā'. Sīn. Mīm.
Those are the signs [*āyāt*] of the
articulate Scripture.[35]
Perhaps thou [Muḥammad] shalt
grieve thyself to death that they
are not believers.
If We wish, We will send down
[*nunazzil*] upon them from heaven a

sign [*āya*]: then to it shall their
necks stay abjectly submissive!
Not a single reminder comes to
them, by the Kindly One brought
forth anew [*muḥdath*], but that from
it they have turned away.
So did they cry lies! And so shall
they have news [*anbāʾ*][36] of that
which they were wont to scorn!
Could they not have looked to the
land ?[37] How many have We produced
therein of every noble type
[*zawj*]!

(1/1–7/6)

The next two verses recur as a refrain seven more times in the long middle section of the sūra (67–68, 103–4, 121–22, 139–40, 158–59, 174–75, 190–91):

Surely in that is a sign [*āya*],[38]
though most of them have not been
believers.
Surely thy Lord—He indeed is the
Mighty and Kindly One [*la-huwa l-ʿazīzu r-raḥīm*]!

(8/7–9/8)

The body of the sūra (āyas 10/9–189) comprises seven narrative subsections: each recounts the essential mission of an earlier messenger-prophet (all of whose careers are treated with more detail in other sūras) and each closes with the refrain just quoted. Each of these seven prophetic stories tends progressively to replicate the other, and each is declared by its refrain to entail a "sign" (*āya*), reiterating the declaration that has just affirmed exactly the same entailment with respect to God's production in the land of "every noble type" (as I have here rendered *zawj*) or, more generally, with respect to Muḥammad's own reception and situation just described (āyas 3/2–7/6). To these matters of the "sign" and the "type" we shall return.

First, a few words may be in order on a question of terminology. In qur'ānic usage the two terms that, above all others, are applied to the mantic recipients and communicators of God's revelation are *nabīy* (pl. *anbiyā', nabīyūn*), "prophet," and *rasūl* (pl. *rusul*), "messenger, apostle" (or its near synonym *mursal* [pl. *mursalūn*], "envoy, emissary").[39] It is true that significant distinctions can often be discerned between *nabīy* and *rasūl* (or *mursal*) in their qurʿānic context.[40] In this essay, however, I have not always scrupulously observed those distinctions and have sometimes used the terms synonymously or in combination. Careful analysis indicates that *nabīy* tends to be applied to biblical figures (including Zachariah, John the Baptist, and Jesus) who "are exclusively among the descendants of Ibrāhīm."[41] The term *rasūl,* on the other hand, which occurs more than four times as often as *nabīy,* usually denotes "above all those who had been sent to a certain folk or community in particular to warn them of impending disaster."[42] But in addition to performing that function, shared with the *nabīy,* a *rasūl* is also to be seen as the proper head or leader of the community.[43] The *rasūl,* writes Willem Bijlefeld, "is God's 'representative' to his people, and as such he has a great responsibility as well as tremendous authority. . . . The 'apostle' is a messenger from among his own people to bring them in their own language the Warning of God: he speaks for God and is so closely linked with God that obedience to the Almighty coincides with obedience to the messenger."[44] As applied to Muḥammad before the Hijra (when this sūra has been dated), "the connotation [of *rasūl*] is primarily that of a messenger sent by God to bring to his own community in its own language *the very same message* which other apostles and communities had received before them."[45] Of the mantic protagonists figuring in these episodes, all but Abraham are explicitly designated *rasūl* within the Qur'ān, and he too shares many features characteristic of messengers.[46]

Qur'ānic revelation gives the names of five (perhaps six) of these personages who are accorded both titles, *nabīy* and *rasūl:* Noah, Ishmael, Moses (with Aaron), and Jesus (and perhaps Jonah who is referred to as *mursal*). It is to this distinguished company of messenger-prophets that Muḥammad is joined, particularly after the Hijra (if the chronology of revelation adopted here and by Bijlefeld be followed), when, Bijlefeld suggests, "the emphatic use of [*nabīy*] . . . coincides with a greater emphasis on the Arabs' descendence from Ibrāhīm and with the first clear references to Ismāʿīl's functioning in the line Ibrāhīm—Ismāʿīl—Arabs."[47]

Regardless of how this assemblage of prophets, messengers, heralds of joy and warning, etc., might have been designated, however, nothing could have been more evident than that collectively they functioned within the world view of the Qur'ān as the unique and unimpeachable channel through which divine *scriptural* revelation had been and was presently being communicated to human societies and, in that capacity, as figures of God-granted authority to whom obedience was due and right. At the same time, though, in the form of a partially schematized series or set of prominent, "historically" verifiable, relatively homogeneous exemplary precedents for divine inspiration and commission, collectively they also provided an unmistakable typological alternative to the contemporary mantic practitioners whose role was more familiar to the Meccan Quraysh. It would have been these latter—the poets, *kuhhān,* sorcerers, etc.—with whom the phenomena of supernatural perception, communication, and intervention were commonly and traditionally associated and with whom these earlier prophetic figures, and Muḥammad, had been mistakenly or deliberately confused.

Such is certainly the case with the seven messenger-prophets whose missions are recounted in sūra 26. Four of them—Moses, Abraham, Noah, Lot—would have been well known to those who had some acquaintance with the Old Testament, whether through reading the scriptural texts or (as seems more likely) through hearing lectors, preachers, or storytellers or attending liturgical recitations. The other three—Hūd, Ṣāliḥ, Shuʿayb—would presumably have been better known, at least as names, chiefly among those familiar with the unwritten *Urgeschichte* of Arabia; or at any rate, the disastrous fates that, in the sūra's pericopes, overtook those messengers' unheeding, disobedient folk would have had somber confirmation in the awe-inspiring ruins and burial sites of vanished peoples.[48]

Returning to the sūra of "The Poets" we observe that the first two of the sūra's seven narrative subsections, comprising sixty-seven and thirty-four verses respectively, are both longer than any of the other five and noticeably different from all of them in content and style, perhaps to some extent in accordance with the special position held by Moses (Mūsā) and Abraham (Ibrāhīm), their respective subjects, in qur'ānic prophetology (and for other reasons I shall go into later).

In āyas 10/9–66 is recounted the familiar episode of Moses, seconded by Aaron (Hārūn), confronting Pharaoh (Firʿawn) with God's message of monotheism and with miraculous magical manifestations of His power, confounding and converting Pharaoh's professional sorcerers, and leading the Children of Israel to safety and Pharaoh's troops to destruction—all explicitly as the result of God's direct intervention in the affairs of the world and the life of His messenger.[49] Moses is far and away the most elaborately developed character in qur'ānic revelation, with almost fifty separate passages and over five hundred āyas given over to mentions and accounts of him. In these passages and verses one can discern perhaps as many as ninety-some discrete incidents and situations involving Moses.[50]

Without entering into the vexed questions of how the various elements in the qur'ānic history of Moses might be chronologically arranged according to one scheme or another or whether, as it seems, revelation of the details of his activity as a full-fledged leader and lawgiver would be assigned for the most part to the Medinan period, I would point out that the features selected for presentation in this passage from the sūra of "The Poets" (incidentally, not at all unfamiliar to readers of Exodus) are notable on at least three counts. First, Moses (with Aaron) is sent by God as His messenger to one of the paramount avatars of supreme political authority known to the ancient and medieval Near East—Pharaoh of Egypt—to *command* that ruler's belief and submission to divine will.[51] Second, among the prophetic credentials with which God has endowed him, Moses exercises a (mantically linked) capacity for wonderworking that impresses the Egyptians of the narrative as magic more potent than that of their own professional sorcerers, a capacity that must have associated his activity in the minds of Muḥammad's listeners with the same jinn and *shayāṭīn* responsible for the mantic effusions of *kuhhān* and poets.[52] Third, Pharaoh's refusal to heed Moses' God-sent message and directive leads directly, as in the Exodus story, to his and his followers' destruction by drowning. This treatment and outcome of the Moses narrative as recounted here give it the character of a "punishment story," a character generally secondary elsewhere in "later" revealed accounts of Moses as leader of the Israelites but predominant in portrayals of the confrontation with Pharaoh and quite appropriate in relation to the typologically conceived stories that follow in this sūra.[53]

The next subsection (āyas 60–102) presents the great patriarchal prophet Abraham.[54] His is a figure not usually associated with the qur'ānic "punishment stories." Here, however, Abraham urges his father and folk to recognize the impotence of their idols—"Do they hear you when you pray or avail you or do you harm?" (72–73)—the unavailing worship of which they cling to and defend, saying, "We found our fathers doing thus" (74).[55] He declares his exclusive attachment to the Lord of the Worlds, proclaims that Lord's potent and efficacious actions, and prays for judgment, inclusion with the righteous, good repute among later generations,[56] admission to Paradise, and—most notably—pardon for his father who "was one of those astray" (86).[57] Almost imperceptibly the prayer turns into a quite extraordinary eschatological vision of the Last Day and the ineluctable and irreversible doom of the perverse idolators (*al-ghāwūn*) who, along with their false gods, are to be cast into Hell, where (in a bit of wry humor) both parties engage in mutual blame and recrimination (compare, perhaps, 28:62–64, 29:25/24). Youakim Moubarac would see this eschatological passage as seemingly dictated by the general unity of the sūra, with its concatenation of "punishment" exempla, so that the crucial prophetic figure of Abraham might be felicitously accommodated here along with the others.[58] Moubarac's suggestion receives some support from Abraham's presentation elsewhere neither as a "warner" of impending punishment (though in some passages he does *intercede* on behalf of Lot and his folk) nor among those, like the other six (or seven, if we include Aaron) in this sūra, who are designated as "messengers" (*rusul*), as distinct from "prophets" (*nabīyūn, anbiyā'*).[59]

As with the preceding account of Moses, certain salient features stand out in the āyas devoted to Abraham. First, just as Moses was sent to command the obedience of the absolutist autocrat Pharaoh, so Abraham here calls upon his father, the focus of agnatic tribal authority, and his kinfolk to face the absurdity and error of their old inherited idolatrous ways—in effect, to throw over the ancestral *sunna* that had perverted and adulterated worship of God alone. Second, that Abraham addresses his predication specifically to his father and prays specifically that his father be pardoned foreshadows in this discourse—and in prophetic history—the directive issued to Muḥammad later in the sūra (214): "Warn your tribe of nearest kin [*wa andhir ʿashīrata-ka l-aqrabīn*]." Third, Abraham's vision of the Last Day and the fate of the unregenerate polytheists unambiguously classes him among mantic (even apocalyptic) prognosticators, like the more familiar *kuhhān;* while his recital of it as integral to prayer and his devotional acknowledgment of God's unique potency set him, as a prophet, apart from most conventional mantic types known to Muḥammad's hearers.

Out of these two longer, more circumstantial narratives can be gleaned some important principles that are further accentuated and made more explicit in the next five subsections. First, it is as conveyors of communiqués received from the Creator Lord, the Lord of the Worlds—that is, as mantics divinely not daemonically inspired—that the messenger Moses (with Aaron) and the prophet Abraham approach their hearers and expect to be heeded, not as overlords or officials acting in their own right or by virtue of their wealth, rank, noble birth, or even personal charisma. Second, because they have been divinely endowed with mantic powers as messenger-prophets, not surprisingly they share with *kuhhān,* poets, and other "lesser" mantic practitioners certain paranormal traits, for example, conjuration, divination, prognostication, and in the case of Moses and Aaron, enhanced verbal virtuousity.[60] Third, the authority of the messenger to command obedience, observance, and respect takes precedence over and, when necessary, supersedes that of absolute monarchs, tribal patriarchs, or venerated ancestral traditions. Fourth, the ultimate penal sanction that attends disregard of the divine messages does not lie within the purview of the messenger-prophet to enforce but rather falls to the responsibility of God, Who can and does impose it during the course of or at the end of history.

The next five subsections of the sūra, comprising eighty-six āyas, are all shorter and of roughly equal length. They present, with a number of striking anaphoric and strophic features, a succession of messengers from both Jewish and Arabian traditions.[61]

Noah (Nūḥ) is sent to summon his brethren to be godfearing. They reject him as one "whom the most abject follow" (111) and threaten him. He prays for deliverance and, with the believers, is saved on the ark, while his folk are drowned (105–20).

Hūd is sent to his brethren ʿĀd to deplore their reckless, arrogant, and violent behavior. He reminds them of God's bounty to them "with flocks and sons, gardens and fountains" (132–33). They scorn him as merely "old-fashioned" and are destroyed (123–39).

Ṣāliḥ is sent to his brethren Thamūd to ask whether their crops and groves and houses carved from stone will secure them against God. He warns them against wreaking havoc in the land.[62] Challenged by them and called "bewitched," he produces as a sign from God a sacrosanct camel, which is to be granted regulated water rights.[63] Despite his command, however, Ṣaliḥ's brethren mistreat and kill the camel and are seized with punishment (141–58).

Lot (Lūt) is sent to his brethren to condemn their sodomy but is answered with threats of expulsion. Detesting their practice, he prays for deliverance for himself and his household. "But for an old woman along with the lingerers" (171), they are indeed saved, when the rest are destroyed with an evil rain (160–73). Finally,

Shuʿayb is sent to his brethren, the Men of the Grove (*aṣḥāb al-ayka;* elsewhere called Midianites) to warn them against persisting in commercial fraud and inequity and causing civil strife and havoc. They accuse him of being bewitched, a mere mortal, and a liar, challenge him to have "pieces of heaven" (*kisafan min as-samāʾi*) fall upon them, and consequently are seized with the punishment of the "Umbrageous Day" (176–89).[64]

Now, although in each of these five passages the messenger in question is distinguished from the others by precise details, it is the shared, repeated elements that stand out and reinforce the typal character of the narratives.[65] Each passage is introduced by an identical strophe consisting of a mise-en-scène and the messenger's quintessential message:[66]

> NN.[67] cried the envoys lies [*kadhdhab-*
> . . . *al-mursalīn*]
> when their brother[68] N. addressed them:
> "Will you not be godfearing [*a-lā*
> *tattaqūn*]?[69]
> I am to you a trustworthy messenger
> [*rasūl amīn*].
> So fear you God and obey you me
> [*fa -ttaqu -llāha wa aṭīʿū-n(ī)*]!
> I ask of you for it no fee [*ajr*]: my
> fee is drawn upon the Lord of the
> Worlds alone."
> (105–9, 123–27, 141–45, 160–64, 176–80)[70]

In addition, the command, "So fear you God and obey you me," recurs a second time in each of the first three subsections, devoted to Noah (110), Hūd (131), and Ṣāliḥ (150) respectively, for a total of eight occurrences of this nonrefrain āya within a passage no longer than eighty-five āyas.[71] Each of the messengers is scorned, insulted, threatened, or rejected, and his injunctions are disobeyed. And as a result, of course, each of the peoples who were warned is ultimately doomed to destruction.

Repetition, then—purposeful, schematic, isomorphous, often verbatim, and patently unmistakable repetition not only of words and phrases but also of entire periods and plot motifs—is the outstanding rhetorical feature of these five subsections (as, needless to say, in a more diffuse fashion it is of qur'ānic discourse in general). What Yuri Lotman says of poetry can, without any difficulty, be applied to the artistry of qur'ānic rhetoric as well: like a refrain, the repeated phrase or period, coming in at different points in the discourse, "and thereby entering into different contexts, . . . continually takes on new semantic and emotional connotations." Above all, on the plane of content, "the repetition of the words only serves to emphasize them."[72] Simply compare the refrain itself, where, for example, the contextual significance and appositeness of the two epithets applied to "your Lord" become progressively, cumulatively, and rhetorically more striking with each successive episode of His "mighty" punishment of peoples disobedient to the messengers whom He so "kindly" had sent to warn them.

But perhaps, relying on the preceding synopses and discussion, one has been led to assume that the narrative portion of "The Poets" falls structurally into a two-to-five pattern: Moses and Abraham versus all the rest.[73] Such may be the prevailing impression resulting from centuries of reading, memorizing, and ritually intoning the *text* of the sūra and *viewing* the two dissimilar episodes as one category and the five similar ones as another in a tabular arrangement, so to speak:

Abraham	Noah
Moses (and Aaron)	Hūd
	Ṣāliḥ
	Lot
	Shuʿayb.

Yet, in fact, if we approach the narratives linearly, as *spoken* discourse *heard* by an audience for the first time (or before texts became widely available), we would perceive a quite different structure. The first three accounts would be heard as three distinct episodes involving three of the best-known and most eminent pentateuchal patriarchs (presented, incidentally, in reverse chronological order): Moses, Abraham, Noah.[74] Then, only with the account of Hūd—*not* with that of Noah—would the strongly repetitive character of the remaining episodes come to the fore. Reiteration requires prior statement, and in the context of this sūra the account of Noah *re*-iterates practically nothing but proceeds as if it were *syntagmatically* coordinated with the two preceding nonsimilar, nonrepetitive accounts. It is only after and as a result of hearing Hūd's story and attending to the elements therein, which, by verbal recurrence and thematic parallel, overtly and audibly relate to Noah's, that we begin to grow aware of repetition and similarity as essential structuring principles (apart from the refrain). It is an awareness that becomes certainty as it is reinforced by the identical phrases and analogous motifs of the succeeding three accounts. The syntagmatic coordination of the first three mutually dissimilar accounts has become effectively and nearly totally supplanted by the *paradigmatic* correlation of the later, almost schematically similar ones; and the story of Hūd serves as a kind of pivotal passage upon which the discourse seems to turn from a homiletic recital of some parenetic exempla to a liturgical recitation of a commemorative litany. The progress in the structure of the discourse from what Lotman calls the "syntagmatic axis" to the "paradigmatic axis of meanings"[75] might be represented as another sort of table:

Moses	Abraham	Noah		
			Hūd	
				Ṣāliḥ
				Lot
				Shuʿayb.

As the episodes tend progressively to replicate one another, the hearer tends to assimilate the earlier, more dissimilar ones to the later ones, and that tendency is reinforced by the identical refrain linking them all. The very rhetorical structure of the entire middle section of the sūra, therefore, the relations of repetition, parallelism, and similarity and the increasingly homologous depictions of the messengers' careers can be said to signify iconically the interrelated and mutually corroborative nature of the chronologically and ethnically disparate "historically factual" sendings of messenger-prophets to disobedient peoples. These verbal and structural features can also be said to signify iconically the process through which one comes to perceive (or learns through revelation to perceive) the essential unity, coherence, and consistency of God's mighty and kindly interventions in history within the apparently untidy, directionless course of human events—the process, in other words, of learning to read and interpret rightly the "signs" of God.[76]

In the last five subsections two of the repeated elements are verbally marked with a particular salience, even in the context of what Lotman calls an "aesthetics of identity":[77] first, the anaphorically privileged phrase "kadhdhab- . . . al-mursalīn [cried the envoys lies],"[78] which introduces each of the five passages; and, second, the eight-times iterated command, "Fear you God and obey you me!"[79] By being verbally embedded in what are represented as events that would have been chronologically, ethnically, and circumstantially altogether disparate and discrete, these repeated elements impart to the five episodes—and through the associative force of the linking refrain, to the preceding two as well—a quality of homogeneity or even equivalence and serve, as it were iconically, to instantiate for the present Messenger's kinfolk the continuity of God's prior involvements in human history with this involvement and the consistency, if not identity, of Muḥammad's message with those delivered to the peoples of the past, though ominously not heeded by them.[80]

In qur'ānic usage the act—or rather, the crime—of *takdhīb,* "crying lies" (when it is not signified absolutely—that is, without object—as in āya 6/5), is represented as being perpetrated chiefly against one of two objects: either, as here, one or the ensemble of messenger-prophets (including Muḥammad) is accused of lying, or the "signs" (āyāt)—verbal and nonverbal—through which God communicates with mankind are branded lies. The first usage obviously is exemplified by the prominent anaphoric recurrences of *kadhdhab-* under consideration, which are foretokened earlier in the sūra by Moses' fear that "they will cry me lies" (12) and are echoed within the stories of Noah (117), Hūd (139), and Shuʿayb (189; cf. 186).

As for the *takdhīb* of God's signs,[81] this usage shows up more than forty times in the Qur'ān, at least four of which are dated by Blachère and Nöldeke prior to the sūra of "The Poets,"[82] and the great majority within what chronologists of revelation call the second Meccan period—as is this sūra itself. Although no form of the expression as such occurs in "The Poets," the sūra presents itself, in the words of Hartwig Hirschfeld, as "a veritable lecture on the sign [*āya*] . . . as elaborate as it is methodically constructed."[83] Already in the opening verse occurs the phrase, "Those are the signs of the articulate Scripture" (or "of the clear [or clarifying] Book"). And closely after follows God's statement, "If We wish, We will send down upon them from heaven a sign" (4/3), which in turn is closely followed by the unrestricted indictment,

"So did they cry lies!" (6/5)—with the verb uttered absolutely (*fa qad kadhdhabū*). This act of *takdhīb* evidently would have taken place in reference to the sign from heaven, "which they were wont to scorn"—a sign not yet sent down upon them or signs previously sent down upon others who had gone before and whose dooms are about to be described.

Immediately thereafter the next āya (7/6) asks rhetorically, in God's voice, whether the unbelievers, who have so agonized the Messenger Muḥammad by their rejection, unbelief, and crying of lies, could "not have looked to the land" to see "how many have We produced therein of every noble *zawj*"—a term that I have here rendered "type." And through the refrain (8/7–9/8), which declares that "surely in that is a sign" and which is repeated after each of the seven messengers' stories, God's production "of every noble *zawj*" (together with the proem as a whole) is linked with and, in fact, assimilated to the succession of narrated episodes that follows. But what could be meant by *zawj* in āya 7/6 that would serve as a sound compositional basis for such a linkage and assimilation? How could God's consolatory remarks on Muḥammad's plight and His *zawj* production be said to entail a "sign" in such a manner that precisely the same entailment would be predicated of each of the seven following pericopes?[84]

The term *zawj* (pl. *azwāj*), which several authorities consider a very early loanword in Arabic from Greek *zygon* or *zeugos,* "yoke," through Aramaic, has a number of senses related to pairing, doubling, or correlation: (one of a) pair, (one of a) couple; a thing (associated with things of the same species or type); spouse (husband *or* wife), mate; associate, comrade; kind, sort, species; fellow, like.[85] Here, since it serves logically as object of God's "producing" or, more precisely, "causing to grow" (*anbatnā,* from *n–b–t:* form IV), many have assumed that *zawj* signifies "species" or "kind" of vegetation.[86] Such an interpretation is not unjustifiable in terms of qur'ānic usage of *zawj* in conjunction with *n–b–t* IV attestable elsewhere (for example, 22:5 and 31:10/9, both instances resulting from God's sending down rain from heaven). But other passages clearly demonstrate that God's "causing to grow" or "producing" may apply to human objects such as Mary, mother of Jesus (3:37/32), and Noah's kinfolk "out of the earth" (71:17/16). The semantic range of *zawj* seems even further extended in 36:36 (B62/N60): "Glory be to Him Who has created all the *azwāj,* such as [or including] what the earth produces [*tunbitu*], their [the unresponsive hearers'] own persons [or themselves], and what they do not know!"[87] This last category of *zawj*, significantly, is left quite vague, enigmatic, and open-ended.

Now, in sūra 26 nothing absolutely precludes our construing "every noble *zawj*" in one of the common denotations of the word, either as cognate—"kind" or "species" (that is, "what the earth produces")—or as complement—"spouse," "mate," or "comrade" (that is, as of human beings, *min anfusi-him* "their own persons" or "themselves")—or even as both. Indeed, without any further context such would undoubtedly be the most plausible understanding. But it is just the further context that, by a process of what Umberto Eco calls "semantic disclosure,"[88] leads me to seek the signification of *zawj* in the third realm of "what they do not know" and to construe it here as correlate or analogue—perhaps "exemplar" or, more pertinently, "type" or "figure" in the exegetic-homiletic sense current in late antiquity among later Old Testament and intertestamental Jews, early Christians, and various gnostic groups.

•

What we see in this usage may, I believe, involve the integration into qur'ānic discourse and the qur'ānic view of history of a phenomenon that had already for several centuries been intimately bound up with religious thought, perception, and expression in general throughout the Judeo-Christian (and Judeo-Christian-influenced) Near Eastern and Mediterranean areas.[89] This was, as Northrop Frye puts it, a "mode of thought and . . . a figure of speech,"[90] a mode of conceiving, interpreting, and depicting, writes Leonard Goppelt, "historical facts—persons, actions, events, and institutions— . . . [as] divinely ordained representations or types of future [or later] realities."[91] "The essence of typology," according to Jean Daniélou, "is to show how past events are a figure of events to come."[92] These "antitypes"—the subsequent realities or "events to come"—could be apprehended as "even greater or more complete" than their correlative preordained types, says Goppelt, "heightening" or "perfecting" them, as he and many other modern Christian theologians insist,[93] or as repetitions, recurrences, or recapitulations of the prefigurative, prerepresentative actualities that constitute their types.[94] Typological or figural interpretation (and representation), then, in Erich Auerbach's words, "establishes a connection between two events or persons in such a way that the first signifies not only itself but also the second, while the second involves or fulfills the first. The two poles of a figure[95] are separated in time, but both, being real events or persons, are within temporality. They are both contained in the flowing stream which is historical life, and only the comprehension, the *intellectus spiritualis,* of their independence is a spiritual act."[96] Furthermore, side by side with the exegetical tradition arose a tradition of typological composition and representation manifesting itself in homiletics, hymnology, devotional and liturgical literature, iconography, and other areas—a tradition that ensured that "the attitude embodied in the figural interpretation became one of the essential elements of the Christian picture of reality, history, and the concrete world in general."[97]

At this point it should be evident that I hold that the qur'ānic accounts of prior messengers and prophets, as they are set forth in this sūra and many others, are expressly intended to be understood as *typological prefigurements* or *prepresentations* of which the person and career of Muḥammad, Prophet and Messenger of God, provide the corresponding *recapitulation* and *fulfillment*—the *antitype*. And too, this idea of "the two poles of a figure," the "type-pair," I strongly suspect underlies the peculiar usage of *zawj* in āya 6/5. That is to say, like each of the succeeding God-revealed pericopes and the God-produced events that they depict, God's production in the land of "every noble *zawj*" is declared to entail a "sign"; that declaration itself, thus, can quite plausibly and appropriately be construed as referring proleptically to the "noble messengers" who are thereafter introduced, in those messengers' role as typal correlates of the Messenger Muḥammad whose recitation this present discourse is.[98] On that interpretation, then, what would be signified through the "sign" entailed by both God's "type" production and all the prophetic pericopes together would be this very typal correlation and the associated fact of God's might in so utterly punishing disobedience to his past messengers and His kindness in sending any messengers at all—including the present one—to communicate His revealed warnings.

Of course, it was probably obvious from first hearing that these cameo narratives had not been revealed and recited solely, or even primarily, for their historical or edificatory value. As many qur'ānic passages make quite explicit[99] and as Muḥammad, several of his contemporaries, and early Muslim generations seem to have assumed,[100] these prominent mantic personages to whom so much revealed qur'ānic discourse is devoted appear to constitute a chain, succession, or cycle of God-sent, divinely inspired men of whom the Prophet of Quraysh was the most recent, if not, in fact, as Islamic tradition strongly maintains, the last and greatest.[101] Modern scholars have frequently noted that in many parallel features of their careers, especially the consistent hostility and rejection with which their missions were received, these messenger-prophets of old are presented within the Qur'ān as precursors of Muḥammad or, more precisely, adumbrations of his persona, deeds, and situation.[102] The "mutual resemblance of men of God" across the centuries is advanced as precedential corroboration of Muḥammad's messengership and his message and retroactive confirmation of those of his predecessors.[103] God plainly declares at the close of the sūra of "Joseph": "In recounting of them [that is, of Joseph and his brethren or, perhaps more immediately, of the messengers in general, who are referred to in the preceding āya] there has been a lesson [*ʿibra*] for those with intelligence: no factitious communication has it been, but rather confirmation of what was before it, full exposition of everything, and guidance and kindness for a folk who believe" (12:111 [B79/N77]).

The prophetic histories serve also, especially in sūras assigned to the middle and late Meccan periods, to console and encourage Muḥammad (and his followers) for the lack of success and the scornful treatment he encountered in his native city; sūra 11:120/121 (B77/N75) presents such encouragement: "And every bit of tidings of the messengers [*anbāʾ ar-rusul*] that We recount to thee is a means whereby We steady thy heart. In these [tidings] there has come to thee the truth and an admonition [*mawʿiẓa*] and warning for the believers." The consolation and encouragement often took the form of explicit emphasis on the correspondences between Muḥammad's situation at Mecca and conditions that had typically (or typologically) prevailed in the case of former prophets and messengers: they, too, had been rejected and called liars or men possessed (for example, 35:4; 6:34; 3:184/181, etc.).[104] And particular stress was laid upon the God-ordained customary dooms that had befallen their unheeding, disobedient peoples, as, for example in sūra 35, "The Creator" (or "The Angels," B88/N86):

> Thou art only a warner [*nadhīr*].
> Surely we have sent thee with the
> truth, as a herald of joy and warning [*bashīran wa nadhīran*]: no

nation but that there has gone
forth to address it a warner.[105]
And if they cry thee lies—well,
before them those cried lies whose
messengers had brought them clear
evidences, holy writs, and illuminant scripture.
Then did I lay hold of those who
disbelieved.[106] And how I did
censure!

(23/21–26/24)

Can we legitimately say, however, that these messenger-prophets who were sent before to other folk function in the discursive context of the Qur'ān as actual "types" or "figures" of Muḥammad in any but a fairly loose sense of the term? Arthur Jeffery adduces extensive qur'ānic evidence to support the view that there emerges in the middle and late Meccan revelations "a pattern of the nature of the prophetic mission" and "the prophetic succession" and that "the stories of the previous prophets, in whose succession [Muḥammad] claims to stand, come to be accommodated to that same pattern."[107] Rudi Paret speaks quite unequivocally of a "Typisierung" of former messengers whose primary value is to furnish us with an "informative schematization," thanks to which "worthwhile inferences about the life and times of the Arabian Prophet can be drawn from the careers of the earlier men of God." If not for that, he rather insensitively claims, this "Typisierung" would have resulted in a "sorry leveling [*armselig Nivellierung*]" of the past, "in its myriad manifestations," to something wherein "Muḥammad always sought out and rediscovered just himself and his own contemporary circumstances."[108] Dealing more particularly with the role of Abraham in the Qur'ān, Moubarac argues that that patriarch-prophet functions more as a "model" or "example" than as a "type"—but as a model or example of the true believer, not of the prophet or messenger or of Muḥammad himself.[109] Yet it is as a "type" of the Messenger-Prophet of Quraysh, addressing God's warning and call to his "tribe of nearest kin," I would argue, that Abraham is cast in this sūra especially.

As discrete, yet correlative sendings by God, the seven messenger-prophets in this sūra are related to each other and, above all, to Muḥammad in an almost wholly atemporal and ahistorical manner (without even any regard for what at least biblically informed critics would consider proper chronological order). This circumstance, which is intrinsic to qur'ānic prophetology, confirms the operation of a well-developed principle of typology that was no less profound and no less essential to the valorization and validation of Mu'hammad's mission than was the Qumrānian community's use of typology for establishing its privileged status at what was thought to be the impending end of time or the early Christian use of it for valorizing and validating Christianity's place in postbiblical history.[110] It can be demonstrated, I am convinced (though not in great detail right here and now), that a typological concept of divine involvements in human history—prefigurative and proleptic when viewed and presented as past events or facts in time, co-occurrent and co-equivalent when viewed and presented as timeless, incommensurable acts of God—permeates and underlies both the qur'ānic vision of that history and the rhetorical mode of qur'ānic discourse which presents it.

I do not mean to suggest in any simplistic way that Muḥammad "borrowed" or that the Qur'ān "was influenced by" Christian, Jewish, or gnostic concepts of typology or some combination thereof. Rather, I suggest that among the predominantly monotheistic milieux of the sixth- and seventh-century Near East there had evolved a reasonably conventionalized, perhaps even sacralized, mode or genre of discourse for representing instances of divine intervention and communication. With H. A. R. Gibb, I would hold that "if the teaching of the Qur'an was to be understood by its first hearers, as is rightly assumed by Muslim scholarship, there must have been not only in existence, but widely enough known in Mecca, an Arabic religious vocabulary applicable to the monotheistic content of the Qur'an." On the basis of qur'ānic evidence and accounts of pre-Islamic missionaries and their homilies, Gibb argues for presuming "the existence of an established style of religious discourse." He notes: "A preacher [like Muḥammad], if he is to be effective, must preach in terms which, on the one hand, are understood by his hearers, and on the other hand, appeal to their emotions. So also the Revelation must, *in its early stages,* use familiar language and traditional imagery, until its hearers have become receptive to a fuller development of religious thought."[111]

Since the second century (maybe even earlier), typological interpretations, speculations, and representations had been essential ingredients of that discourse and the standard stuff of its language and imagery. And in the Christology (and other doctrines) of the New

Testament and the early Church, in the pronouncements of many masters of gnosis, and already in the parenetic, messianic, and apocalyptic teachings of the late Old Testament and intertestamental Judaism, the persons, careers, destinies, and "signs" of earlier prophetic figures had been somewhat abstracted and "homogenized" to the extent that "the prophets" could be spoken of practically as an entity without specifying any one of them.[112] In general it was this ensemble of "the prophets" that became typologically correlated sometimes with the still awaited Messiah or sometimes with Jesus, who was explicitly depicted as an ultimate victim of what had come to be portrayed as their "violent fate" at the hands of a "stiff-necked" Israel.[113] Early Christianity, too, had already expanded the list of those designated "prophet" well beyond those associated with the prophetic books of the Bible, adding, for example, Henoch, Abraham, Jacob, David, Job, etc., to the point, A. J. Wensinck notes, that "in many literary works the words 'prophet' and 'holy one/saint' [*Heilige*] or 'righteous one' are synonyms."[114] Moreover, Christianity took these prophets as typological precursors who had come to be assimilated to and fulfilled in the apostles,[115] thus laying the semantic groundwork for the relatively close association of the two terms *nabīy* and *rasūl* which we find in qur'ānic usage.[116] Furthermore, and perhaps most important from my point of view, the idea had become widespread in the Near East that these "prophets" were not only preachers and holy men but also bearers of ruling authority. Christian popular theology, for instance, had already specified Adam, Noah, Moses, and Jesus as leaders and kings; and many other patriarchs and apostles had been similarly promoted.[117]

In a comparatively recent study of "types of the ruler in the Qur'ān," Heribert Busse has substantively broached the subject of the qur'ānic use of typology. Busse refers to Rudolf Bultmann's view that "the roots of typology lie in the concept of repetition, and as a result it would ultimately have been bound up with cyclical thinking." Maintaining that "salvation history repeats itself in cycles," Busse continues, "Muḥammad himself sees his own fate anticipated in that of his predecessors; yet in the succession of prophets no heightening [*Steigerung*] takes place, if one excludes Muḥammad's taking himself as the last, the 'seal,' of the prophets."[118]

But it would be a mistake, I think, simply to agree with Busse's judgment that the qur'ānic messenger-prophets are presented as a "type" of Muḥammad's own fate, repeated without "heightening."

Certainly, if we restrict our view of Muḥammad's fate to the ongoing intolerable and unresolved experience of disregard, rejection, and disobedience which God addresses in the proem to this sūra and in other "Meccan" passages, we would have to admit that that predicament does merely repeat mutatis mutandis those recounted of his typological correlates. Should the obduracy of the Messenger's people continue, their "future" is known and guaranteed by the recurrent "pasts" of the peoples of former messengers (just as the clear correlation between Muḥammad's "present" and the "pasts" of his typal predecessors authenticates his affinity with them as a God-sent messenger).[119]

In a sense, however, the prevalent tense of qur'ānic discourse is the present of God's action and the prevalent mode is the imperative of His command, issued through the revelations recited by His current Messenger. Antitypal *repetition* of the prefigured punishments is the threat (*waʿīd*) should that command go on being disobeyed. But antitypal *heightening* or *fulfillment*—in the form of personal and communal well-being and reward both here and hereafter—is assuredly the promise (*waʿd*) if the command be obeyed. It is, therefore, the hearers' response to the warning and the command that would have to determine the nature of the typological relationship of their present and future to the recounted pasts of former warned and commanded peoples.

If we accept the view set forth at the outset of this essay that the words of the Qur'ān would have been recited by Muḥammad during the twenty or more years of his career as Prophet and Messenger of God, then we must also recognize that the typology that would be operative here is not so much like that of the New Testament and early Christian Church—that is, reflecting upon established past facts in the life of Jesus, his Apostles, and their first successors and interpretively correlating them with facts from a far remoter Old Testament past. It seems, rather, much more like the sort of "apocalyptic exegesis" that was carried on among the Essenes of the Qumrān community, who approached the Hebrew Scriptures with three principles in mind. "Prophecy," according to Frank Moore Cross, "openly or cryptically refers to the last days. Secondly, the so-called last days are in fact the present, the days of the sect's life. And, finally, the history of ancient Israel's redemption, her offices and institutions, are prototypes of the events and figures of the new Israel."[120] In the "Meccan" sūras, between the representation of the physical destruction that had befallen the disobedient peoples of past prophets and could befall those who disobeyed the present one and the representation of the eschatological punishments imposed upon the unjust and unbelieving at the Last Judgment, there is so little unambiguous distinction as to permit the inference that there may have prevailed among the earliest believers at least a vague apprehension—if not a strong certainty—that the end of time was imminent, perhaps even at hand.[121]

Thus, although Muḥammad had indeed met with scorn, rejection, and disobedience from most of his folk, just as had his typologically cast precursors, the event itself was just not yet over! God's promise to this folk still held good; His threat—delivered by His Messenger in no uncertain terms and borne out by the revealed "historical" evidence he recited—had still not been carried out. God's kindness and mercy to His Prophet's people still prevailed; His might had not yet been unleashed against them. Things could turn out quite differently if "most of them" would become believers, fear God, and obey their Messenger. Whereas the folk addressed by former messenger-prophets had foundered and failed through their disregard and disobedience, the prospect for triumph and success and the continuance of God's kindly beneficence still remained open to Muḥammad's fellow tribesmen of Quraysh, IF they could bring themselves to acknowledge a mantic's authority and obey his inspired commands.

In other words, to be discerned within the Qur'ān's portrayal of Muḥammad's historical situation and dealings with his people, the typological heightening or fulfillment that Busse misses in the correlation of the qur'ānic prophets with the Meccan Messenger must not be sought in the idea of the "seal of the prophets." It must rather be sought precisely in the degree to which that situation could be seen to have resolved the "inner contradiction" upon which (according to some of the later biblical prophets and early Christian exegetes) Israel and the other nations warned by God's messengers had "foundered" and which the Christian Church had for a while hypothetically skirted by pursuing a "kingdom not of this world."[122] That is, it must be sought in the tension generated when a community is summoned to become a people of God, to accept the rule of God, by an agent of God whose very fitness to issue, much less implement, such a summons the community is unwilling, indeed, unequipped and perhaps even unable to recognize.

Hence the striking appositeness of the second verse of this sūra's refrain, "Surely thy Lord—He indeed is the Mighty and Kindly One." Recall that that refrain is repeated not only after each account of a messenger's being sent and the destruction of his unheeding folk but also after God's preliminary references to Muḥammad's distress and the Meccans' crying lies and His summons to contemplate "how many We have produced . . . of every noble type." Reiteratively and cumulatively it impresses upon those who listen and believe the mortal urgency of heeding the *sign* entailed by those accounts—which themselves exemplify and eventuate God's production of "every noble type."

Within the verbal fabric of the prophetic pericopes one utterance and one utterance alone—which also resounds eight times, *just as the refrain itself*—calls out to be perceived and construed as that which is signified by them all. This is the uncompromisingly imperative message explicitly delivered by the last five messengers (twice each by Noah, Hūd, and Ṣāliḥ), but implicitly entailed in the discourse and conduct of the first two, both through the structural linkage effected by the refrain and through the retroflexively assimilative influence exercised by the five mutually replicative narratives. That utterance is the command, "Fear you God and obey you me!" Fearing and protecting oneself from God (or some other supernatural being) was a directive that Muḥammad's contemporaries could understand and, to some extent, perhaps even comply with. But that a mantic figure, however prestigious he might appear, could presume to demand obedience of his folk, of his father, of Pharaoh? And that denying and disobeying a mere mantic could bring down upon whole peoples such utter destruction? The might and power that wrought the destruction, it was possible to admit, could have come from God to avenge the offense to His messenger. This much the succession of "noble types" could corroborate. But whence, the hidebound, stiff-necked, self-sufficient Meccans must have asked, came to such a mantic messenger the *authority* by virtue of which he and his message might be regarded as fit to be obeyed?

•

The entire cycle of prophetic types, as we have seen, operated on a primary level to give value and validity to Muḥammad's mission and to lend actuality, verifiability, and contemporaneity to the potential content of God's consistent and "historically" reiterated threat and promise: the "already" that could substantiate, warrant, and determine the "not yet."[123] But behind practically that entire cycle operated another informing principle that lay much closer to the heart of the socio-political, legal, and religious life of most of the pre-Islamic Arabs. This is the concept and institution of *sunna* (pl., *sunan*): a normative precedent or procedure (or a *corpus* of normative precedents and procedures) "ordained, decreed, instituted, introduced into practice (by a certain person, or—less frequently—by a group of definite persons)," and subsequently inherited, taken over, and observed by others in later generations ("possibly by the community"), entailing a "moral obligation to cling to, or even reproduce, what 'the one (the single individual) who has gone'[124] has done (or advised to do)."[125]

Within the kinship-based societies of the early seventh-century Arabs, then, unregulated as they generally were by written law or well-defined ruling institutions, the enduring, almost sacred authority of the ancestors, in the form of "sunnas to be observed (or followed)" (*sunan muttabaʿa*), held supreme and went for the most part unchallenged. Beliefs, actions, behavior, states of affairs could be judged licit or illicit, proper or improper, insofar as they adhered to or deviated from the "established course" (or "trodden way") of sunna—insofar as, gauged by the inherited standards of sunna, they were *maʿrūf*, "known," "recognizable," and "reputable" or "commendable" or were *munkar*, "unknown," "disavowed," and "reprehensible."[126] The view of Ignaz Goldziher on this question, first published in 1910, is still among the most cogent and perceptive:

> From time immemorial, the Arabs' chief criterion for determining propriety and lawfulness in any aspect of life had been conformity in word and deed to ancestral norm and usage. Whatever is true and just must accord with, and be rooted in, inherited opinion and custom. These constitute the *sunna*. The *sunna* was their law and their *sacra*. It was the sole source of their legal practice and their religion; to forsake it was to transgress against the inviolable rules of hallowed custom. This applied to actions and, for the same reasons, to inherited ideas. In the sphere of ideas, too, the group could accept nothing new that was not in harmony with the views of its ancestors.[127]

"Tribal societies in a state of civilization parallel to that of the Arab tribes of the Jāhilīya," Reuben Levy has written with respect to the *maʿrūf/munkar* dichotomy, "would, in the same way as they did, regard the known and familiar as the good and the strange as the evil."[128] For example, probably far less than the actual deities, personnel, objects, rites, and beliefs per se that were associated with pre-Islamic Arab religion and cult, it was the total integration of these elements into the sacred heritage of the "sunna of those who went before" that most effectively assured their enduring status as "holy" and reinforced in many of Muḥammad's opponents the sense of religious piety, fervor, and propriety that was so offended by his preaching against the veneration of any god but God.[129]

Preaching thus, Muḥammad not only transgressed the bounds of conventional mantic behavior; he also was guilty of flagrant impropriety and innovation. Surely nothing stood out so patently in conflict with sunna and all that it involved as did innovation (*bidʿa, ibtidāʿ, ḥadath*)—especially unwarranted novelty or change for its own sake—and nothing so readily presented itself as unknown or strange and, hence, potentially reprehensible, evil, or even dangerous.[130] In rejecting Muḥammad as God's Messenger, therefore, and his message as imperative revelation from God, the Meccan Quraysh (and other Arab nonbelievers) were behaving quite honestly as stalwart, upright, and respectable members of their society who revered their ancestors and kept faith with the modes, manners, and mores that their ancestors had handed down.[131] "In contrast with their ancient traditions," Goldziher writes, "Muḥammad's prophecy was in their view a *dīn muḥdath,* a brand new—and consequently reprehensible—faith" or observance.[132]

But then, Muḥammad did recite accounts of former messengers and prophets from ages far anterior to the times of the most dimly remembered ancestor. His recitals emphasized the dire fates that had customarily befallen those bygone nations when they scorned and disobeyed the warners sent to them (just as, of course, Muḥammad's fellow tribespeople and townspeople were scorning and disobeying him). By the same token, his appeal was to precisely the same legitimizing principle, sunna, as that which his opponents and critics were striving to defend—though certainly on another plane. For in qur'ānic terms, the wonted impiety, unbelief, and disobedience with which ancient communities had repeatedly and typally received their messengers and prophets, together with their wonted doom, constituted a sunna too—the *sunnat al-awwalīn,* "sunna of the ancients."[133]

Given the relatively familiar evidence picked up from other scriptural traditions and the sobering ocular testimony afforded by the monumental ruins scattered along the caravan routes, Muḥammad's hearers might well have granted a certain "historicity" to this sunna. But to that extent, they would also presumably have had to grant its *priority* to—and, hence, its *precedence* over—the sunna of the ancestors,[134] something they were not so ready to do.

Even more to the point, Muḥammad's revealed recitations established categorically that what had been wont to befall impious, unbelieving, and disobedient ancients was occasioned, from another perspective, by the operation of God's own wonted practice (*sunnat Allāh*) in dealing with those who were sent a messenger to warn them and who persisted in disobedience—that, in other words, *sunnat al-awwalīn* was nothing less than the immanent historical realization of *sunnat Allāh*.[135] Furthermore, it is probable that none—not even the most convinced enemy of Muḥammad—could reasonably have disputed the superior power and dignity of Him Who had "ordained, decreed, instituted, introduced into practice" this unsupersedable and unamendable sunna and Who as creator had surely preceded and preempted all ancestors. Nor is it likely that any could have questioned the preeminent and paradigmatic normative value of whatever He had occasioned. Therefore, the validity, authority, and jurisdiction of such a sunna would accordingly extend beyond any particular tribe or territory or time merely by virtue of the nature of its author.

Out of this discursive, narrative, and parenetic framework, then, through the calculated telling and retelling of stories of former men of God sent with a revealed message (such as we find in "The Poets"), Muḥammad, the Prophet and God's Messenger, like his typological precursors, would emerge as *renovator* of a more venerable, more prestigious, more legitimate sunna—divinely ordained and prophetically proclaimed—and the respected ancestors themselves as *innovators* of those corrupt and aberrant sunnas currently in effect.[136] So, in the world view presented by the Qur'ān, says Johan Bouman, "human history is in essence the history of the prophets and their communities."[137] This depiction stands in stark opposition to the vision of history familiar to most of Muḥammad's Arab contemporaries.[138] History for them was embodied mainly in the narrative accounts of past tribal battles and encounters (*ayyām al-ʿarab,* "the 'days' of the Arabs") and in the poems of the *shuʿarāʾ*, which, whether or not they had been composed in conjunction with the *ayyām*-accounts, were looked to and consulted as "the Arabs' archives" (*dīwān al-ʿarab*). Rather than in heroic ancestors—chieftains, warriors, even outlaws—

and their exploits, all immortalized in jinn-inspired verses, it was in the prophets and messengers that, as Muḥammad's divinely revealed, sign-entailing, cadenced recitations declared, and as Bouman notes, "God had actualized His teaching; in them also does it become possible for man fully to realize his nature and destiny."[139]

We must try to conceive, therefore, just how outrageously offensive, how alarmingly dangerous, how powerfully subversive Muḥammad's revealed message might have seemed to many members of the "pagan" establishment in Mecca and just how egregiously absurd his claims to prophecy and concomitant expectations of obedience would have struck them. Only by trying to do so can we understand something of the concertedness with which they appear to have opposed or ignored him, something of their desperate urge to relegate his recited vaticinations to "safe," generally recognized, and easily dismissable categories of mantic experience,[140] something of the strategic importance of dedicating so much of what many have considered the most interesting and artfully fashioned qur'ānic discourse to recounting the prefigurative and precedent-affirming histories of messengers and prophets from so very long ago.

•

As I have tried to show, qur'ānic discourse about past messenger-prophets and their peoples in general and the sūra of "The Poets" in particular can be said to have been framed in terms of a complex conceptual and ideological configuration, which involves the subtle combination and interaction of two elements: first, a sometimes schematic representation of these divinely inspired and commissioned agents from the past and of their experiences as typological figures of Muḥammad and his experiences and as viable ancient and authoritative alternatives to the mantic poets and *kuhhān* (whom no one seems to have followed and who seem not to have expected "to be obeyed"); and second, a profoundly ingenious restructuring and adaptation of the socially, culturally, and politically vital principle of sunna so as to found upon it the radically new obligation of *obedience* to God's mantic Messenger. Nowhere is the synthesis of these elements more effectively and concisely expressed, I think, than in sūra 86, "The Sand Dunes" (B90/N88; late Meccan): "Say [Muḥammad is commanded]: I have been no innovation among the messengers [*mā kuntu bidʿan mina r-rusuli*] and I know what is to be done neither with me nor with you. I follow only that with which I am inspired and I am only an articulate Warner" (86:9/8).

Through this configuration the warning, message, and way of life preached by Muḥammad, however revolutionary and innovative they might have seemed to his often shortsighted contemporaries, could be presented as legitimately grounded on a foundation of supremely authoritative precedent, as not destroying what already existed but, to a great extent, continuing, developing, reforming, and perfecting it.[141] It might well have been, then, this structural and rhetorical synthesis of typological representation with the principle of normative precedential law or custom—both rooted in the idea that what is present (or future) repeats, if not indeed fulfills, what is past—that provided ideological underpinnings to the qur'ānic program for socio-political habilitation of the divinely inspired mantic and a rationale for affirming his authority and claim to obedience. For in Muḥammad's case at any rate, if not in that of the former prophet-messengers, Islam did become within the course of Revelation and the Messenger's life-time successfully established as a community and nation of believers (comprising Muḥammad's own folk as well), whereas its corresponding prefigurements had foundered and failed; and, for the most part, Muḥammad was finally accepted, heeded, and obeyed as God's Messenger and Prophet, whereas his typal predecessors had not been.[142]

Let us now turn to the conclusion of the sūra and of this essay. After the last recurrence of the refrain (190–91), the quasi-homiletic discourse of "The Poets" turns from narrated exempla of God's *kindly* and merciful sending of messenger-prophets with warnings and His *mighty* and cataclysmic vindication of them after their rejection to the final section, comprising the lessons, conclusions, and important distinctions to be drawn from those exempla (192–227). Since I cannot undertake a systematic explication of these āyas here, I would like to offer a translation of them and to follow it with a few observations and some closing remarks.

And surely it is indeed the
  sending down of the Lord of the
  Worlds [cf. 49:43)—
brought down has it been by the
  Trustworthy Spirit [*ar-rūḥ al-amīn*]

upon thy heart that thou might'st
be one of the warners—
in an articulate Arabic tongue. (195)
And surely it is indeed in the
writs[143] of the ancients.
Or could it not have been for them
a sign [*āya*] that the scholars
[*ʿulamāʾ*] of the Israelites know
it?
Yet had We sent it down upon some
barbarian [*baʿḍ al-aʿjamīn*],[144]
and had he then recited it to them,
they still would not believe it!
Thus it is We have induced it into (200)
miscreants' hearts,
they believing it not till they see
the grievous penalty
when it should befall them
suddenly, while they are unaware,
and they would say, "Shall we be
reprieved?"
So, then, will they rush Our
penalty?
Did'st thou consider: If We (205)
prolong their pleasure for some
years,
then there overcomes them that
which they were threatened with,
will their prolonged pleasure avail
them aught?
Not one city have We destroyed
unless it had warners
to remind, nor have We done wrong!
The daemons [*shayāṭīn*] have not (210)
descended with it.
It is not proper for them, nor are
they able:
surely from hearing they are far
removed indeed!
So call thou not on another god
with God, lest thou be among the
penalized!
And warn thy tribe of nearest kin,

and drop thy wing to those (215)
believers who have followed thee!
But if they disobey thee, say: I
am clear of what you do.
Rely thou upon the Mighty and
Kindly One,
Who sees thee when thou standest
erect
and thy falling prone among the
prostratants,
for surely He is the Hearing, the (220)
Knowing One!
Now, shall I inform you [*hal*
unabbiʾu-kum] on whom the daemons
do descend?
They descend on every peccant falsifier
who all lend ear, though most will
lie.[145]
And the poets [*ash-shuʿarāʾ*]—them
the perverse do follow![146]
Hast thou not seen that in every (225)
valley they are wildering?—
and that they do say what they do
not do?—
save only those who have believed,
done righteous deeds, recalled God
often, and been vindicated[147] after
they were wronged. And those who
did the wrong shall know how
utterly they shall be overthrown!

Note that āyas 192–99 immediately follow the seven progressively more recapitulative figural narratives, and are hence strategically juxtaposed to the sign-affirming refrain.[148] They unequivocally proclaim the transcendent origin of the discourse just recited (as of the Recitation, the Qurʾān itself, as a whole), the altogether nondaemonic agency through which it has reached the reciting Messenger, and the self-evident propriety of its recital in a linguistic form thought to be reserved to poets.[149] In āyas 200–209 Muḥammad's unresponsive, unbelieving hearers are caustically reminded that they have been—and mercifully are still being—warned of the penal retribution to befall them, as harsh, utter, and sure as anything that befell other peoples and cities that had been warned but foundered: Pharaoh's folk, for instance, or the brethren of Noah and of Lot, or ʿĀd, Thamūd, and those of the Grove. Will they continue to take the postponement of their threatened fate as a pretext to cry their Messenger lies, not recognizing this respite for the divine kindness that it is? Must they willfully fail to grasp the entailed "sign," the typological significance of the sequence of "punishment stories" that successively, in iconically reiterative language, represent history as repeated by those who refused to learn its lessons? That God would destroy a folk or a city only after its warner had been persistently and unpardonably disregarded, scorned, and disobeyed constitutes part of a pattern in God's dealings with men that the Qur'ān calls *sunnat Allāh,* as we have seen. The historical verification of this pattern has just been recounted in the form of the sign-entailing "noble types"; and its rhetorical or structural corroboration is hammered home in the crucial patterned verbal correspondences and repetitions of the prophetic pericopes, above all in the resounding command: "Fear you God and obey you me!"

As Irfan Shahîd observes, "Verses 210–220 repeat the statement on the divine nature of the Koran but this time in *negative* terms,"[150] telling us that "the daemons have not descended with it." This denial is supported by categorical assertions, first, that revelation is inappropriate or improper for them to convey; second, that they are incapable of conveying it; and third, that the sources of revelation have been rendered inaccessible to them (an allusion to the myth that guardian angels launch fire and stars against daemons eavesdropping at heaven's gate). In addition, āyas 213–20 seem to parallel 200–209 in the preceding subsection. They are addressed to the Messenger himself, directly and personally; and they admonish him to keep faith with God alone, instruct him to warn his "tribe of nearest kin" (reminding us that he too, like the "noble types" before him, had been sent first to his own brethren), and offer him advice, encouragement, and support. Of particular importance are the words absolving him of responsibility for the failure even of his followers to obey (216).

Thus we are enabled to form an impression of elements that serve to define the role of God's Messenger: observance of the monotheistic imperative before all else, compassion for kin and concern for community, responsibility for proclaiming the message but not for the disobedience of its hearers, reliance upon "the Mighty and Kindly One" (using the verbal correspondence with the refrain to emphasize and reinforce the typological and phenomenal correlation between Muḥammad and former messenger-prophets of the pericopes just recited), and conscientiousness in performing acts of public worship. These elements and others characterize the Warner Muḥammad, upon whose heart "the Trustworthy Spirit" has brought "the sending down of the Lord of the Worlds." Quite a contrast they present to the picture of those "on whom the daemons do descend," who are the subject of the final section (āyas 221–27/28)![151]

Islamic tradition usually identifies "every peccant falsifier" with the *kuhhān*. While I certainly agree that such an identification would be most felicitous and appropriate in the context, I am not always confident that such ad hoc and arbitrary identifications, often imposed by medieval Muslim commentators and exegetes unsupported by any evidence or attestation, can be accepted without serious reservations.[152] There is equally good reason to presume that the expression is used no differently from the way it is used somewhat later, in sūra 45, "Those on Their Knees" (B73/N72), where we find no association with either daemons or poets: "Woe to every peccant falsifier [*affāk athīm*]/who hears God's signs [*āyāt*][153] recited to him, then keeps on arrogantly as if he had not heard them. So announce to him the tidings of a painful penalty!" (7/6–8/7).

In sūra 26, then, the most flagrant "peccant falsifiers" seem to be those who themselves falsely "cry lies" to Muḥammad (6/5) and falsely "cried lies" to the messenger-prophets who prefigured him (12, 105, 123, 141, 160, 176). By thus "giving the lie" to those who would "cry lies" to the Messenger and the message and by imputing to them the same untrustworthy daemonic influence that they would impute to Muḥammad, āyas 222–23 effectively turn the tables on his accusers and undermine their credibility and authority, as they had sought to undermine his.

As for the poets, the *shuʿarāʾ*, it would not be easy to imagine a jibe directed against them—especially the *qaṣīda-*, or ode-poets, the best-known and most eminent among them—more incisive, scathing, and irrefutable than the next three āyas, 224–26. The charge that they are followed by the "perverse, perverted, aberrant" should certainly discredit them as leaders,[154] and their capacity for *leader*-ship would be even further impugned were we simply to consider the denotative implications of "leaders" who would be "wildering in every valley [*anna-hum fī kulli wādin yahīmūn*]."

But their "wildering in every valley" can also be seen to serve as a slightly disingenuous allusion to the primary structuring topos of the conventional pre-Islamic *qaṣīda,* or ode, as rendered by every poet worthy of the name and as heard by audiences just about wherever Arabic prevailed: namely, the seemingly aimless fictive journey that the poet typically represents himself as making by camel (or, rarely, by horse) through the desert with a couple or more companions—a "wildering" journey interrupted and resumed. It is fictively interrupted as a *qaṣīda* opens when the poet—or rather his self-representation or persona—halts at the faded and ruined traces of a long-abandoned tribal encampment to recall nostalgically in verse a pleasurable, often amorous, interlude enjoyed there once upon a time (the *nasīb*); and (with the *takhalluṣ* and *raḥīl*) it is fictively resumed when the persona abruptly breaks off his reminiscences and proceeds, still in the same verse form, to describe in extravagant, yet selective detail the matchless mount on which he rides away—again fictively—to a destination or objective as yet unspecified (but perhaps to be revealed by the end of the ode).[155] Given the almost universally recognized conventionality of this format or schema of the *qaṣīda* as a genre, it is extremely doubtful whether any self-respecting poet would have even pretended to be offering the verses describing his interrupted and resumed journey as autobiographical truth or would have been presumed by any but the most naïve of audiences to be doing so.[156]

It is just as doubtful, therefore, that the next āya, 226, is meant to be taken as accusing the poets of untruthfulness, falsification, or lying *as such:* qur'ānic vocabulary and usage abound in expressions to convey the idea of mendacity—*kadhab,* "lie"; *ifk,* "falsification"; *iftirā',* "fabrication"; etc.—without having to resort to the rather stilted phrase used here.[157] But when the consideration is raised "that they do say what they do not do," it is neither more nor less than an unadorned truism: the very essence and purpose of poetic discourse, as any sympathetic hearer would have affirmed, is for a poet to say—and to say effectively, eloquently, and convincingly—what that poet does not do![158] The āya articulates nothing if not the bald assertion of a generally acknowledged fact which functions not so much (if at all) to "condemn" or even to "criticize" the poets as to *contrast* their role, conduct, and activity as communicators of mantically inspired discourse to those of the messenger-prophets of the preceding stories and especially of Muḥammad the present Messenger.[159]

Whatever else might be said to insult, belittle, or discredit God's messengers and prophets, it could not be said of them, as it could of the poets, "that they do say what they do not do." For what set them and their believing followers apart from and at odds with their cities and folk was the undeniable and only too obvious fact that what they did say they *did* do—as, most recently, āyas 213–20 of this sūra substantiate. No one could have accused Muḥammad of not believing exclusively in the One God, Whose oneness he preached unremittingly to his "tribe of nearest kin," or of taking a fee for his mantic pronouncements, or of withholding alms or neglecting widows and orphans, or of failing to perform the conspicuous acts of worshipful prayer and prostration that seem so to have offended his fellow townspeople's sense of propriety. At least we have heard of no such accusations. The moral and religious imperative with which his every revealed recitation was charged—a feature plainly missing from poetic discourse, brought down by *shayāṭīn,* not by a "Trustworthy Spirit"—seems to have been actualized and manifested in his own role, conduct, and activity. On this basis, and on this basis alone, āya 226 clearly implies, there should have been no *valid* reason or excuse for confusing—or pretending to confuse—the Prophet with a poet.[160]

Why again, then, is it that "the Qur'ān . . . most insistently denies that Muḥammad was either a poet or a *kāhin*"?[161] Why was it so essential that the revelations he received be absolutely dissociated from the verses of the former or the incantatory pronouncements of the latter—so essential that as proof and warranty qur'ānic discourse evolved an elaborate typology of prestigious prophetic alternatives to the familiar jinn-inspired mantics and undertook a complex restructuring of the fundamental notion of sunna? Was it to make sure of eliminating all possibility of confusing or associating God with jinn and *shayāṭīn,* particularly as a source of mantic communication? Of course, but I do not think that is the only—or even the most important—reason. Was it, as Izutsu would hold, to ensure that qur'ānic discourse as mantically communicated revelation be accorded a privileged status, inasmuch as it was grounded in truth and required accession to that truth and commanded ordering of moral, social, and political action in accordance with it, whereas poetry or divination could hold no such status?[162] Certainly, that too was the case.

But in the sūra of "The Poets" and other sūras where the prophetic exempla prevail, in the early descriptions of God's "noble messenger," the "Trustworthy Spirit" who inspired Muḥammad, and in one of the primary injunctions revealed and often repeated in Medina, I find suggested another factor behind this process of denial and dissociation—a factor of possibly even greater moment for our practical understanding of Muḥammad as prophet and statesman, and the institution of the *umma* at Medina. This is the factor of obedience, *ṭāʿa* (verb: *aṭāʿa*).

The qur'ānic vocabulary strictly excludes all beings but God as proper objects for certain verbs that were not so restricted in contemporary usage. Chief among those verbs, in the present context, are *ʿabada,* "to serve, worship" (which can, of course, be directed to improper objects, but with dire consequences), *ḥamida,* "to praise," and *ittaqā,* "to fear, beware of, protect oneself from, guard against." These verbs (and their derivatives) do not, in the Qur'ān, take any other beings—including angels, messengers, and prophets—as their objects. "Obedience," however, could be owed to angels and men, as well as God; and qur'ānic discourse makes it clear, time and again, that messenger-prophets, along with God, could and should be proper objects of the verb *aṭāʿa,* "to obey." The semantic structure of this usage is adumbrated in sūra 81, cited earlier, when Muḥammad's agent of mantic inspiration is characterized as "a noble messenger" who is *muṭāʿ*, "to be obeyed."

Among the Arabs of the Jāhilīya the word *muṭāʿ* had already acquired a somewhat technical sociopolitical sense, inasmuch as it seems to have been applied principally to those sayyids whose authority was virtually uncontested.[163] The phrase *as-sayyid al-muṭāʿ fī qawmi-hi,* "the chieftain who commanded obedience among his fellow tribesmen," occurs with some regularity as a description of important leaders of the pre- and early Islamic period. One figure who was often so described, ʿUyayna b. Ḥiṣn, a prominent bedouin sayyid whose arrogance and recalcitrance caused the Prophet's community at Medina much grief, was said also to have been labeled by Muḥammad himself "the imbecile who is obeyed/commands obedience" (*al-aḥmaq al-muṭāʿ*.[164] To be owed obedience, then, appears to have been a primary badge and perquisite of the office of sayyid, perhaps even regardless of the character and competence of the officeholder.

What became only too evident during the early years of Revelation (if we adhere more or less to the received historical tradition) was that the earthly Messenger Muḥammad was in a position to command the obedience of only the relatively few believers who followed him, and then only to the limited extent that his constrained situation in Meccan society permitted him to exercise that command. As an orphan and dependent, he had had little personal property and status. His marriage to Khadīja had enhanced his situation in both areas but scarcely carried him to the ranks of the political and economic leaders of the tribe and the city. And any chance of attaining a position of influence and power in which he might have been to some extent "obeyed" by his compatriots would most probably have been eliminated once his mantic experiences got under way, since the concrete practical effect of the accusations that he was a poet, a *kāhin,* or "crazy" would have been effectively to render him unfit for public office in the view of those who listened to and believed (or claimed to believe) them.

In the narratives of the earlier prophets and messengers, revealed to Muḥammad during the years just before and after "The Poets," the hearers—believers and unbelievers alike—were confronted with the paradigm of an alternative form of mantic communication. It was a form quite unlike that of the "everyday" jinn-inspired poets and *kuhhān* and one that had as its representatives men who had been endowed with authority not by virtue of wealth or family prestige or their own personal charisma but by virtue of their mantic relationship with God and the certain, truth-based knowledge that God communicated through them, the messenger-prophets, to their communities. This paradigm—a type to be repeated and eventually fulfilled in Muḥammad and a sunna set down in a past more venerably ancient than the time of the Meccans' most dimly remembered ancestors—finds its most explicit, indeed its pivotal, expression in this sūra, where the key "sign"-bearing formula, "Fear you God and OBEY you me," is repeated no fewer than eight times.[165]

But not until after the Hijra, when Muḥammad had actually been accorded a position of some authority, however ambiguous, based at least partially upon recognition of his inspired leadership as Messenger of God, did his revelations include the direct command (about twenty times altogether), "Obey" *or* "Fear you God and obey you the Messenger!" It was only then, too, that the believers themselves came to be defined as "those who obey God and the Messenger." In fact, in a late sūra (4:64/67; B102/N109) the principle is ennunciated quite unequivocally: "We sent never a single messenger, but that he should be obeyed by God's leave."[166]

Yet this new obedience principle could not help but come into conflict with the old inherited principle of obedience to chieftains, and the Qur'ān bears oblique testimony to that conflict through a verse from another late sūra, 33 (B105/N103), referring to the eschatological fate of the Messenger's enemies:

> On the day their faces are over-
>   turned into the fire, they will
>   say, "Ah! Would that we had obeyed
>   God and obeyed the Messenger!"
> And they will have said, "Our
>   Lord, we did indeed obey our
>   sayyids and our elders, but they
>   made us lose the way.
> "Our Lord, bring them penalty
>   twice over, and curse them in a
>   great degree!"
>
> (66/65–68/69)

I have been tracing by a rather circuitous route, through different phases of qur'ānic discourse, the idea of the propriety, even obligation, of giving obedience to the Messenger just *because* of his special mantic links to God and the revealed communications he conveys. This idea had its ideological foundations in the remarkable synthesis that is the sūra of "The Poets," and it found its practical realization in the rule of Muḥammad, the Messenger and Prophet of God, in Medina. There, however, the Meccan-revealed command of the prefigurative messenger-prophets—"Fear you God and obey you me!"—which, one might say, was typologically fulfilled in Muḥammad's Medinan directive, "Obey God and obey the Messenger!" (note: "THE Messenger"), is revealed just once more, in sūra 4 (B102/N100), with a small addition of colossal significance: "Oh, those of you who believe! Obey you God and obey you the Messenger *and those with authority among you* [*wa uli l-amri min-kum*]!" (59/62).

With the death of the Messenger Muḥammad in 632 and the cessation of revealed communications from God, the great debate in the community raged around the question of precisely who would or should constitute "those in authority among you." It might well be asked, who at any time thereafter could merit the obedience that qur'ānic discourse had so painstakingly staked out and so exclusively reserved for God and for His inspired Messenger, himself neither *kāhin* nor poet?[167] Whether that question was definitely resolved then and whether it has ever been resolved are issues for another essay altogether.

CHAPTER 7

The Meaning of *Mutanabbī*

Wolfhart Heinrichs

In the view of the majority of the Muslims, when the Prophet of Islam died, prophecy also ceased.[1] The divine message was final and there was to be no further prophet until the end of time. That the channel of revelation was considered closed had important consequences for the future history of Islamic culture. One was that the corpus of revelational texts—the Qur'ān and, in a slightly different way, the Prophetic Traditions—became the only and exclusive presence of the Divine in this world, and it was the task of the scholars, the students of the divine law, to preserve the texts intact and to understand and expound their meanings. "The scholars are the heirs of the prophets" is an idea found in early ḥadīth.[2] So Islam seemed destined from the beginning to be a scholarly book religion, and that is to a great extent just what it became. Nevertheless, the yearning of many people for a more direct contact with the Divine soon found its expression in the development of *taṣawwuf,* or Islamic mysticism, which on the basis of the Scriptures and the Law they contain places the adept in several additional relationships to God: first and foremost, of course, it sets the adept on the spiritual path of self-purification towards Him; but second and secondarily, it inserts the adept in a chain of masters and disciples (*silsila*) which is meant to connect him or her back to the Prophet and through which esoteric teachings are handed down; and last it makes the adept the possible recipient of divine inspiration (*ilhām*). This *ilhām* is quite different from revelation (which is called *waḥy* in Arabic) in that the addressee of the former is the individual mystic, whereas revelation is aimed at the whole community. Nevertheless, *ilhām* was frowned upon by nonmystical scholars.[3]

Where does poetry stand in relation to all this? First we should note that with the cessation of revelation other varieties of inspiration also became suspect, especially those that had been considered rivals, as it were, of divine revelation—that is, the inspiration of the poets and the soothsayers.[4] That the Prophet himself did not deny the superhuman origin of their utterances and found the jinn-inspired lampoon poets especially dangerous to his cause seems to be clear from traditions in which he is depicted as encouraging his court poet Ḥassān ibn Thābit to hurl poetical invectives against the pagan Meccans and assuring him that Gabriel will be with him.[5] Gabriel is, of course, no less than the messenger of Revelation, and thus a certain parallelism between revelation and inspiration is undeniable. This is one of the reasons that, when revelation stopped, inspiration became implausible, too: the whole mechanism of direct access to superhuman hidden knowledge became questionable. In addition, the source of the reputed supernatural knowledge of the poet naturally became highly suspect: one of the many terms with which the alter ego of the poet in the world of the jinn is designated happens to be *shayṭān* (pl. *shayāṭīn*) and this appellation was soon restricted to the one Satan of the monotheistic religions and identified with Iblis. This usage did not fail to put poetry, in some pious and ascetic circles, in a very bad light. But the main reaction was that the whole idea fell into desuetude and only survived as an idiom in the language: the *shayṭān* of a poet did not mean much more than his poetical talent.[6] It is true that later the notion was taken up again, but as a purely literary device;[7] nobody really believed in it any more. It is, thus, fair to say that inspiration, whether by an angel or by a jinni, is not in any important way considered a source of poetry in the Arab world. In saying this I am admittedly excluding mystical poetry, in which *ilhām,* "inspiration," and dreams may play an important role, but this exclusion is justifiable in that the medieval public would have regarded this poetry as versified doctrine rather than true *shiʿr* (as the Arabs call their poetry); works on literary theory and criticism well-nigh totally disregard it.

Since inspiration as an outside source of poetical knowledge had been discredited, one might perhaps expect that it was transformed and internalized as a special faculty of the poet. And, indeed, there are some attempts in this direction, such as the notion of *ilhām* as aesthetic knowledge, which allows some people to distinguish good from bad poetry or music,[8] or a theory of *ṭabʿ* and *nashāṭ,* "natural talent" and "creative energy," which tells poets how to put their natural resources to use and produce poetry to their liking.[9] But these attempts remained rather rudimentary and did not become a major part of literary theory. By far the most prevalent conception of poetry was to classify it as a craft and a science; technical and scholarly competence were considered indispensable for the poet and became the major focus of attention. In short, the typical poet in Arabic Islamic culture was the *poeta doctus* rather than the *poeta vates*.

Given all this, it is nothing short of surprising to find that one of the most famous Arab poets of the Middle Ages (*the* most famous, if we take the number of commentaries as the criterion) was nicknamed al-Mutanabbī. The title of this essay is, of course, cleverly ambiguous, containing, as it does, two questions: first, what is the meaning of the word *mutanabbī;* and second, what is the meaning of applying this word to this particular poet? The first question can be disposed of very quickly. The word denotes someone "who acts like a prophet." It is the active participle of the verb *tanabbā* (or *tanabbaʾa,* by influence of the Arabic root *n–b–ʾ*), which is a so-called fifth form derived from the noun *nabīy* meaning "prophet" (which latter is a loanword in Arabic from Aramaic *nbīyā* and or Hebrew *nābīʾ*). These fifth forms often have the special meaning of "to behave like, or to claim to be, what the derivational basis says," without, however, necessarily connoting falsity or, worse, fraud.[10] The word *mutanabbī* thus refers to a person who behaves like a prophet, claims to be a prophet, regardless of whether that person is or is not a prophet. Likewise, the fifth-form particle *mutaṭabbib,* derived from *ṭabīb,* "physician," may denote a "practitioner of the medical art" just as well as a fraudulent "quack." It is true, though, that these words have a tendency to acquire the less favorable meaning in usage. In the case of *mutanabbī,* there can be no doubt in the mind of an orthodox Muslim for whom Muḥammad was the final prophet in history that a *mutanabbī* cannot be anything but a "false prophet." Even so, the simple application of this word does not determine anything about the personal convictions of the man to whom it is applied. We shall see that people were aware of this problem.

As for the second question, which is the main topic of the present essay, I will subdivide it into the following separate problems: first, on what basis was this poet called a *mutanabbī;* second, in what context did it make sense to claim prophethood; and third, did his claim to prophethood have any influence on his poetry. Before going into any detail, it seems advisable to give a bare minimum of information on the life and times of al-Mutanabbī. He was born in A.H. 303/A.D. 915 and died in 354/965. He thus witnessed a time in Islamic history which must have been as fascinating as it was disquieting. The Swiss Orientalist Adam Mez has titled his comprehensive study of the tenth century: *The Renaissance of Islam.*[11] This may be a misnomer, inasmuch as we are not dealing here with a comprehensive rediscovery of classical antiquity. It is much more a blossoming of philosophy and science based on a continuous tradition and translation of Greek texts. Yet there are some resemblances between tenth-century Islam and the Italian Renaissance. In both, a noticeable trend toward humanism and individualism shaped the world view and the self-understanding of an elite group of scholars, potentates, and men of letters, and with these al-Mutanabbī's personality seems to have been to a large extent in tune.[12] Another, more superficial similarity is the proliferation of courts all over the Islamic world, which vied with one another in their eagerness to sponsor the arts and sciences and thus brought about a cultural efflorescence that was inversely proportional to the power and unity of the caliphate. Al-Mutanabbī's career is paradigmatic in this respect: whereas in the preceding century poets would normally flock to Baghdad as the center of caliphal power, al-Mutanabbī got his first tenure as court poet in 336/948 at the court of the Hamdanid Sayf al-Dawla in Aleppo, fled to Egypt in 346/957 to sing the praises of the black slave-general Kāfūr who ruled on behalf of the Ikhshidid dynasty, fled to Baghdad in 351/962 and ended up, shortly before his death, at the court of the powerful Buyid ruler ʿAḍud al-Dawla in Shiraz.

The tenth century is, however, also the apogee of what Bernard Lewis in *The Arabs in History* has dubbed the "revolt of Islam."[13] The Sunnī caliphate was beleaguered by an ever-increasing number of Shiite dynasties, some of them friendly, that is, acknowledging the suzerainty of the caliph, such as the Hamdanids in Aleppo and the Buyids in Iraq and Iran, which later became the tutelary rulers over the caliphs themselves. These were moderate Shiites of the Imāmiyya branch. Others belonged to the more extreme and aggressive Ismāʿīliyya branch, which was quite decidedly bent on the overthrow of the existing order. The Fatimid dynasty in Egypt—countercaliphs to the Abbasids—were of this persuasion, as were the Qarmaṭians in

Bahrayn. Both branches, and other extremist Shiites as well, had secret missionary organizations to convert people and incite them to open rebellion. They were particularly successful among the bedouin tribes of the Syrian desert. The Qarmaṭians, once they had established their state in Bahrayn, made devastating raids into southern Iraq and in 317/930 they attacked and conquered Mecca during the pilgrimage, committed an atrocious butchery among pilgrims and inhabitants and carried away the Black Stone of the Kaʿba. Troubled times indeed! The stage is set, enter al-Mutanabbī.[14]

He was born in the Iraqi city of Kufa, and there, with a few interruptions due to Qarmaṭian attacks, he spent his early years. Kufa was originally a garrison city founded by the Arab conquerors not far from the ancient capital of the Sasanian Empire Seleucia-Ctesiphon (or *al-Madāʾin,* "the Cities," as the Arabs called it). For a short while, under the fourth caliph ʿAlī, it had been the capital of the caliphate, and from then on it remained deeply attached to the descendants of ʿAlī and various Shiite beliefs. The military camp attracted a lot of non-Arabs from neighboring al-Madāʾin for menial labor and craftmanship; these gradually became *mawālī,* "clients," of Arab tribes but remained second-class Muslims. One of the religious traditions these people brought with them was ancient gnosticism, which in Kufa became amalgamated with Shiism and thus produced a specifically Islamic variety of gnosticism.[15] Most of what we know about this movement, which over the course of the years split up into many sects, is owed to the accounts of Sunnī and Imāmī heresiographers who named them the *ghulāt,* "exaggerators," for their inordinate veneration of one or the other of the Imāms (descendants—sometimes only spiritual descendants—of ʿAlī who were thought to be the rightful rulers of the caliphate), which did not stop short of deification. Al-Mutanabbī grew up in this milieu, although we do not know whether he espoused any of the various sectarian doctrines with which Kufa abounded. Even his class status, which would allow an educated guess, is not quite clear. His father is said to have been a Juʿfī (that is, belonging to the Arab tribe of Juʿfī), and one source states that he was a trueborn member of that tribe, not a client. On the other hand he is depicted as a water seller with a camel, a rather lowly occupation, and his genealogy is given in two totally different forms, both significantly breaking off with his grandfather. Moreover, he is said to have lived—and his son to have been born—in the *khiṭṭa* (allotment for settlement, town quarter) of the tribe of Kinda, a quarter that is described by one source as being populated by water sellers and weavers.[16] All this points to the possibility that he was not of true Arab descent and that his family thus belonged to the lower strata of society in which gnosticism flourished. It is worth noticing that several heresiarchs of the "exaggerators" bore the tribal name of Juʿfī.[17] On the other hand, there are certain indications that he was somehow connected with the Alid nobility in Kufa: he was nursed by an Alid woman; he frequented the school set up for the children of the *ashrāf,* "nobles," of Kufa; and during his short and abortive career as a religio-political pretender, he is said to have claimed Alid descent.[18]

These, as well as most other bits of information concerning al-Mutanabbī's youth, are too isolated in their attestation to be separately used as the basis for any far-reaching argument, but taken together they enable us to assert the likelihood that al-Mutanabbī was part of the gnostic Shiite circles in Kufa and somehow attached to the Alid nobility of that city. If one is to evaluate the story of his claim to prophethood among the bedouin tribes of the Samāwa desert, the foregoing should, therefore, be taken as the framework within which his rather spectacular behavior should become meaningful. This is no new idea; a Qarmaṭian connection has been proposed for our poet by several scholars, but the information we have is so fragmentary that the vision necessary to fill in the blank spaces may lead the various authors in totally opposite directions: whereas Louis Massignon in his famous article "Mutanabbi, devant le siècle ismaelien de l'Islam" depicts our poet as a (crypto-) Qarmaṭian and Régis Blachère has him as a (pseudo-) Qarmaṭian, the Egyptian scholar Muḥammad Muḥammad Ḥusayn, in a booklet on al-Mutanabbī and the Qarmaṭians, turns him into a fanatic anti-Qarmaṭian.[19] We shall see that although an extremist Shiite connection is very likely, the Qarmaṭian category is probably not a very useful one.

In the following discussion the presumption will be that there actually was a time in the early career of our poet when he claimed to be a prophet. This view has not gone uncontested, especially not by al-Mutanabbī himself, who in his later life apparently circulated various explanations of his nickname that were destined to remove the disgrace and embarrassment it caused, which made him an easy target of ridicule on the part of his enemies. The sources contain, however, at least one story in which our poet comes very close to admitting his faux pas; it is a conversation between al-Mutanabbī and al-Muḥassin al-Tanūkhī (d. 384/994), which took place in Ahwāz in the year 354/

965, a few months before our poet's untimely death. Al-Tanūkhī recounts:

> It frequently occurred to me to ask Abū l-Ṭayyib al-Mutanabbī about his claim to prophethood and the reason for it, namely, whether that was simply a name that had attached itself to him in the way of a nickname or whether it was as it used to be told to us. But I would be too ashamed to do that, because of the multitudes who attended his circle [*majlis*] in Baghdad; I was loath to open up a topic to which he might be averse. Then, when he came to Ahwāz on his way to Fārs, I was alone with him and I had long talks with him and I led him to a point where I said to him: I want to ask you about something I have had in mind for years. I was always too ashamed to talk to you about it because of the many people who were present with you at Baghdad. But now we are in solitude and I simply must ask you about it.—There happened to be in front of me a partial copy of his poetry on which was written "The Poetry of Abū l-Ṭayyib al-Mutanabbī." He said: You want to ask me about the reason for that?—And he put his finger to the writing where it said "al-Mutanabbī." So I said: Yes. He said: That was something that happened in my youth which a certain childishness[20] had brought about.—I had never seen a subtler ambiguous allusion[21] than that, because it would sustain both interpretations: that he had only posed as a prophet and relied on false pretense [*kāna tanabba'a wa-ʿtamada l-kadhib*—the last phrase could also be translated: "and intentionally lied"] or that in his own opinion he had been truthful [*anna ʿindahū annahū kāna ṣādiqan*]. In either case, however, he admitted to [having been] a *mutanabbī*. He [al-Tanūkhī] continued: I saw that this was difficult for him, so I considered it bad to go any further and force him to tell the story in clear detail and so I abstained from it.[22]

Among other things al-Tanūkhī's report suggests to us the various alternatives that he and his contemporaries considered with regard to the reason for al-Mutanabbī's nickname. First, it could have been a nickname pure and simple without a referent in the literal sense. Al-Mutanabbī himself suggested as much to his friend the famous grammarian ibn Jinnī (d. 392/1002); for the latter mentions in his commentary on al-Mutanabbī's *Dīwān* that our poet claimed to have received his nickname on account of one particular line in one of his early poems: "Ana fī ummatin tadārakaha llā—hu gharībun ka-Ṣāliḥin fī Thamūdi [I am in a community—which God may set aright!—a stranger like Ṣāliḥ among the Thamūd]."[23] The poet obviously means to say that, just like the pre-Islamic Arabian prophet Ṣāliḥ, who was not accepted by his people, the Thamūd, to whom he had been sent, he too feels lonely and full of indignation in a society that has completely gone awry. Whether the line also implies that he felt sent by God it is difficult to decide; his pious wish that "God may set [it] aright" by explicitly leaving everything to God seems to indicate that he wanted to avoid this interpretation. In either case, the line would have been quite sufficient to earn him the "title" of Mutanabbī, as this was a time-honored practice with Arab poets: several historians, including ibn al-Kalbī (d. 204/819?), and philologists such as al-Sukkarī (d. 275/888) are known to have compiled whole lists of poets who were named after a word or an idea in one of their lines.[24] It is very likely that al-Mutanabbī used this method of explaining his nickname as a smoke screen to hide embarrassing facts, and indeed, as we shall see, it was not greeted with credulous acceptance by everybody. We should, however, not forget that the line in question can and should be detached from any use that was made of it, either by others (if the nickname was indeed derived from this line) or by the poet himself (if it was only a smoke screen), and that in itself it seems to be in tune with what the sources tell us about his prophetic escapades. The deep sense of alienation ("I am a stranger"), mixed with rebelliousness and resignation, which we find in a large portion of the poem of which his comparison with Ṣāliḥ forms the resounding and climactic last line, should be regarded as the underlying motive of his youthful aberrations, and it may have remained the dominant note of the rest of his life. As ibn Fūrraja (d. after 437/1045), author of the "countercommentary" *Al-Tajannī ʿalā ibn Jinnī* (The accusation of ibn Jinnī), puts it, al-Mutanabbī was a man "bitter in his soul [*murr al-nafs*]."[25]

The sources mention two other explanations of the poet's nickname which also try to circumvent the literal and most obvious meaning of the term, but they have the appearance of little games that he and his environment played to defuse the scandal of its actual meaning and will be relegated here to the notes.[26] The second possibility to which al-Tanūkhī alludes is to assume that the poet at some point in his past had indeed posed as a prophet—either, as al-Tanūkhī clearly sees, as an impostor or as someone who truly believed in his own mission. Short of a confession by the poet himself, this question cannot be decided, but if we assume a man declaring himself a prophet to be truthful, there are again three possibilities to explain his behavior: he may be a simpleton, or mentally disturbed, or a sane person of political ambition and/or with a feeling of moral outrage. All three of these explanations have been applied to the case of al-Mutanabbī, though the first one only by mistake.

A simpleton al-Mutanabbī certainly was not, and the hilarious story in which he is depicted as such is based on a case of mistaken identity. Since I am, however, interested here in the phenomenon of pseudoprophecy in general and not only as it applies to the particular case of our poet, I have some justification to quote it here in full—all the more as the story is typical of a small but recognizable genre within anecdotal *adab* literature, which aims at entertaining the reader with the often ridiculous claims of mentally retarded pseudoprophets and thus forms a genre alongside the better-developed ones that feature the comical feats of misers, parasites, and dunderheads. I follow the version(s) as quoted and commented upon by Kamāl al-Dīn ibn al-ʿAdīm:

> I read in the epistle of ʿAlī b. Mansūr al-Ḥalabī, known as Dawkhala—that is the one that he wrote to Abū l-ʿAlāʾ b. Sulaymān [al-Maʿarrī] and to which the latter replied with his *Risālat al-Ghufrān* (Epistle on forgiveness)[27]—and he says, mentioning ibn Abī l-Azhar and al-Quṭrabbulī and their jointly composed "History" [as his source],[28] that the vizier ʿAlī b. ʿĪsā[29] had him [al-Mutanabbī] brought to his audience and said to him: You are Aḥmad al-Mutanabbī [or: Aḥmad the pseudoprophet]? He replied: I am Aḥmad the Prophet and I have a sign on my belly, the seal of prophethood.—And he showed them something like a wen [*silʿa*] on his belly, whereupon the vizier ordered him to be slapped. So he was slapped and shackled, and he ordered him to be detained in the dungeon.
>
> Later I perused the above-mentioned "History" and in it I read under the events of the year 302 [914–915] the following: In it [that is, the year 302] the vizier ʿAlī b. ʿĪsā sat in court to look into grievances and al-Mutanabbī was brought to his presence—he had been jailed—in order that he be set free. So he [the vizier] interrogated him in the presence of the judges and jurisconsults, and he replied: I am Aḥmad the Prophet and I have a sign on my belly, the seal of prophethood.—And he bared his belly and showed them something like a wen on it, whereupon the vizier ordered him to be slapped. So he was slapped a hundred times and beaten and shackled, and [the vizier] ordered him to be detained in the dungeon.
>
> It became clear to me then that Abū l-Hasan ʿAlī b. Manṣūr al-Ḥalabī had found the mention of Aḥmad al-Mutanabbī in the "History" of ibn Abī l-Azhar and al-Quṭrabbulī and had thought him to be Abū l-Ṭayyib Aḥmad b. al-Ḥusayn; and so he made a monstrous mistake because of his ignorance of history. For in this "History" the above-mentioned

event was in the year 302, and al-Mutanabbī was not even born yet, since his birth, according to the correct opinion, was in the year 303. Some say that his birth was in the year 301 so that he would have been one year old. Abū Muḥammad ʿAbdallāh b. al-Ḥusayn al-Kātib al-Quṭrabbulī and Muḥammad ibn Abī l-Azhar both died before al-Mutanabbī grew up and became known. This Mutanabbī which ʿAlī b. ʿĪsā had summoned before him was a man from Isfahan who had posed as a prophet in the days of [the caliph] al-Muqtadir [reigned 295/908–320/932] and who was called Aḥmad b. ʿAbd al-Raḥīm al-Iṣbahānī. I found him mentioned with this *nisba* in the book which ʿUbaydallāh b. Aḥmad b. [Abī] Ṭāhir wrote as a supplement to the book of his father on the "History of Baghdad."[30]

The rather rough treatment that the sorry hero of this story receives at the hands of the authorities is not all that typical for this genre of anecdotes about pseudoprophets with low IQs; more often the *mutanabbī* would be welcome for his slightly scandalous entertainment value, coupled with harmlessness, and would be made the target of jokes, after which he would be severely admonished to relinquish his claims, possibly with a few lashes for emphasis, and then set free. The man with the cyst must have been particularly loathsome to the "Good Vizier."

A plea of temporary insanity on behalf of our poet has also been tried. Two such attempts are recorded in the sources, one of which is based on the presumption of an actual illness, while the other very much looks like a ruse to save his life. To start with the latter, it is a story told by the poet al-Waḥīd al-Baghdādī (d. 385/995, thus a contemporary of al-Mutanabbī). This man is credited with a commentary on the *Dīwān* of al-Mutanabbī, but what we have of him are notes and corrections on the commentary of ibn Jinnī which have been preserved in one of the manuscripts of that work (marked *ḥ* to set them off from ibn Jinnī's text) and included in the printed edition.[31] As we have seen, ibn Jinnī mentions that al-Mutanabbī used to derive his own nickname from the well-known line in which he likens himself to the prophet Ṣāliḥ. Here al-Waḥīd objects:

He [al-Mutanabbī] used to shield himself with that, for he did in fact pose as a prophet in [the districts of] Jabala and Lādhiqiyya among the bedouins of the Banū l-Qaṣīṣ and he produced for their children a qur'ān [*muṣḥaf*]. When al-Ḥusayn b. Isḥāq[32] heard that, he ordered that he be hidden so that he might be secretly sent away. But a servant from the palace spread his story and the people assembled at his gate to demand him [that is, his release], whereupon he ordered the physician to go outside and say: This is a man who needs bloodletting from both his arms and then vomiting several times in a row and it will also be necessary to extract pumpkinseed oil for him so that he can snuff from it. For there is in him the beginning of melancholy (*mālīkhūliyā*) and that is craziness.—And when the physician had said that, the people dispersed, saying: [He is] a crazy man. Finally, when they no longer paid any attention, he [al-Mutanabbī] left them for Damascus and then Jabal Jarash, where he went into hiding for a while. Then he returned as a horseman on a filly that a man from the tribe of Ṭayyi' had presented to him. On it he betook himself to Abū l-ʿAshā'ir[33] and then he went up from there.[34]

It is regrettable that this report of a contemporary is totally isolated. Al-Waḥīd does not mention his own source, which makes it all the more difficult to assess the trustworthiness of this report. As we shall soon see, that al-Mutanabbī claimed prophethood among the bedouins of the district of Lādhiqiyya (Laodicea, Lattakya) and that he produced a qur'ān is attested in other reports as well. The protective role of al-Ḥusayn b. Isḥāq and the subsequent events present some chronological problems, which will be adumbrated in the context of the other reports. What should be emphasized here is how the danger posed by a (pseudo) prophet—danger, that is, for his own life as well as for political stability and the lives of others—is defused by the presumption of mental illness. In our case it seems that the governor and his physician did not actually believe in al-Mutanabbī's "melancholy" but rather used it to divert the attention of a mob of would-be lynchers (or, possibly, adherents of his prophetic cause, for it is none too clear why the people demanded him).

The other attempt to explain al-Mutanabbī's behavior as a temporary blackout has the authority of the great scholar and scientist al-Bīrūnī (d. after 442/1050) who proffers this explanation in his *Risālat al-taʿallul bi-ijālat al-wahm fī maʿānī nuẓūm ulī l-faḍl* (The pretext of letting one's fancy wander around the meanings of the compositions of excellent men).[35] Al-Bīrūnī's discussion of al-Mutanabbī's nickname as quoted by Kamāl al-Dīn ibn al-ʿAdīm consists of two parts, the first of which I shall treat later. Here is the second part:

He [al-Mutanabbī], in spite of his truthfulness, never told the reason for his nickname. He only came up with some explanation, as Abū

> l-Fatḥ ʿUthmān b. Jinnī reports from him, namely that the reason for it was his line: "I am a stranger in a community—may God set it aright!—like Ṣāliḥ among the Thamūd." Actually, it [the reason for his *laqab*] was that the nerves[36] in his head used to make him wander about and become restless. So he waited for Sayf al-Dawla to be absent on one of his raids and went to the bedouins in the Syrian desert and managed to lead about a thousand men among them astray. This news reached Sayf al-Dawla, so he immediately turned back and swept down upon him. His followers dispersed and he was brought before him as a captive. He said to him: Are you the prophet? He replied: No, I am the *mutanabbī,* that is, predicting that you will feed me and give me something to drink. And when you have done that, I shall be Aḥmad b. al-Ḥusayn.—He was very impressed with his calm composure and his audacity in replying, so he spared his blood and threw him into prison at Ḥimṣ, until his excellence was established to him, whereupon he set him free and attached him to his entourage. And when they went on talking about his claim to prophethood, he took it as a nickname [*talaqqaba bihī*], lest it become a matter of disparagement which would be concealed, whenever someone faced him, and a term of opprobrium with which he would not be addressed openly. The situation then continued on the basis of his having adopted it as a nickname.
>
> I [Yāqūt or ibn al-ʿAdīm] have said: What Abu l-Rayḥān [al-Bīrūnī] says about al-Mutanabbī's waiting for Sayf al-Dawla to be absent on one of his raids, etc., is not correct because none of the Syrians nor any other transmitters have related that anything of this sort emerged from al-Mutanabbī during the days and reign of Sayf al-Dawla in Aleppo and Syria, nor that he jailed him after the latter's attachment to him. All that happened in the days of Lu'lu' al-Ikhshīdī, governor of Ḥimṣ.[37]

Ibn al-ʿAdīm's (or Yāqūt's) criticism is well taken, and it is a little disquieting that a scientist and historian of such well-deserved renown as al-Bīrūnī should have committed such a blunder. It may be that he wrote this work—whose genre, in any case, is not very characteristic of his literary output—at an early age, when important sources like al-Tanūkhī's *Nishwār al-muḥāḍara* (written over a twenty-year period approximately between 360/970 and 380/990) had not yet become available to him. Since this part of the story is easily discredited—all other sources agree that the "prophetic" episode was long before al-Mutanabbī's attachment to the court of Sayf al-Dawla—the information about his pathological restlessness can hardly be accorded more trustworthiness, although it need not be wrong. Suffice it to say, then, that the presumption of a mental disturbance was one of the ways to deal with the phenomenon of *tanabbu*ʾ.

I need not go into detail about the historical facts that can be extracted from the sources concerning his "prophetic" episode, for Blachère has already done as much.[38] The sources he made use of include the few surviving historical-anecdotal texts as well as al-Mutanabbī's poems, which, in the poet's own edition, are more or less chronologically arranged and often introduced by lines specifying some of the circumstances of their composition. What emerges is that after coming to Syria from Baghdad around 318/930, he apparently felt attracted to the city of Lādhiqiyya, to which, in spite of his restlessness and incessant travel, he returned several times: he arrived there for the first time at the end of 319/931, when he addressed three poems to the governor of that city, al-Ḥusayn b. Isḥāq al-Tanūkhī; after a short interval at Tiberias he returned to Lādhiqiyya, when al-Ḥusayn's cousin, ʿAlī b. Ibrāhīm, had become governor, and he praised him for having quelled the rebellion of the bedouins of the Banū l-Qaṣīṣ; finally, after visiting Aleppo and Antioch, he was again back in Lādhiqiyya at the end of 321/933, and it seems to be at this point that he attached himself to one Abū ʿAbdallāh Muʿādh b. Ismāʿīl in whose name we have a colorful account of al-Mutanabbī's prophetic self-proclamation, brimful with improbabilities. (Inasmuch as this is a well-told story, very likely with a historical nucleus, I have added a translation of it in the Appendix to this chapter.) So this may have been the time when he decided on a trial run of his prophetic enterprise, including the working of some miracles![39] If, however, al-Waḥīd's story of al-Mutanabbī's narrow escape is based on fact, then it would seem that our poet had already tested the market on his first visit to Lādhiqiyya, albeit with little success. In any case, it was shortly after his third stay in Lādhiqiyya that he decided to add the political dimension to his self-assumed position of spiritual leadership by joining parts of the Kalb bedouins in the Samāwa desert and inciting them into open rebellion against the authorities. The Banū Kalb were already well accustomed to Shiite agitators of the more extreme variety (Qarmaṭians and others) and very susceptible to the idea of going against the (sedentary) authorities with a little pillage on the side. Soon, Lu'lu' al-Ghūrī, governor of Ḥimṣ on behalf of the Ikhshidids in Egypt, had quite enough of this and moved against him with an army. The bedouins dispersed and our poet was taken prisoner. He spent two miserable years in jail (beginning of 322/934 until the end of 324/936), until he secured his release by means of a poetical petition sent to Lu'lu''s successor, Isḥāq b. Kayghulugh. He was asked to repent publicly and, after his repentance had been duly witnessed, he was set free. From then on, together with his rising fame as a poet, his nickname "al-Mutanabbī" also spread. We have, however, explicit testimony that by the year 315/937 this name was not yet known in his hometown of Kufa.[40]

Unfortunately, the sources tell us little about the specifics of al-Mutanabbī's prophetic teachings and claims, nor do we have any account of the specific charges brought against him, indeed no account of a trial at all. As already mentioned, some scholars (Blachère, Massignon, and Ṭāhā Ḥusayn, among others) have surmised that he must have been a Qarmaṭian or at least a Qarmaṭian-inspired free lance. The time, geography, and technique of his ill-fated attempt to win and change the world would certainly tally well with this assumption, as would his own "insurrectional" (Blachère's term) poetry prior to his rebellion. But in none of this lies a clear-cut proof, and there is indeed one fact which would militate against this idea and that is precisely his prophethood. A Qarmaṭian agitator might be, or claim to be, a propagandist (*dāʿī*) sent by the Imām, or he might claim to be the Imām himself—and al-Mutanabbī may have tried that, too.[41] But it would make little sense for him to pose as a prophet unless he wished to be recognized as the Seventh Imām, Muḥammad b. Ismāʿīl, who was expected to return as the seventh (and last) *nāṭiq,* "Prophet bringing a Law," and who as the Mahdī would rule the whole world in justice. But nothing in the texts dealing with al-Mutanabbī's rebellion would suggest this reading. The question therefore arises: in what denominational context would it be meaningful to claim prophethood? To answer this question, we will now consider the first part of al-Bīrūnī's discussion of this problem as promised earlier.[42] Kamāl al-Dīn ibn al-ʿAdīm reports the following on the authority of Yāqūt:

> Abū l-Rayḥān Muḥammad b. Aḥmad al-Bīrūnī mentions—and I have transcribed it from his own handwriting—that when al-Mutanabbī mentioned in his *qaṣīda Kuffī arānī* the light that, divine in origin, manifested itself in the addressee of his ode and then said: "I am [actually] seeing [you], but I think I am dreaming," and when this [poem] became well known, people said: His Lord has revealed Himself to al-Mutanabbī. And because of this he was thrown into jail. That is the "shackle"[43] that he mentions in his poem *A-yā khaddada llāhu warda l-khudūdi*.

Before taking a closer look at the poem in question, we should quickly note that al-Bīrūnī seems to assume not one but two jailings of our poet, the first of which—the one just mentioned—is not explicitly linked with claims to prophethood. It seems, however, that, simply by juxtaposing this story and the one quoted earlier dealing with his short "prophetic" career, he wishes to indicate a connection between the two, and his feeling may indeed be correct. One should also note in this context that the poem starting *A-yā khaddada* is generally supposed to have been composed when he was in jail for his "prophetic" escapades.[44]

The relevant passage in the incriminating poem alluded to by al-Bīrūnī runs as follows:[45]

> O King, purified as to your substance [which is] from the essence of the Lord of the Divine Dominion, the Highest of whoever soars high.
> [It is] a light whose divinity has appeared in you, so you well-nigh know the knowledge of that which will not be known.
> And it [the light] in you, whenever you speak eloquently, is about to speak from each of your limbs.
> I am seeing [you], but I seem to be dreaming—who could dream of God, so that I would be dreaming of him [now]?!
> The sight [of him] has become too much for me, so that through seeing [him] certainty has become conjecture.

The image and the language used in this panegyric passage is obviously highly hyperbolic, to a degree that it becomes blasphemous: the poet strongly insinuates that the addressee of the praise is like God or is God himself. Now, blasphemous hyperboles are nothing uncommon in the poetry of the so-called "moderns" at the time of the Abbasid caliphate—Abū Nuwās produced famous examples, and there is more of this kind in al-Mutanabbī, too[46]—but this outright deification is an exceptional case. The commentator al-Wāḥidī is clearly embarrassed by this scandal; nevertheless, he gives a justification for the poet, saying "that this is a panegyric that rightly raises suspicion; these are detestable words in a praise of a human being. The reason [for them] is that he wanted to induce the addressee to disclose his religious beliefs [*madhhab*] in the sense that, if he accepted this, one would know that his beliefs were corrupt, and if he disapproved, one would know that his creed was unobjectionable."[47] What al-Wāḥidī suggests cannot easily be proven or disproven; it is, however, not very likely. Of the addressee of the poem we know very little. He was one Abū l-Faḍl (that is all we know of his name), who, according to one tradition, was a *mutafalsif,* "one who studies Greek philosophy," who, the source says, led al-Mutanabbī astray as he led himself astray.[48] The poem is an early one, probably composed at Kufa around 315/927, when the poet was in his early teens. Kufa, as we have seen, was the hotbed of Islamic gnosticism, and we know that in the early tenth century at least one of the gnostic groups, the Ismāʿīliyya, began to rewrite and reinterpret their gnostic myths in the philosophical language of Neoplatonism (al-Nasafī, executed in 331/942, is the earliest Ismāʿīlī author known to us who uses the Neoplatonic system).[49] Under these circumstances a *mutafalsif,* "student of Greek philosophy," would fit in very well. We may thus speculate that he was a gnostic mentor and teacher to al-Mutanabbī. He may have insinuated to the impressionable boy to compose the lines we have heard, or more likely, the poet may have tried to push his mentor to declare himself, but in quite the opposite direction of what the commentator al-Wāḥidī had suggested. However that may be, a closer look at the poetry itself reveals one important fact that has not yet attracted sufficient attention in the discussions about al-Mutanabbī's early beliefs, although it is quite obvious. What al-Mutanabbī describes is clearly the transfiguration of a human being revealing his divinity. This notion is alien to the Ismāʿīliyya, who did not believe in the divinity of ʿAlī and the Imāms, but it is quite common in the tradition of the other important group of gnostics, the Kufan *ghulāt,* the "exaggerators," as they are called by their opponents, precisely because of their deification of the Imāms. In their traditions, which we know better now thanks to the work of Heinz Halm, the miracle of the transfiguration of the Imām in the presence of one of his adherents is quite commonplace. There are moving stories, particularly about the fifth Imām, Muḥammad al-Bāqir (d. 114/732 or 117/735 in Medina). In the book *Ummu l-Kitāb* (The Mother of the Book), which, in its most ancient parts, is one of the two original works of the Kufan "exaggerators" still existing, Muḥammad al-Bāqir is depicted in his transfiguration as transforming himself successively into Muḥammad, ʿAlī, Fāṭima (al-Fāṭir), Ḥasan, and Ḥusayn, the pentade that represents the limbs (*jawāriḥ*) of the eternal God.[50] It may not be fortuitous that "limbs" (though denoted with another word, *ʿuḍw*) play an important role in al-Mutanabbī's description, too. All this is, of course, still a rather tenuous basis for making al-Mutanabbī an "exaggerator," but then there is his claim to prophethood. As we have seen, in all moderate denominations within Islam there is no place for a prophet after the Prophet. The case is different with those who consider the Imāms to be God: any propagandist who promotes their cause and speaks for them can rightfully be called a "prophet," and if we look into the history of the "exaggerators," we find indeed that prophets abound.[51] It thus seems to me likely that when al-Mutanabbī proclaimed himself a prophet, he did so in the tradition of the "exaggerators." We know that various sects of these gnostics, especially the followers of Isḥāq al-Aḥmar (d. 286/899) and Ibn Nuṣayr (d. ca. 250/864), had spread into the area of Aleppo and Lādhiqiyya, so that also from the point of view of the geography of heresies all the facts fall into place.[52] The Nuṣayrīs, of course, still inhabit the hinterland of Lādhiqiyya to this very day. It is not intended here, however, to assign our poet to one or the other of these sects; the sources provide no clues for an answer to this question. Moreover, it would seem that, given his youthful impetuosity and high-soaring aspirations, he would hardly have attached himself to an organized group with fixed doctrines. What is being suggested here, then, is that the gnostic Shiite ideas around him decisively informed his thinking and his *Weltgefühl* and induced him to attempt to save the world along the lines advocated in those circles. One may speculate that he considered Abū l-Faḍl "his" divine imām, and maybe that feeling is what underlies the otherwise strangely faulty account of al-Bīrūnī, but there is no clear connection between his panegyric on Abū l-Faḍl and his "prophethood."

Whether this episode in al-Mutanabbī's life was canceled, as it were, by his official repentance or whether, on the contrary, it had a formative influence on the rest of his life and, more particularly, on his poetry is a question that remains to be studied in depth. Massignon, who was the first to probe this question, was of the opinion that the bitter and haughty tone that pervades so many of al-Mutanabbī's poems betrays the basic feeling of the gnostic initiate (Qarmaṭian, according to him) who knows better.[53] For the time being, I would like to suggest that there was a certain continuity of *Weltgefühl* in spite of his shift from rebellious exuberance to—often equally rebellious—resignation. The bitterness of his soul, which ibn Fūrraja saw, indicates loss and disillusionment ("this world needs salvation, but it has been recalcitrant against my attempt"); after having been unable to conquer the real world as a prophetic leader, his much more successful "subjugation" of the world of poetry was likely only an ersatz for him. And he may have considered it rather maladroit irony when his ardent admirer, Abū l-ʿAlāʾ al-Maʿarrī, with ingenious ambiguity called al-

Mutanabbī's *Dīwān* "The (prophetic) miracle of Aḥmad" (*Muʿjiz Aḥmad*).[54]

Appendix

I [probably ibn al-ʿAdīm] read in a copy I acquired of the poetry of al-Mutanabbī, and on the occasion of his poem *Abā ʿAbdi l-Ilāhi Muʿādhu innī khafīyun ʿanka fī l-hayjâ maqāmī* [Wāḥidī, pp. 84–85][55]

> Abū ʿAbdallāh, my place in battle is hidden from you.
> You mention the momentousness of what is my aspiration and that for it we risk [our] thick heart blood.
> Will calamities take away from the likes of me, will the likes of me shy away from meeting destiny?
> If Time were to come forth against me as a person, my sword would dye the hair of his [Time's!] parting.
> The Nights [=Time] have not achieved their wish and have not passed with my rein in their hand.
> When the eyes of the squadron are filled with me, then woe [to them] in waking and in sleep.

There was mentioned the following: Abū ʿAbdallāh Muʿādh b. Ismāʿīl al-Lādhiqī reported: al-Mutanabbī came to al-Lādhiqiyya in the year 320 and something, when he was still beardless, and he had an abundance of hair down to his earlobes. He attached himself to me, and I honored him and held him in high esteem because of his eloquence and the good composure that I perceived in him. When our relationship had become close and I [once] was alone with him in the house in order to take advantage of looking at him and to derive benefit from his literary culture and when what I saw amazed me, I said: By God! You are a serious young man fit to be the companion of a great ruler.—He said to me: Woe to you! Do you know what you are saying? I am a prophet sent!—I thought that he was joking, then I remembered that, since I had known him, I had never noticed a word of jest from him. So I said: What do you say?—He said: I am a prophet sent.—I said to him: Sent to whom?—He replied: To this community [*umma*], which is straying and leading astray.—I said: To do what?—He said: To fill it with justice just as it is [now] filled with injustice.—I said: By what means?—He said: By showering sustenance and reward, worldly and otherworldly, on those who obey and come and by executing and depriving of sustenance those who disobey and refuse.—I said to him then: That is a dangerous thing [*amrun ʿaẓīmun*], which I am afraid for you lest it become public.—And I reproached him for what he had said, whereupon he spontaneously spoke the following lines *Abā ʿAbdi l-Ilāhi*. . . . Then I said to him: You said that you are a prophet sent to this community. Has anything been revealed to you?—He said: Yes.—I said: So recite to me some of what has been revealed to you.—So he brought forward for me a speech something nicer than which had never reached my ear.—I said: How much of this has been revealed to you?—He replied: 114 admonitions [*ʿibra*].—I asked: And how much is an "admonition"?—And he produced something to the extent of the longest verses in the Qur'ān.—I said: I understand from these "admonitions" that you have an obedience in the heavens. What is it?—He said: I can keep back the abundant rain in order to deprive the rebels and the sinners of their sustenance.—I said: You can stop the rain from the skies?—He said: Yes, by Him Who created them! Wouldn't that be a prophetic miracle?!—I said: By God, certainly!—He said: Now, if I keep it away from a certain place that you can look at and about which you have no doubts, will you then believe in me and regard as true what has been brought to me from my Lord?—I said: Yes, by God!—He said: I'll do it. Don't ask me about anything after this, until I produce for you this miracle, and don't make any of this public, until it becomes public [by itself]. Wait for what you have been promised without asking for it.—After a few days he asked me: Would you like to look at the miracle that has been mentioned?—I said: Yes, by God!—He told me: When I send you one of the servants, ride with him and don't tarry. Let no one go out with you.—I agreed. On a wintery day a few days later the sky became overcast, and, lo, there came his slave and said: My master says to you: Ride to the tryst!—So I rode with him fast and I asked: Whither did your master ride?—He said: Into the desert and none but I went out with him.—The pounding of the rain became intense and he said: Let us hurry that we take shelter with him from this rain, for he is awaiting us on the top of a hill on which no rain hits him.—I said: How did he do it?—He replied: He started looking at the sky, when the black clouds first appeared, saying things that I did not understand. Then he took a whip and let it circle at a place that you will see, on the hill, while mumbling, and the rain was in the area adjacent to him and there was no drop of it on him!—I rushed on with him until I saw him. He was standing on a hill at half a parasang's distance from the town. I approached him and he was standing upright on it with not a single drop on him from that rain, while I was wading in the water up to the knees of my horse, and the rain was absolutely pouring. And I looked at about two hundred square cubits of that hill, dry, with no moisture and no raindrop on it. I greeted him and he returned the greeting and said: What do you see?—I said: Stretch out your hand, for I testify that you are the messenger of God.—He stretched out his hand and I paid him homage, thereby acknowledging his prophethood. Then he said to me: What did this scum tell you, when he called on you?—alluding to his slave. So I explained to him what he had told me on the way, when I had inquired. Thereupon he killed the slave and said: *Ayya maḥallin ar-taqi* . . . [Wāḥidī, p. 60]: "To what height shall I ascend? Of what severity shall I be afraid? For everything God has created, and that He has not created, is as of little account in my aspiration as a single hair in the crown of my head" [Arberry].

I entered into an oath of loyalty with him also for my family, and later the oath of loyalty [*bayʿa*] actually spread through all the cities in Syria. And all this through a most insignificant little trick that he had learned from some of the bedouins, which is called *ṣadḥat al-maṭar* [rain-bead] and with which one can turn the rain away from any spot one wishes, after one has circumscribed it with a stick and has spit on the bead they have. I have seen many of these [people] among the [tribes of] al-Sakūn, Ḥaḍramawt, and Sakāsik, all from Yemen, who do this and do not consider it a significant feat. One of them might even keep the rain away [*yaṣdaḥ*, not in the dictionaries] from his sheep, camels, and kine and from a [whole] town and no raindrop would hit them, and the rain would fall next to the *ṣadḥa* area. This is a kind of magic [*siḥr*]. I have seen them perform even greater magic than that. Later I asked al-Mutanabbī: Have you been among the Sakūn?—He said: Yes, and my father is from them. Have you not herd my line: *A-munsīya s-Sakūna*. . . . From there did he learn what he applied [*jawwaza*?] to the rubble of the people of Syria! After that [episode] several things befell him, fights and imprisonment and moving from place to place, until he ended up at Sayf al-Dawla's and his fame grew.

I [ibn al-ʿAdīm] say: The *ṣadḥa* which he alludes to as preventing the rain is known to this day. Several people whom I trust from among the Yemenites have reported to me that they turn the rain away from the camels and the sheep and the fields of their enemy. The camelherds and shepherds in their lands use it, and it is a kind of magic.

CHAPTER 8

The Poet as Prophet in Medieval Hebrew Literature

Dan Pagis

> What is my strength, what my offense?
> You have beset my home, but why?
> I am no poet, and no prophet,
> A woodcutter am I.

So wrote the modern Hebrew poet H. N. Bialik in 1926 in a bitter poem in which he rejected the tiresome accolades of his admirers, some of whom had claimed that his poems were not "just" admirable works but in fact contained the sparks of true prophecy. If Bialik ultimately rejected the prophetic posture, other modern Hebrew poets did not; on the contrary, some have openly cultivated it (Uri Zvi Greenberg being the foremost example). One might suspect that this connection between poetry and prophecy in modern Hebrew descends directly from biblical or early postbiblical models. Not so. Prophetic postures adopted by twentieth-century Hebrew poets (or attributed to them) were primarily inherited from European Romanticism, with only faint traces of earlier traditions.

Yet it is nonetheless true that such traditions did exist: in talmudic times and, later, throughout the Middle Ages and the Renaissance, Hebrew poets were occasionally compared to prophets, albeit with certain reservations and usually in some figurative sense. Indeed, the question of the relationship between poetry and prophecy had been

This article appears essentially as Professor Pagis wrote it. Since his typescript did not include footnotes, however, I have taken the liberty of providing, where possible, references to primary texts cited, as well as one or two clarifications along the way; no doubt Pagis's own notes would have been more copious [J.K.].

raised specifically by some medieval commentators with regard to the case of biblical poetry and, as we learn from James Kugel's book *The Idea of Biblical Poetry,* several different approaches emerged. To generalize, those commentators who based their idea of poetry on formal, metrical standards, agreed (however reluctantly) to classify the books of Job, Proverbs, and Psalms, as being "close" to poetry, since only these three (but not the prophetic books and others) seemed to show some trace of meter. Other commentators, whose conception of poetry was based not strictly on metrical considerations but on stylistic and rhetorical grounds as well, were inclined also to include the prophetic books in the realm of poetry by virtue of their use of figurative language and florid rhetoric. And medieval literary theorists of various tendencies likewise quoted from the prophets to illustrate individual uses of tropes and figures, which played such an important role in medieval poetic theory.

In any case, the problem of the classification of *biblical* poetry will not directly concern us in what follows. For here I wish to ask not whether biblical poetry and biblical prophecy were seen to overlap in the Middle Ages, but whether medieval Hebrew poetry was itself considered in its own time to have something in common with prophecy—in other words, whether there developed in the Middle Ages a Hebrew poetics that accommodated the analogy between poetry and prophecy, at least in certain respects: inspiration, imagination, and the gift of receiving semidivine visions and imparting them to an audience. Various manifestations of such an analogy between medieval Hebrew poetry and the phenomenon of prophecy are indeed to be found, both within medieval poems themselves and, occasionally, in theoretical treatises as well. But it must be stressed that they are all relatively late: they came into existence within the "Spanish school" of medieval poetry, which itself followed a long period of Hebrew verse of a somewhat different character.

As is well known, the mainstream of early postbiblical Hebrew poetry—Palestinian and Eastern piyyut—was not only exclusively religious in its themes and attitudes but liturgical in its function. In ancient times this poetry could freely replace many of the standard synagogue prayers, serving as the source of variation and innovation in the service.[1] In later periods, even after the standard prayers had become fixed, sections of piyyut were nonetheless still interspersed in them as poetic supplements and embellishments. And certain genres of piyyut, especially the *qerobah,* were fashioned to pick up on the weekly scriptural readings from the Pentateuch and the Prophets, elaborating upon them and stressing their continuing relevance. All this might suggest a ready connection between this poetry and the stuff of prophecy. And yet it was precisely the liturgical stance and function of piyyut that precluded this poetry, rich and varied though it was, from assuming any prophetic posture in its own right. For the payyetan, or liturgical poet, was essentially the congregation's representative (*sĕliaḥ tsibbur*)—in fact, he was often the local cantor—and as such he functioned as the spokesman of the congregation before God and not the spokesman of God before the congregation. Indeed, the payyetan's spokesmanlike role was such that he even suppressed, as a rule, any individual matter concerning himself, to the point of complete self-effacement. Thus, in his liturgical poems if he ever spoke of divine visions, moral admonitions, or the foretelling of the redemption of Israel, he did so with reference to the Bible, indeed, the Bible as filtered through talmudic sources, and he himself never presumed to have been given a prophetic message. The notion of the poet as the recipient of individual inspiration or revelation could flourish only in a different social and literary climate.

Indeed, paradoxical as it may seem, it was only with the emergence of *secular* Hebrew poetry in Spain, in the late tenth century, that the analogy between prophecy and poetry (and secular poetry at that!) could take root.[2] From the eleventh century on, this analogy became commonplace, appearing even in such standard expressions as *nebi'ei hašir,* "the prophets of song," a kenning for "poets." Some of the poetic genres of secular poetry, such as praise poems written for patrons or friends, or boasting poems, provided fertile ground for the use of such similes and metaphors. Thus Moses ibn Ezra: "Poems that soar like eagles, and they alone, like prophesies, stormed the Heavens," or in self-praise: "My poems . . . are as if they were taken from the lips of prophets and inspired by the spirits of the holy ones; the darkness is their ink, the rays of the sun, their pen, and the days are their scroll."[3] Or Judah ha-Levi, also in self-praise: "My verses are a prophecy, and what's more they are written in meter."[4] (Note the humorous hyperbole: his poem is even more beautiful than the prophetic books, which, though sublimely written, are not metrical.)

In the late twelfth and the early thirteenth centuries, the prophetic posture progressed beyond single metaphors to something broader and more structural. This change came about as a result of the new narrative genres that were then emerging in Hebrew, written in rhymed prose interlaced with metrical poems. In this new field some of the best-known works, such as Judah al-Ḥarizi's *Book of Taḥkemoni,* were straitly modeled on the Arabic genre of *maqāma;* others were freer, following different models or inventing their own, and so produced an impressive diversity of narrative techniques, settings, and themes. One of the favorite devices of this poetry was the use of a quasi-prophetic revelation as a literary framework (regardless of the actual subject or tone of the work, which might be serious or humorous, fantastic or didactic): at the outset the author would describe, for example, how he had been commanded by an angel or a heavenly voice to write his book. This fictional device appears in one of the earliest works in this field, *The Offering of Judah the Woman-Hater,* by Judah ibn Shabbetai. The book was undisguisedly meant for pure entertainment, lightly satirizing both women and men, and concluding with a clear statement of the author's humorous intent. Yet it begins with a prophetic vision, modeled on Ezekiel (1:1, 15, etc.; 2:1; 3:12): "Then the spirit took me up and I heard behind me a voice of great rustling . . . and I saw visions of God. . . . Now as I beheld the living creatures, one wheel upon the earth called to me"—all this as the prelude to a hilariously funny series of episodes.

The device became a convention in various rhymed *maqāmas* and related rhymed narratives—prominently so in the aforementioned *Book of Taḥkemoni* by al-Ḥarizi (to which I will return presently), *The Book of Delight* by Joseph ben Meir ibn Zabara, *The Ancient Parable* by Isaac ben Solomon ibn Sahula, and *The Treatise on Morals* by Shem Tob ben Joseph Falaqera. (This last says of its ten-year-old protagonist: "And the spirit of the Lord began to move him in the camp of the prophets and the poets"—a paraphrase of Samson's revelation in the camp of Dan, Jud. 13:25.) There were also authors who satirized the prophetic image or self-image of poets. In his bitter satire *The Touchstone,* Kalonymos ben Kalonymos describes the typical poet of his time: "In polishing his verses he thinks that the Holy Spirit chose him for prophecy sublime/if he can just manage to find a fitting rhyme."[5]

The motif of prophecy as an image for poetry or poetic inspiration thus transgressed the usually clear boundaries of literary genres of the time, appearing both in single short poems (collected in the poet's *dīwān*) as well as in longer, rhymed narratives. This perhaps surprising popularity was itself apparently the result of several deeper, more general features of Hebrew secular poetry in Spain. As already implied, the poetry-prophecy analogy could only develop within the context of a secular (that is, nonliturgical) poetry, indeed, one which took on such broad themes as the individual and society, love and friendship, social praise and satire, descriptions of art and nature, personal complaints and self-praise, the universal fate of mankind and the most intimate details of one's personal life. For within this world, poetry itself could (and did) frequently become the poet's subject, leading him to explore, among other things, the connection to prophecy. Moreover, while prophetic imagery sometimes did deteriorate to mechanical cliches, in at least several instances it is obvious that this topos clearly held special significance for Hebrew poets of the period, since it provided a model for individual inspiration. The then-normative poetics, which blended Arabic rhetoric with biblical elements, usually avoided or completely ignored the problem of poetic inspiration. It concerned itself instead with the rhetorical "making" of poetry, the judicious use of tropes and figures, along with the strict observance of meter and rhyme. As for the more general aspects, this poetics emphasized the persuasive power of poetry and its social task, rather than its personal origin. The role of inspiration, or even imagination, was played down in favor of rhetorical and prosodic skills. Although innate poetical talent was considered a prerequisite, even the most talented poets were supposed to *learn* their craft, training themselves in prosody and the use of tropes and acquainting themselves with the various genres and their conventions.

This, then, was essentially a rather restrictive, rationalistic, Arabized, pseudo-Aristotelian poetics. Accordingly, the poet was usually described as a gifted but careful artisan who produced beautiful artifacts—verbal pearl necklaces or exquisitely crafted golden jewelry. Yet such concepts did not leave things completely static—otherwise the Hebrew secular poetry of Spain would not have produced the masterpieces that it did. All great poets, and most of the minor ones, occasionally transgressed genre boundaries by composing personal autobiographical poems, quite remote from the conventional background. Now such poems often also touched on the urge for self-expression or on poetic inspiration—and in some cases evoked the figure of the prophet in a manner suggesting more than mere literary cliche. The poet as prophet became, rather, an expression of individuality that transgressed the somewhat restrictive normative poetics.

Apart from this, it is to be observed that the motif of poet as prophet emerged naturally from another well-known aspect of the poetry of the Spanish school, namely, its "biblicism." The Bible had, of course, always been the ultimate source for matters of Jewish law and daily practice and was also constantly present in the weekly readings in the synagogue as well as in other aspects of everyday life. But it was only with the emergence of the Spanish school of Hebrew poetry, after centuries of payyetanic liturgical poetry, that the Bible came to be considered as the main, even the only source for poetic language and the only norm of Hebrew as such. Biblical phrases and entire lines were incorporated in poems in new combinations, contexts, and meanings, often producing astonishing effects.

Among the material available for such biblical quotations and half-quotations was much that touched on the poetry-prophecy motif. Biblical passages that connected prophecy with frenzied inspiration, music, and presumably poetry could easily be marshaled for biblical imagery or phrasing in a poem. Such was the case, for example, with the "company of prophets" whom Saul was instructed to meet and join; they were to come down "with harp, tambourine, flute, and lyre before them, prophesying. Then the spirit of the Lord will come mightily upon you, and you shall prophesy" (1 Sam. 10:5–6). Equally significant for medieval poets was a later verse pertaining to the reign of David, which described the commissioned service of "the sons of Asaph, and of Heman, and of Jeduthun, who shall prophesy with lyres, and with harps, and with cymbals" (1 Chron. 25:1). Passages such as these are sometimes alluded to or cited within short, individual poems. On the other hand, the quasi-prophetic framework seen in longer, narrative works (describing, as it were, the author's inspiration for the entire story) mainly drew on other sources, the "writing" prophets Isaiah, Jeremiah, Ezekiel, and the authors of the Twelve Minor Prophets, who frequently describe how they came to be divinely commissioned or inspired.

In considering the two models and sources of secular Hebrew verse in medieval Spain—namely, the Bible (which supplied its language and much of its imagery) and medieval Arabic verse (which was responsible for its poetic norms)—we come to a crucial point. The Spanish school was not based solely on harmonizing these two disparate sources but, in so doing, on highlighting the sense of the tension and strained rivalry between them, a cultural competition that reflected a conscious feeling of revival and national pride among the Jews. Theorists and poets (such as Moses ibn Ezra), although acknowledging Arabic supremacy in the domains of prosody and the richness of language, still took pains to point out the rhetorical and poetic achievements of the Bible, which had of course much preceded Arabic literature and, in Jewish eyes, had surpassed its highest standards of literary style. This championing of the biblical was not carried out by the entire Jewish community: it was accomplished principally by Hebrew poets and writers (but also by Hebrew grammarians and philosophers), who sometimes felt that they had to struggle for its acceptance. This mission of theirs they occasionally described (and probably truly perceived) as *prophetic*. Indeed, poets and writers of *maqāma* took on something of the posture of biblical prophets in pursuing this theme, combining descriptions of personal revelations with jeremiads against the people who neglected the ancient language. At this point, various trends converged: the writers' new individualistic spirit, the readiness for personal inspiration, and a wider national concern springing from a new conception of the Hebrew language and literature. For all this, the poet's mission was still secular and national, unconditioned by matters of *halakhah* and religious legal concerns.

In these works, the Holy Tongue often appears as a key concept or even a personified figure, and "Hebrew" is used in expressions that emphasize its national character. Thus Judah al-Ḥarizi tells us in the first chapter of *Taḥkemoni* that he was encouraged by a "Hebrew youth" to write his book for the glory of the Hebrew language (this youth then turns out to be the main protagonist of all his stories). A century later, Immanuel of Rome, in the introduction to his *Notebooks,* solved the problem of how to collect his dispersed works into a single volume only after "the Lord God of the Hebrews met with me." Both of these phrases are found in the Bible ("Hebrew youth" in Gen. 41:12 and "God of the Hebrews" in Exod. 3:18), but their use here suggests a new sense of the Hebrew poet qua prophet of the neglected language. And this concern with Hebrew (and Jewish sources in general) was to become a leitmotif running through the literary manifestos of many works.

Allow me to illustrate this phenomenon by focusing on two particular striking instances of the intersection of poetry and prophecy in medieval Spain, one from an individual Hebrew poem, the other from a famous *maqāma:*

Around the year 1040, when Solomon ibn Gabirol was nineteen and already well on his way to his achievements in philosophy and Hebrew poetry, he was deeply troubled by the decline of Hebrew as both a sacred and a living language. At first he did not dare to speak up, but then, as he tells it in a moving autobiographical poem, Heaven itself laid this mission on his shoulders.[6] In that very poem he extolls the glory of the Holy Tongue, denounces its neglect by Jews everywhere, and immediately, as it were, sets out to teach its rudiments—hence the autobiographical passage actually forms the introduction to what becomes a long didactic poem about grammar. Of course biblical Hebrew had already been praised, and its teaching urged, by Seʿadya Ga'on in Babylonia some decades earlier, as well as by grammarians in Spain. But the point here is that this endeavor appeared to the young ibn Gabirol as his own *personal prophetic mission,* given to him in a dream, which he describes in the poem.

Indeed, ibn Gabirol presents his vision as a factual experience, not as an allegory, and the manner of its presentation is noteworthy. First, he describes the general situation: Jews speak Arabic or the various languages of Christian countries but are ignorant of the Holy Tongue. This situation hardly augurs well for his own undertaking, since "they know not the prophetic vision, nor do they know the Book: how then will they understand a treatise?"[7] The poet then describes his own frustration and struggle: his heart admonishes him to fight, but fearful that people may mock him because of his youth, he nurses his sorrow in silence. Then comes his revelation, the dream in which he is summoned by a loud voice, calling out to him: "Rise up and do . . . and God's hand will help you. Rise up and do not say, 'I am only a child.' " These last words, of course, echo God's advice to Jeremiah when he is summoned to his prophetic office: "But the Lord said to me, Do not say 'I am only a child' " (Jer. 1:7). The young Gabirol, his spirit uplifted, now knows, as it were, that it is God Himself who has sanctioned his mission: "And so I knew that from the Lord it had been decreed." This too is presented in the poem as fact. Accordingly he sets out to compose his grammatical treatise, and, moreover, to compose it Hebrew, *for the sake of Hebrew,* unlike his predecessors and contemporaries, who wrote their treatises in Arabic, even when they dealt with Hebrew grammar or commentary.

Almost two centuries later, Judah al-Ḥarizi took upon himself a similar mission, but in so doing did not openly present himself as one actually being sent by a voice from Heaven. Instead, in the introduction to his *Taḥkemoni,* he alludes to several prophets who, though at first reluctant to accept their mission, eventually yielded and went on to proclaim the word of the Lord: Moses, Isaiah, Jeremiah, and Jonah. In invoking the example of these reluctant prophets, he plays on the ambiguity of the (now common) poet-as-prophet motif in medieval

Hebrew poetry: but is he merely invoking a standard metaphor or earnestly presenting parallels to what he perceives as his actual mission? In the following I have italicized the biblical allusions to these prophets, which, for Gabirol's audience, would have been unmistakable:

> My intellect aroused me from my sleep of folly and instructed me and said to me: "O you son of man, *what mean you that you sleep!* [Jonah 1:6, when Jonah is awakened aboard the ship]. Open the eyes of your thought and clothe yourself with zeal for the God of Hosts and for the Holy Tongue, which was once the language of prophecy but which has now come down." And I said, "*Alas my lord* [Jer. 1:6, the call of Jeremiah], my solitary wandering has confounded my speech and my thoughts. . . . *Who am I that I should . . . bring forth* the Holy Tongue from its dire straits?" [Exod. 3:11, Moses' answer to God's summons to lead the Israelites out of Egypt]. And he said to me: "*Verily I will be with you.* [Exod. 3:12, God's comforting reply to Moses]. And my arm shall strengthen you among your people."
>
> Then the intellect *put forth his hand and touched my mouth* [Jer. 1:9, God consecrates Jeremiah as a prophet] and kindled the spark of my flame, and said to me: "*Behold, I have put my words in your mouth* [Jer. 1:9, God's words to Jeremiah] and for the vision of poetry *I have set you as a prophet unto the nations* [Jer. 1:5, from the same speech]. *See, I have appointed you to pull down and to destroy* [Jer. 1:10, from the same speech] the houses of folly, *and to build and to plant* [Jer. 1:10, from the same speech] the palaces of poetry, that all the people of the earth may know that the Holy Tongue is incomparable in the clarity of its diction and the pleasantness of its metaphors—that it is as a bride adorned with her jewels. Poetry is her garment and the spice of myrrh is on her skirts. But today, filthy, violent persons among our people have stabbed her with words. . . . Every day she weeps bitterly. . . ." Therefore I have composed this book to show the strength of the Holy Tongue to the holy people whose eyes are bedaubed that they cannot see.[8]

Thus al-Ḥarizi, although he clearly invokes the situation of the reluctant prophet, carefully avoids any literal representation of such a call to himself; yet by means of short quotations from Scripture (a specific trope he was very fond of, as were several other poets of the Spanish school) he seems to imply something similar. It is further to be noted that whereas in the book of Jeremiah God puts out his hand and touches Jeremiah's mouth, ordaining him as a prophet to the nations, to pull down and to destroy, to build and to plant, in this poem it is his "intellect" that touches al-Ḥarizi's mouth and sets him as a prophet unto the nations for the "vision of poetry," appointing him to destroy the "house of folly" and to build the "palaces of poetry." Similarly, whereas Moses protests to God, "Who am I that I should go . . . and bring forth the children of Israel?" al-Ḥarizi's argument is with his own intellect, "Who am I that I should bring forth the Holy Tongue from its dire straits?"

The poet uses the same technique in a witty paraphrase of the story of Abraham's servant, who at the fountain searched for a suitable bride for Isaac and prayed that the maiden who would let down her pitcher and offer him water should be the chosen bride (Gen. 24). al-Ḥarizi metaphorizes the scene and transposes it into a surprising allegory:

> I came this day to the fountain to be refreshed with the love of wisdom, which is better than wine. And I said: "I pray Thee, O awe-inspiring God, make me meet this day the daughters of understanding. . . . Behold, I stand at the fountain of water, and it shall be that the maiden . . . to whom I shall say: 'Give me, I pray you, to drink from the flow of your poetry which trickles from your lips'—if she shall say, 'Drink, and snatch from my lips the fire of love' . . . then I will know that Thou hast desired her for your servant."
>
> I had scarcely finished. . . . And lo! a maiden, pure as the sun, of the daughters of Wisdom, comes forth to draw water and the pitcher is upon her shoulder. . . . She refreshes me with the honey of her lips, and she says to me: "Drink, my lord, from the running waters of my thought. . . ." And I asked: "Whose daughter are you?" . . . She said, "I am an orphan, but my father lives. I was the royal crown but today I am trodden under by every foot. I am the Holy Tongue, your mistress. And if it be pleasing to you, I will be your companion."

Immediately afterward, al-Ḥarizi returns to the motif of prophecy by alluding to Isaiah (8:3), "And I went unto the prophetess; and she conceived, and bare a son."[9] This son turns out to be his book *Taḥkemoni,* a treasure of Hebrew for all and sundry. Certainly the poet as prophet, and the poem as the offspring of the "prophetess" are rhetorical devices. Yet they should not therefore be dismissed as mere convention: if al-Ḥarizi did not exactly follow a call from above in his mission for Hebrew, he did in any case follow a call from within, one that came, as he tells us, from his soul and mind.

Prophetlike visions, literal or metaphorical, were not limited in Hebrew poetry to the topic of the revival of the Hebrew language but, as we have seen, at times served as a means of focusing on the matter of individual poetic inspiration. In the Spanish school this was sometimes merely a playful device, since that school's restrictive poetics emphasized not inspiration but rhetorical skill and artful stylization. This more or less latent interest in self-expression, however, was to become a consistent (though little-known) element in other centers of Hebrew poetry—centers that were partly influenced by Spain but later developed their own style and poetic theory. In these, especially in the Hebrew school of Italy, the concepts of inspiration and imagination continued to develop from the sixteenth century onward; the "daughter of song" (*bat ha-šir*), though actually a native of the Spanish school, now became the Muse, often a *very* individual muse at that. There slowly evolved a different poetics, non-Arabizing and non-Aristotelean, which emphasized the element of the sublime. This Hebrew poetics, hidden in unexpected places, a forgotten precursor of Romanticism, regarded the poet's personality and work as a sublime, semiprophetic expression. Here new elements came into play: mysticism, late religious poetry, and the theory of music. But however related to our topic, this later aspect of poetry and prophecy demands a separate discussion.

CHAPTER 9

The Nature of Prophecy in Geoffrey of Monmouth's *Vita Merlini*

Jan Ziolkowski

At the beginning of the twelfth century the reputation of Myrddin, who is now more often called Merlin, was restricted to Wales.[1] By the middle of the century his renown had spread throughout Western Europe. Merlin's fame during the Middle Ages rested largely upon his prophecies.[2] The only previous figures to win widespread acceptance as true prophets had been prophets of the Old and New Testaments, who had the unimpeachable authority of the Bible, and Sibyls, who were believed to have foretold the coming of Christ and who were known through Virgil's *Aeneid* and other highly respected sources.[3] Not until after the first half of the twelfth century did historically attested medieval prophets such as Hildegard of Bingen and Joachim of Fiore take their places alongside biblical prophets and Sibyls.[4]

The main force behind Merlin's spectacular rise was a single author, Geoffrey of Monmouth, who wrote during the years 1129–1148. Geoffrey laid stress upon Merlin's prophetic powers in all three of his extant works: the *Prophetiae Merlini* (also known as the *Libellus Merlini*), the *Historia regum Britanniae,* and the *Vita Merlini*.[5] In the *Historia* Geoffrey claimed that he had originally intended to finish the *Historia* before dealing with the prophecies of Merlin but that at the urging of Bishop Alexander of Lincoln he had published the *Prophetiae* separately first.[6] When Geoffrey resumed his labors over the *Historia regum*

Among the many thoughtful people who responded to the oral form of this study I acknowledge in particular my colleague Joseph Harris. I owe special thanks to Emery Snyder, my research assistant, for his persistence in gathering materials necessary for this study.

Britanniae, he incorporated the *Prophetiae* together with a dedicatory letter to the Bishop and a prefatory account of his reasons for writing them.[7]

Although the prophecies attributed to Merlin in the *Prophetiae* and *Historia* reflect knowledge of the prophecies ascribed to the Myrddin of Welsh poetry and tradition, the narrative surrounding them seems to have been composed in ignorance of the stories about the Welsh Myrddin. In fact, the Merlin in the narrative portions of the *Prophetiae* and *Historia* is a refashioning of a character named Ambrosius, who originally had no connection with Myrddin.[8] Later Geoffrey became better acquainted with native legends about Myrddin, perhaps through attention to Welsh informants.[9] Eventually he created a poem of more than fifteen hundred hexameters in which he presented a Merlin very different from the one in his earlier prose writings; this later Merlin is not the mentor of Arthur but instead a wild man living in the Caledonian Forest.

That Geoffrey's *Vita Merlini* never attained the success of his earlier works is evident from the numbers of surviving manuscripts—at least 210 in the case of the *Historia,* against only one complete manuscript of the *Vita Merlini*.[10] But the *Vita* lends itself better than either the *Prophetiae* or the *Historia* to an exploration of interplay between prophecy and poetry. In the *Vita* Geoffrey offers a biography of a man whom he categorizes as both a poet and a prophet; Geoffrey routinely refers to Merlin with the lushly ambiguous word *uates;*[11] he describes Merlin's activities with the verbs *cano* and *canto* and his words with the noun *carmen;*[12] and he speaks unhesitatingly of Merlin's predictive powers.[13] Adding to the complexity of the *Vita,* Geoffrey attempts to merge in his portrayal of Merlin at least three quite distinct conceptions of prophecy.

Because the *Vita* remains little known in comparison with the *Historia,* it is worth pausing to summarize the events of the poem. Both a king and a poet-prophet of Wales, Merlin goes mad after three brothers, Merlin's close relatives, perish in a battle. In a frenzy he retreats to the Caledonian woods, where he dwells alone among the beasts until he is discovered by a musician who has been sent by his sister (Queen Ganieda) to retrieve him. After Merlin returns to court and encounters crowds of people, he loses the calmness induced by music and is put in chains to prevent him from fleeing to the woods.

While held against his will at the court, the *uates* on three occasions emits laughs that puzzle those around him.[14] In the first instance he laughs at a leaf in the hair of Ganieda. Upon being promised his freedom if he reveals the cause of his mirth, he explains to King Rodarch that the leaf caught in Ganieda's locks as she lay with a lover in the undergrowth. To repudiate this charge, Ganieda sets out to demonstrate that Merlin is a false prophet (*Vita* 323 "falsus . . . vates"). She has the same boy brought forth three times, but each time in different attire, and each time she asks her brother to describe the death the boy will die. Merlin foretells first death by a fall, then death in a tree, and finally death in a river.[15] Although the inconsistency of the predictions convinces Rodarch that Merlin has lost his wits, subsequent developments confirm Merlin's foreknowledge: the boy falls from a cliff in such a way that one foot lodges in a tree and the rest of his body is submerged in a stream.

Merlin, although Ganieda tries to stop him, leaves the court. Before departing, he declares that his wife (Guendoloena) should remarry. He vows to appear on the wedding day with presents, but he warns any future husband to keep out of his sight at the risk of death. After years in the woods Merlin realizes from reading the stars not only that a political upheaval has occurred but also that Guendoloena is on the verge of remarrying. Mounted on a stag, he sets off to give her a herd of deer. When Merlin glimpses the bridegroom laughing at him, he wrenches off the horns of the stag and, hurling them, kills the man.

Ganieda and Rodarch grow concerned because Merlin, after he has been recaptured, is despondent not to be in the woods. To cheer him they have him led through the town. During his walk Merlin laughs twice, once at a poor man begging for money, once at a young man buying new footgear. After receiving a guarantee that he will be released, Merlin relates to Rodarch that the beggar is seated atop a buried hoard of coins[16] and that the young man will not need new shoes, as he will soon die by drowning. Both insights prove to be true.

Just before Merlin goes back to the woods, Ganieda voices her worries about his unsheltered life. Merlin persuades her to provide him with an observatory equipped with seventy doors, seventy windows, and seventy secretaries to record his prophetic songs. From this vantage point Merlin gazes upon the stars and sings of future happenings. After Rodarch dies, Ganieda resolves to abandon the world and to take up residence with her brother in the woods. Already with Merlin is the sage Thelgesin (that is, Taliesin), who expounds to Merlin upon the constitution of the universe, fishes, and islands. Both discuss the history and future of Britain.

As Merlin speaks of the sorrowful battle between Arthur and Mordred, servants rush in with the news that a spring has welled up miraculously at the foot of a nearby mountain. A draft from the font frees Merlin of both his mental illness and his prophetic powers. Thelgesin offers a disquisition upon curative waters, which in his opinion evidence the dominion of God over nature. After word of Merlin's cure spreads, he is approached by his princes, who invite him to take up his throne again. Merlin refuses their request, on the grounds that he would prefer to purify himself through fasting. As he talks, the princes catch sight of birds flying in an interesting pattern. Merlin holds forth upon the marvelous behavior of birds.

At the conclusion of the lecture a madman rushes in, whom Merlin recognizes as a former friend who had been driven insane by a poison meant for Merlin. After the man (Maeldin) is healed by the spring, he remains with Merlin and Thelgesin. They are joined by Merlin's sister. Filled with the spirit of prophecy after she stares at the windows of the observatory glittering in the sun, Ganieda utters one long political prophecy. The poem closes with the four leading a pious and happy life in the woods.

As even such a cursory précis of the poem suggests, the *Vita* teems with contradictions in its treatment of vaticination. At some times it casts divination and prophecy in a positive light, at others negative; at some times it espouses an orthodox medieval Christian view of prophecy, at others it preserves heterodox pre-Christian conventions of soothsaying. Much of Merlin's behavior during his spell as a madman resembles that of a seer, diviner, or shaman; during other long stretches he is a political prophet; and at the end, when he has been rid of his madness and has become as ascetic and holy as a biblical prophet, he loses his mantic powers altogether. I aim in the remainder of this chapter to examine the nature of Merlin's prophetic powers in the *Vita;* I would like to suggest that the Merlin in the *Vita* is a composite: one part a wild man engaged in shamanlike practices that were widespread in the pre-Christian era, one part a political prophet of a type still found in Wales when Geoffrey wrote, and one part a Christian prophet combining traits of Old Testament prophets and Christian saints.

The term *shamanlike* is a convenient designation for those of Merlin's vaticinatory acts which depart from the primarily predictive powers of a prophet and show traces of an authentically Celtic substratum to the stories related in the *Vita.* It was to the afterlife of such Celtic shamanlike practices that Gerald of Wales, writing about forty years after Geoffrey of Monmouth, referred in his *Description of Wales:*

> Among the Welsh there are certain individuals called *awenyddion* who behave as if they are possessed by devils. You will not find them anywhere else. When you consult them about some problem, they immediately go into a trance and lose control of their senses, as if they are possessed. They do not answer the question put to them in any logical way. Words stream from their mouths, incoherently and apparently meaningless and without any sense at all, but all the same well expressed: and if you listen carefully to what they say you will receive the solution to your problem. . . . If by chance they are questioned a second or a third time on the same matter, they give completely different answers. It is possible that they are speaking through demons which possess them, spirits which are ignorant and yet in some way inspired. . . . When they are going into a trance they invoke the true and living God, and the Holy Trinity, and they pray that they may not be prevented by their sins from revealing the truth.[17]

In *The Journey through Wales* Gerald gave a detailed account of a real Welsh prophet, a man named Meilyr. According to Gerald's report, Meilyr had gone mad when he experienced the opposite of the fairy tale about the princess and the frog: a girl whom he was embracing turned into a monster.

> As he stared at the monster his wits deserted him and he became quite mad. He remained in this condition for many years. Eventually he recovered his health in the church of St. David's, thanks to the virtues of the saintly men of that place. All the same, he retained a very close and most remarkable familiarity with unclean spirits, being able to see them, recognizing them, talking to them and calling them each by his own name, so that with their help he could often prophesy the future. Just as they are, too, he was often mistaken about events in the distant future, or happenings far away in space; but he was less often wrong about matters nearer home or likely to occur within the coming year.[18]

In portraying native prophets Gerald reveals considerable uncertainty about the place of their powers within the framework of Christian theology. In one breath he presents the prophets as demonically possessed, in the next as piously invoking God and the Trinity. In the end he seeks to legitimate them by tracing their origins to the Trojans and by drawing parallels to Old Testament prophets who stripped off their clothes and appeared to lose their reason before they prophesied.[19]

The prophets about whom Gerald writes seem to be partially Christianized representatives of pre-Christian customs. Of course, neither Gerald nor Geoffrey is likely to have been personally acquainted with any true shamans. Like Gerald, Geoffrey could have been aware of men such as Meilyr, who stood halfway between shamanism and sanctity. But Geoffrey's only sure source of knowledge about shamanism would have been legend. In the legend that lay behind the *Vita,* Geoffrey would have encountered a Myrddin who, although showing no signs of a shaman's inner orientation, was reminiscent of a shaman in his conduct.[20] For this reason, a case can be made that Geoffrey's poem belongs to a body of medieval Celtic and Scandinavian literature which was written long after Christianization but which nevertheless preserved vestiges of shamanism in both actions and attitudes.[21]

Shamans derive their powers from spirits.[22] Merlin does not ascribe his own powers to such spirits, but Thelgesin instructs him in the behavior of sublunary creatures that might be considered the learned equivalents of shamanic spirits (764–87). Like a shaman, Merlin undergoes an apprenticeship by breaking away from society and living as an animal (80 and 102–4). Like a shaman, Merlin enters a state in which his soul takes flight from his body; in his own words, "I was taken out of my true self, I was as a spirit and knew the history of people long past and could foretell the future. I knew then the secrets of nature, bird flight, star wanderings, and the way fish glide" (1161–64). Although Geoffrey attributes to Merlin a deep knowledge of birds, he stops short of conceding to Merlin the ability to assume bird form which is characteristic of shamans;[23] but he does raise the issue of bird transformation when he describes the sorceress Morgen (920–25). Geoffrey connects Merlin with another beast rich in shamanic associations, the stag; Merlin's riding of the stag and use of its antlers may be a reflex of the shaman's ride into the other world within the hide of a stag or on the antlers of a stag.[24]

One major component of shamanic ritual lacking in Geoffrey's description of Merlin is the world tree that the shaman mounts in order to mediate between the spirits of the heavens and the people of the earth.[25] Yet this omission can be explained as a conscious decision on Geoffrey's part to alter the stories upon which he based the *Vita:* whereas the world tree plays a part in stories of Celtic wild men who are related to Merlin, Geoffrey had special reasons (to which I shall return) for replacing the tree with an observatory on the ground.

Like Sweeney in the later Irish tale of *Buile Suibhne,* Merlin the madman exemplifies the rationalization by medieval Christians of shamanlike practices.[26] He has the wisdom of a shaman even though he is not shown engaging in non-Christian ecstatic techniques to communicate with spirits. As a person who goes through the rituals of shamanism but who does not share in the spiritual beliefs of shamanism, he is what a shaman might seem to an uncomprehending outsider: a madman.

The nature of Merlin's prophecy changes as the poem progresses. At first he is a seer and astrologer whose perceptions range freely over time and space. His prophetic laughs are proof that he sees what is hidden in the past (Ganieda's adultery), present (the treasure beneath the beggar's feet), and future (the threefold death of the boy and the death of the young man with the new shoes).[27] The strength of his vision across space is revealed when he learns from the stars of his wife's planned remarriage. Yet Merlin seems not to appreciate or to benefit from the value of his gift. His aptitude for seeing and stargazing brings him no happiness except when it buys him freedom. He has vaticinatory powers, but he lacks faith that his powers derive from a higher order.

In the central section of the *Vita* Merlin enlarges the purview of his vaticinations. Whereas during his sojourns at the court of Rodarch his special insights are limited to the fates of single individuals, during his stay in the woods he reveals knowledge of events that will affect masses of people. Although political and national prophecy does not bulk as large in the *Vita* as it did in the *Historia,* nevertheless, nearly a quarter of the *Vita* is taken up with such foretelling (348 lines), and long stretches of the poem repeat many of the predictions in the *Historia;* these prophecies are concerned with the kings of Britain and England, from the death of Arthur to Henry I. The first such prophecy, an abridged version of Merlin's long declaration to Vortigern in the *Historia,* begins with the period from the reign of Maelgwyn (580–595), moves next to civil wars after Rodarch's death (595–626), and then covers the span from the Saxons to Geoffrey's own time (627–688).[28] Merlin's second prophecy renews the theme of foreign domination, but it promises the deliverance of the Britons (941–981). This prophecy of redemption is followed by a long passage of further historical reminiscences and forecasts (982–1135).[29]

The historical prophecies diverge from Merlin's earlier vaticinations not only in their national rather than personal scope but also in their manner of conveying information. Whereas Merlin explains his laughs in plain and simple words, the historical prophecies are related in the metaphoric manner that has been dubbed Galfredian.[30] Prophecies in the Galfredian manner employ animals to indicate kings and other notables. An example of such prophecy comes up as Merlin's first historical prophecy commences: "the nephews of the Cornish boar disrupt everything. They lay ambushes for each other and put one another to death with their evil swords: they cannot wait to succeed lawfully, but seize the crown. The fourth after them will be crueller and harsher. A sea-wolf will engage him and defeat him and drive him in defeat across the Severn into wilder realms. This wolf will lay siege to Cirencester and by means of sparrows raze its walls and houses to the ground" (586–94).

Another discrepancy between the early vaticinations and the political prophecies is in the mode in which their credibility is established. In the "laugh prophecies" Merlin has to prove himself to Rodarch and Ganieda. In the political and national prophecies Merlin's veracity has to be validated to an entirely different audience: readers of the *Vita* in the twelfth and subsequent centuries. To this end, Geoffrey has Merlin make detailed predictions, the accuracy of which can be readily ascertained; the section of the future he has Merlin relate is already past history to Geoffrey's audience, since it lay between Merlin and the time when the poem was composed. In this way Merlin affirms his reliability before he predicts the stretch of the future which lies ahead of the poet and the poet's audience as well as of himself.[31]

Geoffrey puts his most daring historical prophecies into the mouth not of Merlin but of Merlin's sister. As the poem draws to a close, Ganieda reveals in a substantial prophecy (1474–1517) that she has received the spirit that once belonged to her brother. Cloaking her meaning in an authentically Galfredian obscurity, Ganieda describes one battle waged by two lions, two moons, and an Armorican boar and another by stars and wild beasts. There can be no doubt that her prophecy refers to the plight of Britain between 1135 and 1147–1148, particularly to the war between Matilda and Stephen, and yet its meaning is sufficiently opaque that Geoffrey can test the limits of free expression with Ganieda's final bold words: "Iteque Neustrenses [Normans—go!]" (1511).[32]

Geoffrey's translation of recent history into animal metaphors was a form of commentary rather than true prophecy. This innovation was frequently imitated by other authors in succeeding centuries.[33] Even if Geoffrey did not originate all or even most of the material in the historical prophecies, at the very least he deserves recognition for disseminating both the material and the technique from Wales to England and the Continent in his Latin writings.[34]

Another of Geoffrey's achievements in the historical prophecies of the *Vita* was to use verse to memorialize Merlin as a poet-prophet. In an era of low literacy, poets and minstrels had a real chance to influence public opinion through their verse and songs.[35] Geoffrey exalted their potential by giving literary dress to a prophet who was, at least in the *Vita Merlini,* a poet.

The third aspect of Merlin as prophet which needs to be examined in his relationship to Christian prophecy. Geoffrey's *Prophetiae Merlini* posed acute problems to medieval Christians because they were so different from biblical prophecies—and because Merlin himself was so different from the biblical prophets who were memorialized in the exegesis, art, and drama of the Middle Ages. Very soon after the *Vita* came into circulation, medieval schoolmen set out to confront these questions. By the end of the twelfth century they had already produced five systematic commentaries.[36] Between 1174 and 1179 appeared the *Explanationes in prophetiam Merlini* (sometimes attributed to Alan of Lille).[37] Among other concerns, the text considers whether or not Merlin was Christian and whether or not he truly had the gift of prophecy. The author of the treatise inclines to believe that Merlin was a Christian and a bona fide prophet; but even if Merlin was not a Christian, the author points out that Job, the Sibyls, Balaam, Cassandra, and many others who were not Jewish were filled with the prophetic spirit by the Lord.[38] About a decade later Gerald of Wales took upon himself the task of explaining why Merlin, although mad, qualified as a true prophet and why Merlin departed from biblical practice by not adding to his prophecies the words "Thus spake the lord God": "You will object . . . that no such method of prophesying is found in Merlin, so that what he said is merely sorcery. He may well have been a true believer, but, you will say, there is no mention of his sanctity or devoutness. To this I answer that the spirit of prophecy was given not only to the holy but sometimes to unbelievers and Gentiles, to Baal [Balaam] and the Sibyl, for example, and even to the wicked, such as Caiaphas and Baal again."[39] Although Gerald managed to defend the value of the Merlinic prophecies and a broad conception of prophecy, he could not untangle all the problems by himself.[40] They remained for centuries to come.

Geoffrey was aware of the difficulties Merlin raised. In writing the *Prophetiae* and incorporating them into his *Historia* Geoffrey seems not to have fretted over the incompatibilities between Merlin and prophets more acceptable to Christianity; but in the *Vita* he took care to endow Merlin with features of both an Old Testament prophet and a Christian saint.

The influence of the Old Testament can be seen once very clearly, in the peculiar specificity of the seventy doors, windows, and amanuenses that Merlin requests for his sylvan observatory (555–61). This detail, which has attracted frequent comment, but not an explanation, is meaningful if it is taken as an allusion to the seventy elders who accompanied Moses to Mount Sinai and saw the God of Israel, just before God gave the tables of the Law to Moses (Ex. 24:1, 9).[41] Yet the parallel brings out a disparity as great as the similarity between Merlin and Moses; Merlin is a prophet, but his prophetic vision offers no hope of redemption and comes only with his resignation of responsibility toward his people.

Whereas Old Testament prophecy always presupposes the impingement of God upon history,[42] Merlin's tellings and foretellings early in the *Vita* evince a hopelessness that any divine order governs events in the human world. Merlin goes mad from grief at the seeming injustice of the world. In the first stage of his insanity he looks into the past, present, and future, but because he lacks understanding, all that he sees is adultery, death, and the keen irony of poverty amid wealth; and he responds only by laughing bitterly. Later he glimpses the future, but all he notices is civil strife. Unlike an Old Testament prophet, who receives the word of God almost involuntarily but has to decide when and to whom to apply it, Merlin is granted insight into what is hidden without detecting any overarching meaning. When the sage Thelgesin discourses on the glory of creation, Merlin answers with a lament about the failings of humanity.[43] His is a prophecy of despair, a prophecy of which he needs to be cured by a spring that is salvational but in no way resembles the waters that pour forth from the rock of Moses (Num. 20). Although he finally loses his insight into the future, in the process he acquires an appreciation of the divine order that had previously eluded him.[44] Through his study of natural forces he has come to understand that God oversees the operations of the universe—that there is a divine providence. His loss is in fact a gain, as he makes evident by praising God for saving him.[45]

The bonds between the Merlin of the *Vita* and Christian saints are firmer than those between Merlin and Moses. The word *Vita* in the title, usually used to designate a saint's life, signals that either Geoffrey or the copyist sensed in the poem a hagiographic intent. The story of Merlin the wild man belongs to a group of Celtic tales in which the protagonist is known varyingly as Merlin, Myrddin, Lailoken, and Suibhne.[46] In most versions of the story an attempt is made to coordinate the wild man, who often has a talent for prophecy, with a saint. Thus a hagiographic element appears in the Scottish version when Lailoken confesses his guilt to Saint Kentigern and asks him for the Sacrament, in the Irish one when Suibhne Geilt becomes involved with Saint Ronan and Saint Moling.[47] In Geoffrey's *Vita* another approach is taken. No saint is introduced into the story, but Merlin himself puts on saintly trappings. The strongest indications that Geoffrey meant us to view Merlin as a saint come in the behavior attributed to him—in his invocations to God for mercy when he is suffering from his self-inflicted asceticism (87 and 146), in his renunciation of his wife and his devotion to chastity (374), in the moral lesson he derives when he meditates upon the past history of his people (951–52), in his refusal to be swayed by offers of kingship, and in the "saintly resolution" of the poem.[48]

One interpreter has argued that these appropriations from hagiography were the almost inevitable concomitants of the prophecies: since Geoffrey had to endue his prophet with a personality, "la plus convenable, la plus conforme à la prophétie elle-même, est celle d'un saint [the most suitable, the most consistent with prophecy itself, is that of a saint]."[49] An alternative explanation would be that Merlin the prophet in his unaltered native guise was too ambivalent a figure for the Christian Church—and especially for Geoffrey as he became a bishop.[50] Therefore, at the end of his poem Geoffrey stripped Merlin of his prophetic powers and made him a penitent saint in all but name. In the exordium to the *Vita* Geoffrey said that he would sing of both the *rabies* and *musa* of the prophet Merlin; at the end both the madness and the poetry of Merlin have been stilled.

In the *Historia* Geoffrey joined Celtic history with classical history and employed biblical history as a structural model.[51] In the *Vita*

Geoffrey made an even bolder attempt to align Celtic vaticination (which included seeing, astrology, and political prophecy) with the kinds of prophecy customarily associated with the Bible. The *Vita* has been faulted for its awkwardness: "Aussi mal construit que l'*Historia* l'était bien, il n'est fait que de la juxtaposition, sans unité, de vaticinations, d'exposés scientifiques, de tirades déclamatoires, et le récit proprement dit y tient en 600 vers [As poorly constructed as the *Historia* was well constructed, it consists solely of the disorganized juxtaposition of vaticinations, scientific expositions, and declamatory tirades; and the actual story occupies only six hundred verses]."[52] To a certain extent the ungainliness was the inevitable result of diverse sources and inspirations: the poem stands at the intersection of oral and written, Church, classical Latin, and Celtic. But in large part the jumble exists only in the eyes of the beholder. The long ruminations on the universe, fishes, and islands are not as irrelevant as they seem at first blush; they impress upon Merlin that God controls every aspect of nature, that a divine providence determines the course of events. What appears to be a "disorganized juxtaposition" is in reality the record of Merlin's growth from a person with inspiration but without faith to a person without inspiration but with faith.

CHAPTER 10

After the Middle Ages: Prophetic Authority and Human Fallibility in Renaissance Epic

Lawrence F. Rhu

The legacy of medieval ideas about poetry and prophecy had considerable influence in the Renaissance and thereafter, when the connection between the two callings proved a source of both conflict and its transcendence. The imitation of ancient models created predictable problems for Christian poets as their awareness of religious differences from their classical literary ideals increased. Inevitably the idea of the poet's vocation also altered as early modern authors in Europe consciously aimed to follow antiquity's best exemplars of their art while establishing poetic identities in their own right. Prophecy and inspiration naturally became contested concerns because they raise issues of both aesthetics and belief. Prophecy, inasmuch as it involves foresight, causes narrative challenges because of its influence on the interplay of expectation and surprise, those mutually dependent aspects of any plot whose skillful management determines an author's ability to engage and sustain our interest in the progress of his story. Inspiration, a definitive feature of both the prophetic and the poetic callings, gave rise to unavoidable conflict when Christian poets imitated their classical precursors because of the rival theologies that fundamentally distinguished their views of the world. Hayden White notwithstanding,[1] the semantics of some contemporary criticism may still lead us naïvely to assume that form and content are neatly separable elements of a literary composition, so that a poet may simply inherit one while rejecting the other. But the lessons that Torquato Tasso derived from Giovan Giorgio Trissino's clumsy conduct of this transaction with past poetry clearly indicate otherwise; for the latter's efforts to tell a Christian tale in a pagan form produced some odd exchanges between heaven and earth, whose awkwardness and incongruity seem immediately apparent even to the contemporary reader.

In order to explore some of the intersections of poetry and prophecy in the Renaissance, I would like to examine the *Gerusalemme liberata* and *Paradise Lost* and to consider in particular the effects of such intersections on the figure of the poet in these two epics and on their narrative structures. Initially, however, I will take a look at two key authors in the Christian and classical traditions that Renaissance writers inherited, Homer and Dante, to consider their legacy in regard to the two issues under discussion. My choice of these particular precursors reflects Tasso's keen sense of their impingement upon his own efforts as he gives word to it both in his theories of epic poetry and in his practice as a poet in that genre.

For example, when Tasso voices his desire for his patron's favor, immediately after his scrupulously orthodox and apologetic invocation of the muse at the opening of the *Gerusalemme liberata,* he utters virtually the only words of direct self-description that he allows himself in his entire poem, "me peregrino errante" (1.4.3).[2] Granted the manifold meanings of his chosen terms,[3] let us consider how this instance of self-revelation locates Tasso in the line of descent from which he consciously acknowledges his own derivation. "Peregrino" calls Dante to mind and his pilgrimage beyond the grave; and, although "errante" first conjures up Ariosto and thus Tasso's struggles with the "errors" of romance that were an especially prominent feature of the *Orlando furioso,* the term also can lead us to Homer and the rigors of plot structure that his works epitomized for neo-Aristotelian emulators in early modern Europe. For the exemplary design of his narratives regularly serves as a normative touchstone in cinquecento criticism of the frequent vagaries in the storyline of Ariosto's masterwork. But we can reach that destination via Dante as well, since the inspired bard of Greek tradition and the medieval pilgrim found their meeting ground in Dante's Ulysses canto (*Inferno* 26).

This context allows us to see the remarkably different self-images that each of them projects, for here the poet's limitations as an inexperienced wayfarer in wholly unfamiliar surroundings are dramatized in detail. The humbling self-portrait that emerges can readily serve to undermine any exalted ideal of his special calling, because Dante the pilgrim cuts such a childish figure in much of this canto. His eager curiosity, which is certainly akin to Ulysses' own appetite for knowledge, perches him so precariously on the bridge over the eighth *bolgia* that he nearly falls in (43–45).[4] Moreover, his speech reveals a similar immaturity, for when Virgil informs him that sinners are bound in these flames (46–48), he cannot resist replying that he had already figured that out on his own (49–51). When he expresses his wish to hear from the flames of Ulysses and Diomed, the pathetic insistence of a child's pleading sounds in his request (64–66); and the last note that he strikes indicates how deeply Dantesque irony can cut, because his little boy's "look-at-me" pride shows one blissfully unaware of his own folly: "Vedi che del disio ver lei mi piego [See how I am leaning toward it (the flame) with desire]" (69). Though Virgil deems Dante's wish a worthy one and grants it, he tells him, as he closes, to keep still.

This medieval poet actually "has it both ways" on occasions like this, however, since he commands a range of self-expression that runs the gamut from self-exposed fallibility to ear-tingling prophecy. Dante opens *Inferno* 26 with a bitter jeremiad against Florence, five of whose citizens he has just beheld in the previous *bolgia* among the other thieves, yet he closes this twelve-line outburst on a note of personal remorse that modulates his vindictiveness (12). Soon thereafter, he witnesses a sight whose memory amounts to a lesson in self-restraint (21); and, we have already seen, Dante's self-portrait in action as he recounts his experiences on the brink of this fiery pit extends that memory into an object lesson in humility, while he dramatizes a remarkably noble instance of failure due to human pride. Thus, he mixes a moral caveat with a thrilling adventure; he exposes his personal shortcomings while making righteous pronouncements in his own voice; and in the larger terms of the whole *Commedia,* this same author employs nothing less than what Charles Singleton calls "God's way of writing"[5] to assign whatever figures he happens to choose from the whole of history as he knew it to their eternal place in his version of the Christian afterworld—all the while representing himself as a benighted wayfarer ever in need of assistance.

Dante relies on a Christian dialectic that reconstitutes the self through an exposure of its own limitations and inadequacy. This process transforms human identity through self-diminishment and through a reliance on grace that parallels the Homeric poet's dependence on divine inspiration. It is not the poet who speaks, but God Who speaks through him and sponsors the grander claims that the all-too-human author makes upon his audience.

Demodokos in the eighth book of the *Odyssey* provides us with our fullest picture of a traditional bard of the Homeric type. He enjoys a special status in the Phaiakian court which merits particular respect, and he sings stories of heroes and gods while himself enjoying a privileged connection with the latter. Odysseus himself makes a point of paying him exceptional tribute, and he is deeply and visibly affected by two of this poet's three tales because they pertain to his own recent and painful experiences at Troy. The other song, which is by far the longest and occurs between the two accounts of Troy, concerns the adultery of Ares and Aphrodite and portrays divine life in a way that might scandalize a conventional Christian, though it merely titillates most of the divinities who witness their heavenly peers caught *in flagrante delicto.*

The mischief of the gods as Demodokos represents them matters less at the moment than Odysseus's special feeling for the poet, though the Greek attribution of all-too-human foibles to the immortals manifests an acknowledgment of darker forces among the highest, most ideal of their conceptions which bears a relevant kinship to some of the issues that preoccupy me in this essay. Odysseus's particular responsiveness to the poet's performance warrants our immediate attention, however, because it suggests a broader trend in the *Odyssey* which affiliates, if not identifies, the poet with the hero. Moreover, this process indirectly transforms our sense of the poet's role from an exclusively exalted one to a human diversity of possibilities which includes such ambiguous qualities as the cunning and duplicity of Odysseus himself.

The figure of Demodokos helps us to see the Greek singer's lofty station, but the merging of the identities of the poet and the hero in the *Odyssey* stands out more prominently in other sections of the poem—especially books 9 through 12. Odysseus himself tells these tales of his wanderings almost without interruption; and the break in the narrative serves to signal the hero's extended appropriation of the poet's function because Alkinoos, in his earnest request for further stories of adventure, explicitly compares Odysseus to a talented minstrel (11.368).[6] The hero then obliges his host with another book and a half of the epic, wherein Homer and Odysseus again share the same voice.

Alkinoos's comparison of this poem's hero to the sort of performer who sang it accounts for but one in a series of such similes that identify the Ithakan wanderer with a singer of tales. After Odysseus, in disguise as a luckless castaway, has regaled the swineherd Eumaios with a sequence of elaborate fictions about his background and present circumstances, the faithful retainer reports to his mistress Penelope that he has been playing host to a very entertaining guest. He likens his supposedly Cretan visitor's gift for entrancing narration to the songs that gods teach to minstrels who hold their listeners enthralled and reluctant to hear such stories end (17.518–21). Later, when Odysseus, as a beggar in his own home, has patiently waited out the abuse of the suitors and finally has his key weapon in his own hands, he strings the bow that has already foiled his rivals and will cost many of them their lives the way a harper skilled in song strings his lyre (21.406–9).

Homer relates these rather intimately suggestive similes *in propria persona* or, we can fairly imagine, by impersonating the voice of the speaker on that occasion in the narrative sequence. The presence of an audience, plus the fact that the majority of the *Odyssey* unfolds in direct discourse from whatever character "holds the stage" as the story proceeds, highlight the element of self-conscious performance that this poem must have entailed. How, for example, does "Homer," or any other such oral performer, relate to his audience when, as Odysseus in or out of disguise, he lies through his teeth to the hardly deceived goddess of wisdom about who he is and how he happened to turn up on the as yet unnamed island of Ithaka, possessed of abundant loot (123.221–86)? Or when he tries to con Eumaios out of a cloak by fabricating a complete falsehood about the supposedly real Odysseus's having played just such a trick on the gullible Thoas at Troy (14.459–506)?

Such contexts of manifold duplicity, in which the poet's impersonation is compounded by the impersonation by the character he speaks for, welcome us into a hall of mirrors where reflections threaten to multiply ad infinitum or, at least, out of our conceptual control. But if we recall that the poet faces a crowd of listeners who can share his awareness of the complex ironies that come into play on such occasions, we can perceive that a constant, though lively relationship steadily obtains between these multiple fictions and their ultimate source; and the audience and the author, by remaining present to each other, can transcend the terms of make-believe by their implicit ability to recognize each other beyond the context of the ongoing story. That ability inheres in the public setting of a Homeric performance, where "eye contact" could affirm such a conscious complicity. Even a blind bard like Demodokos or the Homer of legend could suggest a similar sense of mutuality, however, by the sort of self-reference that runs through those similes that liken the hero to the poet, and he could certainly draw the audience into an ironic recognition of the author's self-conscious presence at just such moments in the story.

The Aristotelian notion of Homeric self-effacement and the conventional vatic ideal of the poet as a selfless conduit for divine inspiration obscure this element in the *Odyssey.* Tasso's obvious affinity for both of these versions of the poetic vocation conditioned his reading of Homer and shaped his sense of this classical poet whom he so patently imitates on frequent occasions in the *Liberata.* As early as the preface to the *Rinaldo* in 1562, young Tasso alludes to Aristotle's praise of Homer's anonymity as a narrator in a famous passage from the *Poetics* (XXIV [1460a]): "Aristotile chiaramente dica ne la sua *Poetica* che tanto il poeta è migliore, quanto più imita, e tanto imita più quanto men egli come poeta parla. [Aristotle clearly states in his *Poetics* that the better the poet the more he imitates and the more he imitates the less he speaks as a poet]."[7]

The critical tradition of Homer as a virtually nonexistent and certainly unobtrusive presence in his poems springs from this classical source. He is seen as a kind of missing person in his own works, and Tasso obviously shared Aristotle's esteem for this quality in a narrative poet, as becomes evident deductively from a careful look at the *Liberata,* where the poet appears but fleetingly in his own person. With the exception of his request for favor from Alfonso II, these appearances are of the same kind as those of Homer in the *Iliad* and the *Odyssey:* invocations of the Muse and brief vocative addresses to characters in the action. Elsewhere in his early prose, Tasso explicitly makes known his dislike of any further authorial intrusion when he takes Ariosto to task for his frequent and prominent practice of self-reference in personal asides and editorial commentary on the action he relates.[8] Ariosto, in fact, exploits to the fullest extent the pretense that he performs for a live audience like the *cantastorie* who originally imported the legends and lore that Boiardo and he drew upon to write their romances. But Tasso deplores this practice and minimizes any self-consciousness of his role as a poet-performer or as a character in his own poem.

Therefore, to determine Tasso's idea of the poetic vocation and his sense of himself as a poet, we must look outside the *Liberata,* and the abundant theoretical discourses he composed in the process of writing his epic provide a useful field for such an investigation. A famous passage that Joseph Wittreich sometimes quotes to demonstrate the kinship between prophecy and Tasso's idea of the epic as a genre also contains his most notable description of the poet's role.[9] He accepts the convention combining the biblical notion that humankind was created in God's image and the tradition from the same source that imagines God as the Creator; the poet thus becomes a creator after the manner of his Maker, and the poem is the world that he makes. Although this conception stresses craftsmanship, it by no means rules out inspiration, and we encounter in this context an exalted counterpart to Tasso's humble self-portrait as an errant wayfarer at the outset of the *Liberata* when he offers this description of his vocation: "[An excellent poet] is called divine for no other reason except that by working like the supreme Artificer he comes to share His divinity."[10]

Such excursions beyond the borders of a poem have been famously discredited by W. K. Wimsatt and M. C. Beardsley's austere code of critical conduct, the so-called Intentional Fallacy;[11] and the "New Criticism," which strictures like theirs typify, has in turn fallen into disfavor.[12] Although my immediate purpose precludes extensive elaboration of a theoretical rationale for my approach, a few relevant observations of that sort are in order at this point. Tasso's literal-minded reading of Aristotle basically banished him from his own poem in any openly avowed terms; though he believed that the poet is nothing less than a divine craftsman, Tasso is the *deus absconditus* of his own creation. Such absences, of course, promptly invite theorists of the unconscious to explain what isn't (quite) there, and psychoanalytic readers have responded handsomely to this call.[13] Those who question "the self-identity of the *cogito*" and propound the "political" unconscious could likewise apply themselves profitably to the outside determinants of Tasso's inner life. The religious climate of post-Tridentine Italy warrants such scrutiny, especially when comparing Tasso with Milton; and the public discourse of neo-Aristotelianism and its opponents must also be taken into account. This philosophical rivalry set the stage for the literary disputes that consumed so much of Tasso's energy after he first finished the *Liberata;* and although he anticipated this kind of contention even before its completion, the intensity and duration of these debates came as a cruel surprise. Tasso's theoretical writings by no means explain his poetic efforts in any ultimate fashion, but neither are they off limits for those who would venture such explanations. Rather, given the theoretical preoccupations of our moment, they constitute an unusually attractive resource: an extensive poetics that coexists, side by side, with major accomplishments by the same author in the art he seeks to expound in theory.

Prophecy also stands outside the temporality that defines narrative and thus becomes susceptible to similar critiques. Its privileged exemption from the flow of time makes it suspect in terms of mimetic norms that prize credible succession from one event to the next. As both a theorist and a poet Tasso bears witness to the competing pressures of these concerns: for he not only addresses the issues of mimesis and allegory in his poetics; he also inscribes the results of such reflections in the prophetic voices in his own poem. Since Peter the Hermit's major prediction (10.74–78) discharges the conventional obligations of such a figure in a dynastic epic, it can seem merely the predictable routine that his role entails. Tasso pays tribute to his patron's house by having Peter recount, in the future tense, what any informed reader already knows are (supposedly) facts from the past, confirming in the process a truism about all such providential historians: "Nothing succeeds like succession."[14]

But other prophetic utterances give word to the overall structure and theme of the poem in terms that echo Tasso's theoretical concerns in the context of his ongoing narration. In what the poet labels as divinely inspired speech (1.32.3), Peter at the start of the poem asserts Goffredo's rightfully sole dominion over the soldiers of the Cross and expounds the rationale of such a power structure (1.31). In a subsequent dream-vision the late Ugone visits this leader's sleep to provide the ultimate explanation for recalling the truant Rinaldo despite his offense (14.13). He clarifies the young knight's executive function in the hierarchy of duties incumbent upon the chief figures in the Crusade if they are to triumph as God intends. Both prophetic interventions can easily be construed as covert commentaries by the author on his own work, for they bespeak Tasso's preoccupation with unity of plot and meaning which he articulated in his early discourses and in the allegory that he later wrote for his poem. Explanatory interruptions from on high provide a place within the advancing story where Tasso can gloss its intended import without violating the illusion of its self-sufficiency and freedom from authorial intrusions.

In young Tasso's development as a theorist while he was composing the *Liberata,* he evolved from relatively strict Aristotelianism and a predominant concern with unity of plot to Platonic moralizing and an emphasis on the integrity of his poem as an ethical allegory.[15] The course he charts in the process reflects a change in his initial concern with the legacy of Ariosto and the relationship between the genres of romance and epic which he meant appropriately to merge. As the prospect of publication approaches, worries about the reception of his poem and fears of censorship increasingly preoccupy him. A claim to the high-minded ambition of moral allegory becomes an appealing safeguard against his critics, although he by no means forsakes the formalist scruples that neoclassical norms continue to impose upon him.

Unfortunately, Tasso could never completely abandon such concerns, and after the *Liberata* had been published, he labored persistently to revise and perfect his earlier efforts, "to get it right the second time" once and for all. Also, he submitted his theories to a similar revision, elaborating the relationship between history and allegory and researching anew the rules that would harmonize the merger of epic and romance. In the latter effort he had recourse to a figure he remembered from the Ulysses canto of Dante's *Inferno:* the questing hero's passage through the Pillars of Hercules to see the sky the other way around, to see what Dante called *l'altro polo* and Tasso *altre stelle*.[16] In his later discourses he adds, among other things, an opening paragraph to his chapter on plot structure in which he seeks to reconcile the rival traditions of epic and romance and to find the constant, unifying principles behind apparently diverse literary forms. To describe this undertaking he uses the figure of what Dante calls Ulysses' "mad flight" (*folle volo*). But Tasso claims that heavenly guidance, those "other stars" in his terms, as well as enduring truths, can assure the success of an otherwise hazardous adventure that only a fool would trust to mere chance.

Actually, in the *Liberata* Dame Fortune captains just such a voyage through the Pillars of Hercules to Teneriffe in the Canaries to retrieve the erring Rinaldo from his thralldom to Armida. In transit occurs one of those weird moments when poetic prophecy works strange changes upon the time warp, and Fortuna predicts Columbus's discovery of the New World to her eleventh-century passengers, an augury that would come as no surprise to Tasso's *cinquecento* readers (15.31–32). But this journey also manages to close the potentially dangerous gap between the genres of epic and romance which Tasso meant to unify, for Rinaldo's days of solitary emprises and erotic delinquency are fewer the nearer Fortuna's ship draws to his Circe's isle. After an interval in which he appropriately repents and begins to reform, Rinaldo returns to the Christian army and champions the assault upon the Holy City. Once again he adds his due to the joint effort of all the Crusaders, fulfilling the epic role assigned to him from the inception of the poem despite intervening delays.

Although Achilles obviously serves as Tasso's immediate model for Rinaldo's indignant withdrawal from the siege of Jerusalem, in an important way this return parallels what happened to the original Odysseus, before Dante got hold of him. Despite his wanderings, he came back home; and, despite his distinctive identity, he remained, as an epic hero, a character whose corporate identity defines him more decisively than anything that we might call "individuality" or his condition as a solitary person beyond communal bonds and social position: he is his crew's captain, Ithaka's king, and the Greek army's shrewdest tactician. These public distinctions determine his character. Through the inspired bard's song the Muse told us about them in the first place, and the way the story unfolds comes, in a sense, as no surprise. Rather, it comes full circle.

Dante changes all that, however, straightening it out, so to speak, and making Ulysses' voyage a one-way trip to disaster. The dependable cycles of epic are transformed in the *Commedia*'s treatment of this classical hero, whose sad fate also darkly reflects the destiny barely escaped by the fortunate pilgrim. This generic metamorphosis distinguishes Dante's poem in ways that pertain directly to the issues of prophecy and inspiration because temporality and the figure of the poet significantly share in the changes of literary kind which alter our impression of the traditional Greek hero in this new context. As John Freccero points out, "To understand the *Divine Comedy* simply as a religious epic is to dismiss the transformation of the pilgrim as unimportant. To call it a novel, on the other hand, is to miss the confidence of the poet's voice, one of the narrative's distinctive characteristics. Epic and novel exist, side by side, linearity with circularity, in this poetic synthesis which has always been considered a genre apart."[17]

In the *Liberata* prophetic speeches confidently proclaim the requisite unity of the Christian army under one head and the necessary recall of Rinaldo. Summoned from beyond the Pillars of Hercules and from the realm of romance, he takes his fated place among the soldiers of the Cross. Ugone's voice, like that of Peter the Hermit, is undeniably a displaced version of the poet's own as it is inscribed in the prefatory allegory. A rigid code of authorial self-effacement requires such ventriloquism. What becomes of the poet-pilgrim's alternative selves in the *Commedia* eludes Tasso at both extremes. The authoritative voice of prophetic speech is delegated to various proxies within the poem. The potentially suspenseful storyline of a single character facing an uncertain future curves back upon itself and recycles that figure within the heroic ambience of epic action. Strictures of generic propriety, as Tasso narrowly construes them, foreclose the chances of the poem to break radically with the traditions it means to inherit. Occasions for prophecy within the advancing narrative could offer opportunities for a more commanding authorial presence, but similar strictures of austere neoclassicism preclude that option. The innovations of Tasso's creation are kept tightly in check by the severe rules of formalism which he feels obliged to observe, although the ghosts of other impulses can nonetheless be discerned in the carefully disposed stanzas of the tale he tells.

·

Milton's open expressions of regard for Tasso as both a poet and a theorist encourage comparative study of their works.[18] Likewise, their mutual involvement in the inheritance and transformation of a generic tradition provides extensive grounds for comparison of their epics. But critical pursuits that focus upon analogues and literary kinship must also reckon with differences, and in the matters of immediate concern to this essay, prophecy and inspiration, these two Renaissance masters widely diverge. Whereas normative self-effacement strictly constrains Tasso to curtail his own appearances in the *Liberata,* no such reticence at all inhibits Milton. In his initial invocation he appropriates a line from the first proem of the *Orlando furioso,* and the bold claim that he thus asserts typifies the sublime egotism characteristic of the ambitions that impelled him to compose *Paradise Lost.*[19] Although young Tasso respected the popularity that Ariosto's poem had achieved, he pointedly disapproved of its author's unabashed self-reference and also of the lack of decorum that sometimes insinuates itself into supposedly heroic episodes of the *Furioso.*[20] While Milton decisively rejects the brand of heroism that Ariostan romance both celebrates and subverts,[21] he repeats on his own behalf this Italian precursor's foremost boast and situates his own kindred claim with equal prominence in the foreground of his poem.

Milton's proem to book I of *Paradise Lost* is one of four self-revealing excursions that the poet prefixes to key shifts and changes in the action he represents. Also, he is not loath to intervene with brief glosses from his own perspective on the narrative-in-progress. Although classical precedent sanctions this authorial prerogative, Tasso exercises it much more sparingly; and the *Liberata*'s notably guarded induction, like the few brief invocations of the Muse that appear thereafter, bespeaks a severe reserve that sends us elsewhere to inquire about Tasso's aims and struggles with his epic-in-the-making and about his sense of his vocation as a poet. Turning to Tasso's theories, like turning to our own, is not a foolproof method; but, for obvious reasons, it affords us an inviting option when a superior poet has reflected at such length on the art he practices.

In his early poetics, narrative *dispositio* occupies the majority of young Tasso's attention as he takes his stand on the key issue raised by the multiple divagations of Ariostan romance: unity of plot. In this context his assertion of the identity of potentially distinct genres makes him an exemplary forerunner of the encyclopedic inclusiveness that characterizes Milton's major epic. Recent critics, whether they advance the idea of *genera mixta* or of prophecy as an all-encompassing literary kind, read Tasso's openness to variety within a unified narrative framework as an aesthetic norm entirely in keeping with Milton's poetic practice in *Paradise Lost*.[22] The argument for prophecy as the generic model for that poem occasions some questions. One might thus construe Milton's sense of precedents too narrowly, especially if we limit our interest in pre-texts to the single example of Saint John's Apocalypse.[23] Or one might mislabel, as a genre, what could better be described as a perspective. In fact Joseph Wittreich's conception of prophecy embraces so many diverse kinds of writing that no danger of rigid constraints inheres in such an idea as he advances it. Generic distinctions do indeed blur, however, if poems as determinedly different as "Lycidas" and *Paradise Regained* are deemed of the same kind.[24]

While he drew upon various traditions, from classical antiquity to his own age, Milton felt himself the undeniable heir to a great original with unshakable claims to the status of inspired prophecy. From the Pauline assertion that "all scripture is given by inspiration of God" (2 Tim. 3:6)[25] to the Bible-based theology of the Reformation which he inscribed in his own epic (12.502–14), Milton acquired an ideal of Holy Writ which deemed it God's ledger, His Word to humankind. Moreover, Milton's Protestantism gave him direct access to this sacred legacy, which young Tasso considered too holy to provide material for poetic creation. When he reflected upon the proper subject of a heroic poem, he excluded sacred writings upon which church doctrines are founded because their creedal significance would disallow invention, a definitive feature of poetry, as distinct from history, in his view.[26]

Although in the final years of his life he composed his own hexameral account, *Le sette giornate del mondo creato,* it was by no means a triumph; and doctrinal preoccupations, along with a wide range of other tangential concerns, extend its already considerable longueurs. Nothing in Tasso's poetry, really, compares to Milton's relation to the Bible; and this incommensurability in the traditions they bring to bear upon their poetic efforts betokens a world of difference.

In this regard Milton's bold ambition to pursue "things unattempted yet in Prose or Rhyme" signals the revolutionary return to Christian origins before the Church of Rome's dominion placed the clergy between believers and the book upon which their faith was supposedly based. Milton echoes prefaces to vernacular Bibles such as William Tyndale's English New Testament of 1525–1526 and the sentiments of such translators when he briefly suggests what amounts to his own reader-response theory for the student of Scripture: Truth abides in these written records, but it discloses itself only to the spirit's apprehension.[27] This succinct formulation, however, belies a complex and dangerous relationship. The ideal of a tabula rasa, a text cleared of corrupt mediation and tainted interpretation, may lead its reader in unpredictable directions; or vice versa, a demonic self-sufficiency may possess the reading spirit and seduce it into error. Satan, in Milton's poem, is a persuasive master of misconstruction who reinterprets God's word with such compelling falsity as to occasion the Fall.

Milton's own undertakings as an exegete left him open to charges of this sort, especially when he wrote the divorce tracts and relied upon the reinterpretation of Scripture to sponsor his unconventional views. Since his personal dilemma occasioned these revisionary readings, he was inevitably accused of self-serving distortion of established traditions, of Satanic appropriation of the Word to serve his own ends. As a sustained reprise of key segments of the biblical story, from Genesis to Apocalypse, the composition of *Paradise Lost* entailed similar risks, and comparable critiques persist down to our own moment. Among feminist respondents, Mary Nyquist has offered the most insightful commentary I have encountered, but her use of the Documentary Hypothesis involves problems of anachronism.[28] Crystallized by Julius Wellhausen in its most convincing form at the close of the last century, this theory of pentateuchal redaction has itself undergone subsequent revision, but its clear separation of different scriptural tradents definitely postdates the seventeenth century.[29] To speak of a P and J strand in the opening three chapters of Genesis posits a clearer division between what Milton would have seen as apparently divergent accounts within a text unified by a much higher "source." In his *Leviathan* of 1651, Thomas Hobbes had persuasively challenged the attribution of the Torah to Mosaic authorship, and he was by no means the first to express such doubts. But Milton apparently subscribed to this traditional idea, as he reveals in the exordium to *Paradise Lost* by invoking the Heav'nly Muse who inspired

> That Shepherd, who first taught the chosen Seed,
> In the Beginning how the Heav'ns and Earth
> Rose out of *Chaos*.
>
> (1.8–10)

Milton's impulse to harmonize evident inconsistencies in Genesis may mask self-interest, and it does produce a "masculinist" interpretation; but it is indicative of an attitude toward the biblical text as an authentic oracle of the truth which is notably more secure than our present-day scholarly perspectives will allow. The Bible in early modern Europe gave rise to myriad schisms and endless debate, but such divisive controversy derived from the shared agreement about its sacrosanct status as God's holy word. The cold-blooded procedures of source criticism make this special regard simply irrelevant.

Two attitudes toward Scripture particularly affected the composition of *Paradise Lost.* First, the doctrine of accommodation influenced Milton's conception of the deity and his dependence on biblical terms to represent God in his poem.[30] Since Scripture is the language that He chose for Himself in His dialogue with our kind, this verbal means of disclosure, however indirect and metaphorical it may be, provides our chief clues and guidelines for imagining what He is *like.* (Let the terminal preposition in the preceding sentence signify that only comparisons and approximations are available to inhabitants of "the land of unlikeness." Exact equivalences, like the reality itself, are inconceivable.) Second, typology served as the primary exegetical lens through which Milton viewed sacred history and its fulfillment in Christ, and Scripture supplies an exemplary expositor of this sort in Saint Paul. Protestant literalism, however, encouraged Milton to remain faithful to the plain sense of the biblical text, and the tendency for typology and allegory to blur into each other—as they do in Galatians 4:21–31, for example—required vigilant adherence to what the Letter allows.[31]

In book 3 of *Paradise Lost* Milton adapts Isaiah 6 to portray worship among the heavenly host and the angelic praises of Christ's voluntary sacrifice of Himself for sinful humankind. This passage has traditionally given clues, to be followed here, about the ceremonial conduct of adoration and thanksgiving on high; both Christians and Jews have incorporated echoes of this text into their rites and services. But Isaiah's vision of the seraphim at prayer also serves as his inaugural summons to prophecy, and Milton's careful reading of this "call narrative" enables him to extrapolate an exalted ideal of his own role as both a poet and a divine ambassador. A telltale first-person plural in God's audible query—"Whom shall I send, and who will go for *us?*" (Is. 6:8, my italics)—situates the scene of this exchange with the prophet-elect in the divine council, with the Deity in conference with His court in heaven. Milton, in fact, employs his own pronominal shift in both person and number to locate himself as a singer among the angelic host in the company of God:

> Thee Father first they sung Omnipotent. . . .
> Thee next they sang of all Creation first,
> Begotten Son, Divine Similitude. . . .
> Hail Son of God, Savior of Men, thy Name
> Shall be the copious matter of my Song
> Henceforth, and never shall my Harp thy praise
> Forget, nor from thy Father's praise disjoin.
> (3.372, 383–84, 412–17)[32]

Scripture provides the model for this transformation of the poet into a celestial chorister, and the call to prophecy thus exemplifies the poetic vocation. The Bible sanctions this extravagant claim with an authority to which no other text has title, and Milton could avail himself of that sanction in a way that Tasso's post-Tridentine scruples would never allow.

The constraints of religious conservatism and reaction inhibited Tasso in much the same way as did the strictures of neoclassicism which derived from the increasing influence of Aristotle's *Poetics* in the theoretical debates of the mid-Cinquecento. The eighteen-year duration of the Council of Trent and some of the institutions it created, such as the Index of Prohibited Books, symbolize the atmosphere of official vigilance during the period when Tasso grew to manhood and artistic maturity. Both aesthetic and theological legalism must have impinged on the ambitions of most aspiring artists in such an environment; fears of censorship and heresy were not engendered spontaneously out of Tasso's troubled imagination, like Athena out of Zeus's head. This poet voluntarily submitted the *Liberata* to the fastidious philistinism of the clerical critic Silvio Antoniano—"il poetino," as the frustrated young Tasso dubbed him when the painful process of review was under way. He also confessed to the Inquisitor more than once on his own initiative. But the insecurities that occasioned such conduct have a public dimension as well as reflecting private turmoil and inner uncertainty. Paolo Veronese was summoned before the Inquisition for the inclusion of "buffoons, drunkards, dwarfs, Germans, and similar vulgarities" in his *Feast of the House of Levi* during the time that Tasso was first bringing his epic to a conclusion and showing it to his *revisori*.[33] Michelangelo himself came under the most famous and sustained of such attacks for both the indecency of naked bodies and the heresy of figures from pagan mythology in his *Last Judgment* during the decade when Tasso was first formulating his theories about the treatment of Christian subjects in epic poetry. The first, pirated edition of the *Liberata* appeared two years before Bartolommeo Amannati felt prompted to regret the nudity of statues he had carved and wished to make public his repentance.[34]

In this light the nervous apologia in Tasso's initial invocation of the Muse seems symptomatic of his milieu, where official authorities clung tightly to what remained of their previously unthreatened dominion and expected the compliance of their subjects. In seeking inspiration at the outset, Tasso asks pardon for his art, and in his poetics, his uneasiness about invention leads him to rely on history to valorize his claim to credibility.[35] This defensive posture toward his own vocation almost makes him subordinate poetry to a merely decorative function; it nearly becomes an appealing accessory with no integral relation to the substance of his argument in *Gerusalemme liberata:*

> Tu spira al petto mio celesti ardori,
> tu rischiara il mio canto, e tu perdona
> s'intesso fregi al ver, s'adorno in parte
> d'altri diletti, che de' tuoi, le carte.
>
> (1.2.4–8)

Breathe into my breast celestial ardors, illuminate my song, and grant

> me pardon if with the truth I interweave embroiderings, if partly with pleasures other than yours I ornament my pages.[36]

In regard to the prophet's role in the *Liberata,* Tasso could have inherited the habit of making purposeful adjustments upon the historical records of the First Crusade from his primary prose source, William of Tyre's *Historia rerum in partibus transmarinis gestarum.* This chronicle abounds in providential inflections of the events it recounts, and the Christian conquest is regularly represented as foreordained by God. Specifically, William attributes divine origins to speeches by Peter the Hermit, who sometimes voices inspired messages of considerable consequence to the Crusade; on one occasion, which seems entirely William's invention, he cites Isaiah 55:11 to assert the ultimate authority behind Peter's words.[37] But Tasso does not revise historical accounts to accommodate biblical prophecy. He has other models in mind when he adjusts the received version of what actually happened to fit the kind of plot he aspires to reproduce. He resurrects Ademaro, bishop of Puy, from the dead to join the opening muster of the Christian forces in a direct echo of Homer's catalogue of the Greek army at Troy in *Iliad* 2; and he recalls Ugone of Vermandois, a deserter, to take part in the same proud parade of the troops, although William records his abandonment of their mission well before they had reached this stage in their march just as surely as he registers Ademaro's demise.[38]

Milton, of course, includes his classical precursors and follows their examples in his poem, but he also summarily transcends them when the occasion so demands. They are invoked to be denied, but they provide him with great rhetorical power while he puts them securely in their secondary place.

> Descend from Heav'n *Urania,* by that name
> If rightly thou art call'd, whose Voice divine
> Following, above th' *Olympian* Hill I soar,
> Above the flight of *Pegasean* wing.
> The meaning not the Name I call: for thou
> Nor of the Muses nine, nor on the top
> Of old *Olympus* dwell'st, but Heav'nly born . . .
>
> (7.1–7)

This brief passage must epitomize a complex process that pervades the entire fabric of *Paradise Lost* and has attracted particular attention to the portrait of Satan. (For example, Milton ironically echoes in Hell the Homeric catalogue of heroes at Troy when he enumerates the fallen angels who followed Lucifer's lead to that catastrophic conclusion [1.376–521], and he thus subverts the proud display of a definitively epic moment that Tasso reproduces without challenging.)

But a few instances can serve to make some preliminary distinctions between Milton's poetic practice and that of Tasso in the light of my present concern with prophecy and inspiration. The invocation of the Muse in the proem to book 7, already quoted in part, marks the midpoint of the poem; and it reveals the English poet, like his Italian antecedent at the start of the *Liberata,* sifting through his literary choices and accepting only the highest source of inspiration. At such a juncture biblical precedents supply Milton with positive alternatives once pagan options are rejected by the higher reach that a Christian poem requires, whereas this ample reservoir of exalted imagery, perhaps inevitably, remained untapped by the Counter-Reformation poet.

> Before the Hills appeared, or Fountain flow'd,
> Thou with Eternal Wisdom didst converse,
> Wisdom thy Sister, and with her didst play
> In presence of th' Almighty Father, pleas'd
> With thy Celestial Song. Up led by thee
> Into the Heav'n of Heav'ns I have presum'd,
> An Earthly Guest, and drawn Empyreal Air.
>
> (7.8–14)

In the lines that immediately follow this excerpt, Milton, like Tasso, also acknowledges his own liabilities and limitations as he descends to the more consistently earthbound considerations of the second half of his poem, but his art assumes no merely ornamental, almost ancillary role like that Tasso assigns to his own. As we have seen, the Christian dialectic of humility and transcendence vitalizes Dante's voice, but it seems to atrophy with overqualification in Tasso. In Milton it is alive and well, although the Protestant poet threads his way through a labyrinth of options as tortuous as Tasso's.

At the opening of book 7, when Milton invokes the Muse for the third and final time, he calls upon Urania and alludes to a passage from Proverbs (8:22–31, esp. 30) to identify her as Wisdom's companion.

Both of them were present at the Creation, which the poet hopes to recount through this reliance upon an eyewitness. Just as Moses wrote Genesis thanks to the inspiration of the Heav'nly Muse, whose assistance on that occasion Milton remembers and prayerfully requests on his own behalf "in the beginning" of his poem, so Urania is now aptly summoned to provide the necessary aid for the next development in the advancing plot. The Protestant poet can reach past the classics to the biblical text in a gesture that the Catholic poet feels restrained from making, and Milton thereby gains an authority noticeably absent from the artistic self-definition that Tasso presents in more guarded terms. It is not that Milton feels immune from qualifications and uncertainty; the adaptation of Scripture entails an abundance of restraints, and we can often hear the poet consciously working around them. When Milton describes the angelic trumpet blown to announce God's imminent sentence on the fallen pair in Eden, he tentatively projects that instrument's future uses:

> hee blew
> His Trumpet heard on *Oreb* since perhaps
> When God descended, and perhaps once more
> To sound at general Doom.
>
> (11.73–76)

Milton's unwillingness to exceed the terms of Scripture is inscribed in the adverb that he situates in the prominent final position of line seventy-four and then promptly repeats in the next line; and this show of reluctance is by no means a unique instance. The authority of Scripture confers a powerful confidence, but it also requires self-discipline and reserve.

In some ways Milton's dominant attitudes toward biblical interpretation and the imaginative adaptation of Holy Writ likewise reflect this double vision. Typology bespeaks fulfillment and finality, the end of the story as it is shadowed forth along the way. But the theory of accommodation posits indirection and approximation as inevitable in any representation of God: the ultimate reality remains occluded or is only partially available at best. Even typology's sense of completion usually comes from the intermediate perspective of a human exegete and thus involves unavoidable contingencies; and accommodation, it has been noted,[39] can justify the use of images and tales borrowed from nonbiblical literature because they all share the secondary realm of metaphor necessarily inhabited by all mortal speech of things divine. Milton's openness to such a range of options and his skillful combinations of their possibilities enable him to employ the special sanctions of a unique, transcendent source within the polyphonic context of apparently divergent traditions. Therefore, it is an eminently arguable intuition to perceive in Tasso's aesthetic ideals of *discorde concordia* and multiplicity-in-unity a forecast of Milton's attainment in *Paradise Lost* of a generically inclusive epic.[40] But we must keep in mind that Tasso developed these values in the specific historical context of the neo-Aristotelian debates over the vagaries of Ariostan romance and that Milton achieved their realization by means of a unifying discourse inaccessible to Tasso, that of the Bible.

The most sustained review of biblical material in *Paradise Lost* occurs in the final two books when the Archangel Michael descends to the Garden to deliver God's judgment upon Adam and Eve. His account of sacred history picks up where book 10 left off, after the Fall; and the heavenly envoy relates, in varying degrees of detail, the fate of our first parents' heirs from Cain and Abel to the Apocalypse. This painful narrative is all news to Adam, prophecy in fact; but it covers ground thoroughly familiar to Milton's readers, if they know the Bible. The situation here mirrors what John Freccero found in the Ulysses canto of Dante's *Inferno,* where confident foreknowledge and suspenseful temporality combine in the figure of the poet, whose pilgrim self suffers and learns from moment to moment while his vatic voice can rise securely above the ongoing agon.[41] Milton's deft management of his generic options *and* his recourse to Scripture enable him to accomplish a similar fusion of prophetic authority and human fallibility. Adam's tragic experience makes him a postlapsarian exegete, and the promise that he gradually comes to discern in the abridged version of the biblical story told to him by Michael now filters through a fallen consciousness predisposed to misprision and error.

Our quest for the author in the *Gerusalemme liberata* led us outside the poem itself to Tasso's treatises on heroic poetry, which include, among other arguments, the rationale for this poet's almost entire absence from his own poem. In *Paradise Lost,* on the other hand, Milton's own ordeal as a poet claims a prominent share of the significant action that he relates. The four proems contain open self-reflection on the process of composition, which becomes a dramatic part of his poem-in-the-making. Theoretical discourse also enters into the fabric of his work-in-progress. The first three proems are cast as prayerful summonses of three different Muses, after the classical fashion, which the Protestant poet transforms in terms of the Christian dispensation and with the help of biblical allusion. In the fourth proem, Milton-the-theorist speculates on the appropriate theme of an epic and asserts the aptness of tragic matter for heroic song. He conducts the business of Tasso's *Discorsi* in the midst of his advancing narrative between our blissful state in Eden and temptation and the Fall.

Revising Aristotelian *differentiae,* Tasso distinguished epic from tragedy on the basis of the sort of hero suitable for each genre. Wonder is the definitive emotion aroused by epic, and its protagonists must therefore embody extremes of virtue or vice which will promote the appropriate response. Tragedy, on the other hand, needs a central figure whose qualities are more intermediate and thus recognizable, so that the pathos of his or her ordeal can produce its intended effects upon the audience: pity and terror, not wonder.[42] When Satan first describes Adam and Eve among the other creatures in Eden, they meet the epic requirement without stint.

> Two of far nobler shape erect and tall,
> Godlike erect, with native Honor clad
> In naked Majesty seem'd Lords of all,
> And worthy seem'd, for in thir looks Divine
> The image of thir glorious Maker shone.
>
> (4.288–92)

But later, lapsed powers and lost preeminence characterize Adam's fallen condition, and he shows how much he has become one of us in the fallibility he repeatedly reveals in his mistaken responses to Michael's prophetic account of human destiny in books 11 and 12. His nature now better suits what Tasso specified for a tragic hero.

When Joseph Wittreich avers that "in various ways the Book of Revelation is, before the fact, a fulfillment of Tasso's idea of the epic poem,"[43] he has in mind both the multiplicity of literary kinds this prophetic book embraces and the generic polyphony Milton's inspired epic later manages to accommodate. Tasso's treatise thus comes to be seen as containing a forecast of the promise that Milton's masterwork realizes; *Paradise Lost* becomes the antitype of Saint John's Apocalypse, although Wittreich's chronology must first turn back to include the biblical type in Tasso's mediating augury. But it is well to remember that, in discoursing on his literary options, Milton calls the Book of

Revelation a "high and stately tragedy."[44] The genre he discerns in the biblical text is the same one whose presence he announces in his own prefatory poetics to book 9. The tragic agon thus proclaimed serves as a precondition to the prophetic finale and modulates the poet's claim to the authority of God's word through the errors of Adam's responses.

Errori are the solitary wanderings of romance which Tasso eagerly included in his epic after he elaborated the rationale for their presence in heroic song under the sign of *discorde concordia* in his early poetics. The successful marriage of these two genres amounts to the primary innovation in the *Gerusalemme liberata;* and whether the suspense of Rinaldo's solo emprises, like that of Ulysses' travels off course, is ultimately undercut by the foregone conclusion of his return to the epic conflict in the Holy Land remains an engaging question for genre theorists who wonder when the novel, or its forerunners, first appears. Perhaps an imaginary book 13 of *Paradise Lost* can be adduced as a hypothetical fiction for that new form. After Adam and Eve have learned the authorized version of all time, including its end, they still have their lives to live and deeds to add to "the sum of wisdom." As they leave Eden, they enter the realm of mortal time in terms that resonate with reminders of episodes in a romance. They are perched on the brink of fresh experiences and discoveries of another order, which will supply them with material for many new stories. But none of them may readily lay claim to any final authority, such as the thematic and structural patterns of the classical genres of poetry or even the future foretold in the sacred history of scriptural tradition—and so easily misconstrued.

> They hand in hand with wand'ring steps and slow
> Through *Eden* took their solitary way.
>
> (12.648–49)

Notes

1. Poets and Prophets, James L. Kugel

1. Here I might mention my own book, *The Idea of Biblical Poetry* (New Haven, 1981), and those of Michael O'Connor, *Hebrew Verse Structure* (Winona Lake, Ind., 1980), and Adele Berlin, *The Dynamics of Biblical Parallelism* (Bloomington, Ind., 1986).

2. Biblical Hebrew itself has no general categories corresponding to these two terms, nor is there any indication that what we nowadays consider to be the "poetic" parts of the Hebrew Bible were ever viewed as a bloc over against its "prose" parts. See my *Idea of Biblical Poetry*, pp. 69–70.

3. See on this David L. Petersen, *Late Israelite Prophecy: Studies in Deutero-Prophetic Literature and in Chronicles*, Society of Biblical Literature Monograph Series 23 (Missoula, Mont., 1977).

4. Something of the converse may occur in the superscriptions of the collections of *mĕšālîm* found in Prov. 30 and 31; both are apparently referred to by the word *maśśāʾ*, a term that otherwise designates a prophetic oracle.

5. See my *Idea of Biblical Poetry*, pp. 119–27.

6. Jerome, in his Latin translation of the prophets for his Vulgate, apparently adopted some sort of stichographic writing system but warned his readers: "Let no one, when he sees the prophets written down in verses, think that they are read metrically in Hebrew or have something in common with the Psalms or the works of Solomon; but, following the practice that is often found in the works of Demonsthenes and Cicero (who both write in prose, not verse) that they are written down in keeping with periodic style [*ut per cola scribantur et commata*], so I as well, out of regard for the reader's convenience, have distinguished my new translation with a new manner of writing (J. P. Migne, *Patrologia Latina* 28.771).

7. See in general Sid Z. Leiman, *The Canonization of Hebrew Scripture: The Talmudic and Midrashic Evidence*, Transactions of the Connecticut Academy of Arts and Sciences 47 (Hamden, 1976). The separation of Lamentations (traditionally

ascribed to Jeremiah) from the book of Jeremiah proper in many manuscripts following this canonical arrangement may suggest a conscious distinction between prophecy and poetry.

8. See Uriel Simon, *Four Approaches to the Book of Psalms from R. Seʿadya Gaʾon to R. Abraham ibn Ezra* [Hebrew] (Ramat Gan, Israel, 1982).

9. See, e.g., Babylonian Talmud Megilla 32a (Rabbi Yoḥanan's injunction that Scripture and Mishnah must be learned and practiced to a tune); cf. Jer. Talmud Megillah 3:7 and my discussion of it in "Is There But One Song?" *Biblica* 63 (1982): 338 n. 21.

10. Contemporary exegetes read the verbs in this sentence as second person, thus, "Until you arose, Deborah, arose as a mother in Israel" (Revised Standard Version). It may even be that "Deborah" throughout is not a proper name but a title, like "prophetess" (*nĕbîʾāh*).

11. I have examined this topic in greater detail in " 'The Bible as Literature' in Late Antiquity and the Middle Ages," *Hebrew University Studies in Literature and the Arts* 11 (1983): 20–70.

12. Philo of Alexandria, "Life of Moses" 1.23; and "Contemplative Life," p. 3. See my discussion in *Idea of Biblical Poetry,* pp. 128–29, 140.

13. Cf. Acts 7:22—"Pharaoh's daughter adopted him [Moses] and brought him up as her own son, and Moses was educated in all the wisdom of Egypt, and he was powerful in his words and in his actions."

14. Josephus, *Jewish Antiquities* 2.16.4, 4.8.44, 7.12.3.

15. R. H. Conolly, ed., *Didascalia apostolorum* (Oxford, 1929), 12–13.

16. See, e.g., Clement of Alexandria, *Exhortation to the Greeks* 6.59, 7.64. The former passage observes: "For there is a certain divine effluence distilled into all men without exception, but especially into those who spend their lives in thought; wherefore they admit, even though against their will, that God is one, that He is unbegotten and indestructible, that somewhere on high in the outermost spaces of the Heavens, in his own privater watchtower, He truly exists forever."

17. It is true that Elijah finds God not in the strong wind or earthquake or fire but in the "still small voice" (1 Kings 19:12), but as many commentators have suggested, that he does so is certainly a reflex of the Sinai narrative, as well as perhaps an anti-Baal polemic.

18. See on this subject the discussion of Bruce Vawter, *Biblical Inspiration* (Philadelphia, 1972), esp. pp. 8–19.

19. It is perhaps not pointless to stress here that "canonization" (unlike the picture often given in Old Testament introductions and the like) was not an event but a centuries-long process of deciding what texts to teach and copy and what texts to drop, etc., long before the final drawing of boundaries alluded to.

20. Plato, *Dialogues,* trans. Benjamin Jowett (New York, 1892), 1.223–24.

21. Philo, *Special Laws* 1.65, translation in F. H. Colson, *Philo* (Cambridge, Mass., 1937), 5.137.

22. Philo, "Who Is the Heir," pp. 264–65, in Colson, *Philo* 4.419. This passage is particularly reminiscent of another description of prophecy found in Plato, *Timaeus* 71–72: "No man, when he is in his wits, attains prophetic truth and inspiration; but when he receives the inspired word, either his intelligence is enthralled in sleep, or he is demented by some distemper or possession. And he

who would understand what he remembers to have been said, whether in a dream or when he is awake, by the prophetic and inspired nature, or would determine by reason the meaning of the apparitions which he has seen, and what indications they afford to this man or that, of past, present, or future good and evil, must first recover his wits. But while he continues demented he cannot judge of the visions which he sees or the words which he utters" (Plato, *Dialogues* 3.493–94). Note also that this same motif turns up in later rabbinic writings: "Said R. Joshua the Priest . . . Even Elihu prophesied without knowing what he was prophesying, as it is written, 'What my lips know they have spoken clearly' [Job 33:3; i.e., my lips know, but I do not]. R. Elʿazar in the name of R. Yosé b. Zimra: Even Samuel, the master of the prophets, prophesied and did not know, as it is said, '[And Samuel said to the people: . . .] And the Lord sent Jerubaʿal . . . and Samuel . . .' [1 Sam. 12:11]. It does not say 'and sent me,' but 'Samuel,' for he did not know what he was prophesying" (see *Yalqut Šimʿoni* 841 [ad Ps. 90] and parallels).

23. It may have been to others: the version of this story in the anonymous "Letter of Aristeas" (301–7) does not have the translators work independently, but they compare their various versions.

24. Philo, *Moses* 2.37, in Colson, *Philo* 6.466–67.

25. A number of recent works have been devoted to the phenomenon of the sibylline oracles. An excellent short summary of scholarship is J. J. Collins, "The Sibylline Oracles," in *Jewish Writings of the Second Temple Period,* ed. M. E. Stone, Compendia rerum iudaicarum ad Novum Testamentum 2.2 (Philadelphia, 1984), pp. 357–81. See also Collins's translation of the texts (plus introduction and bibliography) in J. H. Charlesworth, *The Old Testament Pseudepigrapha* (Garden City, N.Y., 1983), 1.317–472.

26. Clement of Alexandria, *Miscellanies* 6.5.

27. L. Caecilius Firmianus Lactantius, *Opera omnia,* ed. Samuel Brandt (repr. New York, 1965), pp. 13–14.

28. See in general Domenico Comparetti, *Virgilio nel Medio Evo* (Livorno, 1872).

29. See Harald Hagendahl, *Augustine and the Latin Classics* (Göteborg, 1967), 443; cf. in general his *Latin Fathers and the Classics* (Göteborg, 1958); Jacques Fontaine, *Isidore de Séville et la culture classique* (Paris, 1959); and G. L. Ellspermann, *The Attitude of the Early Christian Latin Writers toward Pagan Literature and Learning* (Washington, D.C., 1949).

30. Again, I have discussed this tendency at length in "The Bible as Literature," esp. pp. 47–57.

31. Sir Philip Sidney, *Defense of Poetry,* reprinted in J. W. Hebel et al., *Tudor Poetry and Prose* (New York, 1953), p. 806.

32. George Puttenhem, *The Arte of English Poesie,* in *English Literary Criticism: The Renaissance,* ed. O. B. Hardison (New York, 1963), p. 153.

33. Thomas Lodge, *A Defense of Poetry* (London, 1853), p. 12. The assertion about Isaiah is, to my knowledge, not to be found in Josephus (or, for that matter, in Origen). On these, see my *Idea of Biblical Poetry,* 140–48. An excellent study of the continuation of this theme into the following century is Barbara Lewalski's *Protestant Poetics and the Seventeenth-Century Religious Lyric* (Princeton, 1979).

34. Here and throughout I refer to George Gregory's widely diffused transla-

tion of Lowth's *Lectures on the Sacred Poetry of the Hebrews* (Boston, 1829), pp. 151, 176, 178–79. It is to be noted that Lowth's argument turns on a subtle twist, without which his claims might easily be denounced as blasphemy. In asserting that biblical prophecy and poetry share "one common name" (i.e., both are "poetry"), he adds in the same breath "one common origin, one common author, the Holy Spirit." Lowth thus simultaneously asserts the communality of biblical poetry and biblical prophecy at the expense (as it were) of stressing the great gulf that separates both from ordinary human creations. He thereby defuses his "prophecy equals poetry" argument for pietists: it becomes a quibble about genre. But having elsewhere in his book exhaustively demonstrated that biblical poetry does not in fact differ from other verse in its "native force and beauty" and that it would be specious, therefore, to argue that such poetry is "not . . . conformable to the principles of science, nor to be circumscribed by any rules of art" (p. 22), he makes clear his own opinion that, however much "the Holy Spirit" differs from human authorship, the gulf separating biblical from other species of poetry is not unbridgeable.

35. Such a classification was necessitated because (semantic) parallelism is only at best—and with great simplification—an intermittent feature of biblical poetry: Lowth's "synthetic" parallelism was in fact a grab bag into which to toss any binary line that was not analyzable as either "synonymous" or "antithetical."

36. Lowth, *Sacred Poetry,* pp. 151, 147.

2. Imagining Prophecy, Alan Cooper

1. David J. Fanning, describing Sviatoslav Richter's performance of Franz Liszt's "Feux Follets," in *Gramophone* (June 1988), 56.

2. Paul Valéry, "Poetry and Abstract Thought," in *The Art of Poetry,* trans. Denise Folliot, Bollingen Series 45.7 (New York, 1958), p. 57.

3. Seamus Heaney, "Feeling into Words," in *Preoccupations: Selected Prose, 1968–1978* (London, 1984), pp. 48–49. Heaney is obviously alluding to Philip Sidney's *Defence of Poetry.* I use the Jan van Dorsten edition (Oxford, 1966), pp. 21–22.

4. Sylvia Plath, "Black Rook in Rainy Weather," in *Collected Poems* (New York, 1981), pp. 56–57.

5. Abraham Joshua Heschel, *The Prophets* (New York, 1975), pt. 1, p. ix, hereafter cited in the text by part and page numbers.

6. Northrop Frye, *The Great Code: The Bible and Literature* (Toronto, 1982), pp. 126–28.

7. Robert Lowth, *Lectures on the Sacred Poetry of the Hebrews,* trans. George Gregory, 4th ed. (London, 1839), pp. 194–95 (lecture 18): "It is sufficiently apparent, that the word *Nabi* was used by the Hebrews in an ambiguous sense, and that it equally denoted a prophet, a poet, or a musician, under the influence of Divine inspiration." For the contrary position, see Johann Gottfried von Herder, *The Spirit of Hebrew Poetry,* trans. James Marsh, Burlington, Vt., 1833), 2.50: "The conception [of the prophet] now given, obviously did not include that of a musician and poet. . . . By the term seers, . . . they were clearly distinguished from minstrels." I shall return to the issue of prophecy and poetry later. For a

splendid discussion of the relationship between inspiration and technique, see K. K. Ruthven, *Critical Assumptions* (Cambridge, 1979), pp. 51–82; also René Wellek and Austin Warren, *Theory of Literature,* 3d ed. (New York, 1970), pp. 81–93.

8. On these alternatives and some mediating positions, see Bernhard Lang, "The Making of Prophets in Israel," in his *Monotheism and the Prophetic Minority* (Sheffield, 1983), pp. 92–113.

9. Herder, *Spirit of Hebrew Poetry* 2.59.

10. Johannes Lindblom, *Prophecy in Ancient Israel* (Philadelphia, 1962), p. 219.

11. As Gene M. Tucker remarks in his comprehensive survey of recent scholarship on prophecy, "Interest in the psychology of prophecy . . . ha[s] receded in recent years" ("Prophecy and the Prophetic Literature," in *The Hebrew Bible and Its Modern Interpreters,* ed. Douglas A. Knight and Gene M. Tucker [Philadelphia, 1985], p. 325). A brief but excellent survey of the state of the question (with bibliography) is Robert R. Wilson, "Biblical Prophecy," in *The Encyclopedia of Religion* (New York, 1987), 12.14–23. For more detail, see John Sawyer, *Prophecy and the Prophets of the Old Testament* (Oxford, 1987). For an insightful critique of recent scholarship, see T. R. Hobbs, "The Search for Prophetic Consciousness: Comments on Method," *Biblical Theology Bulletin* 25 (1985): 136–41. Hobbs remarks that discussions of the "social location" of the prophets typically fail to deal clearly with their "inner motivation and self-consciousness."

12. Harry Austryn Wolfson, "The Veracity of Scripture from Philo to Spinoza," in his *Religious Philosophy: A Group of Essays* (New York, 1965), p. 218.

13. Ibid., pp. 241–45.

14. Morton Smith, "The Present State of Old Testament Studies," *Journal of Biblical Literature* 88 (1969): 20.

15. I use the term *phenomenology* in the general sense of "the comparative study and the classification of different types of religious phenomena." It is also used in more technical ways. See Douglas Allen, "Phenomenology of Religion," in *The Encyclopedia of Religion* 11.273.

16. For historical reconstruction, see, for example, Joseph Blenkinsopp, *A History of Prophecy in Israel* (Philadelphia, 1983). For a history of religious ideas, see, for example, Klaus Koch, *The Prophets,* trans. Margaret Kohl, vol. 1: *The Assyrian Period* (Philadelphia, 1983), and vol. 2. *Babylonian and Persian Periods* (Philadelphia, 1984).

17. See Sid Z. Leiman, *The Canonization of Hebrew Scripture: The Talmudic and Midrashic Evidence,* Transactions of the Connecticut Academy of Arts and Sciences 47 (Hamden, 1976), pp. 28–29. On what it meant to "publish" a book in the ancient world, see Saul Lieberman, *Hellenism in Jewish Palestine,* 2d ed. (New York, 1962), pp. 85–86.

18. See Moshe Greenberg, "The Stabilization of the Text of the Hebrew Bible, Reviewed in the Light of the Biblical Materials from the Judean Desert," *Journal of the American Oriental Society* 76 (1956): 157–67; also Emanuel Tov, "A Modern Textual Outlook Based on the Qumran Scrolls," *Hebrew Union College Annual* 53 (1982): 11–27.

19. See Shemaryahu Talmon, "The Old Testament Text," in *The Cambridge History of the Bible,* vol. 1: *From the Beginnings to Jerome,* ed. P. R. Ackroyd and C. F. Evans (Cambridge, 1970), pp. 159–99.

20. See W. Eugene March, "Prophecy," in *Old Testament Form Criticism,* ed. John H. Hayes, Trinity University Monographs in Religion 2 (San Antonio, Tex., 1974), pp. 141–77; Tucker, "Prophecy and Prophetic Literature," pp. 335–42. For a trenchant and well-documented critique of form criticism, see Meir Weiss, *The Bible from Within* (Jerusalem, 1984), pp. 47–73, 410–16. While Weiss does not deny the existence and importance of literary conventions for biblical authors, he is dubious of the criteria that form critics use to identify biblical genres. Yet even if those critics *could* characterize the genres accurately, he argues, they would still be overemphasizing generalities of form at the expense of the particularities of individual works (esp. pp. 60–63).

21. See Tucker's brief remarks, "Prophecy and Prophetic Literature," pp. 342–45. For more detail, see Douglas A. Knight, *Rediscovering the Traditions of Israel,* Society of Biblical Literature Dissertation Series 9, Rev. ed. (Missoula, Mont., 1975), pp. 26–31 et passim (references in index s.v. "tradition, prophetic"); A. S. Kapelrud, "The Traditio-Historical Study of the Prophets," in *The Productions of Time: Tradition History in Old Testament Scholarship,* ed. Knud Jeppesen and Benedikt Otzen (Sheffield, 1984), pp. 53–66.

22. Blenkinsopp, *A History of Prophecy in Israel,* p. 107.

23. John H. Hayes and Stuart A. Irvine, *Isaiah the Eighth-Century Prophet: His Times and His Preaching* (Nashville, Tenn., 1987), p. 390.

24. See Rudolf Kilian, *Jesaja 1–39,* Erträge der Forschung 200 (Darmstadt, 1983); Hayes and Irvine, *Isaiah,* pp. 387–400. The case of Isaiah is merely exemplary. Every prophetic book raises similar (and sometimes considerably more complex) literary-historical problems.

25. See C. R. North, "Isaiah," in *The Interpreter's Dictionary of the Bible* (Nashville, Tenn., 1962), esp. 2.734–44.

26. Among those who have theorized about disciples, see especially Sigmund Mowinckel, *Prophecy and Tradition: The Prophetic Books in the Light of the Study of the Growth and History of the Tradition* (Oslo, 1946); Alfred Haldar, *Associations of Cult Prophets among the Ancient Semites* (Uppsala, 1945). Mowinckel's position on Isaiah, first advanced in a Norwegian monograph published in 1926, is expounded by Knight, *Rediscovering the Traditions of Israel,* pp. 222–24. Knight remarks: "Isaiah's ministry created a prophetic community which preserved, interpreted, transmitted, and finally set in writing the message of Isaiah. This group of disciples was expressly chosen by Isaiah for the purpose of preserving his message" (p. 223). The prophecies were written down when it was thought that they transcended the specific occasion of their utterance. On the lack of consensus, see the important remarks in Joseph Blenkinsopp, *Prophecy and Canon: A Contribution to the Study of Jewish Origins* (Notre Dame, Ind., 1977), pp. 103–6; also Brevard Childs, *Introduction to the Old Testament as Scripture* (Philadelphia, 1979), pp. 325–38.

27. Emanuel Tov, *The Text-Critical Use of the Septuagint in Biblical Research,* Jerusalem Biblical Studies 3 (Jerusalem, 1981), p. 33. See also Ernst Würthwein, *The Text of the Old Testament,* trans. Errol F. Rhodes (Grand Rapids, Mich., 1979), pp. 103–19.

28. Tov also notes that on occasion "*textual* witnesses reflect different stages in the development of the books and thus contribute to literary rather than textual criticism" (*Text-Critical Use,* p. 33).

29. For a simple example of text criticism at work, consider the second clause of Isaiah 3:12. Authorized Version translates, "and women rule over them." For Hebrew *nāšîm,* "women," the ancient Greek and Aramaic translators apparently read *nōšîm,* "creditors." This reading is reflected in the New English Bible: "and usurers lord it over them." On the other hand, the New Jewish Publication Society translators conjecture an emendation of *nāšîm* to *nĕʿārîm,* "boys," based on a stylistic parallel between 3:12 and 3:4–5. All three renderings make sense, and all three have their supporters among modern scholars.

30. Moshe Greenberg, *Ezekiel 1–20,* Anchor Bible (Garden City, N.Y., 1983), 22, 23. Two good introductions to the state of the text-critical art are Ralph W. Klein, *Textual Criticism of the Old Testament* (Philadelphia, 1974); P. Kyle McCarter, Jr., *Textual Criticism: Recovering the Text of the Hebrew Bible* (Philadelphia, 1986).

31. Robert R. Wilson, *Sociological Approaches to the Old Testament* (Philadelphia, 1984), pp. 67–68. Wilson's major contribution to the study of prophecy is his *Prophecy and Society in Ancient Israel* (Philadelphia, 1980).

32. Lindblom, *Prophecy in Ancient Israel,* p. 108.

33. Wilson, *Prophecy and Society,* pp. 21–134. The ancient Near Eastern texts that are most commonly compared with biblical prophecy are the twenty-eight "prophetic" texts from Mari. See most recently Abraham Malamat, "A Forerunner of Biblical Prophecy: The Mari Documents," in *Ancient Israelite Religion: Essays in Honor of Frank Moore Cross,* ed. Patrick D. Miller, Jr., et al. (Philadelphia, 1987), pp. 33–52 (and note the works cited on p. 48 n. 2). For a brief summary, see Tucker, "Prophecy and Prophetic Literature," pp. 345–47.

34. Thomas W. Overholt, *Prophecy in Cross-Cultural Perspective,* Society of Biblical Literature Sources for Biblical Study 17 (Atlanta, 1986), p. 7.

35. Wilson, *Prophecy and Society,* pp. 133–34. The major influence on Wilson was I. M. Lewis, *Ecstatic Religion* (Baltimore, 1971). I vividly remember the thrill of discovery that accompanied Wilson's presentation of Lewis to his Old Testament seminar at Yale.

36. Wilson, *Prophecy and Society,* pp. 135–308.

37. Gary A. Herion, "The Impact of Modern and Social Science Assumptions on the Reconstruction of Israelite History," *Journal for the Study of the Old Testament* 34 (1986): 10–14.

38. See, for example, Robert P. Carroll, *When Prophecy Failed: Cognitive Dissonance in the Prophetic Traditions of the Old Testament* (New York, 1979); David L. Petersen, *The Roles of Israel's Prophets,* Journal for the Study of the Old Testament Supplement Series 17 (Sheffield, 1981). See the highly critical review of Petersen by David Noel Freedman in *Journal of Biblical Literature* 102 (1983): 464–66. A skeptical attitude toward this whole approach, with special reference to Carroll, has been set forth by Cyril S. Rodd in "On Applying a Sociological Theory to Biblical Studies," *Journal for the Study of the Old Testament* 19 (1981): 95–106. The following is excerpted from Rodd's conclusion (p. 104): "I would claim that the attempt to apply sociological theories to biblical documents is not likely to be fruitful. The chance of testing a hypothesis is so slight as to be negligible. Thus what remains possible is either to accept the theory as valid for the biblical period and then to use it to organize and interpret the evidence [i.e., the method of Wilson, Petersen, and Carroll—AC], . . . or else to use the theories entirely

heuristically to suggest lines of research, which then have to stand or fall on their own merit. The first is illegitimate, the second can be fruitful, but only so long as the researcher does not incorporate in his study assumptions derived from the theory."

39. For an interesting analysis and critique of Heschel's theory of prophecy, see Benjamin Uffenheimer, "Prophecy and Sympathy" [Hebrew], in *Teʿuda II: Bible Studies, Y. M. Grintz in Memoriam,* ed. Benjamin Uffenheimer (Tel Aviv, 1982), pp. 17–35. In general, I do not think that Heschel's work has received the attention it deserves.

40. Alan Cooper, "On Reading the Bible Critically and Otherwise," in *The Future of Biblical Studies: The Hebrew Scriptures,* ed. Richard Elliott Friedman and H. G. M. Williamson, Semeia Studies (Atlanta, 1987), pp. 61, 66. For an excellent account of the theological underpinnings of historical-critical scholarship, see Robert A. Oden, Jr., *The Bible without Theology: The Theological Tradition and Alternatives to It* (San Francisco, 1988). Oden's "alternatives" are predictably derived from the social sciences.

41. For an excellent encapsulation of the contrast, see the remarks of Matitiahu Tsevat, in *Biblical Archaeology Today: Proceedings of the International Congress on Biblical Archaeology, Jerusalem, April 1984* (Jerusalem, 1985), pp. 88–89: "The study of history and the study of literature undertake to answer different questions. The former asks: What was the case? The latter asks: What is meant, or what is the sense, and how is the sense rendered?" For two outstanding examples of the synchronic approach to the prophets which raise grave doubts about the assumptions and achievements of historical criticism, see Moshe Greenberg, "The Vision of Jerusalem in Ezekiel 8–11: A Holistic Interpretation," in *The Divine Helmsman: Studies on God's Control of Human Events, Presented to Lou H. Silberman,* ed. James L. Crenshaw and Samuel Sandmel (New York, 1980), pp. 143–164; idem, "What Are Valid Criteria for Determining Inauthentic Matter in Ezekiel?" in *Ezekiel and His Book: Textual and Literary Criticism and Their Interrelation,* ed. J. Lust, Bibliotheca Ephemeridum Theologicarum Lovaniensium (Leuven, 1986), pp. 123–35. See also Greenberg, *Ezekiel 1–20,* pp. 18–27.

42. Wilson, *Sociological Approaches,* pp. 67–80; see also the summary in Tucker, "Prophecy and Prophetic Literature," pp. 354–55.

43. I want it to be clear that I am approaching the medieval material as a biblicist and not as a medievalist. From the medievalist viewpoint, my use of that material would probably be considered eclectic and idiosyncratic.

44. My translations of the Bible, here and throughout, are based on the New Jewish Publication Society translation.

45. Eliezer de Beaugency, *Kommentar zu Ezechiel und den XII kleinen Propheten,* ed. S. Poznański (Warsaw, 1909), p. 18.

46. Robert P. Carroll, *Jeremiah,* Old Testament Library (Philadelphia, 1986), p. 460.

47. For references to recent scholarly treatments of this topic, see Carroll, *Jeremiah,* p. 450.

48. See Colette Sirat, *A History of Jewish Philosophy in the Middle Ages* (Cambridge, 1985), pp. 28, 51–53; Seʿadya Gaʾon, *Book of Doctrines and Beliefs,* trans. Alexander Altmann, in *Three Jewish Philosophers* (New York, 1965 [orig. 1945]), p.

106. Cf. the view of Abraham ibn Ezra, discussed in Sirat, pp. 108–10: Prophets, in contrast to scientists and astrologers, "know the mysteries of the superior world and can perform in this world miracles that surpass the limits of the natural laws." See also Maimonides, "Epistle to Yemen," trans. Abraham Halkin, in *Crisis and Leadership: Epistles of Maimonides* (Philadelphia, 1985), pp. 113–14.

49. For Qirqisani's remarks and related texts by others, see Ben Zion Dinur, *Yisrael ba-Golah* (Tel Aviv, 1961), 1.2.228–31. The prophet Muḥammad, according to Muslim tradition, was unlettered (*ummi*). This attribute is used to refute the accusation that he composed the Qur'ān himself and then falsely claimed divine origin for it.

50. See especially the superb discussion of Joseph Karo's celestial source—his *maggid*—by R. J. Zwi Werblowsky, *Joseph Karo: Lawyer and Mystic* (Rev. ed.; Philadelphia, 1977), pp. 1–23, 257–86. Rabbi Shelomo b. Adret, *She'elot u-Teshuvot* (Vienna, 1812), pp. 71b–72a, responsum 548. My thanks to Daniel Frank for this reference.

51. B.Shabbat 92a; B.Nedarim 38a. Later commentators generally interpret this statement allegorically. On Maimonides' use of the saying, see (conveniently) Y. Qafiḥ's comments on *Hilkhot Yesodei ha-Torah* 7.1 in his edition of *Sefer ha-Madda'* (Jerusalem, 1984), pp. 156–57 n. 2.

52. Maimonides, *Guide for the Perplexed* 2.32. I refer to the work in the edition of Y. Qafiḥ (Jerusalem, 1972) and cite it in the translation of M[ichael] Friedländer (New York, 1946 [orig. London, 1885]). I prefer the Friedländer translation to the more accurate rendering by Shlomo Pines (Chicago, 1963) because of its greater readability. See also *She'elot R. Ḥoṭer ben Shelomo,* ed. Y. Qafiḥ (Jerusalem, 1984), question 12, pp. 193–94 (= David Blumenthal, *The Philosophic Questions and Answers of Ḥoṭer ben Shelomo* (Leiden, 1981), question 34, pp. 158–59); R. Shimon ben Ṣemaḥ Duran, *Sefer Magen Avot* (Livorno, 1785), p. 74b.

53. Maimonides, *Guide* 2.32 (Friedländer 2.164). See also Abraham ibn Migash, *Sefer Kevod Elohim* 1.26 (Constantinople, 1585; rpr. Jerusalem, 1976), p. 54b. The major alternative to Maimonides' view is that of Yehudah ha-Levi, who argues that all Jews have a genetic predisposition for prophecy (which is why even the most loyal convert can never prophesy), but that it manifests itself outwardly only in those who are "worthy of having the divine light and providence made visible to them." Prophetic revelation, moreover, takes place only in the land of Israel. See *Kuzari* 1.95, 115, 2.8–14 (trans. Hartwig Hirschfeld [New York, 1964], pp. 64–67, 79, 88–92).

54. Joseph Albo, *Sefer ha-Ikkarim* 3.8 (Warsaw ed., pp. 219–20). A nice complement to Albo's remark is Menahem Meiri's explanation of why the books of Daniel and Psalms are not included among the prophetic writings. (The modern scholarly explanation is chronological: Daniel and Psalms were composed after the prophetic canon was closed.) Meiri rejects the usual reason given by the medieval commentators, namely that the Hagiographa manifest a lower order of inspiration than the Prophets. He continues: "We find in this book [of Psalms] numerous psalms that are entirely prophetic of the future, concerning, in particular, the destruction of the Temple and its rebuilding, as well as other future matters. . . . And in Daniel there are powerful and wonderful prophecies, revealing mysteries, some of them clear and some obscured until the end time. . . . The

principle of the matter, in my opinion, is that any prophet who was not commissioned for the purpose of admonishing the people for their evil deeds, or setting them on the upright path, or commanding them in political and military matters—even though that person was a prophet, his words were not included among the prophetic writings." The principal criterion for inclusion in "Prophets," then, is neither the foretelling of the future nor the level of inspiration but the admonitory character of the message. See Meiri's *Peirush le-Sefer Tehillim,* ed. Yosef Hakohen (Jerusalem, 1936), pp. 9–10.

55. Maimonides, *Guide* 2.38 (Friedländer 2.183).

56. Isaac Polgar, *Ezer ha-Dat,* ed. Jacob S. Levinger (Tel Aviv, 1984), pp. 88, 118. See also Sirat, *History of Jewish Philosophy,* pp. 319–22.

57. Duran, *Magen Avot,* p. 75a.

58. John Skinner, *Prophecy and Religion: Studies in the Life of Jeremiah* (Cambridge, 1922), pp. 190–200.

59. Maimonides, *Guide* 2.36 (Friedländer 2.177).

60. *Sifrei* on Deuteronomy, chap. 175 (ed. Finkelstein, p. 221), followed by Rashi on Deuteronomy 18:22 (ed. Berliner, pp. 386–87); Ramban on Deuteronomy 18:21 (ed. Chavel, 2.430–31); Ralbag, *Commentary on the Torah* [Hebrew] (Venice, 1547), pp. 225b–226a, 227b (with considerable elaboration). Also, with an interesting twist, Sforno on Deuteronomy 18:22 (ed. Gottlieb, p. 338).

61. On this point, see Herbert Davidson, "Maimonides' Secret Position on Creation," in *Studies in Medieval Jewish History and Literature,* ed. Isadore Twersky (Cambridge, Mass., 1979), esp. pp. 22–27.

62. *Sifrei* on Deuteronomy, chap. 357 (ed. Finkelstein, p. 430), with parallels.

63. Ḥasdai Crescas, *Sefer Or Adonai* (Ferrara, 1555), 2.4.3.

64. See Robert P. Carroll, *From Chaos to Covenant* (London: 1981), pp. 192–97.

65. Polgar, *Ezer ha-Dat,* p. 116. The Ninevites' repentance reverses the divine decree. See also Rashbam (ed. Rosin, p. 217) and Ḥizquni (ed. Chavel, p. 564) on Deuteronomy 18:22; Elias Bickerman, *Four Strange Books of the Bible* (New York, 1967), pp. 33–48. A classic philosophical statement of this point is by Levi ben Gershom, *The Wars of the Lord* 2.6 (trans. Seymour Feldman [Philadelphia, 1987], 2.59–60): In contrast to the visions of dreamers and diviners, "everything that a prophet transmits is true, although . . . contingent with respect to choice. Accordingly, it is said that the evil predicted by the prophet need not be fulfilled, since it is possible for that man or that nation to avoid it through choice, which has been given as an instrument for this purpose. . . . However, the good that a prophet predicts will doubtless occur, . . . since the human intellect, which is the principle of choice, motivates a person to achieve the good."

66. See the discussion of Qirqisani's retort to this suggestion in Sirat, *History of Jewish Philosophy,* pp. 52–53.

67. Maimonides, *Hilkhot Yesodei ha-Torah* 7.6 (ed. Qafiḥ, p. 159), and *Guide* 2.34 (end), read in the light of 2.6; also explicitly *Guide* 2.36; Ḥoṭer ben Shelomo, ed. Qafiḥ, question 19, pp. 205–6 (= ed. Blumenthal, question 32, pp. 152–54); Duran, *Magen Avot,* p. 15b; Nissim b. Moses, in Sirat, *History of Jewish Philosophy,* p. 281. For a full exposition of Maimonides' theory of prophecy, see Alvin J. Reines, *Maimonides and Abrabanel on Prophecy* (Cincinnati, 1970), pp. xvi–lxiv. See

also the excellent summary statement by Seymour Feldman, in *Wars of the Lord* 2.15–16. The "imagined" character of non-Mosaic prophecy was a sore point for critics of Maimonides. See especially Ramban on Genesis 18:1 (ed. Chavel, 1.103–7); Rabbi Yom Ṭov b. Abraham Alashvili (Riṭva), *Sefer ha-Zikkaron,* ed. K. Kahana (2d ed.; Jerusalem, 1982), pp. 55–62.

68. *Sefer Ruaḥ Ḥen* (Warsaw, 1826), end chap. 4, p. 13a; also Rabbi Abraham ibn Daud, *Sefer ha-Emunah ha-Ramah,* ed. S. Weil (Frankfurt, 1852), p. 29.

69. Maimonides, *Guide* 2.36 (Friedländer 2.175).

70. What little I know about this subject I owe to the kind indulgence of my friend Dr. Joel Goldberg, of the Clark Institute, Toronto. He is, of course, not responsible for my errors. I have also found the following books to be informative and illuminating: Alan Richardson, *Mental Imagery* (London, 1969); Sydney J. Segal, ed., *Imagery: Current Cognitive Approaches* (New York, 1971); P. W. Sheehan, ed., *The Function and Nature of Imagery* (New York, 1972); Edward S. Casey, *Imagining: A Phenomenological Study* (Bloomington, Ind., 1976); Ned Block, ed., *Imagery* (Cambridge, Mass., 1981); Peter E. Morris and Peter J. Hampson, *Imagery and Consciousness* (New York, 1983).

71. See Sydney J. Segal, "Processing of the Stimulus in Imagery and Perception," in Segal, *Imagery,* pp. 69–100; idem, "Assimilation of a Stimulus in the Construction of an Image: The Perky Effect Revisited," in *Function and Nature of Imagery,* ed. Sheehan, pp. 203–30; Block, *Imagery,* p. 47; Morris and Hampson, *Imagery and Consciousness,* pp. 65–90. For a critique of what he calls "apparent indistinguishability," see Casey, *Imagining,* pp. 147–51. Casey's position is that "imagining is unreducible to perceiving as well as independent of it" (p. 177), a radical departure from classical, medieval, and most modern views.

72. In the words of Morris and Hampson (*Imagery and Consciousness,* p. 137), "Although it is generally accepted that there is some equivalence between imagery and perception, it is something of an understatement to assert that there is obviously considerable disagreement among researchers about the nature of the representations and processes used in imagery and perception."

73. A. Graeme Auld, "Prophets and Prophecy in Jeremiah and Kings," *Zeitschrift für die alttestamentliche Wissenschaft* 96 (1984), 66–82; idem, "Prophets through the Looking Glass: Between Writings and Moses," *Journal for the Study of the Old Testament* 27 (1983):3–23.

74. Amos 7:14–15 is also relevant in this connection. A. G. Auld has recently argued (*Amos* [Sheffield, 1986], p. 30) that for the author of that text, "one did not have to be a 'prophet' in order to receive the divine imperative to 'prophesy'; and indeed that such a command did not turn one into a 'prophet.'" (Of course, Amos 3:7 must be deleted for this view to be sustainable.) As in the case of Jeremiah, then, the notion that Amos *was* a prophet might be the product of a tradition that is at odds with the text itself.

75. Robert P. Carroll, "Poets not Prophets: A Response to 'Prophets through the Looking-Glass,'" *Journal for the Study of the Old Testament* 27 (1983):25.

76. Feldman comments in Levi ben Gershom, *Wars of the Lord* 2.14. A collection of the most important medieval texts in English translation can be found in David Bleich, *With Perfect Faith* (New York, 1983), pp. 273–363. For an interesting and relevant study of earlier rabbinic texts, see Robert Goldenberg, "The Problem

of False Prophecy: Talmudic Interpretation of Jeremiah 28 and I Kings 22," in *The Biblical Mosaic: Changing Perspectives*, Semeia Studies (Philadelphia, 1982), pp. 87–103.

77. Isaac Abravanel, *Commentary on the Latter Prophets* [Hebrew] (Rpr. Tel Aviv, n.d.), p. 494. For a detailed account of Abravanel's critique of Maimonides, see Reines, *Maimonides and Abrabanel on Prophecy.*

78. See, for example, Abraham ibn Ezra's commentary on Isaiah 57:19. On the actual etymology of *nĕbîʾîm* (probably from a verb meaning "to call"), see Wilson, *Prophecy and Society*, pp. 136–38.

79. See Y. Tishby, *Messianism in the Time of the Expulsion from Spain and Portugal* [Hebrew] (Jerusalem, 1985), pp. 52–58.

80. Meir Arama, *Sefer Urim ve-Tummim* (Venice, 1603), p. 65b. Arama seems to be transforming a well-known aphorism, "The tongue is the emissary of the mind" or the like (see Israel Davidson, *Otsar ha-Meshalim ve-ha-Pitgamim* [Jerusalem, 1979], pp. 63, 65, nos. 948, 950, 990) into a syllogism: as the prophet is to God, so is the tongue to the mind; in each case, the former is the "emissary and agent of expression" of the latter. Arama's text is difficult here, and I would like to thank my colleagues Ezra Spicehandler and Mark Washofsky, for their helpful criticism of my understanding of it.

81. Maimonides, *Guide* 2.36 (Friedländer 2.173).

82. Text in Rabbi Moshe ben Maimon, *Haqdamot le-Feirush ha-Mishnah* (Jerusalem, 1961), p. 159, translation taken from *Ethical Writings of Maimonides*, ed. R. L. Weiss and C. E. Butterworth (New York, 1975), p. 63. Cf. Maimonides, *Guide* 1.73, prop. X (Friedländer 1.311, 330–339).

83. Harry Austryn Wolfson, *The Philosophy of Spinoza* (New York, 1969), 2.81. See also the detailed discussion of Maimonides' concept of imagination in Yeshayahu Leibowitz et al., *Conversations on the Eight Chapters of Maimonides* [Hebrew] (Jerusalem, 1986), pp. 38–45 et passim.

84. Ibn Daud, *Ha-Emunah ha-Ramah*, p. 29. (All the quotations from ibn Daud in the next two paragraphs are from pp. 29–30.)

85. *Ruaḥ Ḥen*, p. 11b.

86. According to Levi ben Gershom, transmission of prophetic knowledge usually occurs during sleep "because it requires the separation of the intellect or of the imagination or of both of these faculties from the other cognitive faculties of the soul, and this generally occurs during sleep." Moses, as might be expected, "received his prophecies while awake" (*Wars of the Lord*, 2.6 [trans. Feldman, vol. 2.57–58]).

87. Ibn Daud, *Ha-Emunah ha-Ramah*, p. 73.

88. *Ruaḥ Ḥen*, p. 12a; Levi ben Gershom, *Wars of the Lord* 2.6 (trans. Feldman, 2.56).

89. Cf. Sirat, *History of Jewish Philosophy*, pp. 366–67. Note also later manifestations of this view (associated mainly with David Hume), conveniently summarized by Richardson (*Mental Imagery*, pp. 4–6).

90. Crescas, *Or Adonai* 2.4.3.

91. Ḥoṭer ben Shelomo, ed. Qafiḥ, question 12, pp. 193–94 = ed. Blumenthal, question 34, pp. 158–59.

92. Maimonides, *Guide* 2.36 (Friedländer 2.178). See Feldman's important

discussion of this issue in Levi ben Gershom, *Wars of the Lord* 2.21 n. 38. I agree with his statement that "the absence of mediation in Mosaic prophecy refers to the purely *intellectual* reception by Moses of the prophetic emanation; Moses dispensed with the imagination."

93. See, e.g., Crescas, *Or Adonai* 2.4.3: "Although prophecy is generally not something unnatural, the status of Moses exceeds what is natural. It is a wonder among wonders, in order to fix in our minds the perfection and eternity of the Torah."

94. Duran, *Magen Avot,* p. 15b.

95. Levi ben Gershom, *Wars of the Lord* 2.6 (trans. Feldman 2.56).

96. Maimonides, *Guide* 2.45, 36 (Friedländer 2.206, 177).

97. Nissim ben Moses, in Sirat, *History of Jewish Philosophy,* p. 279.

98. *Midrash Tehillim,* ed. Solomon Buber, p. 388; William G. Bruade, trans., *The Midrash on Psalms* (New Haven, Conn., 1959), 2.88.

99. Abravanel, *Commentary on the Latter Prophets,* pp. 40–41. A later, expanded version can be found in Abravanel's commentary on Exodus 15:1 in *Commentary on the Torah* [Hebrew] (repr. Jerusalem, 1964), pp. 122–25. He means compositions that actually bear the title *šîr/šîrâ* or are introduced by a form of the verb *šîr.*

100. See, in general, A. S. P. Woodhouse, "Imagination," in Alex Preminger, ed., *Princeton Encyclopedia of Poetry and Poetics* (Enlarged ed.; Princeton, N.J., 1974), pp. 370–77; also William K. Wimsatt and Cleanth Brooks, *Literary Criticism: A Short History* (New York, 1957), pp. 384–411.

101. J. F. D'Alton, *Roman Literary Theory and Criticism* (New York, 1962), p. 436, and see 435–37, 556–58; Proclus, "On the More Difficult Questions in the *Republic:* The Nature of Poetic Art," in *Classical and Medieval Literary Criticism,* ed. Alex Preminger et al. (New York, 1974), pp. 310–23. See esp. Horace, *Ars poetica,* 309–10 (trans. D. A. Russell, in *Ancient Literary Criticism,* ed. D. A. Russell and M. Winterbottom [Oxford, 1972], p. 288): "Wisdom is the starting-point and source of correct writing. Socratic books will be able to point out to you your material, and once the material is provided the words will follow willingly enough." On the Neoplatonic abandonment of imitation in favor of imagination, see E. E. Sikes, *The Greek View of Poetry* (New York, 1969), pp. 238–39.

102. So, rightly, Dan Pagis, *Secular Poetry and Poetic Theory: Moses ibn Ezra and His Contemporaries* [Hebrew] (Jerusalem, 1970), pp. 47–48. More recently see Joseph Dana, *Poetics of Mediaeval Hebrew Literature according to Moshe ibn Ezra* [Hebrew] (Jerusalem, 1982), pp. 97–105, 217. For an excellent general discussion of "writers as liars," see Ruthven, *Critical Assumptions,* pp. 164–80. The aphorism about "the best part of poetry" is also central to Arabic poetics. See Wolfhart Heinrichs, *Arabische Dichtung und griechische Poetik,* Beiruter Texte und Studien 8 (Beirut, 1969), pp. 56–68; J. C. Bürgel, "Die beste Dichtung ist die lügenreichste," *Oriens* 23–24 (1970–71): 7–102; Vicente Cantarino, *Arabic Poetics in the Golden Age,* Studies in Arabic Literature 4 (Leiden, 1975), pp. 27–40, 80–99.

103. See E. N. Tigerstedt, *Plato's Idea of Poetical Inspiration,* Societas Scientiarum Fennica, Commentationes Humanarum Litterarum 44.2 (Helsinki, 1969), esp. pp. 63–72. A piquant example of the Platonic attitude is the following remark from an essay on Milton by Thomas Macaulay, quoted in Wimsatt and Brooks,

Literary Criticism, pp. 414–15: "Perhaps no person can be a poet, or can even enjoy poetry, without a certain unsoundness of mind. . . . Truth, indeed, is essential to poetry, but it is the truth of madness. The reasonings are just; but the premises are false. . . . Poetry produces an illusion on the eye of the mind, as a magic lantern produces an illusion on the eye of the body. And, as the magic lantern acts best in a dark room, poetry affects its purpose most completely in a dark age."

104. See Cantarino, *Arabic Poetics,* pp. 31–33.

105. James L. Kugel, *The Idea of Biblical Poetry: Parallelism and Its History* (New Haven, Conn., 1981), pp. 204–86.

106. See Brian Hepworth, *Robert Lowth* (Boston, 1978), pp. 47–62; Kugel, *Idea of Biblical Poetry,* pp. 274–86.

107. Lowth, *Lectures on the Sacred Poetry of the Hebrews,* pp. 190–91 (lecture 18).

108. See also James Kugel's attack against "the Bible as literature," in "On the Bible and Literary Criticism," *Prooftexts* 1 (1981): 217–36.

109. David Noel Freedman, "Pottery, Poetry, and Prophecy: An Essay on Biblical Poetry," *Journal of Biblical Literature* 96 (1977): 24.

110. Stephen A. Geller, "Were the Prophets Poets?" *Prooftexts* 3 (1983): 211–21. Geller ignores the many pious commentators who have stressed the Bible's literary excellence. The Jewish exegetes Moses ibn Ezra, Abraham ibn Ezra, and David Qimhi, for example, sought to identify "elegant expression" (*ṣaḥût*) in the Bible. For comparable efforts by Christian scholars, see Luis Alonso Schökel, *Estudios de poética hebrea,* (Barcelona, 1963), pp. 3–8.

111. Robert Alter, *The Art of Biblical Poetry* (New York, 1985), pp. 137–62.

112. See Wimsatt and Brooks, *Literary Criticism,* p. 405; Herbert Grierson, *Milton and Wordsworth: Poets and Prophets* (New York, 1937); Gerard Manley Hopkins, letter to Alexander Baillie, in *A Hopkins Reader,* ed. John Pick (Garden City, N.Y., 1966), p. 129. For a general orientation to the issue, see the stimulating essays in *Poetic Prophecy in Western Literature,* ed. Jan Wojcik and Raymond-Jean Frontain (Rutherford, N.J., 1984).

113. Howard Nemerov, "What Was Modern Poetry? Three Lectures," in his *Figures of Thought: Speculations on the Meaning of Poetry and Other Essays* (Boston, 1978), pp. 190–91, 167, and see 166–83. Cf. Alter's remarks about the "archetypifying force" of prophetic poetry (*The Art of Biblical Poetry,* pp. 146–47). I am a great admirer of Nemerov's biblical poems; see *The Next Room of the Dream* (Chicago, 1962), pp. 30 ("The View from Pisgah"), 43 ("The Fall Again"), 47–52 ("Lot Later"), 73–116 ("Endor"), 119–43 ("Cain"). All are reprinted in *The Collected Poems of Howard Nemerov* (Chicago, 1977).

114. Cooper, "On Reading the Bible," p. 68.

115. Hobbs, "The Search for Prophetic Consciousness," p. 136.

116. *Tanḥuma* Buber *Miqqets,* p. 192 (citing Joel 3:1 as proof). *Tanḥuma Miqqets* 2 (ed. Ets Yosef, p. 49) restricts prophecy in the world to come to Israelites.

3. David the Prophet, James L. Kugel

1. For a discussion of the roots of Acts 2:29–30 and other passages, see J. A. Fitzmyer, "David, 'Being Therefore a Prophet. . . ,' " *Catholic Biblical Quarterly* 34 (1972): 332–39.

2. Although of course this form of psalm exegesis is also characteristic of the Qumran sect and is to be viewed within the overall context of biblical exegesis as practiced there. See in general M. P. Horgan, *Pesharim: Qumran Interpretations of Biblical Books,* Catholic Biblical Quarterly Monograph Series 8 (Washington, D.C., 1979); also Devorah Dimant, "Qumran Sectarian Literature," in M. E. Stone, *Jewish Writings of the Second Temple Period,* ed. M. E. Stone, Compendia Rerum Judaicarum ad Novum Testamentum 2.2 (Philadelphia, 1984), esp. pp. 503–14.

3. David Flusser and Shemuel Safrai, "A Fragment of the Songs of David and Qumran," in *Teʿuda II: Bible Studies, Y. M. Grintz in Memoriam,* ed. Benjamin Uffenheimer (Tel Aviv, 1982), pp. 83–105.

4. See Uriel Simon, *Four Approaches to the Book of Psalms* [Hebrew] (Ramat Gan, Israel, 1982).

5. Fitzmyer, "David 'Being Therefore a Prophet . . .' "

6. J. D. Levenson, "A Technical Meaning for *Nʿ M* in the Hebrew Bible," *Vetus Testamentum* 25 (1985):61–67.

7. Albert Pietersma, "David in the Greek Psalms," *Vetus Testamentum* 30 (1980):213–26.

8. I have discussed the status of music and song in "Topics in the History of the Spirituality of the Psalms," in *Jewish Spirituality from the Bible through the Middle Ages,* ed. Arthur Green (New York, 1986), pp. 113–43.

9. Indeed, Moses himself might have been said to be the founder of these temple rituals, but it was the very absence of their mention in the Pentateuch that made such an assertion problematical in the Chronicler's times.

10. See Patrick D. Miller, Jr., "Trouble and Woe: Interpreting the Biblical Laments," *Interpretation* 37 (1983), 34; also Kugel, "Topics," pp. 116–17.

11. Note also that the great proliferation of pseudepigraphic texts in the last two centuries before the common era may bespeak the same belief that only a well-known prophet or sage or other divinely chosen servant from the past can be a fit author of some book of sacred teaching.

12. It is to be observed in this connection that a number of texts in Chronicles assert that historical records are to be found in the writings of various named prophets (i.e., *nābîʾ*) or seers (*rôʾeh, ḥôzeh*). Thus, 2 Chron. 9:29 observes that the "rest of the deeds of Solomon" are to be found in the "words of Nathan the prophet and in the prophecy [*nĕbûʾāh*] of Ahijah the Shilonite, and in the visions [*ḥăzôt*] of Iddo the seer." Similarly, the deeds of Rehoboam are to be found "written in the words of Shemaya the prophet and Iddo the seer" (2 Chron. 12:15; cf. 1 Chron. 29:29; 2 Chron. 9:29, 13:22, 20:34, 26:22, 32:32, and 33:19; and note the brief discussion in H. G. M. Williamson, *1 and 2 Chronicles* [Grand Rapids, Mich., 1982], pp. 17–19).

13. The situation is complicated somewhat by the superscription of the psalm in question, which, in both the Old Greek and the Masoretic text, connects it with the sons of Korah; but Philo, who apparently cites the line by heart (in fact, he misquotes it) is probably not even aware of the superscription. Cf. Eileen Schuller, *Non-Canonical Psalms from Qumran* (Atlanta, 1986), p. 54 n. 15.

14. This is not to say that he might not have been described as a prophet even earlier. B. Z. Wacholder (*Eupolemus: A Study of Judaeo-Greek Literature* [Cincin-

nati, 1974]) holds that such a reference may have existed in the writings of the second-century B.C.E. historian Eupolemus, though the evidence here is quite inferential; but such a description might in any case flow naturally from a straightforward reading of 2 Sam. 23:1–7 (already discussed). The point is not when "David the prophet" became a possibility but when it began to appear a necessity and so was adopted in some widespread fashion, adopted despite the biblical failure to identify David as a prophet and, in fact, despite the clear separation of (and often opposition between) "king" and "prophet" in biblical history, in David's case as well as others.

15. I have discussed these later stages at length in *The Idea of Biblical Poetry* (New Haven, Conn., 1981).

4. Ancient Greek Poetry, Prophecy, and Concepts of Theory, Gregory Nagy

1. In Homeric poetry, for example, the *aoidos* is described as belonging to the category of the *dēmiourgoi,* "artisans in the *dēmos,*" (*Odyssey* 17.381–85). The word *dēmos,* "administrative district, population," in archaic Greek poetic diction refers to the notion of a local community, with its own traditions, customs, laws, and the like. Other professions that belong to this category of *dēmiourgoi* are the *mantis,* "seer," the *iātēr,* "physician," the *tektōn,* "carpenter," and the *kērux,* "herald" (ibid., in conjunction with 19.135). Cf. Hesiod, *Works and Days* 25–26, where the *aoidos* is juxtaposed with the *tektōn* and the *kerameus,* "potter." The *dēmiourgoi* are socially mobile, as they travel from one *dēmos* to another. There is a reciprocal relationship between the local king and the *dēmiourgoi,* as articulated by the poet (and as presupposed by the *ainos,* "fable," of the Hawk and the Nightingale in Hesiod, *Works and Days* 202–12). For an example of a cognate institution, I cite the Old Irish "people of the craft (*cerd*)," the designation for artisans, including poets, who were juridically immune as they traveled from one *tuath,* "tribe," to another. Old Irish *tuath,* "tribe" (as ruled by a local king), is cognate with Umbrian *touto,* "civitas," and German *Deutsch.* Old Irish *cerd,* "craft," is cognate with Greek *kerdos,* "craft, craftiness, profit"; in the diction of poets such as Pindar, *kerdos* refers to the craft and the potential craftiness of poetry. Cf. N. O. Brown, *Hermes the Thief* (New York, 1947).

2. I offer a detailed discussion in my essay "Hesiod," in *Ancient Writers,* ed. T. J. Luce (New York, 1982), pp. 49–57.

3. Cf. A. L. Ford. *Early Greek Terms for Poetry: Aoidē, Epos, Poiēsis* (Ph.D. diss., Yale University, 1981).

4. J. Kuryłowicz's Fourth Law of Analogy: "Quand à la suite d'une transformation morphologique une forme subit la différentiation, la forme nouvelle correspond à sa fonction primaire (de fondation), la forme ancienne est réservée pour la fonction secondaire (fondée)." See "La nature des procès dits 'analogiques,'" *Acta Linguistica* 5 (1945–49), 15–37; reprinted in *Readings in Linguistics* 2, ed. E. P. Hamp, F. W. Householder, R. Austerlitz (Chicago, 1966), pp. 158–74 (for the Fourth Law, see p. 169 there). By "older form" I mean simply the form that is *already* assigned to a given function, whereas by "newer form" I mean the

form that is *about to be* assigned. As an example, I cite English *quick*, cognate of Latin *vīvus*, "living, alive," which was ousted from the sphere of meaning 'living, alive', becoming semantically specialized in the sense of "lively" and, eventually, "quick" (the older meaning is still evident in such fossils as "the quick and the dead" or "bite the nails to the quick"). There are of course patterns of development that may be described as alternatives to Kuryłowicz's Fourth Law. For one, there will be situations where the competition between newer and older forms leads to the complete ouster of the older form by the newer form. Or else the newer and older forms may achieve coexistence in a suppletive relationship (as in Latin *ferō/ferre/tulī/lātus; tollō, tollere, sustulī, sublātus*) or as morphophonemic variants (on which see F. W. Householder and Gregory Nagy, "Greek," *Current Trends in Linguistics* 9, ed T. A. Sebeok (The Hague, 1962), p. 758.

5. These terms *marked* and *unmarked* have been defined as follows: "The general meaning of a marked category states the presence of a certain (whether positive or negative) property A; the general meaning of the corresponding unmarked category state nothing about the presence of A, and is used chiefly, but not exclusively, to indicate the absence of A" (Roman Jakobson, *Selected Writings* [The Hague, 1971], p. 136). The unmarked category is the general category, which can include the marked category, whereas the reverse situation cannot hold. For example, in an opposition of the English words *interesting* and *boring*, the unmarked members of the opposition is *interesting* because it can be used not only as the opposite of *boring* ("This is interesting, not boring") but also as the general category ("How interesting is this?"). For a useful discussion and bibliography, I cite L. R. Waugh, "Marked and Unmarked: A Choice between Unequals in Semiotic Structure," *Semiotica* 38 (1982): 299–318.

6. On the value of this verb *krainō* as "sanction with authority the accomplishment of a human project and thereby make the project come to be" in expressing the activity of an undifferentiated poet-prophet, see Emile Benveniste, *Le vocabulaire des institutions indo-européennes* (Paris, 1969), 2.35–42.

7. Further discussion in Susan Scheinberg, "The Bee Maidens of the Homeric Hymn to Hermes," *Harvard Studies in Classical Philology* 83 (1979):1–28; also Nagy, "Hesiod," pp. 56–57 n. 2. By "authorizing," the Bee Maidens tell the future: see Benveniste, 2.41.

8. This paragraph is a reworking of what I have argued in Nagy, "Hesiod," p. 57 n. 2.

9. See especially Scheinberg, p. 19.

10. Even the primitive shepherd's pipe, ceded to Hermes when Apollo gets the lyre, is presented as a novelty (*HH* 511–12).

11. Hermes is conventionally represented in the archaic period as a bearded adult. Cf. Walter Burkert, *Greek Religion,* trans. John Raffan (Cambridge, Mass., 1985), p. 158. By contrast, Apollo is an unshorn and beardless ephebe (Burkert, pp. 144–45). Similarly, Dionysus *seems* to be new, not old, but he is in fact both old and new from the standpoint of the myth; similarly, he *seems* to be foreign, not native, but he is in fact both native and foreign from the standpoint of the myth. Cf. Deborah Boedeker, *Aphrodite's Entry into Greek Epic* (Leiden, 1974), pp. 4–5.

12. The testimony of archaic iconography on this theme is neatly articulated in Pausanias 5.18.4.

13. Cf. Gregory Nagy, *The Best of the Achaeans: Concepts of the Hero in Archaic Greek Poetry* (Baltimore, 1979), p. 143.

14. Cf. Walter Burkert, "Apellai und Apollon," *Rheinisches Museum* 118 (1975):1–21.

15. For an extensive discussion with Theognis 15–18 as focus, see Gregory Nagy, "Theognis and Megara: A Poet's Vision of His City," in *Theognis of Megara: Poetry and the Polis,* ed. T. J. Figueira and Gregory Nagy (Baltimore, 1985), pp. 27–29.

16. P. Chantraine, *Dictionnaire étymologique de la langue grecque* (Paris, 1968–80), p. 665.

17. For another such explicit definition, I cite the scholia A to *Iliad* 16.235: "*προφήτας γὰρ λέγουσι τοὺς περὶ τὰ χρηστήρια ἀσχολουμένους καὶ τὰς μαντείας τὰς γινομένας ὑπὸ τῶν ἱερέων ἐκφέροντας* [declarers (*prophētēs* pl.) is the name for those who officiate at oracles and bring forth the mantic utterances (*manteia* pl.) that take place through the agency of the priests]."

18. Joseph Fontenrose, *The Delphic Oracle: Its Responses and Operations, with a Catalogue of Responses* (Berkeley, 1978), p. 218, argues that the official title of the *prophētēs* of the Oracle of Apollo at Delphi was not *prophētēs* but simply *hiereus,* "priest."

19. It is the fact that he is the actor of a speech-act that qualifies the *prophētēs,* "declarer," as a *hupokritēs,* "actor" (Plato, *Timaeus* 72b). A particularly revealing passage is Herodotus 8.135.3, concerning the *prophētēs* of the oracular voice of Apollo at the shrine known as the Ptoön of the Thebans; the official who is actually inspired by Apollo has the title *pro-mantis* (8.135.2). The story has it, as reported by Herodotus, that the *pro-mantis* on one particular occasion made utterances in a non-Greek language (it is made explicit that the utterances were normally in Greek). When they were declared by the *prophētēs,* they were not understood by those present. The story then goes on to report that one Mys took the initiative of writing the words down on a tablet that he impulsively seized from the Thebans who officially accompanied him to consult the oracle. The wording "*ἀπογραψομένους*" and "*συγγραψάμενον,*" in the middle voice, implies that those who consult the oracle not only take notes but commission someone to write a definitive transcript, to be brought back home to their native city.

20. For a minimalist survey of the Pythia's role, see Fontenrose, pp. 196–228.

21. For a collection of testimonia, concerning attempts at bribery, see Fontenrose, p. 224, referring to entries Q137, Q124, and H7 in his catalogue of Delphic responses.

22. *Pace* Fontenrose, pp. 218–19.

23. This possibility, along with others, is discussed by Chantraine, p. 716.

24. I offer an extensive discussion in "*Sēma* and *Noēsis:* Some illustrations," *Arethusa* 16 (1983): 35–55.

25. See François Hartog, *Le miroir d'Hérodote: Essai sur la représentation de l'autre* (Paris, 1980), pp. 368–69.

26. Cognate with English *song*. For extensive commentary on this and the subsequent quotation, see Nagy, "Theognis and Megara," pp. 36–41.

27. By contrast, Herodotus also gives the contemporary Spartan version, according to which Lycurgus got the code from Crete (again, 1.65.4).

28. Or, in the case of athletics, the one who is designated to communicate the sacred message of the victory itself. At Herodotus 1.29.1, Solon gives *theōriā* as the pretext (*pro-phasis*) for his travels, but his other motive, as is made explicit in the narrative, is to prevent his being compelled to undo any aspect of his law code. At 1.30.1, it is made clear that *theōriā* was indeed also his motive. So there are two motives, but only one is made explicit by Solon to his audience; the other motive is kept implicit by Solon but made explicit by Herodotus to *his* audience.

5. Virgil's Messianic Eclogue, Wendell Clausen

1. Servius supposes the Sibyl meant the Etruscan doctrine of ten metallic ages, the last of which was to be ruled by the Sun and end with the extinction of the Etruscan name. See I. S. Ryberg, "Vergil's Golden Age," *Transactions of the American Philological Association* 89 (1958): 115; Bodo Gatz, *Weltalter, goldene Zeit, und sinnverwandte Vorstellungen, Spudasmata* 16 (Hildesheim, 1967), pp. 91–92. It is highly unlikely that the Sibyl mentioned Saturn's reign or Lucina, and out of the question that she made a literary allusion to Aratus. Scholars seem to forget that the Sibyl was not a Hellenistic poet.

2. Greek poets refer to a golden race, Latin poets to a golden age; see H. C. Baldry, "Who Invented the Golden Age?" *Classical Quarterly* 46 (1952): 88–89. In this essay I shall use both terms as seems appropriate.

3. Cf. M. L. West, "Hesiodea," *Classical Quarterly*, n.s. 11 (1961): 133, on Hesiod's *Catalogue of Women* fr. 204.100–4 Merkelbach-West: "Thus the heroic age is not distinguished from the golden race of the *Erga*."

4. Aratus, *Phaenomena* 96–136. A reasonable assumption, as Aratus was widely read in antiquity; not therefore, as it may appear to us, a learned allusion.

5. The identification of **Παρθένος** with **Δίκη** was suggested by Hesiod, *Works and Days* 256: *ἡ δέ τε παρθένος ἐστί Δίκη*; see U. von Wilamowitz-Moellendorff, *Hellenistische Dichtung* (Berlin, 1924), 2.265. In Hesiod, Aidos and Nemesis personified—"their lovely bodies wrapped in white robes" (198)—leave the earth in the iron age, the last. In Aratus, the Virgin leaves the earth in the bronze age, the last in Aratus; Wilamowitz, ibid. 266: "drei Weltalter (mehr konnte er nicht brauchen)."

6. The first Latin poet, in fact, Livius Andronicus fr. 2 Buechner: "pater noster, Saturni filie," translating *Odyssey* 1.45: "*ὦ πάτερ ἡμέτερε Κρονίδη*."

7. Virgil is the first to describe Saturn's reign and Saturn himself as golden: *Georgics* 2.538: "aureus hanc uitam in terris Saturnus agebat"; *Aeneid* 6.792–94: "Augustus Caesar, diui genus, aurea condet/saecula qui rursus Latio regnata per arua/Saturno quondam"—a further development of the fourth eclogue: Augustus will now restore the golden age.

8. Note the urgency of 6 "iam," 7 "iam," 10 "iam."

9. Women in labor implored her aid: Terence, *Adelphoe* 487: "Iuno Lucina, fer opem, serua me obsecro." From the Augustan period on, Lucina was identified, as here, with Diana; see A. S. Pease (1958) on Cicero, *De natura deorum* 2.68.

10. Line 4, that is, the opening line of the original poem; see Felix Jacoby, *Rheinisches Museum* 65 (1910): 77 n. 1; Guenther Jachmann, "Die vierte Ekloge Vergils," *Annali della Scuola Normale Superiore di Pisa* 21 (1952): 49. The style of reference, however, "tuus . . . Apollo," is suitably affectionate and familiar; cf.

Plautus, *Casina* 230: "heia, mea Iuno, non decet esse te tam tristem tuo Ioui"; *Captiui* 157: "Philopolemus tuos" (son); *Mostellaria* 182: "Philolaches tuos" (lover); *Aeneid* 5.52 (Neptune to Venus): "Aeneae . . . tui."

11. See Ronald Syme, *The Roman Revolution* (Oxford, 1939), pp. 217–20.

12. See Appian, *Bellum ciuile* 3.16, 19; also Plutarch, *Antony* 4, 36.

13. Cf. Cicero, *Tusculanae disputationes* 2.22 (Hercules speaking): "haec dextra Lernam taetra mactata excetra/pacauit"; Ovid, *Heroides* 9.13 (Deianira to Hercules): "respice uindicibus pacatum uiribus orbem"; Propertius 3.11.19 (Hercules): "qui pacato statuisset in orbe columnas." Note the "echo" of Virgil in Ovid and Propertius, especially in Ovid. See *Thesaurus Linguae Latinae* s.v.

14. Augustus did not claim descent from Hercules, but comparison with Hercules and Dionysus had become a feature of such encomia; see R. G. Austin (1977) on *Aeneid* 6.801ff.

15. Note the endearment of the repetition εὕδετ', ἐμὰ βρέφεα . . . εὕδετ', ἐμὰ ψυχά and cf. "incipe, parue puer . . . incipe, parue puer."

16. Translation after A. S. F. Gow.

17. Christian Gottlob Heyne (Leipzig, 1776) ad loc.: "est enim res ex eius anni, quo pax facta est, actis dispicienda."

18. "The Idylls of Theocritus," in *The Works and Life of Walter Savage Landor* (London, 1876), 8.361–62.

19. In 35 B.C., as I have argued in *Harvard Studies in Classical Philology* 76 (1972): 201–5.

20. See Jacoby, p. 77 n. 1; and Jachmann, p. 49.

21. As suggested by A. D. Nock; see W. W. Tarn, "Alexander Helios and the Golden Age," *Journal of Roman Studies* 22 (1932): 156 n. 4.

22. Servius Danielis on *Ecl.* 4.11: "Asconius Pedianus a Gallo audisse se refert hanc eclogam in honorem eius factam." Evidently Asconius (9 B.C.–A.D. 76) did not know the identity of the child. Asinius Gallus died in prison in A.D. 33.

23. Thus Virgil's pagan commentator Servius, writing late in the fourth century, has only a vague and confused notion of the historical circumstances and, except for a note on "Sicelides" in line 1, which reveals his essential ignorance, makes no reference to Hellenistic poetry.

24. Lactantius, *Diuinae institutiones* 7.24.11–14, quotes lines 38–41, 28–30, 42–45, 21–22 of the fourth eclogue with the comment: "quae poeta secundum Cumaeae Sibyllae carmina prolocutus ets"; then he quotes *Oracula Sibyllina* 3.787–91, 619–23, 5.281–83. On Lactantius's use of the Sibylline oracles, see M. D. Feld, "The Sibyls of Subiaco: Sweynheym and Pannartz and the 'Editio Princeps' of Lactantius," *Renaissance Studies in Honor of Craig Hugh Smyth* (Florence, 1985), 1.305.

25. From Pierre Paul Courcelle, "Les exégèses chrétiennes de la quatrième eglogue," *Revue des Études Latines* 59 (1957): 298–310.

26. John Conington, *P. Vergili Maronis Opera* (London, 1858), vol. 1.

27. R. S. Conway, "The Messianic Idea in Virgil," in *Virgil's Messianic Eclogue,* ed. Joseph E. B. Mayor (London, 1907), p. 48.

28. Eduard Norden, *Die Geburt des Kindes* (Leipzig, 1924).

29. For a critical, though not unsympathetic, review, see H. J. Rose, *Classical Review* 38 (1924): 200–201.

30. See above, n. 10.

6. A Mantic Manifesto, Michael Zwettler

The following abbreviations are used in the notes:

Bell/Watt, *Intro.* W. Montgomery Watt, ed., *[Richard] Bell's Introduction to the Qur'ān,* Islamic Surveys 8, 2d ed. (Edinburgh, 1970).

CHB 1. P. R. Ackroyd and C. F. Evans, eds. *The Cambridge History of the Bible,* vol. 1: *From the Beginnings to Jerome* (Cambridge, 1970).

EI². *The Encyclopaedia of Islam,* new ed. by "a number of leading orientalists," 5 vols. to date (Leiden, 1960–).

GAPh 2. *Grundriss der arabischen Philologie,* vol. 2: *Literaturwissenschaft,* ed. Helmut Gätje (Wiesbaden, 1987).

GdQ² 1 and 2. Theodor Nöldeke, *Geschichte des Qorans,* 2d ed. revised by Friedrich Schwally, 2 pts. (Leipzig, 1909, 1919). *GdQ²* 3. Gotthelf Bergsträßer and Otto Pretzl, *Die Geschichte des Korantexts* (Leipzig, 1938; rpt. of 1–3, Hildesheim, 1981.

Lane, *Lexicon.* Edward William Lane, *An Arabic-English Lexicon,* book I (1 vol. in 8 pts. [pts. 6–8 and supplement ed. Stanley Lane Poole]; continuous pagination throughout) (1863–93; rpt. New York, 1955–56).

Paret, *Koran.* Rudi Paret, ed., *Der Koran,* Wege der Forschung 326 (Darmstadt, 1975).

RGG³. *Die Religion in Geschichte und Gegenwart: Handwörterbuch für Theologie und Religionswissenschaft,* 3d rev. ed. by Kurt Galling, 6 vols. (Tübingen, 1957–62).

ShEI. *Shorter Encyclopaedia of Islam,* ed. Hamilton A. R. Gibb and Jörg H. Kramers (Leiden, 1965; rpt. Ithaca, N.Y., n.d.).

Sīra. Muḥammad ibn Isḥāq, *Sîrat rasûl Allâh: Das Leben Muhammed's nach Muhammed ibn Ishâk bearbeitet von Abd el-Malik ibn Hischâm,* ed. Ferdinand Wüstenfeld, 2 vols. (vol. 1 in 2 pts.) (1858–60; rpt. Frankfurt, 1961).

WkaS. *Wörterbuch der klassischen arabischen Sprache,* ed. Manfred Ullmann, Anton Spitaler et al., 1 vol. and 17 fascicles of vol. 2 to date (Wiesbaden, 1970–).

1. It may be construed that in taking this view I am not altogether convinced by certain recently advanced theories that the Qur'ān represents an eighth- or even ninth-century compilation of homiletic exempla adapted from Jewish and Christian *Vorlage,* devotional and liturgical anthems, free-floating prophetic "logia," and other materials. See, e.g., Patricia Crone and Michael Cook, *Hagarism: The Making of the Islamic World* (Cambridge, 1977), esp. pts. 1 and 2; John Wansbrough, *Quranic Studies: Sources and Methods of Scriptural Interpretation,* London Oriental Series 31 (Oxford, 1977); Andrew Rippin, "Literary Analysis of *Qur'ān, Tafsīr,* and *Sīra*: The Methodologies of John Wansbrough," in *Approaches to Islam in Religious Studies,* ed. Richard C. Martin (Tucson, Ariz., 1985), pp. 151–63. But cf. also, among others, Angelika Neuwirth, Review of Wansbrough, *Quranic Studies,* in *Die Welt des Islams* 23–24 (1984): 539–42; Tryggve Kronholm, "Dependence and Prophetic Originality in the Koran," *Orientalia Suecana* 31–32 (1982–83): 47–70.

2. Cf., particularly, Angelika Neuwirth, "Zur Struktur der *Yūsuf*-Sure," in *Studien aus Arabistik und Semitistik: Anton Spitaler zum 70. Geburtstag von seinen Schülern überreicht,* ed. Werner Diem and Stefan Wild (Wiesbaden, 1980); idem, *Studien zur Komposition der mekkanischen Suren,* Studien zur Sprache, Geschichte,

und Kultur des islamischen Orients, 10 (Berlin, 1981). See also Irfan Shahîd, "A Contribution to Koranic Exegesis," in *Arabic and Islamic Studies in Honor of Hamilton A. R. Gibb,* ed. George Makdisi (Cambridge, Mass., 1965), pp. 575, 579–80; idem, "Another Contribution to Koranic Exegesis: The *Sūra* of the Poets (XXVI)," *Journal of Arabic Literature* 14 (1983): 4–5. In many respects, I concur with Richard C. Martin who approaches sūra 26 from what he characterizes as a structuralist premise, "namely, that the present *structure* of a text—e.g., of a myth, narrative, poem—*is* itself *significant*" ("Structural Analysis and the Qur'an: Newer Approaches to the Study of Islamic Texts," in *Studies in Qur'an and Tafsir,* ed. Alford T. Welch [= *Journal of the American Academy of Religion* 47.4 (1979)], p. 666 [author's emphasis]). I am not at all sure, however, that Martin clearly distinguishes, or means to distinguish, between *scripture*—as canonical discourse possessed, cognized, revered, dealt with, and augmented by and within a historically established and evolving religious community—and *revelation*—as, materially, more or less the same discourse *prior* to its canonization and "scripturalization," at the point of its production and issuance as a genre of verbal communication or expression which would *perhaps* have been addressed to the formation, delineation, or regulation of such a religious community before or during its embryonic stages. His primary interest as a historian of religions seems to be to arrive at an "interpretation of Sura 26 and of the kind of world it enunciates [that] should be approximately the same for the historian of religions as for the Muslim" (p. 669); that is, he approaches the sūra as part of an established religious tradition, seeking "to take the text of scripture at its face value as an intended, whole expression of that tradition" (p. 668). My primary interest, as an Arabist, Islamist, philologist, and literary critic, is to arrive at an interpretation of the sūra and of the kind of world it enunciates which might approximate that of its initial hearers—believers, unbelievers, and those who may have been religiously indifferent but verbally sensitive and culturally aware.

3. In taking this view, I acknowledge the validity and usefulness—if only as a heuristic exercise—of seeking to establish some sort of chronological arrangement of the revelations such as has been undertaken by a number of scholars over the years. Realizing that no chronological arrangement can pretend to definitiveness or avoid some measure of arbitrariness and subjectivity, I have opted in this instance for the order proposed by Régis Blachère, in *Le Coran,* 2 vols., Islam d'hier et d'aujourd' hui, 4–5 (Paris, 1949–50); and this order corresponds rather closely to that of Theodor Nöldeke, presented in *GdQ*² 1.66–234 (and briefly in the "Inhalt"). Nöldeke's order is conveniently reproduced, together with William Muir's, Hubert Grimme's, and that of the official Egyptian text in Bell/Watt, *Intro.*, pp. 205–13. Sūras will often be cited along with their Blachère and Nöldeke numbers thus: sūra 26 (B58/N56). The best recent discussion of the problems of chronologizing the revelations is by A[lford] T. Welch, "Al-Ḳur'ān," secs. 1–8, *EI*² 5.414b–419a (though I think he accepts Richard Bell's findings a bit too readily). While Welch's critique of the prevailing methodologies of the chronologizers does have much merit and while such methodologies only too often exhibit a degree of self-supporting circularity, Blachère and Nöldeke especially find some strong corroboration in the observable clusters and progressions of features which stand out strikingly in their rearrangements of the sūras and which,

one may be reasonably certain, they had not taken fully into account. Some such features should emerge in the course of this essay. (Incidentally, in presenting the chronological order according to the Egyptian standard edition, Welch, *EI*[2] 5.416a, inadvertently omits two "Meccan" sūras: after LXXXV read XCV, and after LXX read LXIX.)

4. I must at the outset acknowledge my great debt to the pioneer works of Ignaz Goldziher, *Abhandlungen zur arabischen Philologie,* pt. 1 (Leiden, 1896), pp. 1–121, and Paul Arno Eichler, *Die Dschinn, Teufel, und Engel im Koran* (Inaugural diss., Universität Leipzig, 1928) on mantic inspiration among the pre-Islamic Arabs and the role assigned to various categories of supernatural beings in the process. Since Eichler, only Toshihiko Izutsu, *Language and Magic: Studies in the Magical Function of Speech,* Keio University Studies in the Humanities and Social Relations 1 (Tokyo, 1956), and especially *God and Man in the Koran: Semantics of the Koranic Weltanschauung,* Keio University Studies in the Humanities and Social Relations 5 (Tokyo, 1964), has, to my mind, dealt as analytically, insightfully, and thoroughly with questions of inspiration and revelation in connection with the Qur'ān. It surprises me that *God and Man in the Koran* is not better known and appreciated among those concerned with the "Koranic *Weltanschauung,*" particularly Johan Bouman. His identically titled *Gott und Mensch im Koran,* Impulse der Forschung 22 (Darmstadt, 1977), a generally sympathetic, often insightful work, would have lost nothing by reference to Izutsu. I have relied upon the scholarship of many others as well, but here only those whose words and views are expressly adduced will be cited.

5. Cf., in this regard generally, N[ora] K[ershaw] Chadwick, *Poetry and Prophecy* (1942; Cambridge, 1975), pp. 41–57 et passim; Izutsu, *Language,* esp. chaps. 10 and 11; Mircea Eliade, *Shamanism: Archaic Techniques of Ecstasy,* Bollingen Series 76, trans. Willard R. Trask (Princeton, 1964), pp. 93, 96–99, 290, 338, 347, 440, 510–11.

6. I have not taken into consideration here a third type of mantic or quasi-mantic practitioner sometimes mentioned in the Qur'ān in connection with Muḥammad or other messenger-prophets, viz., the sorcerer or *sāḥir.* On "the antithesis of saint and sorcerer [which] underlies much of Late Antique literature," however, do see the powerfully cogent discussion of Peter Brown, *The Making of Late Antiquity* Cambridge, Mass., 1978), esp. pp. 18–24, 59–63 et passim. I will touch briefly on this matter later in the essay.

7. On jinn and *shayāṭīn* in general and on their pre-Islamic and qur'ānic role as agents of mantic inspiration, in particular, see, e.g., Goldziher, *Abhandlungen,* pp. 1–14; Eichler, *Dschinn,* pp. 4–74, esp. 23–29, 61–64; Ernst Zbinden, *Die Djinn des Islam und der altorientalische Geisterglaube* (Bern, 1953), pp. 75–90; A. D. Tritton, "Spirits and Demons in Arabia," *Journal of the Royal Asiatic Society* (1934): 715–27, esp. 722–23; idem, "Shayṭān," *ShEI* 523a–524a; Josef Henninger, "Geisterglaube bei den vorislamischen Arabern," in Henninger, *Arabia Sacra: Aufsätze zur Religionsgeschichte Arabiens und seiner Randgebiete,* Orbis biblicus et orientalis 40 (Freiburg, 1981), pp. 118–69, esp. 118–22, 141–56, addenda and corrigenda to Notes, 131–213; Izutsu, *God and Man,* pp. 169–75; Toufic Fahd, *La divination arabe: Etudes religieuses, sociologiques, et folkloriques sur le milieu natif de l'Islam* (Leiden, 1966), pp. 69–76 et passim; Alford Welch, "Madjnūn," *EI*[2] 5.1101a–1102b. See also A. J.

Wensinck, "The Etymology of the Arabic Djinn (Spirits)," Koninklijke Akademie van Wetenschappen (Amsterdam) *Verslagen en Mededeelingen,* AFd. Letterkunde, 5.4 (1920): 506–14 (on jinn); but cf. Henninger, "Geisterglaube," pp. 156–65, and Arthur Jeffery, *The Foreign Vocabulary of the Qur'ān* (Baroda, India, 1938), pp. 187–90 (on *shayṭān*).

8. Wensinck, "Etymology"; Welch, "Madjnūn."

9. "Wa ka-dhālika ja'alnā li kulli nabīyin 'adūwan shayāṭīna l-insi wa l-jinni yūḥī ba'ḍu-hum ilā ba'ḍin zukhrufa l-qawli ghurūran." See also, e.g., Goldziher, *Abhandlungen,* pp. 7, 106–7; Eichler, *Dschinn,* pp. 24–29, 61–63; Tritton, "Spirits," p. 716; Zbinden, *Djinn,* p. 88; D[uncan] B[lack] Macdonald [and H. Massé], "Djinn," EI^2 2.547a; Izutsu, *God and Man,* p. 178; Fahd, *Divination,* pp. 72–75. On the basis of Blachère's chronology one may observe that the word *jinn* in its various forms occurs exclusively in sūras dated Meccan. The words *shayṭān* and *shayāṭīn,* however, appear first only in the "middle Meccan period" (with a single isolated instance in sūra 81 [B18]) and occur frequently thereafter throughout the course of revelation down to one of the last Medinan sūras, sūra 5 (B116). It is only just that I also acknowledge here my immense debt to the comprehensive and exhaustive concordance to the Qur'ān prepared by Muḥammad Fu'ād 'Abdalbāqī, *Al-Mu'jam al-mufahras li alfāẓ al-Qur'ān al-karīm* (1364/1945; rpt. Cairo, 1378/1958–59).

10. Eichler, *Dschinn,* pp. 23–24; cf. Zbinden, *Djinn,* p. 82; Welch, EI^2 5.1102a.

11. Izutsu, *God and Man,* chap. 7.

12. Michael Zwettler, *The Oral Tradition of Classical Arabic Poetry: Its Character and Implications* (Columbus, Ohio, 1978), chap. 3.

13. On *saj'* in its pre-Islamic and qur'ānic forms, see, e.g., Goldziher, *Abhandlungen,* pp. 57–83; GdQ^2 1.36–44, 63–64, 74–76; Rudi Paret, *Mohammed und der Koran,* 2d ed., Urban Bücher: die wissenschaftliche Taschenbuchreihe 32 (Stuttgart, 1957), pp. 48–51; Régis Blachère, *Introduction au Coran,* 2d ed. (Paris, 1959), pp. 173–79; Izutsu, *God and Man,* p. 183–84; Fahd, *Divination,* pp. 65, 80 n. 3, 151–53; Friedrun R. Müller, *Untersuchungen zur Reimprosa im Koran* (diss., Tübingen, 1969); S. A. Bonebakker, "Religious Prejudice against Poetry in Early Islam," *Medievalia et Humanistica,* n.s. 7 (1976): 77–78, 85–86, 97 n. 56; *GAPh* 2.116–19 with references (A. Neuwirth), 220–23 (H. Horst). The literature on the *kāhin* is extensive. In general see (together with their references), e.g., August Fischer, "Kāhin," *ShEI* 206b–208a; Alfred Haldar, *Associations of Cult Prophets among the Ancient Semites* (Inaugural diss., University of Uppsala, 1945), chap. 4 (with reservations); Henninger, "Geisterglaube," pp. 148–49 and n. 178; Fahd, *Divination,* pp. 91–104 et passim; Fahd, EI^2 4.420b–422a; etc.

14. Jean Lecerf, "The Dream in Popular Culture: Arabic and Islam," in *The Dream and Human Societies,* ed G. E. von Grünebaum and Roger Caillois (Berkeley, Calif., 1966), p. 369. Cf. in this regard David L. Petersen, *The Roles of Israel's Prophets,* Journal for the Study of the Old Testament Supplement Series 17 (Sheffield, 1981), pp. 44–45 (citing I. M. Lewis); also Chadwick, *Poetry,* pp. 64–72; Eliade, *Shamanism,* pp. 23–32.

15. See Henri Lammens, *Le berceau de l'Islam: L'Arabie occidentale à la veille de l'Hégire,* vol. 1: *Le climat—les bédouins* (Rome, 1914), pp. 204–5, 255–58; Lammens, *L'Arabie occidentale avant l'Hégire* (Beirut, 1928), pp. 106–10: "Rien de plus

ordinaire dans l'antiquité, au temps de préhistoire islamique, que la réunion des dignités de *kāhin* et *sayyd* [*sic*] [During the early pre-Islamic period, nothing was more common than combining the offices of *kāhin* and sayyid]" (pp. 106–7). Cf., e.g., Haldar, *Associations,* pp. 164–68, 197–98, 200; Joseph Chelhod, *Introduction à la sociologie de l'Islam: De l'animisme à l'universalisme,* Islam d'hier et d'aujourd'hui 12 (Paris, 1958), pp. 55–56, 62–64, 157 n. 1; Fischer, *ShEI* 207b; Fahd, *Divination,* pp. 118–20 et passim. Josef Henninger ("La société bédouine ancienne," in *L'antica societá beduina,* Universitá di Roma Centro di Studi Semitici, Studi semitici 2, ed and comp. Francesco Gabrieli [Rome, 1959], p. 84), however, maintains that such a combination of functions seems to have been "un phénomène secondaire" (though he subsequently appears to have backed away from this position in "Deux études récentes sur l'Arabie préislamique," *Anthropos* 58 [1963]: 471 and n. 115). Haldar, particularly, wishes to see in such venerable figures as ʿAmr b. Luḥayy, Quṣayy, ʿAmr b. al-Ju'ayd, and Zuhayr b. Janāb representatives of a form of "sacral kingship" ancient in the Near East. (Curiously he omits from consideration the case of Jadhīma al-Abrash, who, established as king along the Middle Euphrates during the third century A.D., is explicitly said to have practiced mantic activities (*kāna . . . qad tanabba'a wa takahhana*] and to have introduced and officiated over idol worship in his realm: Muḥammad b. Jarīr aṭ-Ṭabarī, *Ta'rīkh ar-rusul wa l-mulūk [Annales],* ed. M. J. de Goeje et al., 3 pts. in 15 vols. (Leiden, 1879–1901], pt. 1, p. 752 [cited also in Fahd, *Divination,* p. 102 n. 2, with other references].)

Leaving aside the question of "sacral kings," we should note that the creditable attestations of actual sayyid-*kuhhān* (as opposed to *kuhhān* who would indeed have been consulted on important tribal matters, especially matters of war; cf. Fahd, *Divination,* pp. 119–20) are relatively very few and are confined almost exclusively either to a period—often very remote and semilegendary—predating the mid-sixth century or to the years contemporaneous with or shortly after Muḥammad's Medinan career. In the first instance, given the gradual deurbanization and (re?)bedouinization in the Southwest Asian areas, whose beginnings Werner Caskel ("The Bedouinization of Arabia," in *Studies in Islamic Cultural History,* Comparative Studies of Cultures and Civilizations 2, *American Anthropologist* 56. 2.2, memoir 76 [1954], ed. G. E. von Grünebaum], pp. 36–46) has traced to around the second century A.D., one may deduce that whatever factors of stability of cult and sanctuary and whatever systematization of cult offices, functions, and personnel might have obtained among the Arabs in archaic times (up to and including "sacral kings" or sayyid-*kuhhān*), such factors were no longer prevailing during the sixth and early seventh centuries (at least, not in most of the Arabian peninsula). At that time "the oracular, mantic and augural role of the *kāhin* is for all practical purposes the only one recognized in the evidence we possess, which derives essentially from folklore" (Fahd, *EI*[2] 4.421a). The second instance involves an apparently sudden proliferation of what Islamic tradition generally characterizes as "false prophets": mantic preachers whom the sources often identify as *kuhhān* and who assumed or were accorded roles of leadership in their tribes in contradistinction to or reaction against Muḥammad's new Muslim community at Medina. Whether such mantic leaders of the 630s as Musaylima, Ṭulayḥa, al-Aswad al-ʿAnsī, or Sajāḥ (their female counterpart) are to be construed as imitators or rivals of Muḥammad, motivated by his example and success, or as more or less independent and localized agents responding to a religiously charged "spirit of the times" cannot be considered here. (Cf. J[ulius] Wellhausen, "Prolegomena zur ältesten Geschichte des Islams," in *Skizzen und Vorarbeiten* 6 [Berlin, 1899], pp. 7–37; Geo Widengren, *Muḥammad, the Apostle of God, and His Ascension,* Uppsala Universitets Årsskrift 1955.1 [Uppsala, 1955], pp. 15–17; also articles in *ShEI* and *EI*[2] under the relevant names). What is clear, however, is that in founding their positions at least partially, if not primarily, on putative mantic faculties and directives received from a single High God, these "false prophets," like Muḥammad himself in Mecca, seem to have struck their contemporaries as novel, extraordinary, and anomalous, however much their tribes might have accepted them as useful (cf. Umberto Eco, *A Theory of Semiotics* [Bloomington, Ind., 1976], p. 258) and however much their status may have harked back to some sort of primordial "sacral kingship."

16. Cf. Chadwick, *Poetry,* chap. 2 et passim; Izutsu, *Language,* chaps. 8 and 9; also Eco, *Theory,* p. 215.

17. Eichler, *Dschinn,* pp. 25, 27; Izutsu, *God and Man,* p. 169.

18. See, e.g., most conspicuously, Abū ʿĀmir ibn Shuhayd al-Ashjaʿī al-Andalusī, *Risālat at-Tawābiʿ wa z-zawābiʿ: The Treatise of Familiar Spirits and Demons,* University of California Near Eastern Studies 15, intro., trans., and notes James T. Monroe (Berkeley, 1971), and Monroe's introduction to the translation.

19. Izutsu, *God and Man,* p. 171; cf. p. 183.

20. See Goldziher, *Abhandlungen,* pp. 26–31 et passim; also Izutsu, *Language,* pp. 130–31.

21. Lecerf, "Dream," p. 369.

22. Cf. Henninger, "Geisterglaube," pp. 149–50.

23. Cf. Régis Blachère, "La poésie dans la conscience de la première génération musulmane," *Annales Islamologiques* 4 (1963): 94.

24. Zwettler, *Oral Tradition,* p. 156.

25. Ibid.; cf. C. A. O. van Nieuwenhuijze, "The Prophetic Function in Islam: An Analytic Approach," *Correspondance d'Orient: Études* 1–2 (1962): 125–26. The article continues in vol. 5–6 (1964): 99–119.

26. Muḥammad ibn Isḥāq, in Ṭabarī, pt. 1, p. 1150; trans. adapted from Alfred Guillaume, *The Life of Muḥammad: A Translation of [ibn] Isḥāq's "Sīrat Rasūl Allāh"* (Oxford, 1955), p. 106. This passage was excised—apparently on purpose—from the *Sīra* account as we have it, excerpted and edited by ʿAbdallāh ibn Hishām (d. 218/834).

27. Translations from the Qur'ān are mine, but with a good deal of unabashed adaptation from Arthur J. Arberry, *The Koran Interpreted,* 2 vols. (London, 1955). Verse (āya) numbers are those of the standard Egyptian edition, followed where appropriate, after a slash (/), by those of the 1834 (and thereafter) European edition of Gustave Flügel (on which see, e.g., Arthur Jeffery, "Progress in the Study of the Qur'ān Text" in Paret, *Koran,* p. 400; Bell/Watt, *Intro.,* pp. 60–61, 174, 202–3; A. Neuwirth in *GAPh* 2.113; Welch, *EI*[2] 5.411a; most recently, Arne A. Ambros, "Die Divergenzen zwischen dem Flügel- und dem Azhar-Koran," *Wiener Zeitschrift für die Kunde des Morgenlandes* 78 [1988]: 9–22).

28. For *ḍanīn* many of the earliest qur'ānic codices had the reading *ẓanīn,* "suspected, unreliable, untrustworthy" (see Arthur Jeffery, *Materials for the History of the Text of the Qur'ān: The Old Codices* [Leiden, 1937], pp. 108, 207, 225, 229,

233, 252, 284; Lane, *Lexicon,* p. 1925b; *GdQ*² 3.3 n. 7, 52), with the sense: "Nor as to the Mystery is he suspect." On the double sense of *rajīm,* "accursed" or "pelted with stones," see Eichler, *Dschinn,* pp. 75–76; M[aurice] Gaudefroy-Demombynes, "Radjm," *ShEI* 464a–466b; Fahd, *Divination,* pp. 188–95.

29. Cf. Eichler, *Dschinn,* pp. 123–29, esp. 127–29; Richard Bell, "Muḥammad's Visions," in Paret, *Koran,* pp. 96–99 (with reservations); Widengren, *Muḥammad,* pp. 9–10; E. E. Calverly, "Nafs," *ShEI* 433b–434a; J. Pedersen, "Djabrā'īl," *EI*² 2.362b–364a, specifically 363a.

30. See Izutsu, *God and Man,* pp. 175–79.

31. See, e.g., Carl Brockelmann, "Allah und die Götzen, der Ursprung des islamischen Monotheismus," *Archiv für Religionswissenschaft* 21 (1922): 99–121; Hamilton A. R. Gibb, "Pre-Islamic Monotheism in Arabia," *Harvard Theological Review* 55 (1962): 269–80; W. Montgomery Watt, "Belief in a 'High God' in Pre-Islamic Mecca," *Journal of Semitic Studies* 16 (1971): 35–40.

32. The term *makīn* ("firmly, securely placed; high-stationed; influential") is especially telling in connection with the qur'ānic revelations that jinn and *shayāṭīn* are denied access to heaven and its secrets and are repelled therefrom by fire- and stone-hurling angelic guards (e.g., 15:17–18, 37:7–9, 66:5, 72:8–9; cf. Eichler, *Dschinn,* pp. 30–32). I will discuss the term *muṭā*ʿ later in this essay. On *amīn* and its technical sociocommercial and administrative usage, see H. M. Tilman Nagel, "Some Considerations Concerning the Pre-Islamic and the Islamic Foundations of the Authority of the Caliphate," in *Studies on the First Century of Islamic Society,* Papers on Islamic History 5, ed G. H. A. Juynboll (Carbondale, Ill., 1982), pp. 193–95.

33. Here it may be mentioned that the names of the sūras are all later additions to the scriptural text and reflect some word, feature, or concept that subsequent generations perceived in or associated with a given sūra and adopted as its title; see, e.g., *GdQ*² 3.259–60; Blachère, *Introduction,* pp. 140–41; Bell/Watt, *Intro.,* pp. 58–59; Rudi Paret, *Der Koran: Kommentar und Konkordanz* (Stuttgart, 1971), pp. 545–59; Welch, *EI*² 5.409b–410b. While not all the titles seem apposite, this one certainly is!

34. See Blachère, *Coran,* p. 133; more recently, Neuwirth, *Studien,* pp. 1, 315–16 (especially for the term *Rezitationstext,* which, however appropriate it may be as a functional *Gattungsbestimmung* for the majority of "Meccan" sūras, does not always seem to me adequately to account for the distinctively parenetic, discursive, and polemical quality and form of many of the longer ones, such as "The Poets").

35. These first two āyas are conflated in the Flügel edition. The sūra is introduced with the three Arabic letters *Ṭ, S,* and *M.* On these and the other so-called mysterious letters (or "inchoative elements"—*fawātiḥ*) of the Qur'ān, various combinations of which introduce twenty-nine sūras, see, most recently, Welch, *EI*² 5.412a–414b, with full references; also Paret, *Koran,* chap. 6 (articles by H. Bauer, E. Goossens, M. S. Seale, and A. Jones). The identical or nearly identical phrase, likewise asyndetically juxtaposed to preceding "mysterious letters," opens seven other sūras as well: 10, 12, 13, 15, 27, 28, and 31. A good deal of speculation has been devoted to just what should be deemed the referent of the deictic "those" (*tilka*). For the most part, opinion so far has preferred either the

revealed verses or passages that follow (seeing the letters as more or less extraneous and irrelevant to the content) or the preceding letters themselves in their role as it were of self-signifying graphemic monads of unfolding Scripture. See Welch, *EI*[2] 5.414 et passim (approximately and somewhat impressionistically anticipated by Kenneth Cragg, *The Event of the Qur'ān: Islam in Its Scripture* [London, 1971], pp. 50–53). On *āyāt,* see note 38 herein.

36. Sing. *naba',* "(a piece of) news, information, tidings; announcement." This term, paronomastically if not also etymologically related to *nabīy,* "prophet" (see Josef Horovitz, *Koranische Untersuchungen* [Berlin, 1926], p. 47; Jeffery, *Foreign Vocabulary,* pp. 276–77, with references; Bell/Watt, *Intro.,* pp. 28–29; but cf. also Izutsu, *God and Man,* pp. 181–83; Willem A. Bijlefeld, "A Prophet and More Than a Prophet? Some Observations on the Qur'anic Use of the Terms 'Prophet' and 'Apostle,'" *Muslim World* 59 [1969]: 10–11), occurs some twenty-nine times in the Qur'ān. In almost all the occurrences, singular and plural, it signifies the verbal content of mantic communication—usually the account of a past event involving one of the messenger-prophets, either to be revealed to Muḥammad or intended to reach, through him, the ears of his audience (e.g., 6:34; 9:70/71; 11:100/102, 120/121; 26:69; 38:3/2, 21/20). Sometimes, as here, the content of the "news" or "announcement" is left unspecified (cf. 6:5, 67/66; 20:99; 38:67; and 78:2). Of particular importance are those occurrences that let us know that the "news" mantically communicated to and through the Prophet (*nabīy*) is always news of the "unknowable" or "unseen" world of God, news of "the Mystery," news that would otherwise be unknowable and inaccessible to all human beings—including prophets and messengers—unless imparted to them by God (*anbā' al-ghayb*—3:44/39; 11:49/57; 12:102/103; cf., especially, Izutsu, *God and Man,* p. 182; Bijlefeld, "Prophet," pp. 11–12).

Not irrelevant in this regard, also, would be F. Leemhuis, "About the Meaning of nabba'a and 'anba'a in the Qur'ān," *Akten des VII. Kongresses für Arabistik und Islamwissenschaft (Göttingen, 15. bis 22. August 1974),* Akademie der Wissenschaften in Göttingen, Philologisch-historische Klasse, *Abhandlungen,* 3d ser., no. 98 (1976), pp. 244–49, whose findings on the meaning of *nabba'– (n–b–': * form II) and *anba'– (n–b–':* form IV) in the Qur'ān would seem to confirm the impression that qur'ānic usage has tended to circumscribe the semantic range of these fairly common verbs, generally limiting their application to communications made to, by, or through a *nabīy,* "prophet."

37. Or "earth," as most translators of this verse have it: e.g., Richard Bell, trans., *The Qur'ān Translated,* 2 vols. (1937–39; rpt. Edinburgh, 1960); Mohammed Marmaduke Pickthall, trans., *The Meaning of the Glorious Koran: An Explanatory Translation* (1931; rpt. New York, 1953–); Arberry, *Koran Interpreted;* Rudi Paret, trans., *Der Koran: Übersetzung* (Stuttgart, 1962–63). I have preferred "land" here, however, because of the presence in the Qur'ān of a set of passages that seem to me to be analogous to this one and to call for that sense of *arḍ.* In all of these passages either (1) the question is asked about the unbelievers: "Have they not traversed through the land to observe [*a-fa lam yasīrū fi l-arḍi fa yanẓurū*] how came about the end of the lie-criers [*al-mukadhdhibīn*]?" or "of the miscreants [*al-mujrimīn*]?" or, most frequently, "of those before them [*alladhīna (kānū) min qablihim*]?" whose superiority is stressed; or (2) the unbelievers themselves are imper-

atively directed so to traverse and observe (*sīrū fi l-arḍi thumma/fa -nẓurū*): 6:11; 12:109; 16:36/38; 27:69/71; 30:9/8, 42/41; 35:44/43; 40:21/22, 82; 47:10/11. (The last six instances from 30, 35, 40, and 47 all refer to "those before them," while all the passages but 47:10/11 are dated by most chronological arrangements within the middle or late Meccan period, the period assigned to this sūra.) In all these passages the aforementioned translators choose "land/*Land*," rather than "earth/*Erde*," to render *arḍ*. (Abdullah Yusuf Ali, *The Meaning of the Glorious Qur'ān: Text, Translation and Commentary*, 3d ed., 2 vols. [1938; rpt. Cairo, n.d.]; and T. B. Irving, *The Qur'an: The First American Version* [Brattleboro, Vt., 1985], use "earth" in all cases. Blachère, *Coran*, also uses only "terre," but the French word's semantic extension includes the senses of both "earth" and "land"). The wording of the verse in question, 26:7/6, does differ somewhat from that of the foregoing passages: "a-wa lam yaraw ila l-arḍi kam. . . ." But my choice has been influenced by the really ambiguous usage of *zawj* (to which I shall return) and by the structure of the sūra and the cumulative force of the refrain, which virtually compel us to associate (if not identify) God's production *in the land* of "every noble *zawj*" with the recounted "ends" of lie-criers who went before (to be observed by traversers *through the land*).

38. On the sense and significance of the term *āya* (pl. *āyāt, āy*), "sign, token; exemplum; wonder, miracle; communication; passage, pericope" (only afterward, it seems, did it come specifically to mean a "verse" of qur'ānic revelation), see, e.g., Hartwig Hirschfeld, *New Researches into the Composition and Exegesis of the Qoran*, Asiatic Monographs 3 (London, 1902), pp. 45, 60–61, 72–78; Tor Andrae, "Der Ursprung des Islams und das Christentum," *Kyrkohistorisk Årsskrift* (1923): 149–206; (1924): 213–92; (1925): 45–112 (rpt. in book form, Uppsala, 1926); I use the French trans. by Jules Roche, *Les origines de l'Islam et le Christianisme*, Initiation à l'Islam 8 [Paris, 1953], but cite the original pagination, printed in margin of translated text), here (1925): 70–81, esp. 73–77; Horovitz, *Koranische Untersuchungen*, pp. 4, 25; Richard Bell, *The Origin of Islam in Its Christian Environment*, The Gunning Lectures, Edinburgh University, 1925 (1926; rpt. London, 1968), pp. 108–9, 112; Jeffery, *Foreign Vocabulary*, pp. 72–73; Jeffery, "Āya," *EI²* 1.773b–774a; Izutsu, *God and Man*, pp. 133–47 et passim; Bell/Watt, *Intro.*, pp. 121–27; Kenneth Cragg, *The Mind of the Qur'ān: Chapters in Reflection* (London, 1973), pp. 146–53 et passim; Wansbrough, *Quranic Studies*, pp. 5–7, 18–19; Bouman, *Gott und Mensch*, pp. 91–97; Welch, *EI²* 5.422. On the "sign" of God (especially as "wonder" or "miracle") in pre-Islamic traditions see, e.g., "Wunder," *RGG³* 6.1831–47 (G. Mensching, W. Vollborn, et al.); O. Hofius and C[olin] Brown, "Miracle: Sēmeion," *The New International Dictionary of New Testament Theology*, ed. Colin Brown (Exeter, 1976), 2.626–33. By the early fifth century we find not only that "miracles, prodigies, and marvelous phenomena" are classed by religious writers and Church historians as "signs" of God but also that "the faith allowed many simple events" to be so recognized as well; see, especially with reference to the *Historia ecclesistica* of Rufinus (an augmented translation and adaptation of Eusebius, *Ecclesiastical History*, early fourth century), Françoise Thelamon, *Païens et Chrétiens au IVe siècle: L'apport de l' "Histoire ecclésiastique" de Rufin d'Aquilée* (Paris, 1981), pp. 325–54 et passim (see Index iv, s.vv. *signa* and *signa apostolica*). The complex, sophisticated, and well-developed con-

ception of "signs" in the Qur'ān bears a remarkable—if no more than superficial—resemblance to certain twentieth-century theories of signs or semiotics—such as, e.g., Eco, *Theory,* with which I am most familiar; cf. Terence Hawkes, *Structuralism and Semiotics* (Berkeley, Calif., 1977), pp. 123–50; John N. Deely, Max H. Fisch, et al., in *Sight, Sound, and Sense,* ed. Thomas A. Sebeok (Bloomington, Ind., 1978), pp. 1–110; Jonathan Culler, *The Pursuit of Signs: Semiotics, Literature, Deconstruction* (Ithaca, N.Y., 1981), pp. 18–43; etc. To investigate whether the resemblance runs any deeper might be an interesting, even worthwhile undertaking. Here, however, I am concerned with semiotic theory mainly insofar as it may usefully serve as an interpretive approach.

39. It may of course be quite true that, as many scholars have pointed out, *rasūl* (together with *mursal*) would quite literally and correctly render the Greek word for "one sent (forth)," *apostolos,* and its Syriac equivalent, *šᵉlīḥā* (e.g., A. J. Wensinck, "Muhammed und die Propheten," *Acta orientalia* 2 [1924]: 173–74; Wensinck, "Rasūl," *ShEI* 469b; Horovitz, *Koranische Untersuchungen,* p. 45; Arthur Jeffery, *The Qur'ān as Scripture* [New York, 1952], pp. 19–20; Widengren, *Muḥammad,* pp. 13–15 et passim; Bijlefeld, "Prophet," p. 12; etc.), and that both of the latter terms were used to denote "apostle" in its New Testament, early Christian, and gnostic senses (as well as to denote conventionally "envoy," "emissary," or "messenger"). Nevertheless, I have generally preferred to translate *rasūl* as "messenger," rather than "apostle." One will perhaps grant the validity of arguments advanced in favor of *rasūl* as "apostle." (See especially Widengren. Bijlefeld [p. 12 and n. 55] refers to "a small number of texts [in which] the more general 'messenger' is the only acceptable translation"; in all but those cases Blachère, *Coran,* for instance, uses "apôtre".) Nevertheless, the modern term "apostle" (*apôtre, Apostel,* etc.) has acquired a far more explicitly and exclusively technical religious acceptance than had the Greek, Syriac, and Arabic terms. Furthermore, it still is not satisfactorily explained by those who opt for "apostle" why *rasūl* never occurs in the Qur'ān in reference to the "Apostles" of Jesus, who are called instead *al-ḥawārīyūn* (see Widengren, p. 15; Bijlefeld, p. 12 n. 54; on the latter term, see Jeffery, *Foreign Vocabulary,* pp. 115–16; A. J. Wensinck, "Ḥawārī," *EI²* 3.285). My translational preference by no means implies, however, that I see no parallels or correspondences whatsoever between qur'ānic *rasūl* or *rasūl Allāh,* as applied to Muḥammad and earlier "messengers," and pre-Islamic Christian and gnostic conceptions of apostleship and the apostolate. But that is another question entirely.

40. See esp. Bijlefeld, "Prophet."

41. Ibid., p. 17 (citing Horovitz, *Koranische Untersuchungen,* p. 48–49); cf. pp. 18, 24–25. The precise identity of Idrīs, also a *nabīy,* is still unclear: see Wensinck, "Idrīs," *ShEI* 158b–159a; Georges Vajda, "Idrīs," *EI²* 3.1030a–1031a.

42. Horovitz, *Koranische Untersuchungen,* p. 48. On the frequency of *rasūl* (331 times) and *nabīy* (75 times), see Bijlefeld, "Prophet," pp. 9–13.

43. A. J. Wensinck, "Rasūl," *ShEI* 469b.

44. Bijlefeld, "Prophet," pp. 21, 26.

45. Ibid., p. 23 (my emphasis); cf. Bouman, *Gott und Mensch,* pp. 18–26.

46. See note 59 herein.

47. Bijlefeld, "Prophet," p. 26. On the two terms in general, see, e.g., besides sources already cited, Wensinck, "Muhammed," p. 171–75; Horovitz, *Koranische*

Untersuchungen, pp. 44–51; Horovitz, "Nabī," *ShEI* 427–28 (cf. Heinrich Speyer, *Die biblischen Erzählungen im Qoran*, 2d ed. [1961; rpt. Hildesheim, 1971], p. 416 n. 1); Jeffery, *Qur'ān as Scripture*, pp. 19–22, 27–28, 36–46; Widengren, *Muḥammad*, pp. 7–24, 55–79, et passim (especially on *rasūl* and its early Christian and gnostic parallels); Y[ouakim] Moubarac, *Abraham dans le Coran: L'histoire d'Abraham dans le Coran et la naissance de l'Islam*, Etudes musulmanes 5 (Paris, 1958), pp. 15–25; van Nieuwenhuijze, "Prophetic Function" (1964): 105–8 n. 1; Bell/Watt, *Intro.*, pp. 25–30, 156; Wansbrough, *Quranic Studies*, pp. 54–55; etc. For some understanding of the conception of *prophet* and *apostle* (approximate equivalents of *nabīy* and *rasūl*) during the centuries preceding Islam, see, e.g., G. Mensching et al., "Propheten," *RGG³* 5.608–11, 613–15, 633–35; H. Riesenfeld, "Apostel," *RGG³* 1.497–99; also Widengren, *Muḥammad*, esp. chaps. 1 and 3; Tor Andrae, *Mohammed: The Man and His Faith*, trans. Theophil Menzil, rev. ed. (1955; rpt. New York 1960), pp. 97–107. (I have not taken into consideration here the rather elaborate prophetological speculations of later Muslim scholars after the seventh century; see, e.g., Wensinck, "Muhammed," pp. 169–70 et passim; Seyyed Hossein Nasr, *Ideals and Realities of Islam* (Boston, 1972), pp. 84–91.)

48. See, e.g., Hubert Grimme, *Mohammed*, 2 pts., Darstellungen aus dem Gebiete der nichtchristlishen Religionsgeschichte 7, 11 (Münster, 1892–95), 2.80; Horovitz, *Koranische Untersuchungen*, p. 28 n. 1; Maxime Rodinson, *Mohammed*, trans. Anne Carter (New York, 1974), pp. 63–64, 121–22; Cragg, *Event*, pp. 88, 94.

49. On the complex and multifaceted role played by the figure of Moses in the Qur'ān, see B. Heller, "Mūsā," *ShEI* 414b–415b; Speyer, *Biblischen Erzählungen*, pp. 225–363; Y. Moubarac, "Moïse dans le Coran," in Moubarac, *Le Coran et la critique occidentale*, Pentalogie islamo-chrétienne 2 (Beirut, 1972–73), pp. 127–56; Moubarac, *Abraham*, pp. 20–29. (Karl Prenner's *Muhammad und Musa. Strukturanalytische und theologiegeschichtliche Untersuchungen zu den mekkanischen Musa-Perikopen des Qur'ān* [Altenberge, 1986] came to my attention too late to be utilized for this essay.)

50. Moubarac, "Moïse," pp. 129–30; Moubarac, *Abraham*, pp. 27–28. In contrast, reports and allusions connected with Abraham, the second most prominent figure, account for thirty-seven passages consisting of 245 āyas and about twenty-five separate incidents.

51. See Heribert Busse, "Herrschertypen im Koran," in *Die islamische Welt zwischen Mittelalter und Neuzeit: Festschrift für Hans Robert Roemer zum 65. Geburtstag*, Beiruter Texte und Studien 22, ed. Ulrich Haarmann and Peter Bachmann (Beirut, 1979), pp. 67–70. Note, then, that Moses here is expressly *not* a messenger to the Israelites; cf. Heller, *ShEI* 414b; Moubarac, "Moïse," pp. 133–38; Speyer, *Biblischen Erzählungen*, p. 351.

52. See J[ulius] Wellhausen, *Reste arabischen Heidentums*, 3d ed. (1897/1927; rpt. Berlin, 1961), pp. 159–67; D[uncan] B[lack] Macdonald, "Siḥr," *ShEI* 545b–547b. Cf., for some brief but cogent remarks on the complex and uncertain status of magic among the pre-Islamic Arabs vis-à-vis other more strictly mantic practices, Fahd, *Divination*, pp. 26–27, 42, 90.

53. For the fullest discussion of the "punishment" subgenre of qur'ānic narrative, see Horovitz, *Koranische Untersuchungen*, pp. 10–32; Bell/Watt, *Intro.*, pp. 127–35, esp. 130–31; Welch, *EI²* 5.420b–421a, 424.

54. On Abraham in the Qur'ān, see, e.g., Speyer, *Biblischen Erzählungen,* pp. 120–86; J. Eisenberg and A. J. Wensinck, "Ibrāhīm," *ShEI* 154a–155a; Edmund Beck, "Die Gestalt des Abraham am Wendepunkt der Entwicklung Muhammeds: Analyse von Sure 2:118(124)–135(141)," in Paret, *Koran,* pp. 111–36; Jeffery, *Qur'ān as Scripture,* pp. 75–78; Moubarac, *Abraham;* Moubarac, *Le Coran,* pp. 1–97 (includes, pp. 63–97, reprints of several reviews of Moubarac, *Abraham;* cf. also Maxime Rodinson, "A Critical Survey of Modern Studies on Muhammad," in *Studies on Islam,* ed. and trans. Merlin L. Swartz [Oxford, 1981], pp. 56–58, 81–82 nn. 167–70); Rudi Paret, "Ibrāhīm," *EI*[2] 3.980a–981b; Bouman, *Gott und Mensch,* pp. 76–88.

55. Cf. Speyer, *Biblischen Erzählungen,* p. 133 n. 1.

56. I.e., *lisān ṣidq;* see *WkaS* 2.1.624a; cf. Genesis 12:12.

57. In sūras judged to have been revealed later, this plea that his father be forgiven is rather sharply qualified; see Speyer, *Biblischen Erzählungen,* pp. 144–46 (with references). Moubarac notes: "Dans le Coran, Abraham est essentiellement une personne qui prie. . . . Plus qu'une charactéristique, cela semble être son rôle, sa fonction [In the Qur'an Abraham is essentially a person who prays. . . . More than a characteristic, that seems to be his role, his function]" (*Abraham,* p. 183).

58. Moubarac, *Abraham,* p. 32. But cf. Horovitz, *Koranische Untersuchungen,* pp. 31–32, who notes, with reference to the punitive earthly annihilations of past peoples and the eschatological cataclysms of the Last Day, that one can see "a certain inclination to burst the boundaries between the two."

59. Cf. Moubarac, *Abraham,* pp. 60–62; Bijlefeld, "Prophet," pp. 17, 26. Bijlefeld (p. 26) does observe, however, that Abraham's "function—not with regard to the Arabs, but with regard to his father's community—comes very close to the role of an apostle [messenger]."

60. See 26:16; 20:26/27–34; 28:34–35; also Speyer, *Biblischen Erzählungen,* pp. 260–62. Cf. Exodus 4:10–16.

61. On these messengers and their stories, see the appropriate articles in *ShEI* and *EI*[2] (with references).

62. On the special sociological sense of *fasād/ifsād,* see, perhaps, Paret, *Mohammed,* p. 27; Paret, *Koran: Kommentar,* pp. 13–14. In the latter citation (p. 14), Paret refers to Werner Caskel, *Entdeckungen in Arabien,* Arbeitsgemeinschaft für Forschung des Landes Nordrhein-Westfalen, Geisteswissenschaften, *Abhandlungen* 30 (Cologne, 1954), pp. 11, 27, 32, for information "on the sociological background of the expression." Caskel, however, depended for his interpretation upon emending the Sabaean root *q–s¹–d* (which, Joan Copeland Biella [*Dictionary of Old South Arabic: Sabaean Dialect,* Harvard Semitic Museum, Harvard Semitic Studies 25 (Chico, Calif., 1982), p. 462] notes, has been confirmed as such in some cases from photos) to *f–s¹–d* (which "is not attested except as an alternative reading to qsd" [ibid.; cf. p. 406, s.r. *fsd*]). The root *f–s¹–d* is not even included in A. F. L. Beeston et al., *Sabaic Dictionary (English-French-Arabic),* University of Sanaa, YAR, Publications (Louvain-la-Neuve, 1982), who list only *q–s¹–d* and its derivatives for all attestations—as also does Maria Höfner, *Beleg-Wörterbuch zum Corpus inscriptionum semiticarum, pars IV. . . ,* Veröffentlichungen der Arabischen Kommission 2, Österreichische Akademie der Wissenschaften, Phil.-hist. Klasse, *Sitzungsberichte* 363 [1980]), p. 134.

63. To the best of my knowledge no really adequate explanation has yet been

advanced for the topos of this camel, the water regulations it occasions, and its slaughter by the Thamūdites. As Paret says, "Sind die einzelnen Andeutungen so knapp, daß vieles von der Geschichte der Ṯamūd im dunkel bleibt [Specific clues are so scanty that much of the Thamūd story remains obscure]" (*Koran: Kommentar,* p. 164). Could it perhaps be a question of a symbolic, allegorical, or synechdochic representation of some kind of social or ecological upheaval resulting from conflicts between urban-agrarian and nomadic bedouin groups?

64. On *yawm aẓ-ẓulla,* "the day of the overshadowing (?)," see, e.g., A. S. Yahuda, cited in Paret, *Koran: Kommentar,* p. 371.

65. Cf. Jurij [Yuri] Lotman, *The Structure of the Artistic Text,* Michigan Slavic Contributions 7, trans. Gail Lenhoff and Ronald Vroon (Ann Arbor, Mich., 1977), pp. 131–35.

66. Cf. Welch, *EI*² 5.420b.

67. Here occurs the name of the folk to whom each messenger is sent: Noah's kinfolk (*qawm Nūḥ*), ʿĀd, Thamūd, Lot's kinfolk, and the Men of the Grove, respectively.

68. Cf. Wansbrough, *Quranic Studies,* p. 53. From Deuteronomy 18:15, 18, in conjunction with Acts 3:22 and 7:37, in words ascribed to Moses and cited by Peter the Apostle and Stephen the first Christian martyr, we learn that prophets' being raised up "from among their own brothers" had become a well-established motif in the typology of the prophet for both Jews and Christians. Although in *āya* 177 Shuʿayb is not expressly designated "their brother" (as are the other four), elsewhere, as the messenger sent to Midian, he is so designated (e.g., 7:85/83; 11:84/85; 29:36/35) and, hence, can be assumed to have the same relationship here; cf. *GdQ*² 1.151 n. 9.

69. On the semantic development of *taqwā/ittaqā*ʾ from the idea of "shielding oneself, being on guard" to "fearing God, being pious," see Izutsu, *God and Man,* pp. 234–39; Izutsu, *Ethico-Religious Concepts in the Qurʾān,* McGill Islamic Studies 1 (Montreal, 1966), pp. 195–200; also M. M. Bravmann, *The Spiritual Background of Early Islam: Studies in Ancient Arab Concepts* (Leiden, 1972), pp. 116–18. Cf. Bouman, *Gott und Mensch,* pp. 199–200, stressing the directive to fear God as a dominant theme of the prophetic stories.

70. Compare God's messengers' renunciation of any earthly fee or compensation with the blunt request of the sorcerers summoned by Pharaoh to oppose Moses (41): "Is there a fee for us if we are the ones who overcome?" Cf. Speyer, *Biblischen Erzählungen,* p. 95 n. 5.

71. Cf. Bouman, *Gott und Mensch,* p. 195.

72. Lotman, *Structure,* p. 131, cf. pp. 126–27, 132–33.

73. Cf. Welch, *EI*² 5.420b.

74. If we assume, as I have suggested, that the proem itself, relating Muḥammad's current frustration, rejection, and lack of success, entails the first "sign" (pointed out by the refrain), then the temporal regression of the subsequent three episodes—from Muḥammad's present to Noah's diluvian past—would have made eminently good historical, rhetorical, and structural sense.

75. Lotman, *Structure,* pp. 80–92 et passim.

76. Cf. Tzvetan Todorov, *Symbolism and Interpretation,* trans. Catherine Porter (Ithaca, N.Y., 1982), pp. 35–36: "It is not that 'birds of a feather flock together' (cf.

the French proverb *qui se ressemble s'assemble*), but that 'birds that flock together are of a feather,' that is, resemble each other (*qui s'assemble se ressemble*)."

77. Lotman, *Structure*, p. 290–91.

78. More precisely, *kadhdhab– (k–dh–b:* form II) means "to declare, call, hold, deem someone a liar or something false or a lie; to deny" (cf. *WkaS* 1.94a–95a). See esp. Izutsu, *God and Man*, pp. 136–40; Izutsu, *Ethico-Religious Concepts*, p. 120 et passim.

79. That the command is uttered twice by precisely the *first* three of the later five messengers (as against some other, perhaps more random arrangement) strikes me as significant evidence for the kind of conscious rhetorical patterning to which I wish to call attention. Already many years ago Friedrich Schwally saw fit to distance himself tactfully from Theodor Nöldeke's rather harsh judgment that these repetitions constituted merely "ein ganz naives Verfahren [a quite naïve practice]" (GdQ^2 1.129 n. 3); cf. Ervin Gräf, "Zu den christlichen Einflüssen im Koran," in Paret, *Koran*, p. 189: "Die monotone Wiederholung eines Themas ist nicht ohne weiteres ein Zeichen für das Erschlaffen M[uḥamma]ds schöpferischer Phantasie, sondern liturgischer Stil [The monotonous repetition of a theme is not in and of itself a sign that Muḥammad's creative imagination was flagging, but rather it represents liturgical style]." For a balanced, analytical, yet sensitive discussion of the function of various modes of repetition in establishing the relations that structure verbal art, see Lotman, *Structure*, pp. 94–197 et passim (especially, for the present purposes, pp. 131–33).

Whether we are to discern in the correspondence between the eight iterations of the messengers' command and the eight occurrences of the important sign-focalizing refrain, anything beyond mere coincidence is a question I find most difficult to handle satisfactorily. That this command indeed constitutes the "significant" core matter betokened by these stories (even the first two and the proem where it is not uttered verbatim) I have no doubt—as I hope will be seen. Thus, some sort of a linkage, on the rhetorical level, between the two motifs of "sign" and prophetic command would by no means be unexpected; but I am reluctant to apply to a text like the Qur'ān any approach that smacks of numerology or presumes the operation of a measurable degree of numerical patterning and contrivance.

80. Cf., e.g., Moubarac, *Abraham*, pp. 137–39.

81. It may be noted that while messengers and prophets are invariably signified as direct accusative objects of the verb *kadhdhab-* (or its derivatives), the verb's transitivity with respect to *āyāt* is always expressed through the preposition *bi: kadhdhab- bi (l-)āyāt*.

More generally, one could argue that the unbelievers' very rejection of God's "signs" as lies served, in fact, to validate their "sign-ness." (Cf. K. J. Woollcombe, in G. W. H. Lampe and Woollcombe, *Essays on Typology*, Studies in Biblical Theology 22 [London, 1957], p. 48, commenting on Mark 8:12: "No sign *could* be given to a generation which wilfully closed eyes and ears to the signs of the times, and which refused to admit and proclaim the good news. Indeed their very refusal was itself a sign" [author's emphasis].) So, at least, a semiotician such as Eco might argue. For him, "a sign is everything which can be taken as significantly substituting for something else. This something else does not necessarily have to exist or to actually be somewhere at the moment in which a sign stands in for it. Thus *semiotics is in principle the discipline studying everything which can be used in order to lie.* If something cannot be used to tell a lie, conversely it cannot be used to tell the truth: it cannot in fact be used 'to tell' at all. I think that the definition of 'a theory of the lie' should be taken as a pretty comprehensive program for a general semiotics" (Eco, *Theory,* p. 7 [author's emphasis]; cf. Lotman, *Structure,* pp. 55–56).

82. Viz., 78:28/29 (B26/N33), 54:42 (B50/N49), 37:83/81 (B52/N50), 20:56/58 (B57/N55), compared to sūra 26, "The Poets": B58/N56.

83. Hirschfeld, *New Researches,* pp. 60–61; cf. Shahîd, "Contribution," pp. 576–77.

84. There is a real sense, of course, by no means absent from qur'ānic discourse about God, in which any and all of His creative, providential, and magisterial acts are incommensurate by and with any human standard and must, as divine acts, be of equal, infinite measure, differentiated and circumscribed only insofar as they have to be sensibly, perceptibly, intelligibly manifested or revealed to men. Thus, the apparent heterogeneity and multiplicity—in kind, quality, and magnitude—of the diverse phenomena that the Qur'ān characterizes as being or entailing "signs" (ranging from "ordinary" natural occurrences and processes, prophetic "wonders" and "miracles," and punitive catastrophes that wipe out disobedient nations to the divinely communicated verbal recitals of all these—i.e., to Revelation itself and its prophetic messengers) is only apparent. Understood as signifying hierophanies, these phenomenal reifications and eventualizations of divine agency and will—in effect, immanentizations of transcendence—are essentially equivalent to one another: the differences among "signs" which language suggests and sense and intellect perceive would, on that view, be accidental consequences of human finitude and fallibility. Even Revelation itself, in the form of *linguistic communication* of God's "words," can no more (but certainly no less!) contain and convey His "meaning" (as 18:109 and 31:27/26 make abundantly and poetically clear; cf. Nasr, *Ideals,* pp. 45–49) than can such other "signs" as the alternation of night and day, the "mysterious" sūra-opening letters, the drowning of Noah's kinfolk and Pharaoh's hosts, or the production of "every noble *zawj.*" In other words, there is no *intrinsic* reason to presume any greater degree of homogeneity between God's *zawj* production (*zawj* taken simply in one of its usual acceptations; see further) and the seven "punishment" episodes than would normally accrue from their common "sign-ness." Indeed, fundamental to the Qur'ān's radical restructuring of its hearers' world view is this sacralization of all of phenomenal and historical creation, through which things, processes, utterances, persons, and events in general are invoked to betoken God's will and work (cf. Izutsu, *God and Man,* pp. 134–35; Bouman, *Gott und Mensch,* pp. 91–92; Nasr, *Ideals,* pp. 54–55; Martin, "Structural Analysis," pp. 670, 673–80 passim). Naturally, such a view was blatantly at odds with ideas of the holy prevailing among Muḥammad's compatriots, for whom the temporal, spatial, and psychological boundaries between sacred and profane, cosmos and chaos, would have been reasonably well defined and conventionally observed. (Cf. Mircea Eliade, *The Sacred and the Profane: The Nature of Religion,* trans. Willard R. Trask [New York, 1961], passim, but esp. pp. 11–13, 24–36.) Nevertheless, I am persuaded that there

is *good* reason to construe *zawj* in this context in a special sense (not necessarily excluding its usual senses) and to interpret āya 7/6 as the rhetorically and structurally apt transition from the proem to the recitals of prophetic histories.

85. Jeffery, *Foreign Vocabulary,* pp. 154–55, with references; Lane, *Lexicon,* pp. 1266c–1267b.

86. E.g., Abū l-Qāsim Maḥmūd b. ʿUmar az-Zamakhsharī, *Al-Kashshāf ʿan ḥaqāʾiq at-tanzīl wa ʿuyūn al-awāʾil fī wujūh at-taʾwīl,* 4 vols. (Cairo, 1385/1966), 3.105, line 11; Bell, *Qurʾān Translated* 2.354; Paret, *Koran: Ubersetzung,* p. 300; etc.; cf. *WkaS* 1.145b, lines 12–14.

87. "Subḥāna -lladhī khalaqa l-azwāja kulla-hā mim-mā tunbitu l-arḍu wa min anfusi-him wa mim-mā lā yaʿlamūn."

88. Umberto Eco, *The Role of the Reader* (Bloomington, Ind., 1979), p. 23.

89. The question of typology and typological representation in the Qurʾān, to the best of my knowledge, has been scarcely touched on with any kind of seriousness or depth (for a notable exception, see Busse, "Herrschertypen"). Since to my mind it is an extremely important question, involving fundamental issues of qurʾānic structure, narrative, and prophetology and qurʾānic concepts of history, time, and the nature of God's action, and since it requires a far more extended treatment than can be undertaken here, I hope to deal with it at greater length in a future work. On typology and typological or figural interpretation and representation, especially before the mid–seventh century, see, e.g., for the present, Leonhard Goppelt, *Typos: The Typological Interpretation of the Old Testament in the New,* trans. Donald H. Madvig, with a foreword by E. Earle Ellis (Grand Rapids, Mich., 1982); Erich Auerbach, "Figura," trans. Ralph Manheim, in Auerbach, *Scenes from the Drama of European Literature,* Theory and History of Literature 9 (Minneapolis, 1984), pp. 11–76; Auerbach, *Mimesis: The Representation of Reality in Western Literature,* trans. Willard Trask (1953; rpt. Garden City, N.Y., n.d.), pp. 13, 42–43, 64–66, 490, et passim; Rudolf Bultmann, "Ursprung und Sinn der Typologie als hermeneutischer Methode," in *Pro Regno pro Sanctuario, G. van der Leeuw zum 60. Geburtstag* (Nijkerk-Holland, 1950), pp. 89–100; Jean Daniélou, *Sacramentum futuri: Etudes sur les origines de la typologie biblique* (Paris, 1950), English trans. by Dom Wulstan Hibberd: *From Shadows to Reality: Studies in the Biblical Typology of the Fathers* [London, 1960]; Louis Réau, *Iconographie de l'art chrétien,* vol. 1: *Introduction générale* (Paris, 1955), pp. 192–222; Lampe and Woollcombe, *Essays;* Claus Westermann, ed., *Essays on Old Testament Hermeneutics,* trans. James Luther Mays et al. (Richmond, Va., 1963), esp. essays by G[erhard] von Rad, H[ans W.] Wolff, W[alther] Eichrodt, and W[olfhart] Pannenberg; A. C. Charity, *Events and Their Afterlife: The Dialectics of Christian Typology in the Bible and Dante* (1966; rpt. Cambridge, 1987); F[ranz] Hesse, H. Hakagawa, E[rich] Fascher, "Typologie," *RGG*[3] 6.1094–98; Northrop Frye, *The Great Code: The Bible and Literature* (New York, 1983), esp. pp. 78–138; etc. Except for Auerbach, Daniélou, Réau, and Frye (and *CHB* 1.412–586 passim [several authors]), the works cited tend to deal with the question in theological rather than phenomenological, cultural-historical, *religionswissenschaftlich,* or literary critical terms.

90. Frye, *Great Code,* p. 80, cf. pp. 80–83 et passim.

91. Goppelt, *Typos,* p. 17–18; cf. Eichrodt in *Essays,* ed. Westermann, pp. 226–27.

92. Daniélou, *From Shadows to Reality,* p. 12, cf. p. 52 et passim; Réau, *Iconographie,* p. 195 n. 1. A. C. Charity, too (*Events,* p. 109 n. 1), asserts, as "a basic, perhaps even the basic principle of typology," that "it is primarily events, and not persons or places or things, which are potentially typological, the *res gesta* first, and the *res* or *persona* only in relation to that deed."

93. Goppelt, *Typos,* p. 18, cf. pp. 65, 75, 198–203 et passim; von Rad and Eichrodt in *Essays,* ed. Westermann, pp. 19–22, 233–35; cf. Daniélou, *From Shadows to Reality,* pp. 12, 30–41.

94. See, e.g., Bultmann "Ursprung"; Lampe and Woollcombe, *Essays,* pp. 26–27, 34, 49 et passim; also, perhaps, Auerbach, "Figura," pp. 58–60. Regardless of how early Christian (and non-Christian) groups may in fact have utilized typology in day-to-day teaching and preaching, most modern theological writers (as well as some eminent and orthodox Church Fathers) would probably subscribe to Goppelt's view: "If the antitype does not represent a heightening of the type, if it is merely a repetition of the type, then it can be called typology only in certain instances and in a limited way" (*Typos,* p. 18, cf. p. 62). Such may be the case if the concerns are to preserve conceptual (or doctrinal) purity, maintain theoretical rigor, and observe terminological niceties—concerns that seem not always to have carried much weight among religiously minded majorities before the mid-seventh century (or even well after). But, as Goppelt himself, among others, points out (with some apparent disdain and disapproval), a kind of typology based on recurrence or even mere superficial similarities, often mixed with allegorical and eschatological elements, did prevail widely among intertestamental and early common-era Jewish communities (including the Essenes of Qumran) and did gain ready acceptance in popular Christianity and various heterodoxies (see, e.g., Goppelt, *Typos,* pp. 23–41, 203–5, 226–28; Lampe and Woollcombe, *Essays,* pp. 22–25, 33–36; Auerbach, "Figura," pp. 43–44, 55–56; Johannes Leipoldt and Siegfried Morenz, *Heilige Schriften: Betrachtungen zur Religionsgeschichte der antiken Mittelmeerwelt* [Leipzig, 1953], pp. 141–42, 148–49; Shemaryahu Talmon, *CHB* 1.190; C[harles K.] Barrett, *CHB* 1.387; R[ichard P. C.] Hanson, *CHB* 1.426–29). And, as G. W. H. Lampe suggests, precisely this more heterogeneous brand of typology readily found its way into general religious discourse through "the 'sermon-illustration' method of handling the text of Scripture" (Lampe and Woollcombe, *Essays,* pp. 35–36). But Christian theology especially, it seems to me, could not but focus its typological speculations upon Christ and the Church as antitypes par excellence; and since "Christian typology is Christological," it perforce became a typology whose "basic principle is that there is an imperfect order which prepares for and prefigures an order of perfection" (Jean Daniélou, *From Shadows to Reality,* pp. 25, 31). Therein may well lie the reason for the strong current of rejection directed at Rudolf Bultmann's thesis that (1) typology falls essentially within the conceptual sphere of *repetition, Wiederholung* (though repetition that, he clearly states, may indeed be eschatologized or heightened) rather than of *perfection, Vollendung,* or *fulfillment, Erfüllung* (which are, he holds, intrinsically associated with predictive prophecy and its evidential value), and that (2) it derives from an already ancient cyclical idea of world history involving the repetition or recurrence at the end of time (or the dawn of a new era) of something like or equivalent to that which had been in the beginning of time (or the old era's

distant past) (Bultmann, "Ursprung," esp. pp. 89–90). That such a view may not jibe well with much of Christian doctrine, theology, and historical thinking does not invalidate it as a description of how typological thought, interpretation, and expression may actually have gone on in many—if not most—instances (even though it may be unacceptable to some as a description of how it *ought* to have gone on—or ought to go on). It is my impression, though, that Bultmann's use of *repetition* in his essay is a good deal less naïve and more productive as a characterization of typological processes than his critics often seem willing to grant. (On *repetition* as a much more complex feature within a structural system—specifically, a text—than most of Bultmann's critics take into account, see esp. Lotman, *Structure*, pp. 132–35; cf. Eco, *Theory*, p. 270.)

95. To convey this idea Woollcombe uses the particularly cogent term *type-pair* in Lampe and Woollcombe, *Essays*, pp. 73–75.

96. Auerbach, "Figura," p. 53, as quoted in Auerbach, *Mimesis*, p. 64. I prefer Trask's translation of this passage to Manheim's.

97. Auerbach, "Figura," p. 53, cf. pp. 43–44; also Auerbach, *Mimesis*, pp. 64–66; Lampe and Woollcombe, *Essays*, pp. 12–13; Daniélou, *From Shadows to Reality*, pp. 287–88; Leipoldt and Morenz, *Heilige Schriften*, pp. 147–49; Réau, *Iconographie*, p. 194. In that literature on the subject with which I have become somewhat familiar one finds, with few exceptions, much more consideration given to the principles, "proper" application, and validity of typological or figural interpretation, especially of the Old Testament by New Testament and early Christian writers, than to the actual operation and popular reception of the tradition of such interpretation. And as a result, unfortunately, one generally finds only passing attention given to how these other aspects of the typological attitude manifested themselves.

98. R. Payne Smith, *A Compendious Syriac Dictionary*, ed. J. Payne Smith [Jessie Payne Margoliouth] (1903; rpt. Oxford, 1957), p. 112a, records a Syriac usage, interesting in this connection, *bar zawgā de-š^{e}līḥē*, which is rendered "a fellow-worker with the Apostle(s)." But without further information, greater familiarity with the sources, and more proficiency in the language, I am unable to comment on any possible relation this expression might have with the sense of Arabic *zawj* proposed here.

99. E.g., 73:15–16; 43:6/5–8/7, 44/45; 21:5–9; 6:34, 84–90; 12:109–10; 10:74/75; 51:52; 50:12–13/14; 15:10–15; 14:9–15/18; 40:5, 23/22, 78; 35:23/21–26/24; 4:163/161–165/163; 23:44/46; etc.

100. See, e.g., *Sīra* 1.153–54 (Guillaume, *Life*, p. 107); also A. J. Wensinck, *A Handbook of Early Muhammadan Tradition* (1927; rpt. Leiden, 1971), p. 196–97 (s.v. "Prophet, Prophets"), where many ḥadīth-reports are cited in which a prophetic typology or normative mode of action is presupposed. Cf. also Toufic Fahd, "Problèmes de typologie dans la 'Sîra' d'ibn Isḥâq," in *La vie du Prophète Mahomet*, Colloque de Strasbourg (octobre 1980) (Paris, 1983), pp. 67–75, who suggests how certain features of the biography of Muḥammad might have been framed by early Muslims (many of them converts from Christianity and Judaism) to correspond typologically with features of the lives of great religious figures of the past—especially Moses and Jesus.

101. Cf. Horovitz, *Koranische Untersuchungen*, pp. 53–54; Speyer, *Biblischen*

Erzählungen, pp. 422–23; Jeffery, *Qur'ān as Scripture,* pp. 78–79; Busse, "Herrschertypen," pp. 57–58.

102. For examples and extensive documentation, see, among others, Wensinck, "Muhammed," pp. 175, 188–89; Horovitz, *Koranische Untersuchungen,* pp. 8–9, 18, 29–32 et passim; Karl Ahrens, *Muhammed als Religionsstifter,* Abhandlungen für die Kunde des Morgenlandes 19.4 (Leipzig, 1935), pp. 127–32, esp. 139–46; Johann Fück, "Die Originalität des arabischen Propheten," *Zeitschrift der Deutschen Mogenländischen Gesellschaft* 90 (1936): 518–22 (English trans. in Swartz, *Studies,* pp. 92–95); Jeffery, *Qur'ān as Scripture,* pp. 21–31, 136, esp. 47–51; Régis Blachère, *Le problème de Mahomet* (Paris, 1952), pp. 57–63; Moubarac, *Abraham,* pp. 15–16 et passim; Bell/Watt, *Intro.,* pp. 26, 156; Bouman, *Gott und Mensch,* pp. 16–38 passim, 193–94, 206; etc.

103. The phrase, "gegenseitige Ähnlichkeit der Gottmenschen," is Wensinck's ("Muhammed," p. 124; I am assuming that "Gottmenschen" is likely to be a malapropism for "Gottesmänner"). Cf. *GdQ*[2] 1.119–20: "Überhaupt haben alle diese Propheten untereinander und mit Muhammed eine große Familienähnlichkeit [In general all these prophets bear a strong family resemblance to one another and to Muḥammad]."

104. Cf. Odil Hannes Steck, *Israel und das gewaltsame Geschick der Propheten: Untersuchungen zur Überlieferung des deuteronomistischen Geschichtsbildes im Alten Testament, Spätjudentum und Urchristentum,* Wissenschaftliche Monographien zum Alten und Neuen Testament 23 (Neukirchen-Vluyn, 1967), passim. (I owe this valuable reference to my friend and colleague Professor Sam A. Meier.) See also Charity, *Events,* pp. 59, 66–72, 80, 108, 148–55 et passim (on the concept of a "typology of rejection").

105. Cf. 26:208–9. On this interpretation of *khalā fī-hā,* see Bravmann, *Spiritual Background,* pp. 143–44. On *nadhīr* (or *mundhir*) and *bashīr* (or *mubashshir*), see, e.g., Horovitz, *Koranische Untersuchungen,* p. 47; Bell/Watt, *Intro.,* pp. 26–27.

106. Or "who were ungrateful [*alladhīna kafarū*]."

107. Jeffery, *Qur'ān as Scripture,* pp. 47–53 et passim.

108. Paret, *Mohammed,* pp. 89–91.

109. Moubarac, *Abraham,* pp. 143–48.

110. As I have already indicated, the complex question of the intimate relationship between typological thought and representation and ideas of time and history cannot be dealt with here. For some discussion of the issue, see, e.g., Auerbach, *Mimesis,* pp. 64–65; Charity, *Events,* pp. 17, 51–55, 71–72 et passim (with references cited).

111. Gibb, "Pre-Islamic Monotheism," pp. 269–70, 278, 278–79 (author's emphasis); cf. also Kronholm, "Dependence," pp. 64–65 et passim.

112. See, e.g., Steck, *Israel,* pp. 66–71, 199–201 et passim; Carsten Colpe, "Das Siegel der Propheten," *Orientalia Suecana* 33–35 (1984–86): 72–75.

113. See Steck, *Israel,* pp. 265–316 et passim; also Wensinck, "Muhammed," p. 184; Goppelt, *Typos,* pp. 61–82, 228–29 et passim; Jaroslav Pelikan, *The Christian Tradition: A History of the Development of Doctrine,* vol. 1: *The Emergence of the Catholic Tradition (100–600)* (Chicago, 1971), pp. 209–10.

114. Wensinck, "Muhammed," p. 170.

115. Pelikan, "Emergence," pp. 110–12; Pelikan, *The Christian Tradition: A*

History of the Development of Doctrine, vol. 2: *The Spirit of Eastern Christendom (600–1700)* (Chicago, 1974), pp. 16–19.

116. Early Christian iconography often represented the Old Testament prophets and the New Testament apostles within the same context; see, e.g., Heinrich Paulus, "Apostelbilder," *RGG*³ 1.499; and Erich Dinkler, "Malerei und Plastik I. Spätantike," *RGG*³ 4.636–37. Relatively close, both in time and location, to early seventh-century Arabia would have been the monumental *Transfiguration* apse mosaic in Saint Catherine's monastery on Mount Sinai, dated to the reign of Justinian (mid–sixth century) or possibly a half-century later (discussed and pictured in D. V. Ainalov, *The Hellenistic Origins of Byzantine Art,* trans. Elizabeth Sobolevitch and Serge Sobolevitch, ed. Cyril Mango [New Brunswick, N.J., 1961], pp. 272–74, 279). "The soffit of the arch is decorated with portrait medallions of the apostles. Under the Transfiguration is a series of medallions with representations of the prophets" (ibid., p. 272). Such visual juxtapositions of the two groups could have been even more influential than literary works in effecting their near identification in the popular religious imagination.

117. Wensinck, "Muhammed," pp. 176–77.

118. Busse, "Herrschertypen," p. 57 (citing F. Hesse's summary of Bultmann's position in "Typologie I. Im AT," *RGG*³ 6.1094). It is still quite debatable whether the term "seal of the prophets [*khātam an-nabīyīn*]" (33:40) is to be understood as the "last" of them or their "confirmation" or "authentication"; see, e.g., Horovitz, *Koranische Untersuchungen,* pp. 53–54; Jeffery, *Foreign Vocabulary,* pp. 120–21; Speyer, *Biblischen Erzählungen,* pp. 422–23; Blachère, *Coran,* p. 992 n. 40. On the concept in general, in the context of the Near Eastern religious Weltanschauung before Islam, see esp. Colpe, "Siegel."

119. Cf. Charity, *Events,* pp. 153–54 (also 66–71, 80, 108, et passim), speaking of a "typology of rejection." A thorough evaluation of Charity's complex theses and their applicability to a study of qur'ānic typology cannot be undertaken here.

120. Frank Moore Cross, *Canaanite Myth and Hebrew Epic: Essays in the History of the Religion of Israel* (Cambridge, Mass., 1973), p. 333; cf. G. Vermes, *CHB* 1.226, and C. K. Barnett, *CHB* 1.386–89, 395–96.

121. See, among others, Horovitz, *Koranische Untersuchungen,* pp. 31–32; W. Mongomery Watt, *Muhammad at Mecca* (Oxford, 1960), pp. 65–66; etc.

122. Cf. Rudolf Bultmann, "Weissagung und Erfüllung," in Bultmann, *Glauben und Verstehen: Gesammelte Aufsätze* (Tübingen, 1952), 1.162–86, esp. 183–84. (English trans. by James C. G. Greig in *Essays,* ed. Westermann, pp. 50–75). The term *Scheitern,* "shipwreck, foundering; failure," is Bultmann's (pp. 183–86). J. Greig (in Westermann, *Essays,* pp. 72–75) translates it as "miscarriage"—not, I think, an entirely felicitous choice.

123. Cf. Charity, *Events,* pp. 153–54.

124. Arabic: *man maḍā* or *al-māḍī,* "an individual personality of the past, sometimes known and definite (as in the instance of the Prophet), sometimes unknown, and hence merely symbolic" (Bravmann, *Spiritual Background,* p. 163).

125. Bravmann, *Spiritual Background,* pp. 155, 160, 163, and cf. pp. 123–77 passim. Bravmann has effectively argued for reinterpreting the term in this sense, stressing its *primary* association with an act or practice instituted as a norm by a specific person or group, which only *secondarily* may have come to be loosely

identified as "the general custom," "the normative usage," or "the customary practice of the community" (*Spiritual Background,* pp. 151–52, 164–68, as against, particularly, the prevailing opinions of D. S. Margoliouth and Joseph Schacht). Every *sunna,* then, would seem to have come into effect as a *bidʿa* or *ḥadath,* an (unwarranted) "innovation," discretely (and perhaps discreetly, as well!) introduced. (See ibid., p. 162, on the verb *aḥdatha—ḥ-d-th:* form IV—as a term for "creating a *sunna.*")

126. It is no accident that these societally grounded terms of communal approbation and disapprobation—*maʿrūf* and *munkar*—became a major feature of what Izutsu calls "the basic moral dichotomy" of the qur'ānic Weltanschauung (*Ethico-Religious Concepts,* pp. 105, 213–17).

127. Ignaz Goldziher, *Vorlesungen über den Islam,* 2d ed., ed. Franz Babinger, Religionswissenschaftliche Bibliothek 1 (1925; rpt. Heidelberg, 1963), pp. 254–55 (English trans. by Andras Hamori and Ruth Hamori, *Introduction to Islamic Theology and Law* [Princeton, 1981], pp. 230–31).

128. Reuben Levy, *The Social Structure of Islam* (Cambridge, 1957), p. 194; cf. Izutsu, *Ethico-Religious Concepts,* pp. 213–17.

129. See, e.g., Goldziher, *Vorlesungen,* p. 255; C. H. Becker, *Islamstudien: Vom Werden und Wesen der islamischen Welt* (Leipzig, 1924), 1.337; Chelhod, *Introduction,* pp. 81–82. Cf. Brown, *Making,* pp. 36–39, 49–50, 99–100.

130. See, e.g., Ignaz Goldiher, *Muhammedanische Studien,* 2 vols. (Halle, 1889–90), 1.41–42, 2.13–17 (English trans. by C. R. Barber and S. M. Stern, *Muslim Studies,* 2 vols [London, 1967–71]). Cf. Ramsay MacMullen, *Roman Government's Response to Crisis, A.D. 235–337* (New Haven, Conn., 1976), p. 43, speaking of the Roman Empire during the third and early fourth centuries: "A Christian raged in vain against the inflexible veneration accorded by pagans to their own past. 'They take refuge in the judgment of the ancient forebears who, they allege, were wise, and made test, and knew what was best.' On exactly the same grounds, a pagan raged against the first Christian emperor because he was a 'changer,' *novator*—not (and precisely here lay the heart of the problem in the third century) a *renovator.* It was in that little 're-' that so many claims to leadership and gratitude were made. . . . Whatever was long approved was right." See also van Nieuwenhuijze, "Prophetic Function" (1962): 128–29; (1964): 113 (p. 111 n. 1 continued).

131. Many passages from sūras dated in the middle and late Meccan period, like āya 74 from this sūra, make it clear that the Meccans (as well as their typological predecessors, the folk of the earlier messenger-prophets) justified their resistance to the prophetic message and their disobedience in terms of their righteous adherence to the ways, beliefs, and gods of their fathers: e.g., 53:23; 43:22/21–24/23; 21:53/54; 11:62/65, 87/89, 109/111; 14:10/12; 10:78/79; 7:28/27, 70/68.

132. Goldziher, *Vorlesungen,* p. 255.

133. E.g., 15:13; 18:55/53; 35:43/42. Cf. 17:77/79: "The sunna of such of our messengers as We did send before you [*sunnata man qad arsalnā qabla-ka min rusulinā*]."

134. At least, such seems to have been the theory underlying the ideologically charged term *sunnat al-awwalīn.* That the theory's plausibility and validity were not immediately embraced by the Meccans and others lay, in my opinion, in its apparently deliberate course of divorcing the idea of *sunna* from the central all-

pervasive principle of blood kinship to which, in the social and cultural context, it was inseparably wedded. Here, I am convinced, can be seen one phase of the massive campaign embedded in qur'ānic discourse to elevate allegiance (*dīn*) to God and His Messenger above tribal loyalty and the kinship bond (*ṣilat ar-raḥim*) as the primary generating, sustaining, and sanctioning force through which community membership was to be determined and delimited. This campaign was not a mere matter of substituting a "bond of faith" or "religion" for a "bond of blood," as has frequently been asserted—especially inasmuch as at the time the two ideas would not have involved mutually exclusive phenomena, attitudes, or sets of obligations. Rather it reflected an incredibly complex, nuanced, multifaceted strategy designed to co-opt, expand, reorient, transform, and subvert existing terms, concepts, systems, institutions, and frames of reference in a manner and to a degree that cannot possibly be dealt with in this essay. I would only suggest that in the manifest operation of this strategy from the "earliest" to the "latest" revelations lies the strongest case for the proposition that Muḥammad's message was destined, maybe from the outset, for an audience ultimately far beyond his local one at Mecca (cf., among others, Frantz Buhl, "Fasste Muḥammed seine Verkündigung als eine universelle, auch für Nichtaraber bestimmte Religion auf?" *Islamica* 2 [1926]: 135–49; S. D. Goitein, "The Concept of Mankind in Islam," in *History and the Idea of Mankind,* ed. W. Warren Wagar [Albuquerque, N.M., 1972], pp. 76–79; van Nieuwenhuijze, "Prophetic Function" [1964]: 111–14; H. M. Tilman Nagel, *Staat und Glaubensgemeinschaft im Islam: Geschichte der politischen Ordnungsvorstellungen der Muslime,* 2 vols. [Zürich, 1981], 1.55–81). Most of the Meccans, after all, came to heed the message only when its efficacy had made itself felt elsewhere, where the principle of blood kinship may perhaps have been less all-pervasive or more diluted or may not have become so rigidly ossified into urbanized conventions as seems to have happened at Mecca.

135. The expression *sunnat Allāh* (once in the form *sunnati-nā,* "Our sunna") occurs nine times in the Qur'ān: 17:77/79; 40:85; 35:43/41–42 (bis); 33:38, 62 (bis); 48:23 (bis). Sūras 17, 40, and 35 are considered to be late Meccan, and 33 and 48 are considered late Medinan. In all these occurrences, God's sunna is characterized as (1) having taken effect or become established procedure long ago (see Bravmann, *Spiritual Background,* pp. 139–51, esp. 143–44) and (2) being subject neither to amendment nor to supersedence (so I construe the legal sense of *taḥwīl* and *tabdīl,* as, e.g., in 35:43: "Fa lan tajida li-sunnati -llāhi tabdīlan wa lan tajida li-sunnati -llāhi taḥwīlan [You will not find God's sunna superseded nor will you find God's sunna amended]"). Cf. Charity, *Events,* pp. 27–29, 52–58, et passim, on the "steadfastness" of God and the "normativeness" and "newness" of His acts in Judeo-Christian typology.

Thus, it is not quite accurate to hold, as Wensinck did (*ShEI* 552a), that "the two expressions"—i.e., *sunnat al-awwalīn* and *sunnat Allāh*—"are synonymous insofar as they refer to Allah's punishment of earlier generations who met the preaching of prophets sent to them with unbelief or scorn" (cf. Paret, *Koran: Kommentar,* p. 188). It may also be noted, however, that, with one debatable exception (17:77/79) the term *sunna* occurs in the Qur'ān *only* in one or the other of these two expressions and *never* with reference to the ancestral or tribal sunna that Islam was to co-opt, amend, and supersede.

136. Cf. G. E. von Grünebaum, "Von Muḥammads Wirkung und Originalität," *Wiener Zeitschrift für die Kunde des Morgenlandes* 44 (1937): 43–45.

137. Bouman, *Gott und Mensch,* p. 192.

138. Cf., e.g., von Grünebaum, "Von Muḥammads Wirkung," pp. 44–46.

139. Bouman, *Gott und Mensch,* p. 192.

140. Ironically, and hardly fortuitously, it was the discourse of poets and *kuhhān* which was most frequently and naturally appealed to to attest or support tribal sunna. Might it not have seemed paradoxical to some, then, to categorize as a conventional mantic one whose discourse so uncompromisingly subordinated all tribal sunnas to the sunna of God?

141. Cf. Albrecht Alt, "God of the Fathers," in Alt, *Essays on Old Testament History and Religion,* trans. R. A. Wilson (Garden City, N.Y., 1968), p. 5.

142. As Eco says, "Even prophets have to be socially *accepted* in order to be right; if not, they are wrong" (*Theory,* p. 256 [author's emphasis]).

143. On the sense of *zubur,* see, e.g., Horovitz, *Koranische Untersuchungen,* p. 69; Ahrens, *Muhammed,* p. 132; Jeffery, *Foreign Vocabulary,* pp. 148–49.

144. Literally, "some non-Arab, some speaker of an incomprehensible language"; see, e.g., Izutsu, *God and Man,* pp. 187–88; F. Gabrieli, "ʿAdjam," *EI*[2] 1.206; Zwettler, *Oral Tradition,* pp. 161–64, 186 n. 144.

145. Alternatively, "They descend on every peccant falsifier, / [the daemons] lending ear, though most [daemons] will lie." This interpretation would perhaps eliminate the logical quibble raised by one's wondering how only *most* falsifiers would lie (see, e.g., az-Zamakhsharī, *Kashshāf* 3.132–33, esp. 133, lines 2–4.

146. Formerly, influenced by arguments advanced by Irfan Shahîd ("Contribution," pp. 566–72, 577–78), I rendered this āya thus: "And the poets!—Attending them (are) those who lead astray [i.e., the demons, *al-ġāwūn*]" (Zwettler, *Oral Tradition,* p. 157, and cf. p. 185 n. 134). I no longer find sufficient ground to think that *ghāwūn* here means anything but what it seems ordinarily to mean and what it most likely means in its five other occurrences in the Qurʾān, two of which are to be found in this sūra (91, 94): viz., "errant, aberrant, perverted, perverse, astray, disoriented"—i.e., as the active participle of the form I verb *ghawā* in its *intransitive* sense (cf. 7:175/174; 15:42; 37:32/31). Nor, given the evidence based on qurʾānic usage, am I convinced by Shahîd's arguments in "Another Contribution," pp. 2–6. Shahîd is quite correct that *ghawā* can also be used in a *transitive* sense, meaning "to pervert, lead astray"; but while it is true that "examples for the use of *ghawā* rather than *aghwā,* the commoner [form IV] transitive form, are not lacking" ("Contribution," p. 569), such examples are entirely lacking in the Qurʾān, where the two forms occur only in complementary distribution; see 5:16/15; 11:34/36; 15:39; 20:121/119; 38:82/83; 52:2; and esp., e.g., 27:63, where the daemons respond: "rabba-nā hāʾulāʾi -lladhīna aghwaynā aghwaynā-hum ka-mā ghawaynā [Our Lord, these whom we perverted we perverted as we ourselves were perverse (*or* have been perverted)]." I cannot agree with his suggestion that *ghāwīn* (not *al-ghāwūn*) occurs in 37:32/31 "in what is most probably its transitive sense" ("Contribution," p. 569). The verse—"fa aghwaynā-kum in-nā kunnā ghāwīn"—must be read in its full context and in conjunction with, e.g., 15:39–42; 28:63; and 38:82/83–85; then it becomes clear that it must be rendered; as most translations have it: "So we perverted them, for we ourselves were perverse/perverted." (Cf.

Shahîd's own dictum ["Contribution," p. 578]: "Coherence with the lexicology of the Koran itself must remain the firmest of all supports for any interpretation on the lexical level.") Who consequently would have been signified by *al-ghāwūn* in the present āya is a different question. It may indeed refer to the *shayāṭīn,* but in the same sense as the verb *ghawā* is used with them as subject, not in the sense of "perverters, those who lead astray" (which qur'ānic usage indicates would be *mughwūn/mughwīn*). On the basis of āyas 91 and 94 of this sūra, however, I suspect it to be the idolatrous unbelievers, rather than the daemons, contrary to my earlier opinion. Cf. Paret, *Koran: Kommentar,* p. 372; Michael B. Schub, "Qur'ān 26:224 /ġāwūnᵃ/ = 'Fundamentally Disoriented': An Orientalist Note," *Journal of Arabic Literature* 18 [1987]: 79–80. Martin, "Structural Analysis," pp. 677, 681 n. 8, seems to have misunderstood both the meaning of the āya and Shahîd's interpretation of it, which he says he adopts.

147. Pace Schub. On the interpretation of *intaṣarū* as "to take vengeance, avenge oneself," see Shahîd, "Contribution," pp. 574–75.

148. For other discussions of the structure of this third section of the sūra, taking a somewhat different tack from mine, see Shahîd, "Contribution," pp. 576–77; Martin, "Structural Analysis," pp. 676–78.

149. See Zwettler, *Oral Tradition,* pp. 156–66 (pace Shahîd, "Another Contribution," pp. 19–20).

150. Shahîd, "Contribution," p. 576.

151. In addition to Shahîd's 1965 and 1983 discussions of these āyas ("Contribution" and "Another Contribution"), other important studies include Blachère, "Poésie"; and Bonebakker, "Religious Prejudice," esp. pp. 77–81. Renate Jacobi ("Dichtung und Lüge in der arabischen Literaturtheorie," *Der Islam* 49 [1972]: 85–86) deals briefly with the āyas themselves, but her primary concern is with their influence on the development of later Islamic attitudes toward the general question of mendacity or "fictiveness" in poetry. In that regard she is of the opinion "daß die Koranverse gegen die Dichter im allgemeinen nicht als eine definitorische Aussage über die Dichtung aufgefaßt worden sind, sondern nur als eine Warnung vor mißbräuchlicher Anwendung oder übertriebener Wertschätzung [that in general the qur'ānic verses against the poets have been construed not as a regulatory pronouncement on poetry but rather just as a warning against using it improperly or attaching excessive value to it]" (pp. 90–91).

152. Compare, e.g., in many commentaries on the *Fātiḥa,* the prayer that opens the Qur'ān, the polemical and quite gratuitous identification of "those who have incurred wrath [*al-maghḍūb ʿalay-him*]" with the Jews and "those astray [*aḍ-ḍāllīn*]" with the Christians (cf. Blachère, *Coran,* p. 127–28 n. 7; Paret, *Koran: Kommentar,* p. 12; Mahmoud M. Ayoub, "The Prayer of Islam: A Presentation of Sūrat al-Fātiḥa in Muslim Exegesis," in Welch, ed., *Studies,* pp. 645–46).

153. Or "verses"? Cf. Bell/Watt, *Intro.,* pp. 126–27. One might well explore the intimate relationship, both in the Qur'ān and in Arabic and old Semitic usage, between *hearing* and *obedience,* a particularly important conjunction with regard to orally delivered revealed commands: e.g., "We hear and obey [*samiʿnā wa aṭaʿnā*]," "To hear is to obey [*as-samʿa wa ṭ-ṭāʿata*]," and the like. The words occur in close, apparently idiomatic, conjunction in five passages: 2:285; 4:46/49; 5:7/10; 24:51/50; and 44:16 (in the imperative, "Hear and obey!). "We hear"—*samiʿnā*—also

occurs twice in ironic conjunction with "we disobey"—*ʿaṣaynā*—refering to the Israelites' reception of the Law at Sinai. See esp. Joseph Horovitz, "Jewish Proper Names and Derivatives in the Koran," *Hebrew Union College Annual* 2 (1925): 214; Speyer, *Biblischen Erzählungen*, pp. 301–3.

154. Cf. Shahîd, "Contribution," pp. 370–71. Shahîd argues ("Another Contribution," p. 2) against interpreting *al-ghāwūn* in āya 224 "as an erring group of human beings following the poets," because such an interpretation "does not correspond with the facts of pre-Islamic Arab literary and social life, in which there was no place for poets with followers." His point is true, of course, as I have tried to set forth; but as an argument, it entirely misses the irony of the qurʾānic turn of phrase (and moreover, it clashes rather jarringly with arguments advanced by him on p. 7 defending the poets as "a much-respected group").

155. D. S. Margoliouth ("The Origins of Arabic Poetry," *Journal of the Royal Asiatic Society* [1925]: 418–19, 443–44) noted the correlation between āya 225 and the itinerant fiction that sustained the classical Arabic *qaṣīda,* but incredibly he considered it as evidence supporting his untenable theory that practically all of what we would think of as pre-Islamic poetry consisted of later Islamic fabrications prompted in part by this single qurʾānic verse. Cf. other interpretations of this āya in Blachère, "Poésie," p. 94 n. 2; Shahîd, "Contribution," pp. 570–71; Bonebakker, "Religious Prejudice," p. 79–80 (essentially repeating Blachère).

156. Minimal confirmation can be found in the famous opening hemistich of the "suspended ode" (*muʿallaqa*) of ʿAntara b. Shaddād, which (assuming its authenticity) dates from the sixth century: "Have the poets left a single spot for a patch to be sewn?" (trans. Arberry). On conventions (not to be confused with so-called stereotypes) and conventionality in the pre-Islamic *qaṣīda,* see, e.g., Fuat Sezgin, *Geschichte des arabischen Schriftums,* vol. 2: *Poesie bis ca. 430 H.* (Leiden, 1975), pp. 7–11 with references. On the more complex question of the *qaṣīda* and the mode and "reliability" of its representation, on the one hand, of the "actual world" of the poet and his audience and, on the other, of the poet's own person, psyche, and experiences, see, among others, G. E. von Grünebaum, *Die Wirklichkeitweite der früharabischen Dichtung: Eine literaturwissenschaftliche Untersuchung,* Wiener Zeitschrift für die Kunde des Morgenlandes, Beiheft 3 (Vienna, 1937); G. Müller, *Ich bin Labīd und das ist mein Ziel: Zum Problem der Selbstbehauptung in der altarabischen Qaside,* Berliner Islamstudien 1 (Wiesbaden, 1981); also Renate Jacobi in *GAPh* 2.23–31 passim.

157. Irfan Shahîd seems to be aware of this when he notes, with respect to "*yaqūlūna mā lā yafʿalūn* [they do say what they do not do]," that "the two verbs together make up a phrase which describes a situation more complex than the simple one of telling lies" (Shahîd, "Another Contribution," p. 7). Unfortunately, however, the interpretation he advances, on the basis of arguments that are not always pertinent, lucid, or consistent, does not seem to me to be plausible. In the first place, despite the observation just cited, he proceeds to treat the verse as if it were somehow a "denunciation" of the poets' "mendacity," and in a note (p. 7 n. 15) excludes the possibility that the words might refer to "certain elements in pre-Islamic poetry [that] could conceivably but erroneously be equated with mendacity"—such as *fakhr* (poetry of boasting and self-praise) or the hyperbolic claims of panegyric. Yet, as will be seen, while such examples "cannot be simply equated

with mendacity" (as Shahîd, rightly maintains), they are precisely cases of poets' saying "what they do not do"! But even more arbitrary seems the decision to interpret āya 226 as a reference "to the well-known *taḥaddī/iʿjāz* problem, the challenge that the Koran flung to its opponents to produce something like it and their failure to do so" (p. 8). Leaving aside most of the "supporting arguments," I must question Shahîd's claim that sūra 61 ("The Ranks"; B100/N98): 2–3 (the only passage where a similar phrase occurs—here twice in the second-person plural), "provides the desiderated key to understanding the exact meaning of the identical phrase in sūra XXVI, namely failure to fulfil a promise or to perform in a contest" (p. 8 n. 18). The āyas can be rendered as follows: "Oh, those of you who believe! Why do you say what you do not do [*lima taqūlūna mā lā tafʿalūn*]?/ Gravely odious is it to God that you should say what you do not do [*an taqūlū mā lā tafʿalūn*]!" Relying on only a single "occasion of revelation [*sabab an-nuzūl*]" adduced by exegetes for these āyas, Shahîd posits categorically that they constitute "an expression of dissatisfaction with, and a rebuke to, the Muslims who had promised much before the battle of Uḥud but did not fulfil their promises" (ibid.). Irrespective of the reliability of the *asbāb an-nuzūl* as keys to understanding qurʾānic discourse, one must note that, e.g., az-Zamakhsharī (one of Shahîd's primary sources) offers at least three other alternatives to the single one selected by Shahîd: exaggerated or false claims of prowess in battle (= *fakhr?:* "Men used to say 'I killed' and 'I stabbed' and 'I struck' and 'I withstood,' when they had done no such things"), attribution to oneself of the feats of others or the hypocritical protestations of the *munāfiqūn* (*Kashshāf* 4.96_{14}–97_{1}). In general, I cannot agree with the sometimes oversimplified views on poetry and poets and, especially, on the problem of *taḥaddī/iʿjāz* (in either its qurʾānic or its later Islamic form), which are so confidently and peremptorily set forth in "Another Contribution"; nor can I accept the interpretation of āya 226 which makes up a substantial portion of that contribution.

158. The frequently cited aphorism "The finest poetry is the most mendacious [*aḥsanu* [or *khayru*] *sh-shiʿri akdhabu-hu*]" is not to be attested in available sources before Qudāma b. Jaʿfar (d. 922), according to R. Jacobi, "Dichtung," p. 92. The concept of the intrinsic fictiveness of poetry underlying it, however, must have been much older.

159. On the level of contrast, too, might we not be expected to associate the rather paltry ruined traces that the poet's "wildering" fictively takes him past and where he stops (*al-wuqūf ʿala l-aṭlāl*) with the incomparably more imposing—and visibly, palpably real—ruins of cities and folk destroyed in punishment for disobedience to God's messengers (cf. Moubarac, *Abraham,* p. 132 n. 1), to whom the earlier pericopes refer?

160. I do not intend here to discuss the final verse (two verses in the Flügel version), not because I consider it extraneous to the sūra (quite the contrary!) or possibly a later addition to it but because to do so would unnecessarily lengthen an already long essay without contributing a great deal to the thesis under consideration. On āya 227/227–28 see, e.g., Blachère, "Poésie"; Shahîd, "Contribution," pp. 572–75; Shahîd, "Another Contribution," pp. 12–18.

161. Zwettler, *Oral Tradition,* p. 156.

162. Izutsu, *God and Man,* pp. 172–84.

163. See especially Lammens, *Berceau,* pp. 206–10, 252–75, et passim. Lammens cites many examples indicating that *muṭāʿ* was used very much as an "epithète emphatique," above all of the sayyid and occasionally of the leader in war (*qāʾid*): pp. 197 n. 1, 207 n. 6, 256 n. 7, 258, 262 nn. 1 and 5, 268 and n. 2. The word *rabb,* meaning "master" or "lord" par excellence, was often defined in medieval sources as *sayyid muṭāʿ* (e.g., Lane, *Lexicon,* p. 1003b, citing ibn al-Anbārī and the *Tāj al-ʿarūs;* Lammens, *Berceau,* p. 205 n. 1), suggesting that the combination of the two terms was fairly well established in early Arabic usage.

164. ʿAmr b. Baḥr al-Jāḥiẓ, *Al-Bayān wa t-tabyīn,* 4 vols., ed. ʿAbdassalām Muḥammad Hārūn (Cairo, 1380–81/1960–61), 2.253; cf. M. J. Kister, "Mecca and the Tribes of Arabia: Some Notes on Their Relations," in *Studies in Islamic History and Civilization in Honour of Professor David Ayalon* (Jerusalem/Leiden, 1986), pp. 40–42.

165. Cf. also Horovitz, *Koranische Untersuchungen,* pp. 40–41. The formula occurs once earlier in the Meccan period, in 71:3 (B53/N51), and only twice later, 43:62 (B63/N61) and 3:50/43 (B99/N97), both times uttered by Jesus. (In 20:90/92 [B57/N55], Aaron addresses the Israelites worshiping the golden calf, "Follow me and obey my command"; but he does not link obedience with fear of God.)

166. "Wa mā arsalnā min rasūlin illā li yuṭāʿa bi idhni -llāh."

167. Cf. Brown, *Making,* p. 16: "For to vest a fellow human being with powers and claims to loyalty associated with the supernatural, and especially a human being whose claim was not rendered unchallengeable by obvious coercive powers, is a momentous decision for a society made up of small face-to-face groups to make." Brown stresses and carefully analyzes, in a way that bears much relevance for this essay, Late Antique society's "acute awareness of the disruption and dominance within the group that might come from allowing a fellow member to wield new forms of power within it. . . . To decide that a man was a saint and not a sorcerer, the community had to overcome severe inhibitions and to release the well-tried defensive mechanisms with which ancient men were armed to hold new forms of supernatural power in check" (pp. 21–22).

7. The Meaning of *Mutanabbī*, Wolfhart Heinrichs

1. Instead of saying "Muslims" it would be more precise to use a circumlocution such as "people claiming adherence to Islam," because groups that do believe in prophets after Muḥammad are considered unbelievers by the rest. This same dilemma prompted al-Ashʿarī (d. 324/935), one of the founders of orthodox Sunnī theology, to title his heresiographical work: *Maqālāt al-islāmiyyīn wa-khtilāf al-muṣallīn* (The doctrines of those who claim Islam and the disagreement of those who perform the ritual prayer), thus avoiding prejudicing the question of who can rightfully be called a Muslim. Note that *takfīr* "declaring someone who calls himself Muslim an unbeliever" is generally discouraged in Islam if doubts concerning his status vis-à-vis God remain.

2. For references, see A. J. Wensinck et al., *Concordance de la tradition musulmane,* 7 vols. (Leiden, 1936–69), 4.321, 1–3.

3. Cf. Duncan B. Macdonald, "Ilhām," *Encyclopaedia of Islam,* new ed. (Leiden, 1960–), which is, however, rather brief and unsatisfactory. As an alterna-

tive way of acquiring knowledge—and one preferred by the Sufis—*ilhām* is contrasted with *taʿallum* "learning" and described at some length by the great pro-Sufi theologian al-Ghazālī (d. 505/1111) in the chapter titled *Sharḥ ʿajāʾib al-qalb* (Exposition of the wonders of the heart), in his most famous work, *Iḥyāʾ ʿulūm al-dīn* (Revivification of the religious sciences). The paragraph in question has been translated into English by Richard J. McCarthy, S. J., *Freedom and Fulfillment* (Boston, 1980), pp. 378–81. Authors who were unsympathetic to the Sufi claim of deriving knowledge from inspiration often prefer to speak of *al-wasāwis wa-l-khaṭarāt* (or vice versa), which Bayard Dodge in his translation of ibn al-Nadīm, *Al-Fihrist* ([Book catalogue], written in 377/988) renders somewhat harshly as "mental seizures and hallucinations," see *The Fihrist of al-Nadīm* (New York, 1970), 1.455. *Khaṭarāt* simply means "sudden notions" and does not imply a specific source, whereas the term *wasāwis* usually refers to the "whisperings," "insinuations" of the Devil; inspiration is thus discredited by throwing doubt on its source. The staunch traditionalist ibn al-Jawzī (d. 597/1200) in his *Talbīs Iblīs* (Delusion of the Devil), where he dismisses the writings of the Sufis, quotes the eponym of his school Aḥmad b. Ḥanbal (d. 241/855) as saying that the first two generations of Islam did not talk about *al-wasāwis wa-l-khaṭarāt,* thus indicating that for him this was an illegitimate source of knowledge. See D. S. Margoliouth, trans., "The Devil's Delusion of ibn al-Jauzi," *Islamic Culture* 10 (1936): 358.

4. See Michael Zwettler's contribution to the present volume.

5. On this role of Gabriel, see Wolfhart Heinrichs, *Arabische Dichtung und griechische Poetik* (Wiesbaden, 1969), pp. 34–35. Cf. also Irfan Shahîd, "Arabic Poetry as the Vehicle of Religious Propaganda in Early Islam," in: *Prédication et propagande au Moyen Age: Islam, Byzance, Occident,* Penn-Paris-Dumbarton Oaks Colloquia 3, ed. George Makdisi et al. (Paris, 1983), pp. 29–40, esp. 36–37, where, however, the author could be understood as suggesting that Gabriel continued to be the source of inspiration for later Muslim poets. As far as I am aware, this is not the case—at least not in the Arab world; Persian poets later resuscitated the idea and declared themselves to be inspired by an angel (the qur'ānic Gabriel or the Zoroastrian Sarōsh) or by Khiḍr.

6. For the various uses of *shayṭān* in this context, cf. Ignaz Goldziher, *Abhandlungen zur arabischen Philologie,* pt. 1 (Leiden, 1896), pp. 7–14.

7. Thus in the famous *Treatise of Familiar Spirits and Demons (Risālat al-Tawābiʿ wa l-zawābiʿ),* in which the Andalusian poet ibn Shuhayd (d. 426/1035) tells how he is taken by his own familiar spirit to the land of the jinn where he meets the jinnic alter egos of the famous poets of the past. The work has been translated by James T. Monroe (Berkeley, Calif., 1971).

8. Thus in the epistemological chapter at the beginning of the *Fundamentals of Religion* by the theologian ʿAbd al-Qāhir al-Baghdādī (d. 429/1038), cf. *K. Uṣūl al-dīn* (Istanbul, 1346/1928), pp. 14–15.

9. Cf. Heinrichs, *Arabische Dichtung,* pp. 47–48.

10. This particular meaning of the fifth form has not yet received adequate treatment in the available grammars. William Wright, *A Grammar of the Arabic Language,* 3d ed., 2 vols. (Cambridge, 1955), 1.36D–37B, does not explicitly mention it, but his examples contain relevant material, such as our *tanabbaʾa* "to give oneself out as a prophet" and *taḥallama* "to try to acquire, or to affect,

clemency." In the latter case, Wright has nicely brought out the semantic vacillation between honest effort and affectation. Wolfdietrich Fischer, *Grammatik des klassischen Arabisch* (Wiesbaden, 1972), p. 88, defines the meaning of this class of fifth-form verbs as "feigning" (*Sich-Verstellen*), which seems too one-sided. Arab grammarians have identified the semantic common denominator as *takalluf,* which itself is a fifth form, again with two meanings: "to exert oneself" and "to affect, to feign." Raḍīy al-Dīn al-Astarābādhī (d. 686/1287), one of the most insightful grammatical commentators, prefers instead the notion of "attribution" (*intisāb*), i.e., the subject of the verb (e.g., *taḥallama*) attributes him/herself to the notion of *ḥilm* "clemency" or, in other words, ascribes to him/herself this quality. This definition has indeed the advantage of neutralizing the awkward dichotomy "exertion" vs. "simulation," since it covers both. See his *Sharḥ Shāfiyat Ibn al-Ḥājib,* ed. Muḥammad Nūr al-Ḥasan et al., 4 vols. (Beirut, 1395/1975), vol. 1, pp. 104–5.

11. Adam Mez, *Die Renaissance des Islams,* ed. Heinrich Reckendorf (Heidelberg, 1922); Eng. trans., *The Renaissance of Islam,* trans. S. Khuda Bukhsh and David S. Margoliouth (Patna, India, 1937).

12. The most recent comprehensive treatment of the intellectual life of this period can be found in Joel Kraemer's two volumes *Humanism in the Renaissance of Islam* (Leiden, 1986) and *Philosophy in the Renaissance of Islam* (Leiden, 1986).

13. Bernard Lewis, *The Arabs in History* (1950; rpt. London, 1958), p. 99, chapter head of chap. 6; it is in quotation marks, thus presumably meant to be an allusion to the title of Shelley's poem. The chapter itself deals with the various movements of discontent and rebellion against the established—Abbasid—order which culminated in the Ismāʿīlī states of the tenth century.

14. Al-Mutanabbī is one of the few medieval Arab poets on whom there is a book-length study in a Western language: Régis Blachère, *Un poète arabe du IVe siècle de l'Hégire (Xe siècle de J.-C.): Abou ṭ-Ṭayyib al-Motanabbī* (Paris, 1935). The subtitle of this book (*Essai d'histoire littéraire*) indicates the biographical-literary approach chosen by the author. There are several similar attempts by modern Arab scholars, particularly the three substantial studies by Maḥmūd Muḥammad Shākir, ʿAbd al-Wahhāb ʿAzzām, and Ṭāhā Ḥusayn, which were published in connection with al-Mutanabbī's millenary in 1936 (= A.H. 1354; he died in A.H. 354). Particularly useful is the second edition of Maḥmūd M. Shākir, *Al-Mutanabbī,* 2 vols. (Cairo, 1977), which contains the author's narrative and documentation of the literary feud that was sparked by his book, as well as—and more important for us—three ancient and hitherto unpublished biographies of our poet, which were taken from the following sources: *Bughyat al-ṭalab fī taʾrīkh Ḥalab* (The goal of the search: On the history of Aleppo), by the Aleppine historian Kamāl al-Dīn ibn al-ʿAdīm (d. 660/1262); *Taʾrīkh madīnat Dimashq* (The history of the city of Damascus), by ibn ʿAsākir (d. 571/1176); and *Al-Muqaffā* (The sequence), an enormous unfinished work by the Egyptian historian al-Maqrīzī (d. 845/1442) which was meant to contain the biographies of all the famous people who ever lived in Egypt. All three works are admittedly rather late, but they contain material from earlier sources that are lost to us. Ibn al-ʿAdīm, in particular, has proven very valuable because of his erudition and his meticulousness in indicating his sources. Extremely helpful for our purposes is also the collection of relevant

ancient texts by ʿAbdallāh al-Jubūrī, *Abū l-Ṭayyib al-Mutanabbī fī āthār al-dārisīn*, vol. 1 (Baghdad, 1977).

15. For this account, I rely on the most recent research by Heinz Halm, especially *Die islamische Gnosis: die extreme Schia und die ʿAlawiten* (Zürich, 1982). For the role of al-Madāʾ in and Kufa as hotbeds of early Islamic gnosticism, see pp. 16–18.

16. The most trustworthy account of al-Mutanabbī's pedigree seems to be the one offered by the grammarian and "mutanabbiologist" Abū l-Hasan ʿAlī b. ʿĪsâ al-Rabaʿī (d. 420/1030), who knew the poet in Shīrāz; it occurs in Kamāl al-Dīn ibn al-ʿAdīm, *Bughyat al-ṭalab,* in Shākir, *Al-Mutanabbī* 2.251:

> Our friend Abū l-Durr Yāqūt b. ʿAbdallāh al-Rūmī, the client of al-Ḥamawī al-Baghdādī, has told us the following: I saw the *Dīwān* of Abū l-Ṭayyib al-Mutanabbī in the handwriting of Abū l-Hasan ʿAlī b. ʿĪsā al-Rabaʿī, and at the beginning he says: What I know about the genealogy of Abū l-Ṭayyib is that he is Aḥmad b. al-Ḥusayn b. Murra b. ʿAbd al-Jabbār al-Juʿfī. He used to conceal his pedigree and I once asked him about his reason for suppressing it and he said: I constantly stay [alight] with the clans and tribes of the desert Arabs and I do not want that they recognize me [i.e., as belonging to a certain tribe] for fear lest there be a blood-vengeance on their part against my people.—The above [al-Rabaʿī says] is what I consider the correct genealogy. [Al-Rabaʿī] continues: Once I crossed the bridge in Baghdad together with the poet Abū l-Ḥasan Muḥammad b. ʿUbayd Allāh al-Salāmī and among the group of beggars on it there was a blind man. Al-Salāmī said to me: This blind man is the brother of al-Mutanabbī.—So I approached him and asked him about all this, and he verified it and recounted the same genealogy, then he said: At this point our geneaology breaks off.—His [i.e., al-Mutanabbī's] birth was at Kufa in [the quarter of] Kinda in the year 303. He was nursed by a woman of ʿAlid descent from the clan of ʿUbayd Allāh.

This is, by the way, the only report that makes mention of a brother of al-Mutanabbī; his being a beggar may be taken, though not necessarily so, as another indication of the low status of his family. The quarter of Kinda where our poet is said to have been born is described by Abū l-Ḥusayn ibn al-Najjār (d. 402/1011), author of a "History of Kufa," as consisting of three thousand houses inhabited by water sellers and weavers; thus quoted from ibn al-Najjār's lost work by Abū l-Qāsim ʿAbdallāh b. ʿAbd al-Raḥmān al-Iṣfahānī (d. after 410/1019): *Al-Wāḍiḥ fī mushkilāt shiʿr al-Mutanabbī* (The lucid one on the difficulties in the poetry of al-Mutanabbī), ed. Muḥammad al-Ṭāhir ibn ʿĀshūr (Tunis, 1968), p. 6. Although this is certainly exaggeration and not meant to be taken literally, it probably reflects the preponderant character of that quarter and tallies well with the reports that the poet's father earned his living as a water seller. One should note here that Shākir considers these reports to be slanderous inventions on the part of the famous prose writer al-Muḥassin al-Tanūkhī (d. 384/994), who is the authority for some of these reports and who belonged to the Baghdadi circle of literary men who were inimical to al-Mutanabbī. The only oddity in these reports is that the poet's father appears in them bearing the name of ʿĪdān, not al-Ḥusayn. There is, however, independent attestation of this name in a story that the scribe Muḥammad b. ʿAlī b. Naṣr al-Thaʿlabī (d. 437/1045) included in his collection of eyewitness reports titled *Al-Mufāwaḍa* (The conversation), which tells us how the poet al-Nāmī (d. 399/1008) lost his position as a favorite of the Hamdanid prince Sayf al-Dawla of Aleppo to the newcomer al-Mutanabbī and how, full of indignation, the former asked his princely supporter: Why do you prefer the son of ʿĪdān the water seller to me? (in Shākir, *Al Mutanabbī* 2.322). The uniqueness of the name, a point in favor of its authenticity, has occasioned misspellings in the sources and discussions of the correct vocalization; it has the abstruse meaning of "tall palm-tree trunks," and it is quite obviously a nickname (*laqab*), although we know nothing about its reason. That this man was of true Juʿfī descent is claimed in a report transmitted by the same al-Muḥassin al-Tanūkhī whom Shākir supposes to have been inimical to our poet (see ibid. 2.256)! We do not know why he lived in the quarter of Kinda, but it should be pointed out that the quarter of Madhḥij which is the larger genealogical unit comprising Juʿfī was located next to Kinda on its western side (see Louis Massignon, "Explication du plan de Kufa (Irak)," in Massignon, *Opera minora,* ed. Youakim Moubarac, 3 vols. [Beirut, 1963], 3.35–60, map on p. 36).

17. Among others Jābir b. Yazīd al-Juʿfī, al-Mufaḍḍal b. ʿUmar al-Juʿfī, and Muḥammad b. al-Mufaḍḍal al-Juʿfī; cf. Halm, pp. 96, 214, and 302.

18. The sources are al-Rabaʿī (Shākir, *Al-Mutanabbī* 2.251), al-Iṣfahānī (*Al-Wāḍiḥ,* p. 6), and al-Muḥassin al-Tanūkhī (Shākir, 2.256).

19. Louis Massignon, "Mutanabbi, devant le siècle ismaelien de l'Islam," in *Al Mutanabbi: Recueil publié à l'occasion de son millénaire* (Beirut, 1936), pp. 1–17, rpt. in Massignon, *Opera minora,* 1.488–98; Blachère, *Un poète,* particularly pp. 55–86; Muḥammad Muḥammad Ḥusayn, *Al-Mutanabbī wa-l-Qarāmiṭa* (Riyadh, 1401/1981), pp. 73–76.

20. I follow the reading *ṣabwa* in al-Muḥassin al-Tanūkhī, *Nishwār al-Muḥāḍara,* ed. ʿAbbūd al-Shālijī, 8 vols. (Beirut, 1393/1973), 8.198. If the variant *ṣ–w–r–h* is adopted, which appears in all other versions of the report known to me (even in the earlier edition of the relevant *Nishwār* section by D. S. Margoliouth, *K. Jāmiʿ al-tawārīkh al-musammā bi-K. Nishwār. . . , al-juzʾ al-thāmin* [Damascus, 1348/1930], p. 118, penult.), it should probably be read *ṣawra* "a certain inclination, desire" rather than *ṣūra* "a certain form/shape/quality," as Shākir reads it. He equates it with *ṣifa* "quality" and has it refer back to "youth"; see *Al-Mutanabbī* 2.214. Note that *ṣabwa* also has the connotation of "foolish desire," which makes it a near synonym of *ṣawra.*

21. The manuscript here has the meaningless *dahthama* for which Shākir in a footnote suggests the emendation *rahsama,* which the dictionaries explain as "information left incomplete and allusive."

22. Al-Maqrīzī, *Al-Muqaffā,* in Shākir, *Al-Mutanabbî* 2.344. There are several versions of this story, and I must confess that I have chosen this particular one, in spite of its late attestation, for no better reason than its literary qualities. Al-Muḥassin al-Tanūkhī who had this interview with al-Mutanabbī has recorded the same event in his own collection of stories and anecdotes (*Nishwār* 8.198) as follows: "As for myself, I asked him in Ahwāz in the year 354, when he was passing through on his way to Fārs, during a long conversation between the two

of us about the meaning of *al-Mutanabbī,* because I wanted to hear from him whether or not he had posed as a prophet. He answered me with a reply that was meant to lead me to the wrong conclusion [*bi-jawābin mughāliṭin lī*] which was that he said: That was something that happened in my youth which a certain childishness had brought about.—I was too ashamed to press him any further and I desisted." Al-Maqrīzī's more elaborate report is not necessarily semiapocryphal; we know that apart from the material contained in *Nishwār al-muḥāḍara,* there are other pieces of information on al-Mutanabbī that are traced back to al-Tanūkhī. The latter may certainly have told this story on several occasions, as it was sure to be of great interest to the general public, and in so doing, he would have created several chains of transmission.

23. Ibn Jinnī, *Al-Fasr* (The explanation), ed. Ṣafā Khulūṣī 2 vols. to date (Baghdad, 1398/1975), 2.322. As ibn Jinnī phrases it, "He used to say that through this verse he had been named al-Mutanabbī." The anthologist and literary historian al-Thaʿālibī (d. 429/1038) in *Yatīmat al-dahr fī maḥāsin ahl al-ʿaṣr* (The unique pearl of the time on the beauties of contemporary men), ed. Muḥammad Muḥyī al-Dīn ʿAbd al-Ḥamīd, 4 vols., 2d ed. (Cairo, 1375/1956–1377/1958), 1.129, quotes ibn Jinnī somewhat differently:

> I heard Abū l-Ṭayyib say: I have been nicknamed al-Mutanabbī only because of my saying:
>
> "I am the companion of generosity, the lord of the rhymes, the poison of the enemies and the anger of the envious.
>
> "I am in a community, etc."
>
> And in this *qaṣīda* he also says:
>
> "My stay in the land of Naḥla [place near Baalbek] was nothing short of the stay of the Messiah among the Jews."

This last-mentioned verse, which occurs much earlier in the poem, is, of course, similar in meaning to the Ṣāliḥ simile and the famous poet and Mutanabbī admirer Abū l-ʿAlāʾ al-Maʿarrī (d. 449/1057) in his *Muʿjiz Aḥmad* (The miracle of Aḥmad), a commentary on the *Dīwān* of al-Mutanabbī, says that some people allege this line to be the cause of his nickname, while others prefer the Ṣāliḥ line (quoted by Ṣafā Khulūṣī in his ed. of ibn Jinnī, *Al-Fasr* 2.314 n.55).

24. Cf. Fuat Sezgin, *Geschichte des arabischen Schrifttums,* 9 vols. to date (Leiden 1967–), 2.98–100.

25. Quoted by ibn al-ʿAdīm, in Shākir, *Al-Mutanabbī,* 2.277; and by ibn ʿAsākir, ibid., 2.334.

26. One is a tradition that Abū l-ʿAlāʾ al-Maʿarrī, *Risālat al-Ghufrān* (The epistle on forgiveness), ed. ʿĀʾisha ʿAbd al-Raḥmān Bint al-Shāṭiʾ, 4th ed. (Cairo, n.d.), p. 418, claims to have heard: "Whenever he [al-Mutanabbī] was asked about the truth of this nickname, he would say: that is (derived) from *al-nabwa* meaning 'the elevated part of the land.'" I know of no other testimony for this story and it may easily have been invented by al-Maʿarrī, who surely knew that even the word *nabīy,* "prophet," was derived by some philologists from this very root. Our poet's nickname would then mean something like "the one who is elevated above others."

The other story is traced back by ibn al-ʿAdīm (Shākir, 2.267–268) to the famous historian and philosopher Miskawayh (d. 421/1030), who relates that al-Mutanabbī was asked (in his presence, it seems): "For whom have you claimed prophethood? He said: For the poets. They said: Every prophet has a miracle, so what is your miracle? He said: This line: 'One of the calamities of the world for a noble man is that he sees that he must befriend an enemy of his [*Wa-min nakadi l-dunyā ʿalā l-ḥurri an yarā ʿadūwan lahū mā min ṣadāqatihī buddu*].' " Although this line does not strike the reader as an example of inimitable and flawless poetry (and, in fact, has been criticized for its illogical use of *ṣadāqa,* "friendship," rather than *mudārāt,* "flattery,"), the protest and bitterness pervading it again chime in well with the dim view he takes of contemporary society, and it is thus probably not without reason that our poet selected this particular line for his *muʿjiza.*

27. The man "known as Dawkhala" is better known as ibn al-Qāriḥ (d. after 421/1030). His epistle was published together with al-Maʿarrī's much more voluminous reply, the *Risālat al-Ghufrān* (see pp. 21–68). The relevant passage is on pp. 29–30, the wording being somewhat different from that of ibn al-ʿAdīm, who must have quoted from memory.

28. For this "History" we seem to have attestation only in ibn al-Qāriḥ and ibn al-ʿAdīm. Ibn Abī l-Azhar (d. after 313/925–26) is mentioned in the *Fihrist,* trans. Dodge, 1.323–24, but no suitable title is listed among his works. Al-Quṭrabbulī is identified by Bint al-Shāṭiʾ in her ed. of al-Maʿarrī's *R. al-Ghufrān,* p. 418, with Abū l-Ḥasan Aḥmad b. ʿAbdallāh b. al-Ḥusayn al-Quṭrabbulī (no dates given); see *Fihrist,* trans. Dodge, 1.272, where he is indeed credited with a "history up to his own days." Ibn al-ʿAdīm, however, who claims to have read this "history," gives Abū Muḥammad ʿAbdallāh b. al-Ḥusayn as the author's name, presumably the father of Aḥmad. Cf. also on this question Franz Rosenthal, *A History of Muslim Historiography,* 2d ed. (Leiden, 1968), p. 73 n. 1.

29. High state official and twice vizier to the Abbasid caliph al-Muqtadir. He died in 334/946 at the age of eighty-nine.

30. In Shākir, 2.268–69; on ʿUbaydallāh (d. 313/925–26), son of the more famous ibn Abī Ṭāhir Ṭayfūr (d. 380/893), see Rosenthal, *Muslim Historiography,* p. 462 n. 2.

31. Hellmut Ritter ("Philologica XIII: Arabische Handschriften in Anatolien und Istanbul," *Oriens* 2 [1949]: 270) surmises that ibn Jinnī may have critically used al-Waḥīd's commentary (thus also Sezgin, *Geschichte des arabischen Schrifttums* 2.491–92). It seems, however, that al-Waḥīd often explicitly refers to ibn Jinnī's observations, leading us to assume that al-Waḥīd himself or someone else incorporated his notes into ibn Jinnī's text; such incorporation is also borne out by the reference to al-Waḥīd's work as *Iṣlāḥ* "Correction" in the manuscript Ritter describes.

32. Governor of Lādhiqiyya (d. ca. 368/978), panegyrized by al-Mutanabbī; see Blachère, *Un poète,* pp. 44–45.

33. Governor of Anṭākiyā for his cousin Sayf al-Dawla, the Hamdanid ruler of Aleppo.

34. Ibn Jinnī, *Fasr* 2.322. The text as printed in this edition is marred by a number of misreadings and misprints. I read *badw Banī l-Qaṣīṣ* for *tadwīn al-qiṣaṣ* (lines 4–5); *khufyatin* for *khuffayhi* (line 6; although the latter may have some merit

in view of the phrase *rajaʿa fārisan* in line 12); *bābihī* for *mā bihī* (line 7); *Jarash* for *Ḥaras* (line 11), *fa-ghāba* for *fa-ghuliba* (?) (line 11).

35. This title is not mentioned in connection with the passage I am quoting here, but it occurs in another passage quoted by ibn al-ʿAdīm on the authority of Y āqūt, *Muʿjam al-udabāʾ*, ed. Ahmad Farīd Rifāʿī (Cairo, 1937), 17.185, line 12, and *ijāla* in Margoliouth's edition as cited in Carl Brockelmann, *Geschichte der arabischen Litteratur,* supplement, vol. 1 (Leiden, 1936), p. 875. I have opted for this Yāqūt, *Muʿjam al-udabāʾ*, ed. Ahmad Farīd Rifāʿī (Cairo, 1937), 17.185, line 12, and *ijāla* in Margoliouth's edition as cited in Carl Brockelmann, *Geschichte der arabischen Litteratur,* supplement, vol. 1 (Leiden, 1936), p. 875. I have opted for this last variant, but as with my translation of the title, tentatively, since we are in the dark about the intentions of the author in this work that is mostly lost to us.

36. The word is *khuyūṭ,* literally "threads." The dictionaries give *khayṭ al-raqaba,* lit. "the thread of the neck," as meaning the "spinal cord." The tentative translation "nerves" is based on this definition.

37. The quotation is in Shākir, 2.258.

38. See Blachère, *Un poète,* pp. 57–84. I follow Blachère's chronology of these events, although there is some disagreement among scholars.

39. Three of them are told by al-Maʿarrī, *Risālat al-Ghufrān,* pp. 423–24. The three "miraculous" events (riding a recalcitrant camel, healing a penknife cut by spitting on it, and killing a barking dog by remote control) are such that one can vividly see al-Maʿarrī's tongue-in-cheek attitude in telling them.

40. The poet and scholar al-Nāshiʾ al-Aṣghar (d. 365/975 or 366/977) recounts that during that year al-Mutanabbī attended his poetry *majlis* in Kufa, when he was not yet famous and his nickname not yet known. See Yāqūt, *Muʿjam al-udabāʾ* (Cairo, n.d.), 13.290–91.

41. Al-Muḥassin al-Tanūkhī recounts a meeting with the qadi Abū l-Ḥasan ibn Umm Shaybān al-Hāshimī al-Kūfī two years after al-Mutanabbī's death. During this meeting the qadi tells him: "When al-Mutanabbī had gone out to the Kalb [bedouins] and stayed among them, he [first] claimed to be of ʿAlawī-Ḥasanī descent, then he claimed prophethood after that, and finally he again claimed to be an ʿAlawī, until it was duly recorded by legal witnesses in Damascus against him that he was lying in both his claims [*sic!*]" (see al-Khaṭīb al-Baghdādī, *Taʾrīkh Baghdād,* here quoted from al-Jubūrī, p. 143; this particular story is not included in al-Tanūkhī's *Nishwār al-muḥāḍara*).

Claiming descent from ʿAlī probably meant that he wished to be recognized as the imām, the legitimate temporal and spiritual ruler of the world (a position that in the beliefs of the Shiite "exaggerators" was likely to be higher than that of a prophet!). Al-Mutanabbī's wavering indecision in the claims he made as portrayed in this story has prompted some scholars, including Shākir, to dispute the authenticity of this report and to assume interpolations. I can see no improbability that a high-strung and megalomaniacal young man is somewhat uncertain about how far he can go. He may also have been reacting to responses of his audience about which we obviously know nothing. It should be noted that ibn Umm Shaybān was appointed grand qadi of Egypt and parts of Syria in 336/947–48 (see ibn Ḥajar al-ʿAsqalānī: *Rafʿ al-iṣr ʿan quḍāt Miṣr,* in al-Kindī, *K. al-Wulāt wa-K. al-Quḍāt,* ed. Rhuvon Guest (Leyden London, 1912), p. 574, ll. 10–11), so he may easily have had access to the court records on al-Mutanabbī's case, which had happened only a little more than a decade before.

42. The text is in Shākir, 2.257 (no. 22).

43. I read *wa-huwa l-wathāq* for *wa-l-wathāq*. For the poem, see *Dīwān* with commentary by al-Wāḥidī, ed. Friedrich Dieterici (Berlin, 1861), pp. 80–84 (no. 30). It does not contain the word *wathāq;* however, *quyūd,* "fetters," occurs in line 21.

44. Cf. Blachère, *Un poète,* p. 83.

45. Cf. *Dīwān,* pp. 19–20 (lines 13–17).

46. See Muhalhil b. Yamūt, *Sariqāt Abī Nuwās* (The plagiarisms of Abū Nuwās), ed. Muḥammad Muṣṭafā Haddāra (Cairo, 1957), pp. 144–46, a collection of so-called *kufriyyāt,* "verses of unbelief," from the poetry of Abū Nuwās, and al-Thaʿālibī, *Yatīma* 1.184–86, a collection of lines from al-Mutanabbī documenting "feeble belief and weak religion."

47. Dīwān, p. 19, commentary on line 13.

48. Cf. Blachère, *Un poète,* p. 30.

49. Heinz Halm, *Kosmologie und Heilslehre der frühen Ismāʿīlīya* (Wiesbaden, 1978), p. 128.

50. Halm, *Islamische Gnosis,* pp. 132–33.

51. Halm, *Islamische Gnosis,* pp. 54 (Hamza b. ʿAmmāra, prophet for the divine Muḥammad ibn al-Ḥanafiyya), 200, 202, 203 (Abū l-Khaṭṭāb, prophet for the divine Jaʿfar al-Ṣādiq), 206 (Bazīgh b. Mūsā, prophet for Jaʿfar), 208 (al-Sarīy al-Aqṣam, apostle for Jaʿfar), 237 (Muḥammad b. Bashīr, prophet for the divine Mūsā al-Kāẓim), 278 (ʿAlī b. Ḥasaka, prophet for the divine ʿAlī al-Hādī). It should be noted that among the earlier "exaggerators" another type of prophecy—more "normal" and not explicitly connected with a divine imām—was claimed by the heresiarchs Bayān b. Simʿān (pp. 57–60), Abū Manṣūr al-ʿIjlī (p. 86), and al-Mughīra b. Saʿīd (p. 90), but this seems to be less relevant for the case of al-Mutanabbī.

52. For the Isḥāqīs, see Halm, *Islamische Gnosis,* p. 278; for the Nuṣayrīs, see ibid., p. 297 (the fourth sheikh of the Nuṣayrīs al-Khaṣībī [d. 346/957–58 or 358/969] active at the Hamdanid court in Aleppo).

53. Massignon, "Mutanabbi, devant le siècle ismaelien."

54. Also the title of al-Maʿarrī's commentary on the *Dīwān.* Aḥmad, of course, refers both to al-Mutanabbī and, obliquely, to the Prophet Muḥammad whose alternative name it was.

55. The original of this story is given in ibn al-ʿAdīm, in Shākir, 2.261–64; also in al-Maqrīzī, as printed in Shākir, 2.346–49; and in Yūsuf al-Badīʿī, *Al-Ṣubḥ al-munabbī ʿan ḥaythiyyat al-Mutanabbī,* ed. Muṣṭafā al-Saqqā et al. (Cairo, 1963), pp. 52–55. Ibn al-ʿAdīm mentions that he found the story in a copy of al-Mutanabbī's *Dīwān.*

8. The Poet as Prophet in Medieval Hebrew Literature, Dan Pagis

1. A full-length survey of this subject in Hebrew is Ezra Fleischer, *Hebrew Liturgical Poetry in the Middle Ages* (Jerusalem, 1975). Two brief general treatments of the subject in English are Jefim Schirmann, "Problems of the Study of Post-

Biblical Hebrew Poetry," *Proceedings of the Israel Academy of Science and the Humanities* 2 (1967):228–36; and Dan Pagis, "Trends in the Study of Medieval Hebrew Literature," *Association for Jewish Studies Review* 4 (1979): 125–41.

2. No doubt Professor Pagis would have pointed out here, as he had elsewhere, that the name "secular" for this poetry is somewhat misleading, since some of it is clearly of a religious character; but it is "secular" in the sense of "nonliturgical": it was not meant for recitation as part of the synagogue service—J.K.

3. Moses ibn Ezra, *Širei ha-ḥol,* ed. Hayim H. Brody (Berlin, 1932), 1.97, 111.

4. Yehudah ha-Levi, *Diwan,* ed. Hayim Brody (Berlin: Schocken, 1927), 1.55.

5. See Jefim Schirmann, *Ha-širah ha-ʿivrit bisfarad uv-provans* (Tel Aviv, 1961), pt. 2, p. 515.

6. Solomon ibn Gabirol, "Maḥberet ha-ʿAnaq," in Solomon ibn Gabirol, *Širei ha-ḥol,* ed. Hayim Brody and Jefim Schirmann (Jerusalem, 1975), 169–72.

7. Ibid.

8. For the Hebrew text, see Judah al-Ḥarizi, *Taḥkemoni,* ed. Y. Toporovski (Tel Aviv, 1952), pp. 8–10.

9. Ibid.

9. The Nature of Prophecy in Geoffrey of Monmouth's *Vita Merlini,* Jan Ziolkowski

1. On Myrddin/Merlin, see, first, three studies by A. O. H. Jarman: "Early Stages in the Development of the Myrddin Legend," in *Astudiaethau ar yr Hengerdd: Studies in Old Welsh Poetry: Cyflwynedig i Syr Idris Foster,* ed. Rachel Bromwich and R. Brinley Jones (Cardiff, 1978), pp. 326–49; *The Legend of Merlin* (Cardiff, 1960); and "The Welsh Myrddin Poems," in *Arthurian Literature in the Middle Ages: A Collaborative History,* ed. Roger Sherman Loomis (Oxford, 1959), pp. 20–30.

2. See Paul Zumthor, *Merlin le prophète: Un thème de la littérature polémique de l'historiographie et des romans* (Lausanne, 1943).

3. On the Sibyls, see William L. Kinter and Joseph R. Keller, *The Sibyl: Prophetess of Antiquity and Medieval Fay* (Philadelphia, 1967).

4. A new overview of medieval prophecy is long overdue. Until one appears, see Paul Alphandéry, "Prophètes et ministère prophétique dans le moyen-âge latin," *Revue d'Histoire et de Philosophie Religieuses* (1932): 334–59; J. J. I. von Döllinger, *Fables Respecting the Popes in the Middle Ages; Together with the Prophetic Spirit and the Prophecies of the Christian Era,* trans. Alfred Plummer and Henry B. Smith (New York, 1872), pp. 273–392; Marjorie E. Reeves, "History and Prophecy in Medieval Thought," *Medievalia et Humanistica: Studies in Medieval and Renaissance Culture,* n.s. 5 (1974): 51–75; and R. W. Southern, "Aspects of the European Tradition of Historical Writing: 3. History as Prophecy," *Transactions of the Royal Historical Society,* 5th ser., 22 (1972): 159–80.

5. On the date of the *Vita Merlini,* contrast John J. Parry, "The Date of the *Vita Merlini,*" *Modern Philology* 22 (1924–25): 413–15; and Lewis Thorpe, "The Last Years of Geoffrey of Monmouth," in *Mélanges de langue et littérature français du Moyen Age offerts à Pierre Jonin,* Senefiance 7 (Aix-en-Provence, 1979), pp. 661–72.

6. For different points of view on the truthfulness of Geoffrey's statement, see Caroline D. Eckhardt, "The *Prophetia Merlini* of Geoffrey of Monmouth: Latin Manuscript Copies," *Manuscripta* 26 (1982): 167–76; H. C. Leach, "*De Libello Merlini*," *Modern Philology* 8 (1911): 607–10; Bernard Meehan, "Geoffrey of Monmouth, *Prophecies of Merlin:* New Manuscript Evidence," *Bulletin of the Board of Celtic Studies, Cardiff* 28 (1978): 37–46; John J. Parry and Robert A. Caldwell, "Geoffrey of Monmouth," in *Arthurian Literature in the Middle Ages: A Collaborative History,* ed. Roger Sherman Loomis (Oxford, 1959), pp. 75–76; and J. S. P. Tatlock, *The Legendary History of Britain* (Berkeley, Calif., 1950), pp. 418–21.

7. These three elements constitute book 7 of the *Historia* as it is divided in one set of editions: for example, see *The Historia Regum Britanniae of Geoffrey of Monmouth with Contributions to the Study of Its Place in Early British History,* ed. Acton Griscom and R. E. Jones (New York, 1929). In another set of editions these three elements compose sections 109–17: for example, see *The Historia Regum Britannie of Geoffrey of Monmouth, I: A Single-Manuscript Edition from Bern, Burgerbibliothek, MS. 568,* ed. Neil Wright (Cambridge, 1985).

8. See H. Munro Chadwick and N. Kershaw Chadwick, *The Growth of Literature* (Cambridge, 1932), 1.123–32; and Jarman, "Early Stages in the Development of the Myrddin Legend," pp. 348–49.

9. For an essay on Geoffrey's knowledge of Celtic and other languages, see T. D. Crawford, "On the Linguistic Competence of Geoffrey of Monmouth," *Medium Aevum* 51 (1982): 152–61.

10. On manuscripts of the *Historia,* see Wright's remarks in his edition, p. 1. On manuscripts of the *Vita,* see Geoffrey of Monmouth, *Vita Merlini: Life of Merlin,* ed. and trans. Basil Clarke (Cardiff, 1973), pp. 43–45. All references to the *Vita* will refer to the line numbers and text in this edition, to be cited hereafter in my text.

11. For applications of the word to Merlin, see the *Vita,* lines 1, 7, 21, 199, 201, 236, 238, 249, 262, 270, 280, 323, 368, 429, 466, 474, 481, 494, 507, 532, 533, 732, 1393, and 1465. On the nuances of the word in classical Latin, see J. K. Newman, *The Concept of Vates in Augustan Poetry,* Collection Latomus 89 (Brussels, 1967). The identification of the *uates* with prophecy, poetry, and madness was of course still commonplace in the Middle Ages: for example, see Isidore, *Etymologiarum sive originum libri XX,* 8.7.2 (lines 5–6) and 8.7.3 (lines 12–17), ed. W. M. Lindsay, 2 vols. (Oxford, 1911).

12. On *canere,* see lines 579 and 681; on *cantare,* see 1014; and on *carmen,* see 561.

13. See lines 579 ("que tunc ventura sciebat"), 1014 ("cantare futura"), and 1521 ("res precantare futuras": of Ganieda).

14. On these laughs, see Alexander Haggerty Krappe, "Le rire du prophète," in *Studies in English and Philology: A Miscellany in Honor of Frederick Klaeber,* ed. Kemp Malone and Martin B. Ruud (Minneapolis, 1929), pp. 340–61; Lucy Allen Paton, "The Story of Grisandole: A Study in the Legend of Merlin," *Publications of the Modern Language Association of America* 22, n.s. 15 (1907): 234–76; and Zumthor, *Merlin le prophète,* pp. 45–47.

15. For a study of this motif, see Kenneth H. Jackson, "The Motive of the Threefold Death in the Story of Suibhne Geilt," in J. Ryan, ed., *Féilsgríbhinn Eóin Mhic Néill* (Dublin, 1940), pp. 535–50.

16. The passage leaves ambiguous whether or not the beggar knew of the hoard. If he did know, then Merlin's laugh was a reaction to the irony of the beggar's deceitfulness; if the beggar did not know, then the laugh was a response to the cruel irony of fate.

17. Gerald of Wales, *Descriptio Kambriae,* book 1, chap. 16, ed. James F. Dimock, Rolls Series (London, 1868), pp. 194–95; *The Journey through Wales and The Description of Wales,* trans. Lewis Thorpe (Harmondsworth, Eng., 1978), pp. 246–47. The word *awenyddion* is the plural of *awenydd,* a word that means poet-prophet and that derives from *awen* ("in-spiration") "oracular frenzy."

18. Gerald of Wales, *Itinerarium Kambriae,* book 1, chap. 5, *The Journey and The Description,* trans. Thorpe, pp. 116–17.

19. See Gerald of Wales, *Descriptio Kambriae,* book 2, chap. 16, ed. Dimock, p. 196; *The Journey and The Description,* trans. Thorpe, pp. 247–51 (with reference to 1 Sam. 19:18–24 and 10:5–6).

20. A similar argument has been made for the Irish *Buile Suibhne,* see Brigit Beneš, "Spuren von Schamanismus in der Sage *Buile Suibhne,*" *Zeitschrift für celtische Philologie* 28 (1960–61): 309–10. To my knowledge, the only attempt to take this approach to the figure of Merlin is Nikolai Tolstoy's thought-provoking, but extremely eccentric book *The Quest for Merlin* (London, 1985), esp. pp. 135–60.

21. For seminal studies, see Beneš, "Spuren von Schamanismus," pp. 309–34; Peter Buchholz, "Schamanistischen Züge in der altisländischen Überlieferung" (Inaugural diss., Westfälische Wilhelms-Universität, 1968); Peter Buchholz, "Shamanism—the Testimony of Old Icelandic Literary Tradition," *Mediaeval Scandinavia* 4 (1971): 7–20; N. Kershaw Chadwick, *Poetry and Prophecy* (Cambridge, 1942); Patrick K. Ford, *The Poetry of Llywarch Hen* (Berkeley, Calif., 1974), pp. 58–62; and Åke Ohlmarks, *Studien zum Problem des Schamanismus* (Lund, Sweden, 1939), pp. 310–50.

22. The basic study of shamanism remains Mircea Eliade, *Le chamanisme et les techniques archaïques de l'extase* (Paris, 1951), trans. by Willard R. Trask as *Shamanism: Archaic Techniques of Ecstasy,* Bollingen Series 76 (Princeton, N.J., 1964).

23. See Hans Findeisen, *Schamanentum dargestellt am Beispiel der Besessenheitspriester nordeurasiatischer Völker,* Urban-Bücher: Die wissenschaftliche Taschenbuchreihe 28 (Zurich, 1957), pp. 80–85.

24. See Findeisen, *Schamanentum,* pp. 80–85; Tolstoy, *The Quest for Merlin,* pp. 147–48. For the stag in related Irish tales, see Josef Weisweiler, "Vorindogermanische Schichten der irischen Heldensage," *Zeitschrift für celtische Philologie* 24 (1953–54): 35–55.

25. On the shaman-tree, see Findeisen, *Schamanentum,* pp. 112–20; Ohlmarks, *Studien zum Problem des Schamanismus,* pp. 129–31; and Tolstoy, *The Quest for Merlin,* p. 152.

26. For the text and a translation, see *Buile Suibne* (*The Frenzy of Suibhne: Being the Adventures of Suibhne Geilt, a Middle-Irish Romance,* ed. and trans. J. G. O'Keeffe, Irish Texts Society 12 (London, 1913). For a statement on the accommodation between the shamanlike and the Christian in the *Buile Suibne,* see Beneš, "Spuren von Schamanismus," p. 321. For further examination of Sweeney's shamanlike qualities, see Joseph Falaky Nagy, "The Wisdom of the *Geilt,*" *Éigse* 19 (1982–83): 48–51.

27. The range of Merlin's vision is compatible with the act of *prophetia* as it was understood by patristic and medieval theologians. For pertinent quotations from Gregory the Great and Peter the Venerable, see J. P. Torrell, "La notion de prophétie et la méthode apologétique dans le *Contra Saracenos* de Pierre le Vénérable," *Studia Monastica* 17 (1975): 260–61.

28. For concise summaries of the political prophecies, see *Vita,* ed. Clarke, pp. 16–21.

29. See *Vita,* ed. Clarke, pp. 21–21.

30. The term was given currency by Rupert Taylor (*The Political Prophecy in England* [New York, 1911]), who discusses extensively the *Libellus, Historia,* and *Vita.* For correctives to his view that Geoffrey was the inventor of animal metaphors in prophecy, see Tatlock, *Legendary History of Britain,* pp. 406–417; and Zumthor, *Merlin le prophète,* pp. 26–30.

31. This point was made by Adrian Morey and C. N. L. Brooke, *Gilbert Foliot and His Letters* (Cambridge, 1965), pp. 157–58.

32. See *Vita,* ed. Clarke, pp. 153–54.

33. See Taylor, *Political Prophecy in England,* p. 16.

34. For a study of the place Geoffrey's writings occupy in the tradition of Welsh vaticination, see Margaret Enid Griffiths, *Early Vaticination in Welsh with English Parallels,* ed. T. Gwynn Jones (Cardiff, 1937), pp. 57–83.

35. See Robert Bartlett, *Gerald of Wales, 1146–1223* (Oxford, 1982), p. 63.

36. See Zumthor, *Merlin le prophète,* pp. 78–79.

37. On this text, see G. Raynaud de Lage, *Alain de Lille: Poète du XIIe siècle,* Université de Montréal Publications de l'Institut d'études médiévales 12 (Montreal, 1951), pp. 13–15.

38. *Prophetia anglicana et romana, hoc est Merlini Ambrosii Britanni, ex incubo olim, ante annos mille ducentos in Anglia nati vaticinia a Galfredo* (Frankfurt, 1603 and 1608), discussed by Zumthor, *Merlin le prophète,* p. 79. On the use of Balaam in considerations of Merlin's standing as a prophet, see Zumthor, p. 90.

39. See Gerald of Wales, *Descriptio Kambriae,* book 2, chap. 16, ed. Dimock, pp. 197–98; *The Journey and The Description,* trans. Thorpe, p. 249.

40. See Zumthor, *Merlin le prophète,* p. 88.

41. For expressions of puzzlement or attempted explanations, see *Vita,* ed. Clarke, p. 140; Tolstoy, *Quest for Merlin,* pp. 116–17 (who perceives a vague memory of Stonehenge!); and Zumthor, *Merlin le prophète,* p. 41.

42. See *The Interpreter's Dictionary of the Bible: An Illustrated Encyclopedia,* ed. George Arthur Buttrick (Nashville, 1962), 3.905.

43. See Penelope B. R. Doob, *Nebuchadnezzar's Children: Conventions of Madness in Middle English Literature* (New Haven, Conn., 1974), p. 156.

44. Ibid., pp. 153–58.

45. Ibid., p. 157.

46. The exact interrelationship among these tales has been a matter of unending contention: see John Carey, "Suibhne Geilt and Tuán mac Cairill," *Éigse* 20 (1984): 93–105; James Carney, *Studies in Irish Literature and History* (Dublin, 1955), pp. 129–64, 385–93; Chadwick and Chadwick, *The Growth of Literature,* 1.108–14; Edmond Faral, *La légende arthurienne: Etudes et documents,* vol. 2: *Geoffroy de Monmouth: La légende arthurienne à Glastonbury,* Bibliothèque de l'Ecole des hautes études, Sciences historiques et philologiques 256 (Paris, 1929), pp. 347–63; Ken-

neth Jackson, "A Further Note on Suibhne Geilt and Merlin," *Eigse* 7 (1953–55): 112–16; Kenneth Jackson, "The Motive of the Threefold Death"; Ferdinand Lot, "Etudes sur Merlin: I. Les sources de la *Vita Merlini* de Gaufrei de Monmouth," *Annales de Bretagne* 15 (1899–1900): 336–47; John J. Parry, "Celtic Tradition and the *Vita Merlini*," *Philological Quarterly* 4 (1925): 193–207; Tolstoy, *The Quest for Merlin*, pp. 192–98; and H. Ward, "Lailoken (or Merlin Silvester)," *Romania* 22 (1893): 504–25.

47. See Jarman, "Early Stages," pp. 328–29.

48. On the hagiographic side, see *Vita*, ed. Clarke, p. 2; Jarman, "Early Stages," p. 330; Zumthor, *Merlin le prophète*, p. 43.

49. Zumthor, *Merlin le prophète*, p. 45.

50. See *Vita*, ed. Clarke, p. 21.

51. For this reading of the *Historia*, see Paul Feuerherd, *Geoffroy von Monmouth und das Alte Testament mit Berücksichtigung der Historia Britonum des Nennius* (Halle, 1915).

52. Zumthor, *Merlin le prophète*, p. 37.

10. After the Middle Ages, Lawrence F. Rhu

1. Hayden White, "Interpretation in History," in his *Tropics of Discourse: Essays in Cultural Criticism* (Baltimore, Md., 1978), pp. 51–80.

2. All citations refer to Lanfranco Caretti's edition of *Gerusalemme liberata* (Torino, 1971).

3. See Charles Klopp, " 'Peregrino' and 'Errante' in the *Gerusalemme liberata*," *MLN* 94 (1979): 61–76.

4. All citations refer to C. H. Grandgent's revised edition of *La divina commedia* (Boston, 1933).

5. Charles S. Singleton, *Dante Studies* 1 (Cambridge, Mass., 1954), p. vii.

6. All citations refer to *The Odyssey*, with an English translation by A. T. Murray, 2 vols. (Cambridge, Mass., 1966).

7. *Aristotle* XXIII, ed. W. Hamilton Fyfe, Loeb Classical Library (Cambridge, Mass., 1957), 96–97; Torquato Tasso, *Rinaldo*, a cura di Luigi Bonfigli (Bari, Italy, 1936), p. 5.

8. Torquato Tasso, *Discorsi dell'arte poetica e del poema eroico*, a cura di Luigi Poma (Bari, Italy, 1965), pp. 20–21.

9. Joseph A. Wittreich, Jr., " 'A Poet amongst Poets': Milton and the Tradition of Prophecy" in *Milton and the Line of Vision* (Madison, Wis., 1975), p. 130; idem, *Visionary Poetics: Milton's Tradition and His Legacy* (San Marino, Calif., 1979), pp. 11–12.

10. "Non per altro divino è detto se non perchè, al supremo Artefice nelle sue operazioni assomigliandosi, della sua divinità viene a partecipare." (Tasso, *Discorsi dell'arte poetica e del poema eroico*, pp. 36, 140.) This statement is virtually identical in both the early and late discourses. Wittreich quotes the translation of the *Discorsi del poema eroico* (1594) by Mariella Cavalchini and Irene Samuel (Torquato Tasso, *Discourses on the Heroic Poem* [Oxford, 1973], p. 73). I prefer to use the *Discorsi dell'arte poetica* (ca. 1564) in relation to the *Liberata*, which was finished in 1575–76, because chronology better justifies making that connection. Although there is

much overlap between the two versions, the second, revised and expanded edition applies more appropriately to Tasso's *Gerusalemme conquistata* (1593). See my "Tasso's First Discourse as a Guide to the *Gerusalemme liberata*," *Journal of the Rocky Mountain Medieval and Renaissance Association* 7 (1986): 65–81.

11. See *Twentieth-Century Criticism*, ed. David Lodge (London, 1972), pp. 303–19.

12. Terry Eagleton, *Literary Theory: An Introduction* (Minneapolis, 1983), pp. 46–53.

13. Margaret W. Ferguson, *Trials of Desire: Renaissance Defenses of Poetry* (New Haven, Conn., 1983); Sergio Zatti, *L'uniforme cristiano e il multiforme pagano: Saggio sulla "Gerusalemme liberata"* (Milan, 1983).

14. Marjorie Garber, "'What's Past Is Prologue': Temporality and Prophecy in Shakespeare's History Plays," in *Renaissance Genres: Essays on Theory, History, and Interpretation*, ed. Barbara Lewalski (Cambridge, Mass., 1986), p. 320.

15. See my "From Aristotle to Allegory: Young Tasso's Evolving Vision of the *Gerusalemme liberata*," *Italica* (Summer 1988): 111–30.

16. *Inferno* 26:127; *Discorsi* 116.

17. John Freccero, *Dante: The Poetics of Conversion* (Cambridge, Mass., 1986), p. 138.

18. E.g., "The Reason of Church Government Urged against the Prelaty," 668, and "Of Education," 637, in *John Milton: Complete Poems and Major Prose*, ed. Merritt Y. Hughes (New York, 1957).

19. "Cosa non detta in prosa mai né in rima" (1.2.2); "Things unattempted yet in Prose or Rhyme" (1.16). All citations of the Italian refer to Lanfranco Caretti's edition of the *Orlando furioso* (Torino, 1971). All citations of the English refer to *John Milton: Complete Poems and Major Prose*, ed. Hughes.

20. *Discorsi*, 22–23, 20–21, 41.

21. *Paradise Lost* 10.25–43.

22. Barbara K. Lewalski, "The Genres of *Paradise Lost*: Literary Genre as a Means of Accommodation," *Milton Studies* 17 (Pittsburgh, 1983): 76–77. Also see Wittreich, "'Poet amongst Poets,'" p. 130; and idem, *Visionary Poetics*, pp. 11–12.

23. See C. A. Patrides, "'Something like Prophetick Strain': Apocalyptic Configurations in Milton," in *The Apocalypse in English and Renaissance Literature*, ed. Patrides and Joseph Wittreich (Ithaca, N.Y., 1984), 214–17.

24. See Leland Ryken, "*Paradise Lost* and Its Biblical Epic Models," in *Milton and the Scriptural Tradition: The Bible into Poetry*, ed. James H. Sims and Ryken (Columbia, Mo., 1984), 74.

25. All biblical citations refer to the Authorized Version of 1611.

26. *Discorsi* 9.

27. *Paradise Lost* 12.511–14.

28. Mary Nyquist, "The Genesis of a Gendered Subjectivity in the Divorce Tracts and in *Paradise Lost*," in *Re-membering Milton: Essays on the Texts and Traditions*, ed. Nyquist and Margaret W. Ferguson (New York, 1987), pp. 108, 116–17.

29. John H. Hayes, *An Introduction to Old Testament Study* (Nashville, Tenn., 1979), pp. 106–20, 155–97; James King West, *Introduction to the Old Testament*, 2d ed. (New York, 1981), pp. 59–76.

30. Barbara K. Lewalski, *Paradise Lost and the Rhetoric of Literary Forms* (Princeton, N.J., 1985), 110–14.

31. H. R. MacCallum, "Milton and Figurative Interpretation of the Bible," *University of Toronto Quarterly* 31 (1962): 397–415.

32. See Sister M. Christopher Pecheux, "The Council Scenes in *Paradise Lost,*" in *Milton and the Scriptural Tradition,* p. 101.

33. Frederick Hartt, *History of Italian Renaissance Art* (New York, 1979), 631.

34. Anthony Blunt, *Artistic Theory in Italy, 1450–1600* (Oxford, 1940), 114, 120–21.

35. *Discorsi,* pp. 4–5.

36. Translation by Ralph Nash in Torquato Tasso, *Jerusalem Delivered* (Detroit, 1987).

37. William of Tyre, *A History of Deeds Done beyond the Sea,* trans. and annotated by Emily A. Babcock and A. C. Krey (New York, 1943), 376 and n. 48.

38. Ibid., 298–99; *Gerusalemme liberata* 1.37–38.

39. Barbara K. Lewalski, *Paradise Lost and the Rhetoric of Literary Forms,* p. 113.

40. *Discorsi* 36. See Wittreich, " 'Poet amongst Poets' "; idem, *Visionary Poetics;* Lewalski, "Genres of *Paradise Lost.*"

41. See Freccero, *Dante.*

42. *Discorsi* 11–13.

43. Wittreich, *Visionary Poetics,* p. 18.

44. Milton, "The Reason of Church Government," in *Complete Poems and Major Prose,* p. 669.

Contributors

Wendell Clausen is Pope Professor of the Latin Language and Literature in the Department of Classics, Harvard University. He has prepared a critical edition of Persius and Juvenal (1959), coedited the *Cambridge History of Classical Literature* (1982), and is the author of *Virgil's Aeneid and the Tradition of Hellenistic Poetry* (1987). He is currently working on a commentary on Virgil's *Eclogues*.

Alan Cooper is Professor of Bible at Hebrew Union College–Jewish Institute of Religion, Cincinnati, Ohio. He is writing a Psalms commentary for the Anchor Bible.

Wolfhart Heinrichs is Professor of Arabic in the Department of Near Eastern Languages and Civilizations, Harvard University. His publications include *Arabische Dichtung und griechische Poetik* (1969), *The Hand of the Northwind: Opinions on Metaphor and the Early Meaning of* Istiʿāra *in Arabic Poetics* (1977), and "On the Genesis of the *Haqīqa-Majāz* Dichotomy," *Studia Islamica* 59 (1984). He is presently working on a comprehensive study of medieval Arabic literary theory.

James L. Kugel is Starr Professor of Hebrew Literature and chairman of the Department of Near Eastern Languages and Civilizations, Harvard University. He is the author of *The Techniques of Strangeness* (1971), *The Idea of Biblical Poetry: Parallelism and Its History* (1981), *Early Biblical Interpretation* (1986), and *In Potiphar's House: The Interpretive Life of Biblical Texts* (1990).

Gregory Nagy is the Francis Jones Professor of Classical Greek Literature and Professor of Comparative Literature at Harvard University. He is the author of *The Best of the Achaeans: Concepts of the Hero in Archaic Greek Poetry* (1979), *Pindar's Homer: The Lyric Possession of an Epic Past* (1990), and *Greek Mythology and Poetics* (1990). He is currently chairman of Harvard's undergraduate literature concentration.

Dan Pagis was Professor of Medieval and Renaissance Hebrew Literature, the Hebrew University of Jerusalem. He was the author of numerous ground-breaking literary studies in Hebrew, including *Innovation and Tradition in the Secular Hebrew Poetry of Spain and Italy* (1976) and *The History of the Hebrew Riddle in Italy and Holland* (1986). But he was best known in Israel for his poetry and is ranked among the finest Hebrew poets of the century. English translations of his poetry include *Poems* (1972), *Selected Poems of T. Carmi and Dan Pagis* (1976), and *Points of Departure* (1981). He died in 1986.

Lawrence F. Rhu is Assistant Professor of English at the University of South Carolina, Columbia. His essays on Renaissance literature have appeared in various publications. At present he is writing a book on the genesis and development of Torquato Tasso's narrative theory and its relations to his achievement as an epic poet.

Jan Ziolkowski is Professor of Medieval Latin and of Comparative Literature at Harvard University. His books include *Alan of Lille's Grammar of Sex: The Meaning of Grammar to a Twelfth-Century Intellectual* (1985), *Nigel of Canterbury: Miracles of the Virgin Mary, in Verse* (1986), *Jezebel: A Norman Latin Poem of the Early Eleventh Century* (1989), and *On Philology* (1990).

Michael J. Zwettler is Associate Professor of Arabic literature and Arabic studies in the department of Judaic and Near Eastern Languages and Literatures at the Ohio State University. He is the author of *The Oral Tradition of Classical Arabic Poetry: Its Character and Implications* (1978) as well as a number of essays on classical and early medieval Arabic literature. He is now at work on a major study of the earliest known document in Arabic, a tomb inscription of the early fourth century of the common era.

Index

Abraham (biblical figure), 87–89, 92, 93, 101
Abravanel, 37–38, 42–43
Abū l-Faḍl, 134, 136
Akiba, Rabbi, 11
Albo, Joseph, 35
Amos (biblical prophet), 6, 26–28
Antony, 67, 70
aoidos (singer), 56–57
Apollo, 58–59, 64, 66–67, 71
Arama, Meir, 38
Aratus, 65–66
Ariosto, 164, 174
Aristotle and Aristotelianism, 42, 144, 150, 168, 170, 177, 183
Augustine, Saint, 12, 19, 72
Augustus, 68

Balaam (biblical figure), 6, 36, 48, 159–60
Ben Sira, 52–53
Bialik, H. N., 140
Biblicism, in medieval Spain, 144
Bīrūnī, al-, 130, 133–34

Callimachus, 68–69
Canonization of the Bible, 8–9, 15
Cassiodorus, 12
Christ, Jesus, 19, 72, 101, 176
Clement of Alexandria, 18
Crescas, Ḥasdai, 36, 40

Daniel (biblical prophet), 46
Dante, 1, 164, 171–72
David (biblical figure), 145
  author of Psalms, 49, 51
  as prophet, 10, 21, 45–55
  "Songs of," 46–47
  Temple impresario, 47, 51
Dead Sea Scrolls, 8, 9, 30, 46–48, 50, 54, 102
Deborah, Song of, 11
Delphi, 59, 61–62
Donne, John, 22
Dreams and visions, 20, 31, 39–40, 60, 62, 121, 133–34, 141, 147–49
Duran, Shimon b. Ṣemaḥ, 36, 40

Eliezer de Beaugency, 34
Eusebius of Caesarea, 13
Ezekiel (biblical prophet), 7, 34, 37, 41, 143, 145

Falaqera, Shem-Tov b. Joseph, 143
False prophecy. *See* Lying and falsehood; Prophecy: false
Faltonia Proba, 19

Gabriel (angel), 81, 83, 121
Geoffrey of Monmouth, 151–62
Gerald of Wales, 155
Golden Age, 65–66, 70
Greenberg, Uri Zvi, 140

ha-Levi, Judah, 142
Hananiah (biblical figure), 40–41
Ḥarizi, Judah al-, 143, 146–49
Ḥassan ibn Thābit, 121
Herder, J. G., 24

Library of Congress Cataloging-in-Publication Data

Poetry and prophecy : the beginnings of a literary tradition / edited
by James L. Kugel.
p. cm. — (Myth and poetics)
Includes bibliographical references and index.
ISBN 0-8014-2310-4 (cloth: alk. paper). — ISBN 0-8014-9568-8 (pbk.: alk. paper)
1. Prophecy in literature. 2. Mythology in literature. 3. Poetry—History and criticism. I. Kugel, James L. II. Series.
PN1077.P58 1990
809'.93353—dc20 90-55128

For Jeff Dwyer and Elizabeth O'Grady—
my Irish agents extraO'rdinaire
—R.M.

For Cheryl, Cassidy and Grace
—R.R.

This is a Borzoi Book published by Alfred A. Knopf

Visit us on the Web! www.randomhouse.com/kids
Educators and librarians, for a variety of teaching tools, visit us at www.randomhouse.com/teachers

Library of Congress Cataloging-in-Publication Data
Michelson, Richard.
Busing Brewster / by Richard Michelson ; illustrated by R. G. Roth. — 1st ed.
p. cm.
Summary: Bused across town to a school in a white neighborhood of Boston in 1974, a young African American boy named Brewster describes his first day in first grade. Includes historical notes on the court-ordered busing.
ISBN 978-0-375-83334-2 (trade) — ISBN 978-0-375-93334-9 (lib. bdg.)
[1. Busing for school integration—Fiction. 2. School integration—Fiction. 3. Race relations—Fiction. 4. African Americans—Fiction. 5. Boston (Mass.)—History—20th century—Fiction.] I. Roth, R. G., ill. II. Title.
PZ7.M581915Bu 2010
[Fic]—dc22
2009022626

The text of this book is set in Bailey Sans.
The illustrations were created using ink, watercolor, and collage.

MANUFACTURED IN MALAYSIA
May 2010
10 9 8 7 6 5 4 3 2 1
First Edition

Random House Children's Books supports the First Amendment and celebrates the right to read.

Busing Brewster

By Richard Michelson

Pictures by R. G. Roth

Alfred A. Knopf
NEW YORK

All summer I've been playing on the school playground with Bryan. I climb the fence by myself, and Bryan catches me on the other side.

"I'll be back soon, Brewster," he tells me. He runs off with Jules and Big Earl, but I don't mind. There's plenty to do.

I find a stick and swing it like Hammerin' Hank.

I make believe I'm hitting homers, but it's just Jules throwing a rock high over my head. Uh-oh. I hope that isn't Miss Evelyn's window. Miss Evelyn's gonna teach me the first grade at Franklin.

"She's mean," Bryan tells me. "She yells like somebody's always setting off her fire alarm."

He squints his eyes and pretends to put on glasses. "You'll learn to read, if it's over my dead body," he screeches.

Big Earl laughs like he's ready to bust a gut.

Bryan makes fun of everybody. Mama says Miss Evelyn's nice.

When we get back home, Mama's on the stoop waving a letter.

"You boys are going to Central!" she tells us.

Bryan moves away before she can hug him. I don't move away, but I look at Bryan and I don't hug Mama back.

All night Bryan's punching his pillow.

"Central's the white school," he says.

"I ain't waking up at six."

"Sittin' an hour on the bus."

"Ain't no Negroes at Central."

"At least I won't have Miss Evelyn," I say. I squinch up my eyes and circle my fingers to make glasses.

Bryan doesn't laugh. "Miss Evelyn's nice," he says.

I'm up by five-thirty, but Mama's already frying eggs. "Don't you worry, Brewster," she tells me. "You're going to like Central. They've got rooms for art and music and a roof that doesn't leak. There's even a swimming pool inside the building and a real library bursting full of books."

I don't know how to read, or how to swim. But I'm glad Mama's happy.

"Maybe you'll be president someday, Brewster," she tells me. And she looks at me proud, like I already am.

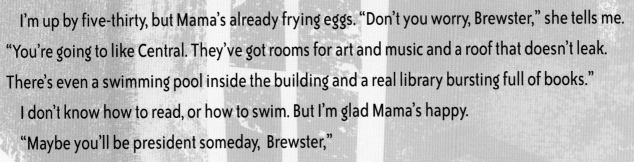

By the time we turn the corner, Jules is already waiting at the bus stop. Bryan drops my hand and runs ahead. The bus turns right at the Jewish cemetery. We pass a bar and then a Catholic church.

I can't wait till we get to Central. Maybe I'll learn how to swim. I wish Mama had bought me a bathing suit.

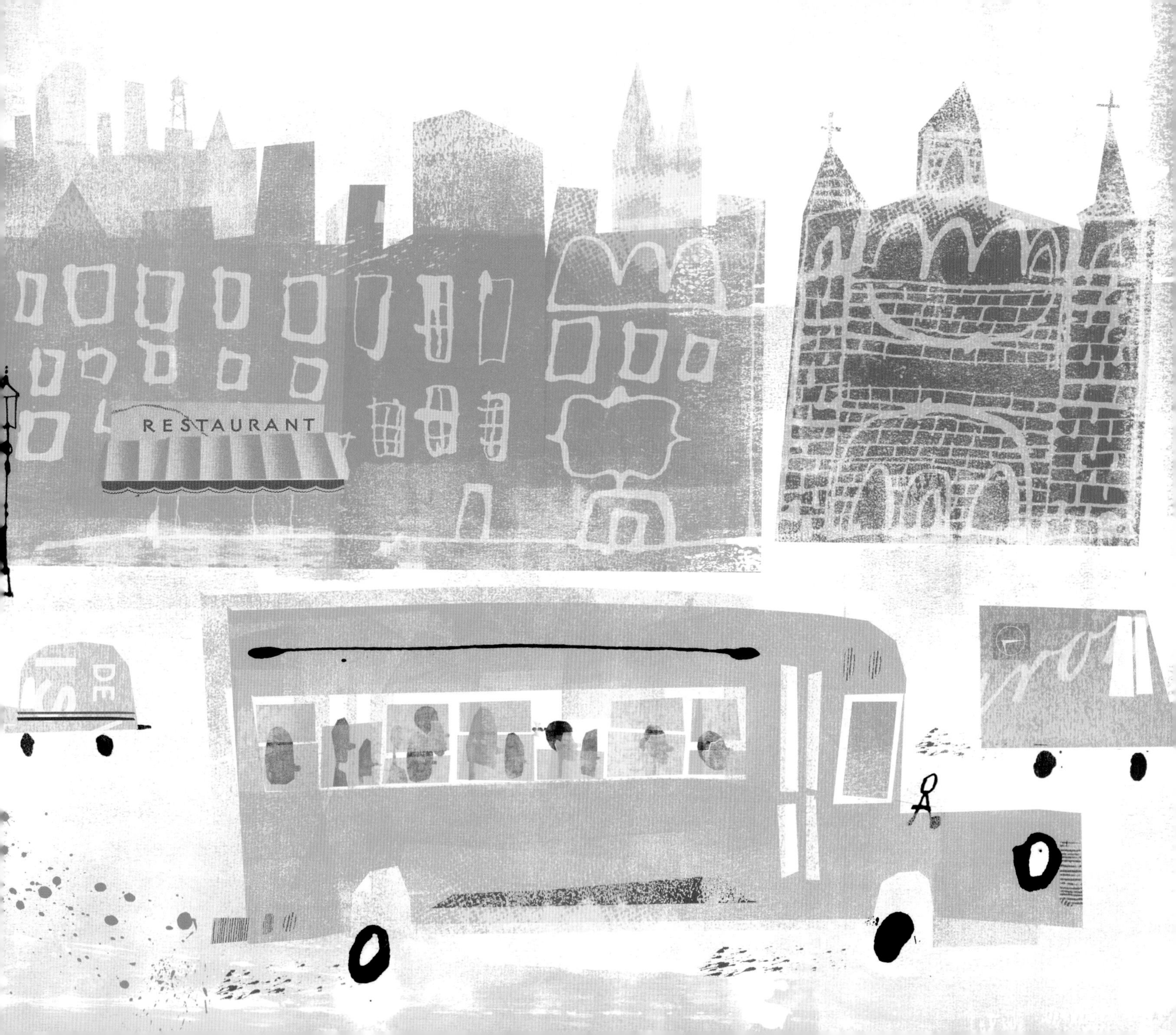
RESTAURANT
DE

"What's that sign say?" I ask Bryan. There's white people lined up on both sides of the street.

"Welcome to Central," Bryan answers.

But then I see him give Jules one of his "better don't tell on me" looks.

SMASH! BAM! CRASH!

I didn't even see the rock. I just heard the glass shatter.

Bryan squishes me down under the seat. "Wish we could stay at Franklin," Bryan says. From down here Franklin seems a million miles away.

There's two policemen standing at the Central door, but inside is the whitest hall I ever saw.

There are brand-new shiny lockers lining one whole wall.

There's even a water fountain and it's making me thirsty.

I'm drinking when somebody shoves me from behind. "Wish your kind all stayed at Franklin," he says.

"We like it right here, Freckle-face." It's Bryan, pushing him back.

Now all the older kids are yelling. One of the cops rushes over. "Well now, lads," he says, "if it's trouble you're wanting, you can follow me."

If Big Earl were here,
he'd be busting a gut.

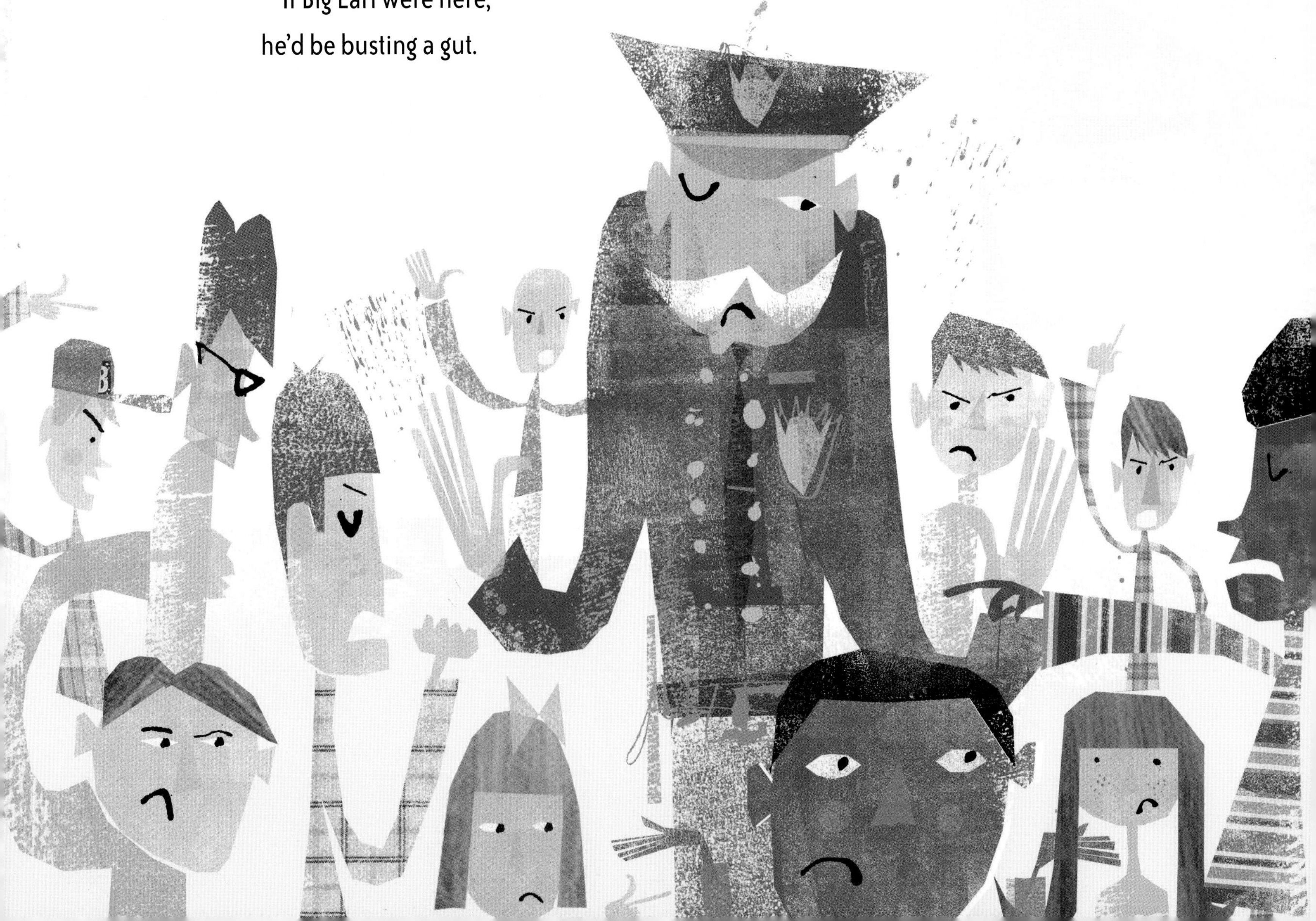

We're spending the whole first day in the library. Bryan says it's called detention, but I don't mind. I've never seen so many books. I find one with a rocket ship on the cover. I turn all the pages and then start again from the front.

I wish I knew what it said.

Miss O'Grady's the librarian. She looks just like Miss Evelyn. "Perhaps you'll be an astronaut someday, Brewster," she says. She brings me a book about the moon landing.

"Mama hopes I'll be president," I say proudly. I feel stupid as soon as I say it. Even I know there's never been a Negro president.

But Miss O'Grady doesn't laugh. "You'll be going from here to Harvard, then," she says, sitting down next to me. "So we'd better begin by teaching you how to read."

Behind her, I see Bryan squint his eyes and pretend to put on glasses. When Freckle-face busts a gut, he sounds just like Big Earl.

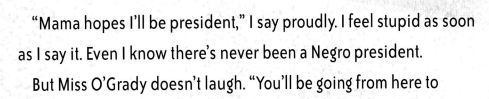

Miss O'Grady reads us a book about some man called Kennedy. "Every child deserves an education," she says. "It wasn't long ago that folks didn't want the Irish in their schools. And just because Kennedy was Irish Catholic, people said he'd never be president. But he proved them wrong."

I look over at Freckle-face, but he isn't even listening. He keeps whispering to Bryan and laughing. When the bell rings, they both run out the door.

"I wish you could teach me the first grade," I tell Miss O'Grady.

"You'll do just fine, Mr. President," she says. But she makes me promise to visit her in the library every day.

I'm almost back on the bus when I see Freckle-face standing with his daddy. I start to wave, but he looks away.

"Wish them coloreds all stayed at Franklin," I hear his daddy say.

Mama's waiting on the stoop when we get back home. "How was your first day at Central?" she asks.

Bryan moves away before she can hug him. He shrugs and runs off to meet Big Earl at the playground.

I don't want to worry Mama, either, so I give her a big hug. "I spent the whole day in the library," I tell her. "Someday I'm going to be president."

Mama looks at me proud, like I already am.

"Maybe tomorrow," I say, "I'll learn how to swim."

Author's Note

Brewster is a composite of many young African American children who, in the 1970s, were bused to previously segregated all-white schools. Segregation generally meant that there were schools for black children and different (better) schools for white children. If an African American child lived near an all-white school, he or she would be forced to travel to a black school, even if it was inferior and far away.

The U.S. Supreme Court had outlawed segregated schools in 1954 (*Brown v. Board of Education*). But even after their ruling, most schools, in reality, were still segregated as, throughout the country, children went to class near their home, and most neighborhoods were not integrated.

In 1971, in an attempt to further integrate schools, the Supreme Court permitted "forced busing." Now, instead of being *allowed* to attend a white school if one was near their home, some black children *chose* or were *forced* to attend a white school, even if none were nearby. To make room for the incoming black students, some white students too had to be bused outside their neighborhoods. This often led to resentment, and occasionally to violence. While much opposition was racially motivated, many blacks and whites honestly preferred that their children attend local schools; parents were unwilling to see their children used as pawns in a social experiment, however worthy. Forced busing failed on many levels, but there is no denying that many black students were provided with opportunities they would not otherwise have had.

In the end, of course, a good education almost always comes down to caring individuals: a loving family that fosters curiosity, and the many librarians and teachers who, like the fictional Miss O'Grady, believe that all children who want to do something important with their lives deserve an equal opportunity.

Brewster dreams of becoming president. Barack Obama was elected the first African American president of the United States in 2008. I wrote this story five years earlier, in 2003. While Miss O'Grady and Brewster's mother might not have been surprised, it never occurred to me while writing *Busing Brewster* that such a historic event would become a reality in my lifetime, much less before the book's publication. My words have taken on a greater resonance than I intended, which is what authors hope for.

In a 2005 speech to the American Library Association, the then Senator Obama gave "an apology for all those times I couldn't keep myself out of trouble and ended up sitting in the library on a time-out." He went on to say that "the moment we persuade a child, any child, to cross that threshold into a library, we've changed their lives forever, and for the better. . . . We all have a responsibility as parents and librarians, educators and citizens, to instill in our children a love of reading so that we can give them the chance to fulfill their dreams."

Maybe even to become president!

Brewster